SHANAHAN LIBRARY
MARYMOUNT MANHATTAN COLLEGE
221 EAST 71 STREET
NEW YORK, NY 10021

D1279289

OCCUPATIONAL GHETTOS

STUDIES IN
SOCIAL INEQUALITY

EDITOR

David B. Grusky STANFORD UNIVERSITY
Paula England STANFORD UNIVERSITY

EDITORIAL BOARD

Hans-Peter Blossfeld
Mary C. Brinton
Thomas DiPrete
Michael Hout
Andrew Walder
Mary Waters

OCCUPATIONAL GHETTOS

THE WORLDWIDE SEGREGATION
OF WOMEN AND MEN

Maria Charles and David B. Grusky

STANFORD UNIVERSITY PRESS
STANFORD, CALIFORNIA
2004

Stanford University Press
Stanford, California

© 2004 by the Board of Trustees of the Leland Stanford Junior
University. All rights reserved.

Printed in the United States of America on acid-free, archival-
quality paper

Library of Congress Cataloging-in-Publication Data

Charles, Maria, 1960–
Occupational ghettos : the worldwide segregation of women and
    men / Maria Charles and David B. Grusky.
        p. cm.
    Includes bibliographical references and index.
    ISBN 0-8047-3634-0 (cloth : alk. paper)
        1. Sexual division of labor.   2. Sex role in the work
    environment.   3. Sex discrimination in employment.
    4. Social stratification.   5. Sex discrimination against
    women.   6. Sexual division of labor—Statistics.   I. Title:
    Worldwide segregation of women and men.   II. Grusky,
    David B.   III. Title.
    HD6060.6 .C48 2004
    306.3'615—dc22   2003023988

Original Printing 2004

Last figure below indicates year of this printing:
13   12   11   10   09   08   07   06   05   04

Typeset by G&S Book Services in 10/14 Sabon

FOR OUR CHILDREN

Nico, Elena, and Natasha

Max and Dashiel

CONTENTS

TABLES AND FIGURES

Tables

ACKNOWLEDGMENTS

The personal world in which we live and wrote this book reveals the contradictory forces for change and stability that we seek to understand here. There is of course much integrative change within this microcosm: Most obviously, our collaboration with each other and with our contributors can be seen as a shining example of gender integration, one that reflects the emergence of sociology as a truly gender-integrated profession. At the same time, we recognize that our discipline may be on the road to wholesale feminization and that many of its subfields, such as the one to which we contribute here, are already regarded as "essentially" female in method or topic. We also see evidence of both change and stability in the gender composition of the support workers who made this book possible. While the pool of graduate students upon which we relied for research assistance was quite gender-balanced, our administrative support was almost exclusively female, and our computer support almost exclusively male. The household services that we purchased to free up time for our research were provided by women, while the deans and "chairpersons" who oversaw our academic lives were largely men. These experiences suggest that gender integration of the professions may be accompanied by intra-occupational differentiation and segregation, that gender distinctions are eroding more within elite than within nonelite occupations, that a great many occupations remain "hypersegregated" despite a spectacular rise of egalitarian values and culture in recent decades, and that such persisting hypersegregation reflects durable essentialist beliefs about what constitutes intrinsically female or male pursuits. This striking coexistence of change and stability is what we hope to illuminate in this book.

We owe intellectual debts to numerous friends and colleagues who have inspired, supported, and sometimes challenged our work. Rather than the usual perfunctory fare, much of their commentary on our research engaged seriously with our theories, our methods, and our sometimes perplexing results. In particular, this book is much the better for the contributions of Karen Aschaffenburg, David Baker, Jim Baron, Karen Bradley, Mary Brinton, Marlis Buchmann, Diane Burton, Lisa Catanzarite, Mariko Lin Chang, Clifford Clogg, Raymond Clémençon, Shelley Correll, Thomas DiPrete, Paula England, Leo Goodman, Joon Han, Robert Hauser, Jerry Herting, Michael Hout, Jerry Jacobs, Janne Jonsson, Rebecca Klatch, Robert Mare, John Meyer, Winifred Poster, Chiqui Ramirez, Barbara Reskin, Manuela Romero, Ákos Róna-Tas, Patricia Roos, Rachel Rosenfeld, Jesper Sørensen, Szonja Szelényi, Marta Tienda, Christena Turner, Kim Weeden, and Yu Xie. We are also grateful to colleagues in our respective departments for broadening our intellectual horizons and for much professional and moral support over the years.

Many talented students assisted with parts of this project. We thank Nielan Barnes, Paula Gutiérrez, Michael Haedicke, Susan Halebsky Dimock, Mark Jones, Jodie Lawston, Asaf Levanon, Patrick McLeod, Lida Nedilsky, Colin Ong-Dean, Jeanne Powers, and Marisa Smith for their contributions. We wish them well as they embark upon professional careers of their own.

We have benefited from excellent administrative support at our universities. Overworked though they sometimes were, Jessica Henning and Elizabeth Heitner at Cornell University and Barbara Stewart, Martha Neal-Brown, and Nora Bodrian at UC San Diego helped us keep our administrative and financial affairs in good order.

The skilled editorial staff at Stanford University Press (SUP) was exceedingly patient with a project that was long in coming, even by the generous standards of academic publishing. We thank in particular our editors and assistant editors: Kate Wahl, Laura Comay, Nathan MacBrien, Patricia Katayama, and Carmen Borbon-Wu. We also gratefully acknowledge important contributions of the SUP production team, especially Judith Hibbard and our excellent copy editor, Janet Mowery.

The international data analyzed throughout this book were assembled with the assistance of Sylvie Lagarde (France), Ulrich Greiner (Germany), Leif Haldorson (Sweden), Jan Boruvka (Switzerland), Margaret Wort (United Kingdom), and Mariko Lin Chang and Joon Han (Japan). We also received helpful advice and statistical documentation from Peter Elias, Harry Ganzeboom, Magnus Nermo, and Yoshimichi ("Mitch") Sato.

The research reported here was supported by the National Science Foundation; the Spencer Foundation; the UC San Diego Committee on Research; the UC San Diego Faculty Career Development Office; the UC Hellman Faculty Fellowship Program; the UC Center for German and European Studies; the Stanford Center for the Study of Families, Children, and Youth; the Stanford University Dean's Research Fund; and Cornell University.

We dedicate this book to our (respective) children. We thank them for the humor, joy, and balance that they bring to our lives, and for all the distractions, both planned and unplanned, that they have afforded us over the years. May they each perceive and enjoy a wide range of life choices.

Finally, we are deeply grateful to our spouses, Raymond Clémençon and Szonja Szelényi, for their many intellectual contributions and, equally important, for their steady friendship, love, and support over the years. This book is their product as well as our own.

Maria Charles and David Grusky
May 2004

INTRODUCTION

CHAPTER ONE

The Four Puzzles of Sex Segregation

The rise of egalitarian values and associated egalitarian institutional reforms is a distinctive feature of modernity and postmodernity. This development, which may be dated at least to the Enlightenment, intensified throughout the twentieth century as formal legal rights were extended to previously excluded groups (such as women), wide-reaching institutional reforms were implemented to equalize life chances (such as antidiscrimination legislation), and anti-egalitarian doctrines (such as racism) were challenged. These processes of equalization, dramatic though they are, obviously do not exhaust the story of modernity and postmodernity. As is well known, this story is replete with counterpoints in which the forces for egalitarianism have been resisted, sometimes violently (as with the recurrence of eugenics and fascism) and sometimes in quieter but still profound ways (as in the persistence of residential segregation).

This book is about one of those quieter counterpoints that is currently playing out in the domain of gender stratification. At first blush, the forces for equalization may appear to be straightforwardly triumphing in this domain, as evidenced by (a) the rapid diffusion of egalitarian views on gender roles (see, e.g., Smith 1999), (b) the withering away of the long-standing gender gap in college attendance and graduation (e.g., Jacobs 1996; K. Bradley 2000), and (c) the steady increase in rates of female labor force participation (e.g., Brewster and Rindfuss 2000).[1] These developments, while spectacular and unprecedented, have nonetheless been coupled with equally spectacular forms of resistance to equalization, especially within the workplace. Most notably, women and men continue to work in very different occupations, with women crowding into a relatively small number of female-typed occupations (teacher, secretary, nurse).[2] If one sought, for example, to undo all sex segregation by reallocating women to less segregated occupations, a full 52 percent of the employed women in the United States would have to be shifted out of their current occupational category (Jacobs 2003). This extreme sex segregation is typical of what prevails throughout the advanced industrial world. Because sex segregation is so extreme, and because it colors the life chances and life experiences of so many women and men, we characterize the contemporary occupational structure as "hypersegregated" (see Massey and Denton 1993 for a related usage).

Why is the occupational structure so resistant to egalitarian forces and pressures? It could be argued that fundamental institutional change is inevitably prolonged and that full integration will ultimately be achieved through ongoing reform efforts (Jackson 1998). Although we cannot rule out the possibility of full integration in the distant future, we would stress that this outcome is by no means inevitable under prevailing policies, practices, and commitments. That is, rather than viewing sex segregation as a residual that is destined to wither away under contemporary egalitarian pressures, it is best regarded as an organic feature of modern economies that is ideologically consistent with egalitarianism, at least as the latter is understood today. In this sense, there is a deep structure to sex segregation that makes it a viable long-term feature of modern economies, even as pressures for equalization mount in other domains of the gender stratification system.

The foregoing interpretation is consistent with the relatively slow pace of integrative change, the failure of conventional egalitarian policy to reduce segregation, and the long-term persistence of pockets of extreme segregation ("occupational ghettos"). We briefly review each of these pieces of supporting evidence in the following paragraphs.

Slow pace of change.   The clearest evidence of resistance to egalitarian pressures emerges in comparing the rate of desegregative change with corresponding rates of change elsewhere in the gender stratification system. As indicated in Figure 1.1, the moderate declines in occupational sex segregation over the past thirty years stand in stark contrast to the more precipitous changes in (a) attitudes toward gender roles, (b) rates of female labor force participation, and (c) the gender gap in educational investments. These differences in the pacing of change indicate that the segregation regime has

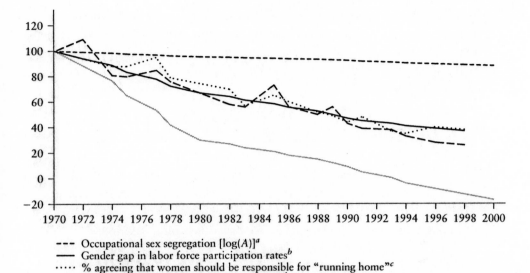

Figure 1.1   Parameters of Gender Stratification, 1970–2000.

[a]Weeden, Table 5.3 this volume. The trends under *A*, *D*, and *D$_s$* are similar for this time period (see Chapter 5 for details).
[b]U.S. Census Bureau, *Statistical Abstract of the United States*, Table 569, 2001 (*http://www.census.gov/prod/2002pubs/01statab/labor.pdf*). Gap calculated as ln[(male %)/(female %)].
[c]General Social Surveys. NORC-GSS, Cumulative Data File, 1972–2000. In 1970, the GSS did not administer this item, so a linear trend model is used to estimate the 1970 data point ($R^2 = .92$).
[d]General Social Surveys. NORC-GSS, Cumulative Data File, 1972–2000. In 1970, the GSS did not administer this item, so a linear trend model is used to estimate the 1970 data point ($R^2 = .91$).
[e]*http://www.census.gov/population/socdemo/education/tabA-2.pdf*. Gap calculated as ln[(male %)/(female %)].
[f]All times series pertain to the rate of change since 1970 (from a standardized starting point of 100).

been shielded from the equalizing forces that have played out more dramatically in other domains.

The failure of egalitarianism.   As a parallel line of evidence, one might ask whether countries that have committed most explicitly to family-friendly policies, anti-discrimination legislation, and other forms of egalitarianism have made substantial headway in reducing sex segregation. If they have, it is suggestive that conventional egalitarian commitments, at least when carried out to their logical extremes, can serve to more quickly root out residual segregative processes. The available evidence is largely disappointing on this front. For example, Sweden is well known for its egalitarian and family-friendly policies, yet it remains deeply sex-segregated to the present day. Obversely, countries that are commonly viewed as bastions of conservative gender practice, such as Japan and Italy, do *not* show up as especially segregated.

Unevenness of change. There is, to be sure, clear and substantial evidence of desegregation in many sectors of the occupational structure (in Sweden and elsewhere), yet any careful observer of this process has to be struck by its unevenness, with some occupations proving to be almost entirely resistant to egalitarian pressures (secretary, nursery school teacher). Moreover, when male-dominated occupations do embark on what appears to be integrative trajectories, the influx of women often continues on well past the point of gender parity; and a new form of resegregation (of the female-dominated variety) then ensues (e.g., Reskin and Roos 1990). These results are again suggestive that sex segregation, far from being a holdover, is actively advanced by dynamics that are part and parcel of modern industrialism.

We therefore pose the following puzzle: Why has sex segregation proven resistant to egalitarian pressures, even as other forms of gender inequality have given way? Although we return to this puzzle repeatedly, it is also important to recognize that it is merely one part of a larger complex of puzzling findings that scholars of segregation have recently reported. The following three puzzles might also be cited: (a) the common view that male power and privilege allows men to dominate the best occupations fails to accord with the typical patterning of contemporary sex segregation; (b) the highest levels of segregation are often found in socially and culturally progressive countries (such as Sweden) rather than in their more traditional counterparts (such as Japan); and (c) the cross-national evidence on sex segregation has been diversely interpreted, with quantitative scholars emphasizing the commonalities in segregation regimes, and researchers working in ethnographic or area studies traditions emphasizing, by contrast, how segregation regimes are culturally constructed and accordingly idiosyncratic and variable. Taken together, these findings seem to suggest a topsy-turvy world in which males do not straightforwardly dominate the best jobs, family-friendly policies have a perverse segregating effect, and contemporary gender regimes continue to have a highly-segregated "1950s feel" even into the twenty-first century.

We argue that these puzzles have emerged because conventional theories and methods blind us to the multidimensional structure of segregation. By advancing a two-dimensional conceptualization of sex segregation and a matching methodological approach, we seek to resolve the puzzles and build an alternative understanding of the development of segregation regimes. We carry out this work on three fronts. First, we lay out the standard "evolutionary theory" of sex segregation in the clearest possible terms, allowing us to expose some of the inconsistencies between this theory and the available evidence on sex segregation. We next advance an alternative account that solves the foregoing puzzles and thus squares better with the available evidence. We argue that gender inequality is driven by two distinct dynamics, a horizontal dynamic that segregates men and women across the manual-nonmanual divide, and a vertical dynamic that allocates men to the most desirable occupations on both sides of this divide. Finally, we develop and apply new models of sex segregation that allow competing representations of the structure of segregation to be explicitly contrasted, thus moving beyond conventional index-based approaches that rest on untested (and seemingly implausible) assumptions about this structure. These models are applied to newly constructed arrays of high-quality comparative data that allow us to produce far more detailed and comprehensive comparisons than were heretofore possible.

It is well to ask whether such a careful scrutiny of sex segregation is warranted. The main rationale for revisiting the comparative data with our more rigorous modeling approach is the growing evidence that segregation is the smoking gun that accounts for many other forms of gender-based advantage and disadvantage. In their pathbreaking work, Petersen and Morgan (1995) demonstrate that much of the gender wage gap (63.8 percent) is attributable to the segregation of men and women into different occupations, implying that the study of gender-based inequalities reduces in large part to the study of occupational segregation.[3] Moreover, the occupational structure is not merely the "backbone" of the economic reward system (Parkin 1971, p. 18), but it also serves as the main conduit through which working conditions, lifestyles, and consumption practices are determined (Grusky and Sørensen 1998; also see Parsons 1954, pp. 326–29; Duncan 1968, pp. 689–90; Hauser and Featherman 1977, p. 4). Although one could redress gender-based inequalities by recalibrating how occupations disburse economic and noneconomic rewards ("comparable-worth adjustments"), this approach has not garnered much legal support (see Nelson and Bridges 1999). In this context, efforts to reduce gender inequalities must focus on eliminating segregation rather than equalizing remuneration for occupations that are, except with regard to sex-typing, perfectly equivalent. As a precursor to that effort, there is much to be said for exploring the underlying structure of segregation, a task to which this book is dedicated.[4]

THE FOUR PUZZLES OF CONTEMPORARY SEGREGATION RESEARCH

In recent years, segregation scholars have been mired in debates about the methodology of segregation measurement, while discussions about the most pressing substantive issues have played out largely in the background, if at all. These methodological discussions have been exceedingly fruitful (see Chapter 2 for a review). However, our own view is that the most fundamental methodological problems have now been resolved, allowing the field to return to substantive problems that have languished. We therefore turn to the four empirical puzzles that were described in cursory fashion in the preceding discussion. In this stock-taking exercise, we lay the groundwork for our larger claim that standard narratives about the underlying structure of segregation are incomplete, misleading, and at times contradictory.

Puzzle #1: Do men dominate the best occupations?

It is useful to begin by asking whether the underlying structure of sex segregation is consistent with conventional accounts of segregation. In many such accounts, it is simply presumed that the best occupations will be dominated by men, either because women have disproportionate domestic responsibilities that reduce their incentive to invest in demanding careers (e.g., G. Becker 1991), or because employers exercise their tastes for discrimination through "glass ceiling" personnel policies and other forms of male-biased queuing in the labor market (e.g., Reskin and Roos 1990). There is clearly much merit in these accounts. However, insofar as one seeks to understand the structure of sex segregation, their usefulness is arguably limited because the correlation between the socioeconomic status of occupations and their gender composition is weak.[5] In reacting to this result, some commentators have questioned whether socioeconomic scales adequately measure occupational desirability, thereby implying that the anticipated relationship might well emerge if only a proper gradational scale were deployed (e.g., England 1979). While we agree that socioeconomic scales are imperfect (see Hauser and Warren 2001), we suggest that the weakness of the socioeconomic effect arises not merely because of measurement error but also because sex segregation is not entirely socioeconomic in structure.

The key to resolving this puzzle rests with the distinction between vertical and horizontal forms of segregation and, in particular, the interaction between these two forms (see Semyonov and Jones 1999; Blackburn, Jarman, and Brooks 2000).[6] The anticipated socioeconomic effect appears, after all, *within* each of the two horizontal sectors; indeed, it explains much of the segregation within the nonmanual sector (i.e., men are disproportionately allocated to professional and managerial occupations), and it likewise explains much of the segregation within the manual sector (i.e., men are disproportionately allocated to craft occupations). Although the socioeconomic account accordingly holds within each sector, it cannot explain the disproportionate allocation of women to the nonmanual sector itself (because this sector is, on average, higher in socioeconomic status than the manual sector). There are, accordingly, three types of segregation that can in principle vary independently of one another: (a) the extent to which men dominate the most desirable occupations in the nonmanual sector ("nonmanual vertical segregation"), (b) the extent to which men dominate the most desirable occupations in the manual sector ("manual vertical segregation"), and (c) the extent to which women are disproportionately allocated to nonmanual occupations ("horizontal segregation"). Throughout this book, reference is often made to these three fundamental segregation components because they govern much of the systematic cross-national, temporal, and cross-group variability in segregation regimes.

Puzzle #2: Is there a worldwide segregation regime?

There is also much room for further research on the extent and patterning of cross-national variability in sex segregation. Among quantitative analysts of survey data, the prevailing view is that substantial commonalities in the underlying structure of segregation can be identified (at least for advanced industrial countries), with women dominating lower nonmanual occupations and men dominating craft and management occupations. This characterization accords, for example, with the early comparative analyses of Roos (1985), as well as with contemporary analyses drawing on more recent surveys (e.g., ILO 1989; Charles 1992, 1998; Rubery, Smith, and Fagan 1999; Nermo 2000; United Nations 2000). By contrast, scholars working in the area studies tradition tend to presume that sex segregation takes on more contingent and idiosyncratic forms, with their narratives typically emphasizing how the contours of segregation are affected by the distinctive cultures, political traditions, and institutional practices that emerge and live on within nation-states. For example, scholars of Eastern Europe and the former Soviet Union have emphasized that socialist full-employment policies served to desegregate the high-level technical sector, as women streamed into medical, engineering, and related technical occupations in record numbers (e.g., Dodge 1971; Blekher 1979). We might likewise cite well-developed literatures on the putative distinctiveness of segregative practices and outcomes in Japan (Brinton 1993), the United States (Milkman 1987), Great Britain (H. Bradley 1989), India (Poster 1998), Switzerland (Charles 2000), Germany (Rosenfeld and Trappe 2000), and many other countries (e.g., Ruggie 1984; Crompton, Le Feuvre, and Birkelund 1999).

We review these literatures in more detail in Chapters 2 and 3. At this point, we merely point out that the two literatures coexist and that, with few exceptions (e.g., Chang 2000), segregation scholars have not sought to adjudicate between them in any systematic way. It is high time, then, for a comprehensive comparative analysis of the sort that we seek to present here. In this sense, the main problem on the comparative front is not so much that segregation narratives are incomplete or poorly developed (although indeed they are), but that the field lacks an adequate evidentiary base upon which compelling narratives might be built. We develop this base in Chapters 3 and 4 by identifying a core structure in terms of three basic components of sex segregation. With this core structure in hand, it becomes possible to examine both (a) the extent to which segregation regimes vary around a common theme, and (b) the characteristic ways in which this variability is expressed. The foregoing empirical work allows us to build a comprehensive narrative that identifies the sources of the common core as well as the sources of the observed variability around that core.

Puzzle #3: Why are gender-egalitarian countries extremely segregated?

In its present form, the comparative literature is underdeveloped and leaves ample room for further research on the shape of the common core, but there can be little doubt that, however the core is conceived, it will reveal pockets of extreme segregation. Although present-day segregation is sometimes represented as a mere holdover from a less egalitarian past, it is difficult to reconcile this view with results indicating that sex segregation is especially prominent in countries with egalitarian ideological climates, family-friendly state policies, and other institutional practices that may be regarded as prototypically modern (such as low levels of fertility and high rates of female labor force participation). In the 1980s and early 1990s, a series of path-breaking studies revealed that Sweden and similarly "progressive" Scandinavian countries were highly segregated, whereas Japan, Portugal, Italy, Greece, and other countries with more traditional gender politics and policies were, by comparison, rather less segregated (Roos 1985; Charles 1990, 1992; Rosenfeld and Kalleberg 1991; Jacobs and Lim 1992). This pattern also shows up in more recent cross-national comparisons (e.g., Anker 1998; Blackburn, Jarman, and Brooks 2000; Melkas and Anker 2001).

These results are clearly counterintuitive and, as such, demonstrate the role of sociological research in moving beyond common-sense understandings. At the same time, it is important to provide some account of the counterintuitive results; and on this more ambitious explanatory front the current literature falls somewhat short. We devote much of Chapter 4 to the task of incorporating the explanatory account offered by Charles (1992, 1998) into our two-dimensional model of segregation. The main argument pressed in Chapter 4 (and in the current chapter) is that egalitarian policies can serve to delegitimate vertical forms of segregation, but that this desegregating effect is muted and ultimately offset because (a) the logic of egalitarian policy is not inconsistent with the persistence or even the growth of horizontal forms of segregation, and (b) the egalitarianism of Sweden and other Scandinavian countries has emerged in the context of a strong "postindustrial economy" that unleashes processes that actually increase horizontal segregation as well as vertical inequalities in the nonmanual sector. The distinction between vertical and horizontal segregation proves, then, to be crucial in making sense of the effects of seemingly gender-egalitarian policies and practices.

Puzzle #4: Why has integration occurred relatively slowly and in such piecemeal fashion?

The available evidence from the United States, Europe, and Japan suggests that occupational sex segregation has declined since 1970, but at a modest rate relative to the more dramatic and precipitous increases in female labor force participation and educational attainment (Gross 1968; G. Williams 1979; England 1981; Beller 1984; Blossfeld 1984; Handl 1984; Albeda 1986; Bianchi and Rytina 1986; Jacobs 1989a, 1999; Reskin and Roos 1990; Hakim 1992; Brinton 1993; Nermo 1996; Anker 1998; Rubery, Smith, and Fagan 1999; Jacobs 2003).[7] Moreover, while professional and managerial occupations appear to have desegregated relatively rapidly, some female-typed occupations have proven resistant to change and others have become more deeply female-typed (Cohn 1985; Gwartney-Gibbs 1988; Reskin and Roos 1990; Rubery and Fagan 1995; Jonung 1998; Rubery 1998). The core puzzle for scholars of trend is to understand why change has been so slow and why certain occupations have remained hypersegregated.

In understanding this empirical puzzle, it again proves useful to distinguish between vertical and horizontal forms of segregation, because the former is more directly undermined by the rise of egalitarian institutional practices than the latter. We also examine whether trends vary across countries (the United States, Japan, and Switzerland) that differ in their cultural and political commitment to reducing gender inequality. The United States is distinctive for its long history of liberal feminism and its early legal provisions for gender equality (including equal opportunity laws and affirmative action policies), whereas Japanese society and government have been more resistant to such formal egalitarianism and the institutional reforms associated with it (at least until recently). As a final point of comparison, we examine trends in sex segregation in Switzerland, a case of interest because our previous analyses (Charles and Grusky 1995) revealed it to be highly segregated relative to other industrialized countries. These comparisons lend new insight into how gender regimes evolve in the context of differential starting points and differential commitments to formal egalitarianism.

CONCEPTUALIZING SEX SEGREGATION

The preceding discussion suggests that various empirical puzzles have emerged in the literature because stratification scholars tend to treat sex segregation in unidimensional terms and accordingly fail to appreciate that a complex amalgam of processes underlies gender inequality and renders some forms of segregation more entrenched than others. Although the tendency to represent segregation unidimensionally is widespread, it emerges especially clearly in classical theorizing about long-term trends in inequality. For example, structural-functional theorists typically treat all forms of segregation and inequality in undifferentiated terms, with the assumption being that "ascription" is a generic residue destined to wither away either because discriminatory tastes are inefficient and costly or because bureaucratic forms of social organization have diffused widely and serve to undermine discriminatory practices (see, e.g., Kerr et al. 1960; Goode 1963; Parsons 1970).[8] In similar fashion, neoinstitutionalists assume that egalitarian practices and organizational forms will gradually diffuse and generate across-the-board reductions in segregation, although the main impetus for such diffusion is not the intrinsic efficiency of universalistic practices but rather the characteristically modern commitment to cultural *stories* about their efficiency (e.g., Ramirez 1987; Meyer 2001). Finally, some early feminist scholars conceptualized occupational sex segregation as one of the main outcomes of "patriarchal" forms of social organization, where the latter refers to the various social relations that "create solidarity and interdependence among men and enable them to dominate women" (Hartmann 1981, p. 14; Huber 1988). This approach typically treats both patriarchy and inequality in monolithic terms and thus draws scholars into weaving stories about the extent of segregation rather than its many dimensions and their differential responsiveness to egalitarian forces.

These various theories share, then, the prejudice that the explanandum of interest (segregation) may be represented in unidimensional terms, but they differ in their claims about the extent or pacing of change in this explanandum. If segregation is seen as persistent or ubiquitous, then reference is made to the strength and durability of patriarchal norms, institutions, or values (Hartmann 1981; Chafetz 1988; Ridgeway 1997; J. Williams 2000). If segregation is seen as relatively weak or declining in strength, this is attributed to (a) the gradual displacement of traditional gender roles and ideologies with universalistic values, (b) the diffusion of bureaucratic forms of organization, or (c) the discrimination-eroding discipline of the competitive market (Goode 1963; Ramirez 1987; see also Jackson 1998). These discrepant interpretations are typically evaluated by applying scalar measures of segregation that likewise presume unidimensionality (such as the index of dissimilarity). There is accordingly a close correspondence between classical unidimensional theorizing and the methodologies that have to date been adopted to describe and compare sex segregation.

This unidimensional orientation is not nearly so dominant in other sectors of the field. Indeed, when the agenda shifts from describing segregation to explaining it, the literature does become explicitly multidimensional. In individual-level models of hiring and promotion, much is typically made of the distinction between (a) segregation arising from demand-side discrimination, and (b) segregation arising from the supply-side effects of preferences, expectations, and investment decisions (such as investments in education). In some evolutionary stories, the discriminatory component of segregation is seen as withering away (by virtue of competitive forces and bureaucratization), leaving a residue of pure supply-side segregation that presumably has real staying power even within modern stratification regimes.

The main difficulty with this approach is that discrimination cannot be easily ascertained in the nonexperimental context. The usual approach is to equate discrimination with the residual gender gap that persists after applying controls for education, experience, and other human capital investments (but see Goldin and Rouse 2000 for new quasi-experimental approaches). While much important research has come out of this conventional operationalization of discrimination, it suffers from the obvious problem that supply-side investment decisions are themselves shaped by expectations about future domestic responsibilities as well as the perceived structure of discrimination in the labor market. Within this literature, scholars often fret about omitted human capital variables and the consequent upward bias in the discrimination effect, but they should perhaps be equally troubled by the countervailing bias that arises from ignoring the "feedback effects" of discrimination on expectations and investments. To be sure, these feedback effects are well known and frequently discussed (e.g., Blau and Kahn, forthcoming), yet their full implications seem underappreciated. There is ample room, then, to question the deep disciplinary commitment to the seductive but impossible task of distinguishing between segregation that is induced by discrimination and that which is induced by supply-side forces.

The distinction between horizontal and vertical segregation is, by contrast, readily operationalized and arguably more useful in understanding both the dynamics of segregation and its variability across countries. In the following sections, we consider these two dimensions of segregation in turn, laying out some of the mechanisms that generate and maintain them. We suggest that horizontal and vertical segregation are principally cultural and institutional phenomena that reflect two deeply rooted ideological tenets.

The first, *gender essentialism*, represents women as more competent than men in service, nurturance, and social interaction. The second, *male primacy*, represents men as more status worthy than women and accordingly more appropriate for positions of authority and domination (e.g., Kilbourne et al. 2001; Ridgeway, forthcoming). Although biological differences between the sexes (women's reproductive role, men's greater physical strength) may have contributed to the initial development of these principles, they have subsequently become ideologically and institutionally entrenched and have accordingly taken on lives of their own (e.g., Firestone 1970; Chafetz 1984; Collins et al. 1993; Huber 1999).[9]

Horizontal Inequalities and Gender Essentialism

We begin by asking why there is "horizontal segregation." Why, in other words, do women crowd into the nonmanual sector and men crowd into the manual sector? In understanding such segregation, one has to be struck by the strong correspondence between (a) the traits that are regarded as distinctively male or female (gender essentialism) and (b) the task requirements of manual and nonmanual labor. We explore the implications of this correspondence below.

Although prevailing characterizations of male and female traits are complex and multifaceted, a core feature of such characterizations is that women are presumed to excel in personal service, nurturance, and interpersonal interaction, while men are presumed to excel in interaction with things (rather than people) and in strenuous or physical labor (Zaretsky 1986; H. Bradley 1989; Eagly and Mladinic 1994; Conway et al. 1996; Elvin-Nowak and Thomsson 2001; Gerson 2002; Fitzsimons 2002).[10] These stereotypes about natural male and female characteristics are disseminated and perpetuated through popular culture and the media,[11] through social interaction in which significant others (parents, peers, teachers) implicitly or explicitly support such interpretations, and through micro-level cognitive processes in which individuals pursue and remember evidence that is consistent with their preexisting stereotypes and ignore, discount, or forget evidence that undermines them (Fiske 1998; Reskin 2000).[12] The main claim that we wish to advance is that horizontal segregation is maintained and reproduced in large part because (a) nonmanual occupations embody characteristics (such as service orientation) that are regarded as prototypically female, and (b) manual occupations embody characteristics (such as strenu-

TABLE 1.1
Mechanisms Underlying Horizontal
and Vertical Segregation

| | TYPE OF SEGREGATION | |
Mechanisms	Horizontal	Vertical
A. Cultural Mechanisms		
1. Employer discrimination	X	X
2. Institutional discrimination	X	X
3. Internalization		
a. Preferences	X	
b. Self-evaluation	X	X
4. Expected sanctions	X	X
5. Labor force commitment		X
B. Other Mechanisms		
1. Statistical discrimination	X	X
2. Networks	X	X

ousness and physicality) that are regarded as prototypically male (see, e.g., Lorber 1993; Milkman and Townsley 1994; C. Tilly 1998; Crompton 2001; Fitzsimons 2002).[13] This linkage between gender essentialism and horizontal segregation arises through the intermediary processes listed in Table 1.1 and elaborated in the following paragraphs.

Before discussing these intermediary processes, it bears noting that our culturalist position is of the weak-form variety, with at least three types of qualifiers limiting its reach. First, we appreciate that many individuals, far from being oversocialized and unreflective, in fact engage with commonplace stereotypes in oppositional or combative ways. That is, we regard principles of gender essentialism as consensual only in the limited sense that most everyone recognizes them as a feature of the social world and often acts in terms of them, even though many men and women may not personally endorse or approve of them (see Ridgeway, forthcoming). Second, we are altogether agnostic on the matter of historical origins, with our culturalism extending only to the limited claim that, whatever its historical origins may be, gender essentialism serves at present to maintain high levels of horizontal segregation in existing occupations and to generate it afresh in new occupations that emerge in the division of labor. Third, the relationship between occupational task content and segregation is not unidirectional and determinist, but rather has what might be termed "dialectical" features. As we argue, the task content of new occupations is a principal determinant of their initial sex composition (meaning that nurturing occupations are more likely to become female-dominated), but at the same time occupations tend to grow and change in ways that bring their task content into better alignment with their initial sex composition (meaning that female-dominated occupations are more likely to become nurturing).

We are therefore pressing a weak-form argument in which (a) internalization is understood to be partial and often shallow, (b) noncultural forces are admissible as "first causes," and (c) reciprocal effects between task content and sex composition are fully incorporated. To be sure, a strong-form culturalist position could be advanced on all three of these fronts, but doing so is unnecessary for our argument.

Bearing these caveats in mind, we can now turn to the social processes that serve as intermediary links between gender essentialism (the foregoing package of "stereotypes" about gender differences) and the generation and maintenance of horizontal segregation. In some essentialist accounts, scholars merely make reference to the correspondence between occupational task content and sex composition, almost as if the mechanisms through which such correspondence is secured were obvious. We show that these mechanisms are, to the contrary, unobvious and often complicated. Moreover, insofar as intervening mechanisms are made explicit, one can more plausibly predict and understand the forces for change and variability in horizontal segregation. We accordingly proceed by first laying out the mechanisms that express cultural (i.e., "gender essentialist") forces and then turn to other sources of horizontal segregation that arise from noncultural forces.

Employer discrimination. We begin with the demand-side effects of gender stereotypes on employer preferences and perceptions. If personnel managers have indeed internalized essentialist stereotypes, they will tend to hire, fire, and promote in accord with such stereotypes, thereby generating horizontal segregation in its many forms (Reskin and Roos 1990). These tastes for discrimination can be present even among employers and managers who consciously disavow them or who regard their gender-based hiring as an efficient adaptation to objective gender-based differences in productivity (see, esp., Reskin 2000, p. 322). That is, employers who presume to be engaging in statistical discrimination may in fact be discriminating in ways that are *not* undergirded by true gender differences in productivity, given that stereotyping of the sort generated by essentialist accounts can predispose observers toward interpretations that blind them to disconfirming evidence and therefore prevent them from appreciating that their assumptions about gender-based differences are off the mark (Fiske 1998).

Institutional discrimination. The foregoing essentialist views are also institutionally embedded in personnel practices, educational systems, and firm-internal promotion ladders. For example, the underrepresentation of women in the manual sector is sustained not merely by the pure discrimination of employers and personnel managers, but also by the institutionalization of such discrimination in the form of laws and regulations prohibiting women from heavy lifting. In the United States, such laws were deemed unconstitutional in 1970, yet Bielby and Baron (1984) have shown that organizational practices excluding women from physically strenuous jobs remained largely unchanged thereafter. The institutionalization of gender essentialism thus allows horizontal segregation to live on even when the underlying essentialist tastes begin to dissipate.

Preferences. We do not wish to suggest that the effects of gender essentialism operate entirely or even predominantly on the demand side. To the contrary, just as gender stereotypes generate tastes for discrimination by employers, so too do they shape the preferences of workers. Through the usual processes of socialization, children internalize the sex-typed expectations of others, thereby converting these expectations into durable sex-typed aspirations and preferences, some of which operate at the subconscious level.

When girls internalize essentialist stereotypes that associate males with physical labor, they become less likely to prefer and aspire to physically strenuous work, to embark on the requisite training for such work, or to persist in such work in the face of difficulties. This mechanism accordingly presumes that gender-specific preferences are internalized early in life, affect subsequent investment decisions and aspirations, and form a stable component of the adult personality (Parsons and Bales 1955; Chodorow 1978; Bourdieu 2001; see also Xie and Shauman 2003 on the segregative effects of individual choice over the life course).

Self-evaluation. Essentialist beliefs can also affect how workers come to understand their skills and abilities (see Table 1.1). As Correll (2004) cleverly shows, women tend to regard themselves as less competent than men at male-typed tasks, even when objectively they are just as competent. This mechanism implies that women eschew physical work not merely because, relative to men, they find it less desirable (a preference-based mechanism), but also because they believe that they are less competent at it. Even in the absence of sex-specific preferences, internalized beliefs about gender difference can thus result in biased self-evaluations of performance, thereby contributing to horizontal segregation. This mechanism capitalizes on deeply internalized meritocratic presuppositions; indeed, even if men and women resolve to pursue only those occupations for which they believe themselves qualified, horizontal segregation will be generated because beliefs about abilities and qualifications are themselves sex-typed (regardless of whether there is any objective foundation for such sex-typing).

Expected sanctions. Although internalization is, then, an important pathway through which essentialism expresses itself, it also operates through the real and anticipated sanctions associated with nonconforming action. Because gender is omnirelevant to social life, many types of behaviors are evaluated against prevailing standards of femininity and masculinity, and such evaluations obviously alter the attractiveness of displaying such behaviors. It follows that workers who transgress norms about gender-appropriate labor are subject to sanctions of various sorts (see, e.g., Goffman 1977; West and Zimmerman 1987; Fenstermaker and West 2002).

The sanctions may range from the quiet disapproval of parents (when, for example, a son announces his desire to become a nurse) to overt discrimination against gender-atypical coworkers (when, for example, construction workers harass a female coworker). These negative reactions generate a feedback effect because they come to be anticipated and thereby shape individual aspirations, preferences, and human capital investments (see Kanter 1977; Blair-Loy 2001; and Kennelly 2002 on the behavioral manifestations of gender stereotyping within firms). In this sense, even those who disavow essentialist beliefs must take them into account because they believe that others still embrace such beliefs, that others still evaluate them in terms of such beliefs, and that others will still sanction them for failing to conform to such beliefs. This tendency to attribute essentialist beliefs to others renders essentialism especially pernicious by allowing it to live on even as feminist "opinion leaders" come to question it (see Fenstermaker and West 2001, pp. 29–30).

The preceding processes constitute the main mechanisms through which gender essentialism contributes to horizontal segregation. We appreciate, however, that horizontal segregation is also generated by mechanisms that are unrelated to gender essentialism (see panel B, Table 1.1). For example, because women tend to have less upper-body strength than men, horizontal segregation may partly reflect differential capacities for physical labor. In some mining, construction, and laboring occupations, the core job tasks may require more physical strength than the average woman possesses, leading employers to discriminate against all women in hiring for them. By virtue of the usual processes of statistical discrimination, small sex differences in physical strength can be parlayed into more extreme forms of sex segregation, such that even women who are physically capable of performing the work are disqualified.

Likewise, horizontal segregation is also perpetuated by various inertial forces, such as the tendency for men to have a disproportionate number of friends, peers, and other network ties in the manual sector. Because much hiring occurs via informal networks, male manual workers will draw their male friends and peers into similar lines of work, thereby generating horizontal segregation anew. Again, this network mechanism is not directly related to gender essentialism, but it does reproduce and amplify forms of segregation that have their sources in essentialist processes.

We stress, in conclusion, that the relationship between occupational task content and segregation is neither unidirectional nor determinist. Although the task content of new occupations is perhaps the principal determinant of their initial sex composition, we suspect that occupations tend to grow and change in ways that bring their task content into better alignment with the initial demographic composition. This dialectical relationship is clearly revealed in the evolution of the craft and mass-manufacturing sectors. When production moved from home to factory during the eighteenth and nineteenth centuries, an ideology of "separate spheres" was consolidated, and the blue-collar workplace accordingly emerged and evolved under the presumption that men alone would work in it.[14] This "separate spheres" ideal, by which married women were excluded from paid work and men served as breadwinners, was buttressed by protective labor laws and exclusionary labor-union practices, many of which remained in effect until the 1970s in the United States. It was under these historical circumstances that employment structures (full-time, lifelong), pay practices (the family wage), and work cultures (masculine bravado) crystallized in many of the skilled craft and mass-manufacturing sectors that dominated the industrial economy (Kessler-Harris 1982; Milkman 1987).[15] In this sense, the blue-collar sector developed a "male" culture and institutional structure as an adjustment to its initial male composition, thus creating the conditions for an enduring male-typing of this sector even as the presumption of separate spheres began to lose force (see Clement and Myles 1994, pp. 22–23).

The staying power of horizontal sex segregation may therefore be attributed to the inertial effects of such adjustment processes as well as to the generative mechanisms summarized in Table 1.1. Although the causal relationship between task content and gender composition is accordingly bidirectional, this relationship is in either case grounded in essentialist representations about the types of traits that are fundamentally male or female. We argue in the following sections that modern norms of equality have proven to be quite compatible with such essentialist representations (see, e.g., Berkovitch 1999; Elvin-Nowak and Thomsson 2001).

Vertical Inequalities and Male Primacy

We turn next to the question of why men are disproportionately allocated to the best-paid and most desirable occupations in both the nonmanual and manual sectors. In accounting for this vertical segregation, we again understand the main forces at work as being cultural in form, but now the relevant cultural principle is the long-standing belief that men are more status worthy than women and accordingly better suited for positions of authority and domination. As Ridgeway (forthcoming) notes, ideologies of difference ("gender-role essentialism") tend to be converted into ideologies of hierarchy ("male primacy"), with the implication that members of both groups "come to agree (or concede) that, as a matter of social reality, one group is more respected and status worthy than the other" (p. 9).[16] Despite the rise of universalistic ideals, there persist deeply rooted and widely shared cultural beliefs that men's traits are more valuable than women's, that men are generally more competent than women, and that men are better suited than women for positions involving the exercise of authority and power (Deaux and Kite 1987; Ridgeway 1997). We are arguing, then, that vertical segregation is maintained and reproduced in part because it is consistent with the cultural value of male primacy.

For some theorists, this link between values of male primacy and segregation practices is regarded as self-evident (e.g., Firestone 1970), but again we think that the underlying mechanisms are usefully elaborated. As indicated in Table 1.1, the premise of male primacy generates vertical segregation through several cultural mechanisms, some of which are directly analogous to those that generate horizontal segregation. For example, the "employer discrimination" mechanism operates for both types of segregation, given that employers not only internalize (a) the essentialist view that women are fundamentally caring and supportive and hence appropriately assigned to nurturant tasks, but also (b) the corollary assumption that men are especially competent and therefore appropriately assigned to high-status positions in both the nonmanual and manual sectors.[17] The "self-evaluation" mechanism, which again relies on internalization, likewise operates similarly for vertical and horizontal forms of segregation (line A3(b)). That is, women presumably evaluate themselves as less competent for all kinds of male-typed tasks, those involving physical labor as well as those involving the exercise of authority and autonomy.

It is equally clear that some generative mechanisms operate differently across the two forms of segregation. Most notably, legal and regulative forces play a less prominent role in generating vertical segregation, because formal prohibitions have historically precluded women from heavy lifting but not from occupying high-status positions per se. We also suspect that the "preferences" mechanism plays a relatively weak role in generating vertical segregation. While some women may reconcile themselves to discrimination of the "male primacy" variety and hence opt out of pursuing more desirable positions, this process entails a realistic adaptation to discrimination and expected sanctions (line A4) rather than any intrinsic preference for lesser positions. For other women, real "submissive dispositions" may also be in play (Bourdieu 2001); and it is accordingly premature to summarily rule out the possibility that a deeper preference mechanism accounts, in part, for the tendency of women to crowd into subordinate occupations.

Although a preferences account of vertical segregation requires one to postulate gender-specific tastes, a "commitment mechanism" can, by contrast, account for such segregation more economically (line A5). The latter mechanism emphasizes differences in labor force commitment that emerge from the sex-typed household division of labor. Because women continue to be disproportionately responsible for domestic duties (even in two-earner households), their commitment to the formal labor force is often reduced, and they may therefore select themselves out of competition for high-status positions that are typically demanding, stressful, and thereby inconsistent with the domestic responsibilities that women expect to assume. This line of argumentation, while closely associated with neoclassical economic formulations (see, e.g., G. Becker 1985, 1991), can also be motivated by functionalist, culturalist, and feminist perspectives on work-family relations (e.g., Parsons and Bales 1955; Rose 1992; Hartmann 1976; Chafetz 1988; Walby 1990; Hakim 2000; Williams 2000; Blair-Loy 2003). Whatever the mechanism through which domestic responsibilities have an effect, the important point for our purposes is that such responsibilities better explain vertical than horizontal forms of segregation (see Table 1.1).

The conventional evolutionary account implies that presumptions of male primacy are gradually weakening as universalism and egalitarianism diffuse and ascriptive status hierarchies become delegitimized. We argue in the following that such forces serve principally to undermine the presumption of male primacy rather than gender essentialism; and, consequently, vertical forms of segregation are especially susceptible to weakening. This weakening occurs, for example, with declines in individual and institutional discrimination, external sanctioning, and biased self-evaluations, as well as through structural changes that undermine the commitment mechanism (such as state-provided child care and family-friendly workplaces). At the same time, we suggest that egalitarian pressures do not operate evenly throughout the occupational structure, but rather are most apparent in the more meritocratic cultures of elite nonmanual occupations (such as professions and management). We elaborate on the rise of gender egalitarianism in the next section.

Effects of Gender Egalitarianism

The decades since the 1960s have been characterized by growing national and international attention to issues of gender equality. In contemporary discourse, the presumption that women are full citizens with the same rights and responsibilities as men is increasingly prevalent, as evidenced by changing popular attitudes about gender and the sexual division of labor, increased public discussion of women's rights and roles, the proliferation of national and international feminist organizations, and the rise of rules, laws, and related provisions aimed at increasing gender equality in families, educational institutions, and political arenas (Pietilä and Vickers 1990; Evans and Mason 1996; Inglehart 1997; Inglehart and Norris 2003; Ramirez, Soysal, and Shanahan 1997; Berkovitch 1999; K. Bradley and Charles 2003). These egalitarian principles are also expressed within modern labor markets in the form of universalistic hiring practices (credentialism, equal opportunity programs) and bureaucratized pay scales and promotion procedures (Meyer and Rowan 1977; DiMaggio and Powell 1983; Dobbin et al. 1993; Jackson 1998; Reskin and McBrier 2000).

For our purposes, it suffices to simply review these well-known developments while remaining largely agnostic as to their causes. In functionalist and neoclassical economic accounts, universalistic practices are presumed to spread because they are intrinsically efficient, meaning that discriminating firms are less profitable and will either adopt meritocratic forms of allocation or face the risk of elimination from the market (K. Davis and Moore 1945; Kerr et al. 1960; Goode 1963; Treiman 1970; D. Bell 1973; see Inglehart and Baker 2000 for a less deterministic version). As meritocratic organizational practices and legal equality mandates proliferate, a cultural commitment to universalistic principles often emerges and comes to be taken for granted, even among employers and workers who did not originally espouse egalitarian goals (Goode 1963; Parsons 1970). Nonetheless, functionalists treat these cultural principles as rooted, first and foremost, in the exigencies of modern industrial or postindustrial production.

The conventional opposing view, best expressed within the neoinstitutionalist tradition, understands the emergence of egalitarian norms and institutions as a primarily *cultural* phenomenon, grounded in Western ideals of progress, justice, and equality that continue to be endogenously "worked out" irrespective of their real efficiency (Ramirez 1987; Meyer et al. 1997; Berkovitch 1999; Meyer 2001; Ramirez and Wotipka 2001). According to these accounts, universalistic and gender-egalitarian ideals have progressively penetrated international society and have diffused cross-nationally, with the momentum for cross-national change intensifying in recent years because of the spread of world markets and the increasing scope and visibility of supranational bodies, international conventions, and treaties. Indeed, virtually all of the major international bodies, including the United Nations, the World Health Organization, and the World Bank, now affirm gender equality as a fundamental social goal.

The resulting diffusion of egalitarian premises, unprecedented though it is, obviously remains partial and incomplete, with important and persisting national, regional, and occupational differences in the degree to which such ideals have been accepted and institutionalized. This variability may be understood as arising from differences in (a) the penetration of the "market principle" and hence the extent of competitive pressures, (b) the extent to which preexisting cultural commitments are consistent with or receptive to egalitarian formulations, and (c) the extent to which preexisting institutional forms are consistent with or receptive to universalistic organizational arrangements. The literature exploring the sources of these differences is at once rich and inconclusive (see, e.g., Lipset, Bendix, and Zetterberg 1959; Kerr et al. 1960; Ruggie 1984; Orloff 1993; Sainsbury 1996; Wuthnow 1989; Lamont 2000).

We are especially interested in how this rise of egalitarianism undermines vertical forms of segregation. This effect would appear to play out in two main ways. First, symbolic representations of equal "personhood" shape individual cognition and, ultimately, come to be embodied in individual and collective action. As liberal norms of individual equality and equal opportunity become more pervasive and deeply rooted, men's and women's educational, familial, and labor market choices, and employers' decisions about hiring, placement, and promotion will be influenced less often, and to a lesser degree, by norms of male primacy.[18] In the parlance of Table 1.1, it follows that women will become more likely to evaluate themselves as capable of performing high-status tasks (line A3(b)), that employers will gradually shed their tastes for vertical discrimination against women (line A1), that institutional discrimination will be delegitimized and gradually eliminated (line A2), and that women will, in turn, increasingly pursue high-status positions as their expectations of discrimination and other external sanctions recede (line A4).

Although a strict neoinstitutionalist position emphasizes that these changes arise from a growing cultural commitment to egalitarianism, we suggest that market forces are also implicated. That is, employers will be less likely to support vertical segregation not merely by virtue of their own shifting cultural premises but also because, in a society where egalitarianism has spread and become institutionalized, there are nontrivial legal, financial, and public-relations penalties imposed on discriminatory firms. The second effect, then, of the rise of egalitarianism is a substantial change in the costs of discrimination, a change to which employers must attend even if their own tastes for egalitarianism lag behind those of the labor market at large.

If neoinstitutionalist and neoclassical accounts are fused in this way, it becomes apparent that the costs of exercising discriminatory tastes (see G. Becker 1971) are a function of the institutional and cultural environment in which employers operate. Indeed, insofar as discrimination has a market cost, it is partly because the social and cultural diffusion of egalitarian practices makes it costly. To be sure, neoclassical economists correctly stress that, regardless of the institutional and cultural setting, discriminatory employers will overpay for the preferred category of labor and thereby operate less efficiently. But such "pure" (i.e., institution-free) costs of discrimination are probably swamped by the social costs of attempting to operate a discriminatory firm in an environment that has delegitimated vertical discrimination. The long persistence of discriminatory practices throughout the nineteenth and early twentieth centuries is consistent with this claim that employers can readily overcome such pure inefficiencies and will fundamentally rethink their hiring and promotion practices only when confronted with an additional layer of social costs.

The spread of egalitarianism thus reduces vertical segregation, both because tastes for vertical discrimination recede and because its social costs increase. We are, however, skeptical of accounts that assume that egalitarianism will weaken all forms of segregation equally. There are, to the contrary, two main fronts of resistance: (a) the cultural content of egalitarianism speaks principally to issues of male primacy and does not, therefore, directly delegitimate horizontal forms of segregation, and (b) the manual sector has been rather less receptive than the nonmanual sector to egalitarian principles.

The first form of resistance reflects the specific *content* of gender-egalitarian mandates. The vision of "women's rights" that is embodied in modern social agendas is by and large a liberal individualistic one, with men and women viewed as autonomous agents entitled to equal rights, opportunities, and treatment. In this sense, egalitarian mandates are understood largely in procedural terms as norms against ascriptive discrimination on the basis of class, race, or gender. These ideals are difficult to reconcile with blatant male bias in hiring and promotion and with overtly discriminatory practices that have historically protected male monopolies in such key public institutions as higher education, the polity, and the labor market. When women are culturally redefined as equal citizens entitled to the same basic rights as men, and when *formal* legal and organizational barriers to full female participation in educational and market institutions are weakened or eliminated, increasing numbers of women will acquire the human and social capital necessary for gaining access to high-status occupations.

However, even though this commitment to procedural equality is part and parcel of liberal individualism, the individual "selves" at the center of liberal theory remain social and cultural entities with fundamentally gendered outlooks and identities. The modern form of egalitarianism that has emerged accordingly allows men and women to understand their roles and competencies in ways that are consistent with standard essentialist visions of masculinity and femininity (Bourdieu 2001; see also Loury 2002 for a similar argument about racial inequality).[19] Consequently, despite the spread of procedural provisions for "equal opportunity," cultural stereotypes about gender differences will maintain their influence on family, educational, and occupational preferences and choices (Table 1.1, line A3 (a)).

These essentialist stereotypes also serve to maintain residual forms of employer discrimination (line A1). The norm of procedural equality may be gradually institutionalized in the workplace and therefore delegitimate blatant discrimination by employers, but more subtle forms of discrimination arising from essentialist prejudices (such as the presumption that women are more nurturant) can and do live on. In the labor market, this essentialist coloring of employer tastes and worker preferences is manifested in persistent horizontal distinctions, specifically the ongoing "hypersegregation" of manual and nonmanual work.[20]

We conclude that deeply rooted and widely shared cultural beliefs about gender difference are ideologically compatible with liberal egalitarian norms. This durable essentialism supports gender-typical identities and behaviors and thereby preserves horizontal sex segregation in modern labor markets. With the rise of formal equality, women increasingly enter higher education and the paid labor market, but they do so in ways that are consistent with their essentialist preferences, with the essentialist sanctions imposed by others, and with the essentialist prejudices of employers. It follows that sex segregation in the modern period is shaped by "different but equal" conceptualizations of gender and social justice (see also Charles and Bradley 2002 on sex segregation across fields of study).[21]

If our first point, then, is that a "different but equal" form of egalitarianism has taken hold, our second point is that even this restrictive form has not spread uniformly throughout the occupational structure. There is, in particular, rather more tolerance for vertical segregation in the manual sector, where men continue to dominate the most desirable skilled craft positions while women are allocated to less desirable semiskilled, laboring, or service positions.

This difference arises partly because the nonmanual workplace is subject to closer public scrutiny. That is, nonmanual employers who continue to segregate on the vertical principle face substantial social costs, if only because the public visibility of elite professional and managerial positions heightens political pressures to conform to equal opportunity laws and norms of gender equality. Moreover, because qualification for managerial and professional jobs can often be formally demonstrated on the basis of educational credentials, processes governing allocation to these positions are likely to be more meritocratic. Finally, women seeking elite professional and managerial occupations tend to be highly educated and strongly committed to the formal labor force, meaning that they have more interest in and resources for insisting on equal opportunity than do those who view their market role as secondary (see Hakim 2000 on the heterogeneity in the female labor force). The foregoing arguments imply that nonmanual employers who discriminate will face considerable social disapprobation.[22]

Effects of Economic Structure

The segregation regime is obviously affected by economic as well as cultural forces. We suspect that *service-sector expansion* and *economic rationalization* are especially important sources of economic change in segregation regimes, and we accordingly focus on these sources throughout this book. Although other economic and structural forces are at work, we argue that at least some of them are a direct consequence of service-sector expansion and economic rationalization.

The service sector comprises industries devoted to providing services rather than producing goods. The expansion of this sector affects the structure of occupational sex segregation because of (a) changes in the industrial composition of occupations (the "compositional effect"), and (b) workplace adaptations that make the routine nonmanual sector the default province of women with substantial domestic responsibilities (the "adaptive effect"). The compositional effect arises because some market-based services are functionally and symbolically similar to traditional domestic activities of women (especially personal service industries), and because such services often demand emotional labor or interpersonal skills that are female-typed (retail sales, banking, and communication industries). As the service sector grows, the industrial mix of some occupations becomes increasingly service-based, and female representation therefore increases in such occupations (Oppenheimer 1970; Hartmann 1976; Izraeli 1979; Semyonov and Scott 1983; H. Bradley 1989; Cotter, Hermsen, and Vanneman 2001).[23] The occupations of clerk and manager, for example, should become feminized to the extent that they are increasingly performed in service industries that tend to recruit or attract women. This process of industry-driven feminization contributes to horizontal segregation because the compositional effect plays out principally in nonmanual occupations.[24]

The adaptive effect is likewise predicated on the expansion of service-sector activities, but the focus shifts to the second-order structural and cultural changes that this expansion brings about in the workplace. These adaptive changes become necessary because service-sector expansion raises the demand for labor to the point that it can no longer be met by simply drawing further on the largely tapped supply of single women. Instead, employers often turn to nonemployed wives and mothers as an alternative supply of labor, especially in the rapidly-expanding routine nonmanual sector.[25] This new labor force has substantial domestic responsibilities that create pressure for such adaptations as part-time work, flexible scheduling, and reduced penalties for intermittency (Oppenheimer 1973; L. Tilly and Scott 1978; Ruggie 1984; Kuhn and Bluestone 1987; Reskin and Roos 1990). In this fashion, the structure and culture of the routine nonmanual workplace becomes increasingly female-oriented, much as the craft workplace adapted to the needs and requirements of male labor in the eighteenth and nineteenth centuries. Through these adaptive changes the routine nonmanual sector gradually becomes the default "home" for female labor. It follows that service-sector expansion in Sweden and other postindustrial welfare states has the dual effect of raising rates of female labor force participation while also strengthening vertical segregation by feminizing the lower nonmanual sector.

The process of postindustrialization classically involves not merely service-sector expansion but "economic rationalization" as well. We are referring here to ongoing differentiation in the division of labor, the consequent increase in functional specialization, and the associated routinization of job tasks and personnel practices in some economic sectors (Braverman 1974; Thurow 1975; Bluestone et al. 1981; Tienda, Smith, and Ortiz 1987). These processes are revealed, for example, in the replacement of proprietor-run specialty stores and service establishments (restaurants, laundries, hotels) with large discount stores and chains. As independent entrepreneurs disappear, clerical and sales jobs are typically routinized and deskilled, and women are actively recruited to fill them (Davies 1975; L. Tilly and Scott 1978; Reskin and Roos 1990). The main effect of economic rationalization has thus been to feminize lower nonmanual work and thereby increase vertical segregation within the nonmanual sector. However, rationalization also generates new opportunities for elite, career-committed women in the managerial sector, which grows in response to problems with coordinating and supervising the additional lower-level workers.

We conclude that growing demands for female-typed nonmanual labor are principally met by drawing in women who have a less substantial commitment to the labor force. By contrast, the female labor force of less developed countries is more stringently "culled," meaning that women who enter the nonagricultural labor market in these countries are typically highly educated and strongly committed to their market careers.[26] As service jobs in the formal economy proliferate, the female labor force grows and comes to include a larger share of workers with extensive family responsibilities, less education, and more traditional gender-role ideals (K. Davis 1984; H. Bradley 1989; Goldin 1990; Charles 1992; Charles and Grusky 1995; Hakim 2000). This influx of "less elite" women into the formal economy generates relatively high levels of vertical segregation in the nonmanual sector of postindustrial economies.[27] By implication, the "pink collar" occupational ghetto should not be regarded as a holdover, but rather as an organic outcome of postindustrial economic restructuring.

Other Macro-Level Effects

Although the preceding forces are, in our view, the dominant ones at work, we know that other social, demographic, and economic forces also affect the structure of occupational segregation. For example, the growing representation of women in elite educational institutions and in the formal labor market should change attitudes about gender roles and thereby undermine individual and institutional discrimination, raise female aspirations and self-evaluations, and reduce the extent to which market behavior is conditioned by expectations of gender discrimination and stereotypes (K. Davis 1984; Ramirez 1987). Likewise, emerging parity in the human capital investments of men and women undermines the rationale for a gender-based division of household labor, while delays in the onset of childbearing and associated reductions in overall fertility allow women to better compete with men for demanding professional and managerial positions. Finally, direct political interventions (such as affirmative action) can affect patterns of sex segregation, as can the emergence of a woman-friendly public sector, the decline of male-biased union policies, and the diffusion of occupational closure tactics that are comparatively universalistic (such as formal licensing). To this point, we have implied that such variables are best viewed as *outcomes* of the grander forces of egalitarianism and postindustrialism, yet we must bear in mind that they are also independent *catalysts* for further weakening of anti-egalitarian culture and gender.

We do not attempt here to sort out the complicated relationships between variables of this sort (see Charles 1992, 1998, for relevant analyses; also, Blalock 1967; Thurow 1975; Semyonov and Shenhav 1988). Rather, we wish merely to stress that the tendency for various gender-equalizing developments to cluster together in time and location is not entirely accidental, but instead suggests that larger egalitarian commitments undergird these developments. In this sense, egalitarianism provides the requisite cultural support for all manner of gender-equalizing institutional change (including political interventions, growing gender parity in education, delays in the onset of childbearing), and absent such cultural support it seems doubtful that these changes would have so quickly diffused.

METHODOLOGICAL ISSUES

The foregoing hypotheses about the structure of sex segregation cannot be adequately addressed using standard comparative methods and data. Instead, analysts must use measures that preserve information on the occupation-specific contours of segregation (especially its vertical and horizontal components), while also employing data that are detailed enough to allow segregation to be explored at both aggregate and disaggregate occupational levels. The main purpose of this book is to characterize the structure of segregation that emerges when these simple methodological strictures are followed.

We have argued elsewhere (Charles and Grusky 1995; Grusky and Charles 1998, 2001) that comparative analyses of sex segregation have been limited by three methodological weaknesses. First, the multidimensionality of segregation regimes cannot be adequately captured when they are characterized, as is conventionally the case, with the index of dissimilarity ("D"), the size-standardized index of dissimilarity, or any other scalar index values. Second, such conventional indices are sensitive to temporal or intercountry differences in (a) the occupational structure (the relative sizes of occupations), or (b) rates of female labor force participation (the relative sizes of the gender categories). Finally, by relying on highly aggregate occupational categories, previous comparative studies have left open the possibility that the appearance of cross-national variability in segregation regimes is merely an artifact of differences in the composition of the categories. We review in more detail each of these methodological problems in the remainder of this section.

Summary indices.   The practice of using summary indices is consistent with the prevailing conceptualization of sex segregation as a unidimensional quantity that increases or decreases in across-the-board fashion depending on the level of "gender equality" in any given historical or national context.[28] Indeed, because conventional indices retain no information about *patterns* of segregation, they rest on the implicit assumption that segregation differs only in degree and follows a historically and cross-nationally invariant profile. This assumption is, however, at odds with existing evidence suggesting (a) substantial cross-national variability in the patterning of occupational sex segregation (Haavio-Mannila 1989; Charles 1992; Charles and Grusky 1995), and (b) idiosyncratic changes over time in the sex-typing of particular occupations (Davies 1975; Strober 1984; Reskin and Roos 1990; Crompton, Le Feuvre, and Birkelund 1999). We deploy a new modeling framework that allows the empirical viability of index-based representations to be formally tested (see Chapter 2).

Margin-free indices.   The standard indices are also flawed for comparative purposes because they confound variability in sex segregation with variability in the occupational structure and in rates of female labor force participation.[29] It is well known that D is sensitive to changes in the occupational structure. Although there is a long history of efforts to repair this defect (e.g., F. Blau and Hendricks 1979; Silber 1989; Watts 1992; Siltanen, Jarman, and Blackburn 1995), none of the proposed repairs can eliminate the dependency without, ironically, introducing a new dependency on rates of female labor force participation (Grusky and Charles 1998; see also Chapter 2).[30]

We have therefore developed a new "margin-free" index, A, that is unaffected by variability in rates of female labor force participation and in the sizes of the occupational categories. We should stress, however, that this index is no panacea; in fact, we caution against the exclusive use of *any* scalar measure, given that segregation profiles are only rarely invariant and that cross-table variation cannot, therefore, typically be captured with a single parameter (see Chapters 2 and 3). It follows that A should be used judiciously in conjunction with modeling that can better reveal the underlying structure of segregation regimes.

Disaggregate analyses. The field of comparative segregation analysis has long been hampered by problems of data availability, comparability, and validity. Because of these problems, previous comparative and historical research has been mainly based on highly aggregated occupational data (e.g., Charles 1992; Jacobs and Lim 1992), on impressionistic or qualitative studies (e.g., Blekher 1979), or on classificatory schemes that are cross-nationally or historically variable (e.g., Hakim 1994; Anker 1998). We have taken here the more ambitious approach of assembling an archive of highly detailed and cross-nationally harmonized occupational data for ten industrial market economies (see Chapters 3 and 4). This approach allows us to offer a richer and more systematic description of cross-national variability in men's and women's occupational roles than has previously been possible.[31]

The resulting archive of segregation data is, alas, cross-sectional in structure because it proved infeasible to assemble a harmonized time series of segregation data for all ten countries. We therefore proceed by carrying out trend analyses in three countries of particular theoretical interest (the United States, Japan, Switzerland). Although our modeling approach has been frequently applied to cross-national segregation data (Charles 1990, 1992, 1998; Charles and Grusky 1995; Grusky and Charles 1998, 2001; Nermo 2000;

Chang, 2004), it has not been exploited to the same extent for the purposes of trend analysis (cf. Weeden 1998). For reasons of data availability and quality, these analyses are limited to the second half of the twentieth century, except in the United States (where a longer, high-quality time series is available).[32]

OVERVIEW

The remaining chapters of this book engage more systematically with the preceding issues. We begin in Chapter 2 by reviewing the characteristic methodologies of comparative and historical sex-segregation research and explaining why these methodologies are theoretically and empirically unsatisfactory. We then introduce our remedy, a structural modeling approach, that makes it possible to uncover commonalities and differences in segregation patterns after eliminating the confounding effects of variability in the occupational structure and in rates of female labor force participation. This chapter introduces the core models and measures employed throughout this volume and shows how they relate to conventional theoretical accounts of the causes and contours of occupational sex segregation.

We then turn to issues of cross-national variability by applying these models to our ten-country data set. In Chapter 3, we provide a detailed portrait of the underlying structure of sex segregation in industrial market economies, taking care to distinguish between patterns that appear at the level of detailed occupations and those that appear at the level of major occupations. We find much evidence of variability at the detailed level that is attributable to cross-national differences in the task content of occupations, in the availability of women workers when occupations expand, in the types of occupations that serve as "models" for the purposes of sex-typing, and in other idiosyncratic features of national labor markets, institutions, and occupational structures. We also find significant commonalities at the major occupational level that appear to proceed from the universality of horizontal and vertical processes of segregation. These two processes, generated by the mechanisms listed in Table 1.1, combine to create a characteristic segregation profile in all advanced industrial societies.

In Chapter 4, we use the same international data archive to formally test our arguments about (a) the multidimensionality of sex segregation, and (b) the causes underlying cross-national variability in vertical and horizontal sex segregation. When the segregation profile is explicitly modeled, we find that the characteristic patterning of this profile (at the major occupational level) can indeed be "decomposed" into horizontal and vertical components, with both components reliably appearing in all countries. Although there is much cross-national commonality in these segregation profiles, the variability that does appear can be attributed, in part, to differences in the strength of vertical and horizontal inequalities. These differences in strength may in turn be understood as reflecting international differences in the strength of postindustrialism and cultural egalitarianism. We find, for example, that postindustrialization has the predicted "perverse effect" of increasing both horizontal segregation and vertical segregation (among nonmanual occupations). At the same time, gender egalitarianism is associated with low levels of vertical sex segregation (again in the nonmanual sector), but not with correspondingly low levels of horizontal sex segregation. The latter results make it clear that sex segregation is fundamentally multidimensional and that the logic of egalitarianism does not mechanically reduce all forms of segregation.

The long-term evolution of sex segregation in the United States, Japan, and Switzerland is examined in Chapters 5, 6, and 7. These chapters, some of which are authored and coauthored by our colleagues, focus on three advanced industrialized nations with markedly different cultural traditions, social structures, geopolitical contexts, and histories. The United States is distinguished by its high levels of female labor force participation and university enrollment and by its long-standing legislative and grassroots commitment to formal gender equality. By contrast, Japan is distinguished by its relatively traditional economic structure, with postindustrialization beginning later and proceeding more slowly than in the United States. We also chose to examine sex segregation in Switzerland because our previous comparative analyses indicated that it is extremely segregated and hence potentially useful in understanding how inequality is generated and sustained (see, e.g., Charles and Grusky 1995).[33]

Through historical case studies in three distinct contexts, we learn how particular national characteristics interact with international secular pressures (such as gender egalitarianism and economic restructuring) to generate cross-national variability in the structure of occupational sex segregation. For the most part, the resulting analyses reveal the predicted changes in vertical and horizontal segregation, although those changes are muted or amplified in response to local market and institutional forces.

In the first temporal analysis (Chapter 5), Kim Weeden examines trends in sex segregation in the United States, drawing on detailed and aggregate occupational data compiled from ten decennial censuses spanning the period between 1910 and 2000. The results from these analyses indicate that major changes in segregation partly coincided with commonly referenced historical "punctuation points" (World War II, the feminist movement) but also played out during other periods as well. The main trends at the aggregate level are (a) rising female representation in managerial and professional occupations in the post-1970 period (declining vertical segregation in the nonmanual sector); (b) a gradual feminization of sales occupations throughout the twentieth century; and (c) a more dramatic desegregation of craft, clerical, and service work during the Great Depression. Although many detailed occupations have integrated over the course of the twentieth century, the timing and patterning of this process was quite variable. These results are accordingly inconsistent with conventional evolutionary accounts that presume that segregation declines gradually and uniformly as ascription in its many forms becomes delegitimated.

In Chapter 6, Maria Charles, Mariko Chang, and Joon Han explore the development of sex segregation in Japan from 1950 to 1995. As in the United States, the results indicate that vertical segregation has declined modestly over the last quarter-century, with such declines again most apparent in the nonmanual sector. By contrast, horizontal segregation proves to be far more resistant to change, as women continue to flow into sales and clerical occupations and thereby increase the overrepresentation of women in the nonmanual sector. Historically, horizontal segregation in Japan has been comparatively weak, given that young Japanese men often take clerical jobs and that older Japanese women (so-called "reentrants") have been employed for manufacturing jobs. This characteristically Japanese form of sex segregation shows, however, signs of change, with Japan accordingly evincing an increasingly Westernized pattern of strong horizontal segregation.

The final historical case study, presented in Chapter 7, addresses the evolution of sex segregation in Switzerland between 1970 and 2000. In this chapter we extend our modeling approach to examine segregation by both gender and citizenship status, allowing us to identify how women fare when another subordinate group, foreign workers, coexists in the labor market. We find that vertical segregation (in the nonmanual sector) weakened in Switzerland despite this competition; that is, native women's access to prestigious male-dominated occupations improved substantially in Switzerland, often at the expense of foreign men. This integration was nonetheless slow in coming because of the delayed emergence of gender-egalitarian values and because attractive associate professional positions were so readily available that they siphoned off women who might have otherwise pursued more prestigious positions. The effect of postindustrialization was, by contrast, more deeply modified by the presence of foreign workers. Although the rising demand for associate professional and clerical workers generated the expected postindustrial feminization of these occupations, this segregative effect was partly held in check by employers' reliance on foreign men.

In Chapter 8, Kim Weeden and Jesper Sørensen develop models for cross-classifications of industry, occupation, and sex, thus allowing them to tease out the net effects of occupational and industrial segregation. These models yield results that are consistent with our argument that service-sector expansion has segregation-enhancing effects. That is, women prove to be strongly overrepresented in service industries, even net of interindustry differences in occupational composition. This chapter also provides evidence of substantial interindustry variability in patterns of male and female occupational segregation. The two-dimensional models of segregation introduced here can be readily generalized to study sex segregation across other dimensions, including employment situation (public vs. private sector), work status (full-time vs. part-time), class of worker (self-employed vs. salaried), and establishment size.

The concluding chapter summarizes our main findings, reviews our solutions to each of the empirical puzzles posed at the beginning of this chapter, and outlines future research that might usefully be undertaken. The theme of the conclusion, and indeed the book itself, is that hypersegregation can be expected to persist indefinitely because it expresses essentialist premises that are entirely consistent with modern variants of gender egalitarianism. We turn now to laying out the methodological apparatus that makes it possible to prosecute this argument.

CHAPTER TWO

Toward Linking Theory and Method:
A New Approach to Understanding
Variability in Sex Segregation

The history of comparative research on occupational sex segregation is long and distinguished (see, e.g., Roos 1985; Tienda, Smith, and Ortiz 1987; Goldin 1990; Reskin and Roos 1990; Rosenfeld and Kalleberg 1991; Jacobs and Lim 1992; Charles 1992, 1998; Hakim 1994; Anker 1998; Rubery, Smith, and Fagan 1999; Blackburn, Jarman, and Brooks 2000; Chang 2000; McCall 2001). The staying power of this research tradition is perhaps surprising because it has not been energized by methodological innovations of the sort that have emerged in other high-growth areas of inequality research. In fact, the methods used by comparative segregation scholars have remained largely unchanged for nearly a half-century, with the index of dissimilarity and its close cousins still playing a featured role. To be sure, log-linear and log-multiplicative models have begun to supplant index-based approaches (see, e.g., Charles 1998; Weeden 1998; Chang 2000, 2004; Nermo 2000), but there remains much resistance to these new methods (e.g., Watts 1998; Jacobs 2001). This resistance is unfortunate because a modeling framework allows for greater flexibility in operationalizing and testing different representations of segregation regimes and different forms of historical and cross-national variability in those regimes.

The purpose of this chapter is to briefly review the methodological state of affairs in the field and to indicate why it is problematic. We then introduce our modeling approach and review its advantages in adjudicating between competing accounts of the structure of segregation regimes. Although measurement and theory have typically developed independently in the field, we suggest in this chapter that much is gained by bringing them together. We proceed therefore by combining a technical discussion of measurement issues with a substantive discussion of the features of segregation regimes that our measures ought to capture.

CONVENTIONAL MEASUREMENT TOOLS

The analytic approaches that drive research subfields often bear the imprint of the methodologies that happened to be popular when these subfields took off. In the case of sex segregation research, the first burst of activity occurred when the index of dissimilarity (D) was emerging victorious from a "ten-year index war" (see Peach 1975, p. 3), and the field has labored under the yoke of D ever since. This index, for all its usefulness, has had the unfortunate effect of cutting off methodological innovation, so much so that the concept of segregation has sometimes come to be equated with D itself.

It is instructive to examine the formula for the index of dissimilarity. While D may be expressed in various ways, the following definition is the conventional one:

$$D = \sum_{j=1}^{J} |(F_j/F) - (M_j/M)| \times 100 \times \frac{1}{2}, \tag{2.1}$$

where J refers to the total number of occupations, M_j and F_j refer to the number of men and women in the jth occupation, and M and F refer to the number of men and women in the labor force as a whole. We can interpret D as the percentage of men or women that would have to be removed from the labor force to bring about a perfect correspondence between the sex composition of each occupation and that of the entire labor force (Cortese, Falk, and Cohen 1976). When D is calculated, one is effectively comparing the existing distribution against a perfectly sex-neutral one, with the difference between these distributions characterized by the number of workers who must be excised from the former to generate the latter.

The popularity of D may be partly attributed to the relative ease with which it can be calculated. Moreover, by equating the concept of segregation with the number of workers who are affected by it, D has the (putative) virtue of a concretely individualistic referent. This referent has proved so appealing that alternative approaches have frequently been criticized for failing to have a "readily interpretable meaning" (Jacobs 2001, p. 538), a criticism that, we suspect, is motivated mainly by the absence of the preferred *individualistic* interpretation. It is striking in this regard that the concept of segregation has evolved so idiosyncratically. By contrast, other key labor market concepts, such as discrimination and ascription, have been conceptualized and operationalized in straightforwardly parametric terms; and there has typically been little, if any, interest in calculating the number of workers that the process in question has hypothetically affected.[1]

The more important point for our purposes is that an individualistic conceptualization of segregation necessarily produces a margin-dependent index. Indeed, the main shortcoming of D, a shortcoming that has prompted numerous efforts to revise it, is its sensitivity to cross-national or historical variability in the relative sizes of occupational categories. The value of D will decline, for example, whenever highly segregated occupations (such as craft workers) grow smaller and hence contribute less to the overall index value. Because D is margin-dependent, any changes in D may proceed either from changes in the occupational structure or from more fundamental institutional changes in patterns of socialization, in the aspirations of men or women, or in the determinants of hiring, firing, or promotion. If one presumes, as almost all segregation researchers do, that the "segregation regime" pertains to the joint distribution of sex and occupation, it is then problematic to purport to measure segregation with an index that is affected by changes in the occupational structure alone.

Although this margin dependence has motivated many attempts to formulate alternative indices, the best-known and most frequently used alternative is the so-called size-standardized index of dissimilarity (D_s). This variant of D is calculated as follows:

$$D_s = \sum_{j=1}^{J} \left| \left[\left(\frac{F_j}{M_j + F_j} \right) \middle/ \sum_{j=1}^{J} \left(\frac{F_j}{M_j + F_j} \right) \right] - \left[\left(\frac{M_j}{M_j + F_j} \right) \middle/ \sum_{j=1}^{J} \left(\frac{M_j}{M_j + F_j} \right) \right] \right|$$
$$\times 100 \times \frac{1}{2} \tag{2.2}$$

with all terms defined as before. Until recently, it was not well known that this standardization merely trades off one form of margin dependence for another, eliminating a dependence on the occupational distribution at the cost of introducing a new dependence on the gender distribution (Charles and Grusky 1995; Grusky and Charles 1998). That is, because D_s is sensitive to multiplicative transformations of the sex ratio, its value will typically change

TABLE 2.1
Marginal Dependencies of Various Segregation Indices

		OCCUPATIONAL COMPOSITION	
		Margin-Dependent	*Margin-Free*
GENDER COMPOSITION OF LABOR FORCE	*Margin-Dependent*	Isolation index Interaction index Variance ratio index WE index Sex-ratio index	Size-standardized dissimilarity index I_p index and decomposition Marginal matching index
	Margin-Free	Atkinson index Gini index Index of dissimilarity Lieberson's diversity index	Odds ratios (or functions of them)

NOTE: The interaction and isolation indices are often denoted xP^*y and xP^*x (see Lieberson 1981). The variance ratio index has been labeled S (Zoloth 1976), η^2 (Duncan and Duncan 1955), and the "revised index of isolation" (W. Bell 1954). The diversity index was introduced by Lieberson (1969); the WE index was introduced by the OECD (1980); the sex-ratio index was introduced by Hakim in 1981 (described in Hakim 1992); and the marginal matching index was introduced by Blackburn, Jarman, and Siltanen (1993). The Atkinson index was reviewed by James and Taeuber (1985). See Coulter 1989 for a review of related indices. See Watts 1998 and Grusky and Charles 1998 on the I_p index and its decomposition.

when rates of female labor force participation change. The size-standardized index has thus failed to fully realize the margin-free conceptualization of sex segregation that most scholars in the field have implicitly adopted.

As can be seen in Table 2.1, all conventional segregation indices are margin-dependent, not just D and D_s but a wide range of other popular indices as well. When margin-dependent measures are used, it has to be borne in mind that any variability that is observed (across countries, time periods, or other contexts) can arise not merely from variability in the joint distribution of gender and occupation, but also from variability in either distribution taken singly. Moreover, because conventional indices are sensitive to marginal shifts, it becomes impossible to tease out the causal relationship between sex segregation and such shifts. This is unfortunate because these causal relationships are prominently featured in conventional theorizing about segregation (see, e.g., Oppenheimer 1970; Hakim 2000).

As problematic as such marginal dependencies are, the more fundamental failure of index-based approaches is that they reduce all differences between the male and female occupational distributions to a single parameter, no matter how complicated these differences may be. Put differently, summary indices can reveal differences in the degree of segregation, but not differences in the pattern of segregation. There is much evidence suggesting that differences in pattern are too substantial to ignore (e.g., Charles 1992; Grusky and Charles 1998; Weeden 1998; Nermo 2000). This chapter introduces a framework for characterizing differences across countries, time periods, or regions when these cannot be captured in a single parameter pertaining to the strength of segregation.

A NEW MARGIN-FREE INDEX

We have issued two methodological recommendations aimed at addressing the shortcomings of conventional segregation measures (see Grusky and Charles 1998; Charles and Grusky 1995). First, insofar as segregation scholars insist on an index-based approach, we recommend a new index, A, that is margin-free and therefore better captures prevailing conceptions of segregation. This index may be expressed as follows:

$$A = \exp\left(1/J \times \sum_{j=1}^{J} \left\{ \ln(F_j/M_j) - \left[1/J \times \sum_{j=1}^{J} \ln(F_j/M_j) \right] \right\}^2 \right)^{1/2} \qquad (2.3)$$

where all terms are defined as before. The value of A expresses the extent to which occupation-specific sex ratios deviate from the mean of such ratios calculated across all occupations. If the exponent of A is taken, the resulting value may be interpreted as the multiplicative factor by which males or females are, on average, overrepresented in the occupational categories being analyzed. It follows that A equals zero and $\exp(A)$ equals one when the labor market is perfectly integrated.[2]

Because A is margin-free (see Appendix 2.1), it can be used to compare countries or time periods with different occupational structures or different rates of female labor force participation, thereby solving one of the most pressing methodological problems in the field. This index should therefore replace conventional indices, such as D_s, that have been represented as margin-free but in fact are not. By contrast, some of the classic margin-dependent measures, such as D, were never intended to be margin-free and cannot be faulted on those terms. These classic measures remain useful because they characterize the differences between male and female occupational distributions in appealingly individualistic terms, and because they allow scholars to maintain continuity with prior analysis.

There is, however, no possibility of rendering D or related individualistic measures (see, e.g., Watts 1998) free of all forms of margin-dependence, decades of methodological tinkering notwithstanding. Insofar as margin-free analysis is desired, segregation scholars have no choice but to supplement D with measures based on odds-ratios, thus leading them directly to A (Grusky and Charles 1998). We have introduced A because segregation scholars have long been oriented toward indices and will likely continue using them regardless of whether they can adequately represent the complexity of segregation arrays. We admit, then, to a rather pragmatic rationale for A.

Although likely to go unheeded, our second and more important recommendation is that segregation scholars supplement all index-based analysis (including that based on A) with explicit modeling of segregation arrays because doing so uncovers the structure of these arrays in more revealing ways than conventional indices permit. In some circumstances, the segregation profile may take on the same basic shape in all countries or time periods, thus making it possible to characterize differences with a single parameter pertaining to the degree of segregation (see below for details). However, our earlier research has shown that segregation regimes typically vary in kind as well as degree (Charles and Grusky 1995; Grusky and Charles 2001), meaning that A will not frequently suffice as a stand-alone measurement tool.

We have therefore proposed a general modeling approach that allows segregation scholars to explicitly test the adequacy of scalar measures and, when necessary, to characterize the qualitative (that is, occupation-specific) contours of sex segregation. This general modeling framework, which we introduce in the following section, is applied throughout the book to analyze cross-national variability in sex segregation as well as variability over time. We also introduce extensions to these basic models in some of the subsequent chapters.

TABLE 2.2

A Typology of Cross-National and Historical Similarity in Sex-Segregation Regimes

Regimes	Forms of Similarity in Marginal Effects[a]	Forms of Similarity in Sex Segregation[b]	Forces Underlying Similarity or Variability	Compatible Theories	Defensible Indices
A. Margin-Invariant Forms					
1. Complete similarity	Gender, occupational	Strength, pattern	None	None	D, D_s, A
2. Demand-side similarity	Occupational	Strength, pattern	None	None	D, A
3. Supply-side similarity	Gender	Strength, pattern	Occupational labeling	Oppenheimer	D_s, A
B. Margin-Varying Forms					
4. Universal association	None	Strength, pattern	Universal sex roles, patriarchy	Chodorow; Firestone	A
5. Multiplicative shift	None	Pattern	Variability in egalitarianism	Parsons; Goode	A
6. Multilevel	None	Minor-category strength, minor-category pattern	Macro-institutional forces	Brinton; Charles; Chang	None[c]
7. Saturated	None	None	Micro- and macro-institutional forces	Tilly and Scott; Bradley	None[c]

[a] The gender margin refers to the gender composition of the labor force; the occupational margin refers to the occupational composition of the economy.

[b] Here and throughout the book, "sex segregation" refers to the association between occupation and sex. The "strength" of sex segregation refers to the extent to which women and men are allocated to different occupations; the "pattern" of sex segregation refers to the occupation-specific contours of this association. "Minor categories" are the detailed occupations that comprise aggregate occupational groups.

[c] If an index must be used, A should be chosen.

FORMS OF VARIABILITY AND SIMILARITY
IN SEX SEGREGATION REGIMES

We proceed by distinguishing seven types of cross-contextual similarity and variability in sex segregation regimes and demonstrating that such types are often associated with specific "theories" about the forces accounting for sex segregation (see Table 2.2). The first three specifications place constraints on marginal effects by assuming invariance across contexts in the gender composition of the labor force, the occupational composition of the economy, or both. The next four specifications allow for variability across contexts in these marginal effects. Although we will show that conventional indices are defensible under some of these formulations (see Table 2.2, right-hand column), one cannot determine whether the requisite conditions are in place without first explicitly modeling the data. This implies that even the most diehard defender of indices cannot avoid some amount of modeling.

We lead off by considering a particularly extreme form of invariance in which the cell proportions in a sex-segregation array are identical across all contexts (countries or time periods). If this form of invariance holds perfectly, the observed counts in the segregation array will be identical across contexts up to a scale factor that adjusts for variability in the size of the sample. As we have noted elsewhere (Grusky and Charles 1998), such extreme invariance will be observed only when (a) the marginal effects for gender and occupation are invariant, and (b) the strength and pattern of sex segregation (the sex-by-occupation association) are likewise invariant. These various parameters are generated by such fundamentally different sociological forces that one would be hard-pressed to identify a theory that treats them all of a piece. The best candidate might be a general "theory" of traditional societies that presumes a highly integrated economy in which all forms of labor market change occur extremely slowly. For example, a time series of segregation arrays from the medieval period might well exhibit type 1 invariance, given that the occupational mix in medieval societies presumably changed only slowly, as did rates of female labor force participation and patterns of occupational sex-typing. In the contemporary context, this extreme form of invariance will not typically be found, as the forces for economic and labor market change are obviously more substantial. It is ironic that contemporary indices are nonetheless well suited to detecting such invariance; that is, when type 1 similarity holds, scholars can safely use a wide variety of conventional segregation indices, all of which will properly reveal the invariance in the data (see line 1).

Under type 2 ("demand-side") similarity, the marginal effects for gender are allowed to vary, but all other aspects of type 1 similarity are preserved. This model does *not* imply that the observed occupational margins ($[F_j + M_j]/N$) or the observed occupation-specific sex ratios (F_j/M_j) are necessarily invariant. Rather, it merely implies that any variability in these quantities is entirely attributable to variability in the gender composition of the labor force, with rising female participation serving to (a) increase the relative size of occupations that draw disproportionately from the female labor force, and (b) increase the occupation-specific sex ratios by a constant factor (across all occupations). While supply-side forces are surely important, we doubt that many segregation scholars would take the extreme position that they drive *all* cross-national and historical variability in the occupational structure and in occupation-specific sex ratios. The usefulness of D for comparative purposes nonetheless rests on this assumption. As Table 2.2 indicates, D can be defended as a useful comparative measure only in the unlikely event that type 1 or type 2 invariance holds, as otherwise differences in D will be generated, in part, by variability in occupational demand.

Under type 3 ("supply-side") similarity, the marginal effects for occupations are allowed to vary, but all other aspects of the type 1 specification are preserved. This formulation implies that occupations are identically sex-typed in all contexts (F_j/M_j does not vary by context) and that the gender composition of the labor force (F/M) adjusts to accommodate the "structural need" for female labor. If, for example, the demand for routine non-manual workers (secretaries, clerks) increases, wages in this sector would presumably rise and thereby motivate women whose reservation wage is now met to enter the labor market. The latter mechanism underlies the longstanding argument that rates of female labor force participation have increased in recent decades in response to labor shortages in rapidly growing "female-demanding" occupations (esp. Oppenheimer 1970, 1973; see also Semyonov and Scott 1983; Jones and Rosenfeld 1989; Cotter et al. 1998; Nermo 2000). When type 3 similarity holds, the gender effect is (by definition) invariant across contexts, and D_s will therefore properly detect the simple structure of the data. The test for type 3 invariance is therefore of considerable interest; and, absent such an empirical test, one might well suggest that we dismissed D_s prematurely in our earlier research (Charles and Grusky 1995).

Although a convincing rationale for type 3 invariance can thus be found in the literature, most of the theorizing in the field refers, if only implicitly, to the structure of association after marginal effects are purged. The remaining models in panel B of Table 2.2 impose various constraints on this association while allowing marginal effects to freely vary. The "universal association" model, which is our natural starting point in panel B, presumes that the strength and patterning of occupational sex segregation is invariant across contexts (see line 4). Under this type 4 specification, a family resemblance in segregation regimes ultimately emerges, but such resemblance is "genotypical" in structure and accordingly reveals itself only after (phenotypical) variability in marginal effects is parsed out. This model may be motivated, at least in part, by conventional explanatory accounts of sex segregation (see Table 1.1), since such accounts tend to emphasize the generic forces that cause segregation rather than ways in which these forces are modified across societies or over time.[3] These theories are especially relevant insofar as they explicitly treat the forces underlying segregation as universal or self-perpetuating. For example, theories of patriarchy emphasize the universal power of men to dominate women and the consequent ubiquity of vertical segregation (e.g., Firestone 1970; Hartmann 1976; Strober 1984; Walby 1986; Reskin and Roos 1990), while theories of sex-typing emphasize the deep-rooted identification of women with reproductive, service, and nurturing tasks and the consequent ubiquity of horizontal segregation (e.g., Oakley 1974; Beck-Gernsheim and Ostner 1978; Chodorow 1978; Polachek 1981; Fitzsimons 2002). If type 4 similarity does obtain, it would be obscured by indices that are sensitive to the margins (D, D_s) but would be properly reflected in indices, such as A, that are margin-free (see Table 2.2, line 4).

In this sense, conventional explanatory theories may be seen as consistent with type 4 similarity, but only with the additional caveat that the contours of the (putatively) shared regime are themselves a matter of disagreement. We have sought to review these explanatory theories comprehensively in Chapter 1. As indicated in Table 1.1, some of these theories account for the overrepresentation of women in occupations involving service, reproduction, and nurturing (horizontal segregation), while others account for the underrepresentation of women in the most desirable occupations in the manual and nonmanual sectors (vertical segregation). Typically, each of these theories is regarded as a self-standing and sufficient account of segregation, yet we suspect that the shared segregation profile will reveal the interleaving of horizontal and vertical segregation that, for the most part, may be regarded as complementary rather than mutually exclusive. The analyses presented in Chapters 3 and 4 explore how vertical and horizontal forms of segregation combine in industrial market economies to generate a hybrid profile.

If the universal association model proves to be inconsistent with the data, we can conclude that the strength or patterning of segregation differs across contexts. As indicated in line 5, the "multiplicative shift" formulation constrains the occupation-specific contours of sex segregation (the "segregation profile") to be invariant across contexts, but allows the strength of segregation to vary. This specification can be used to test the widely accepted assumption that historical or cross-national variability in segregation takes the form of differences in degree rather than kind. If the type 5 assumption is on the mark, it becomes possible to capture historical or cross-national variability with a margin-free index (e.g., A).

Although the rationale for index-based analysis rests on the plausibility of a type 5 formulation, segregation scholars have hardly rushed to make an empirical or even theoretical case for it. Indeed, because index-based approaches have been so dominant in the field, scholars have simply defaulted to them without considering whether they can adequately capture the structure of change and stability. If pressed for a theoretical justification, most segregation scholars would probably argue that labor markets, though they differ in many ways, are most usefully understood as differing in the extent to which basic egalitarian practices have been institutionalized on both the supply side (through preference formation) and the demand side (through employer discrimination). As egalitarianism diffuses, the proximate mechanisms underlying segregation (preference formation, discrimination) will gradually erode, and the overall amount of segregation should accordingly decline. This formulation suggests, then, that segregative practices throughout the labor market are the institutional realization of systemwide values regarding the legitimacy or illegitimacy of gender-based inequality (Parsons 1970; Goode 1963; Jackson 1998). The latter account might be contrasted with one that treats segregation regimes as more loosely coupled; that is, egalitarian practices in one sector of the occupational structure may coincide with discriminatory practices in another, thereby leading to more complex patterns of cross-national or historical difference than type 5 similarity allows. In Chapter 1, we hypothesized that precisely such complexities may obtain, with horizontal forms of segregation likely to be relatively resistant to the "different but equal" variant of egalitarianism that has diffused in the contemporary period.

As should be obvious by now, our approach involves progressively peeling away layers of surface variability, with the objective being to determine whether a more fundamental invariance will in the end reveal itself. If a type 5 formulation fails to fit the data, an invariant segregation pattern may still emerge at the detailed occupational level after more idiosyncratic patterns of segregation at the aggregate occupational level are parsed out. In raising this possibility, our suspicion is that relatively contingent macro-level forces may introduce considerable variability in how men and women are distributed across aggregate categories, whereas the universal facts of patriarchy allow males to always and everywhere dominate the most desirable detailed occupations *within* these major categories. This line of argumentation, while not explicitly laid out in the literature, is consistent with institutionalist approaches describing how macro-level forces tend to influence the extent and patterning of segregation at the major-category level. For example, Brinton (1988) has argued that Japanese women are especially likely to work in the semiskilled manual sector, where the returns to firm-specific capital are so limited that workers returning from extended family-related leaves are only trivially penalized. We might also cite stories about female "overcrowding" in the Scandinavian service sector (Ruggie 1984; Charles 1992), the American managerial sector (Chang 2000), and the Turkish professional sector (Charles and Grusky 1995). Although countries and historical periods may differ, then, in patterns of labor supply to aggregate occupational groupings, this contextual variability is presumably overlaid on the more fundamental conditions of patriarchy that guarantee micro-level male advantage in the competition for desirable occupations within major categories.

The empirical foundations of sex-segregation research are so poorly developed that the obverse argument is no less credible. That is, one might plausibly suggest that aggregate patterns of segregation take on much the same shape in all times and places, whereas labor practices at the detailed occupational level are subject to idiosyncrasies of many kinds, most notably those reflecting (a) the particular constellation of tasks assigned to a detailed occupation (and the associated desirability of that occupation), (b) the types of labor that were available when the detailed occupation expanded and carried out its formative recruiting, and (c) the types of firms, industries, or occupations that served as "models" for employment practices when the detailed occupation was established or expanded (see Stinchcombe 1965 for related argumentation). The foregoing considerations imply a form of path dependency whereby early decisions regarding the gender-typing of a detailed occupation are determined by considerations specific to particular countries or time periods. By contrast, major-category segregation may be determined by more fundamental and less variable forces, such as the cultural processes underlying horizontal and vertical inequality (see Table 1.1). This line of reasoning suggests that the deep structure in segregation data will only be uncovered by first filtering out context-specific noise at the detailed occupational level.

We are left, finally, with the extreme position that no deep structure exists and that contextual variability is accordingly too complex to be captured even by the weakened formulations that we have just rehearsed. The historical record indicates, of course, that segregation of *some* kind is universal, yet many scholars have emphasized that it takes on historically or cross-nationally contingent forms that can only be understood through careful qualitative study (Dodge 1971; L. Tilly and Scott 1978; Blekher 1979; A. Scott 1986; H. Bradley 1989). This position has been compellingly argued; however, given that its adherents draw principally on case studies, one cannot know whether the cited idiosyncrasies are isolated examples or indicative of more pervasive variation, nor can one formally test for the more complex and subtle forms of contextual similarity that we have outlined in Table 2.2. The results presented in the following chapters provide the first comprehensive evidence of the extent to which distinctive cultures, institutions, and historical forces affect the contours of sex segregation.

SEX-SEGREGATION MODELS

We turn now to the task of representing the preceding models more formally. Throughout this section, we assume that the segregation data take the form of a three-way cross-classification with i indexing gender, j indexing occupation, and k indexing context (either countries or time periods). The models presented in subsequent chapters often allow for additional dimensions (such as industry, cohort, or citizenship status), but a three-way formulation suffices to introduce the main features of our modeling approach.

We begin with a simple model in which cell proportions are constrained to be the same across all contexts (Table 2.2, line 1). This model can be generated by fitting a full set of occupation-by-gender terms (δ_{ij}) as well as a full set of marginal effects (α_k) that inflate or deflate the implied cell proportions up to the sample size prevailing in each context. The resulting specification may be represented as follows:

$$m_{ijk} = \alpha_k \delta_{ij}, \tag{2.4}$$

where α_k is the grand mean in the kth context, and δ_{ij} is the interaction term for the ijth cell. This model can be identified by constraining α_1 to equal 1.

The next two models allow for variability across contexts in the marginal effects for gender or occupation (see Table 2.2, lines 2 and 3). These models take the following form:

$$m_{ijk} = \alpha_k \beta_{ik} \delta_{ij}, \tag{2.5}$$
$$m_{ijk} = \alpha_k \gamma_{jk} \delta_{ij}, \tag{2.6}$$

where β_{ik} is the context-specific marginal effect for the ith gender, γ_{jk} is the context-specific marginal effect for the jth occupation, and all other terms are defined as before. In the model of demand-side similarity (equation 2.5), the marginal effects for occupation are constrained to be invariant across contexts, implying that the proportion of all men (or all women) falling into the jth occupation (the "outflow rate") is the same across contexts. The model of "supply-side similarity" (equation 2.6) likewise implies that the ratio of men to women in the jth occupation (the "inflow rate") is the same in all contexts. We can identify these models by constraining α_1, β_{1k}, β_{i1}, γ_{1k}, and γ_{j1} to equal 1.

The remaining models of Table 2.2 allow the marginal effects for both occupation and gender to freely vary. The universal association model, for example, combines such variability in marginal effects with the constraint that all sex-by-occupation interactions ("sex segregation") are identical across contexts. This constraint generates the following model:

$$m_{ijk} = \alpha_k \beta_{ik} \gamma_{jk} \delta_{ij}, \tag{2.7}$$

where δ_{ij} is the sex-by-occupation interaction term for the ijth cell in each context. The marginal effects for this model are identified by constraining the parameters for the first row or column to equal one ($\beta_{1k} = \gamma_{1k} = 1$), and the sex-by-occupation interaction effects are identified by constraining the parameters in the first row and column to equal one ($\delta_{1j} = \delta_{i1} = 1$).

If the universal association model fails to fit, we might ask whether cross-national or historical variability arises from simple differences in the *degree* of sex segregation (see Table 2.2, line 5). This multiplicative shift model is consistent with the standard practice of summarizing contextual variability in a single parameter (an index). We can test for simple shift effects with the following log-multiplicative specification:

$$m_{ijk} = \alpha_k \beta_{ik} \gamma_{jk} e^{\Phi_k Z_i \nu_j} \tag{2.8}$$

where Φ_k is the multiplicative shift effect for the kth context, Z_i is an indicator variable for gender ($Z_1 = 0$ and $Z_2 = 1$), and ν_j is the scale value for the jth occupation. The scale values in equation 2.8 can be identified by constraining them to sum to zero ($\sum_{j=1}^{J} \nu_j = 0$), while the shift effects can be identified by constraining Φ_1 to equal one. If this specification fits the data, it follows that Φ_k can be used to represent historical or cross-national variability in the underlying strength of sex segregation; and we have therefore defined a new index, A_M, that equals the product of Φ_k and $\exp[\{\sum_{j=1}^{J}(\nu_j^2/J)\}^{1/2}]$.[4] We have demonstrated elsewhere that A and A_M are equivalent when the multiplicative shift model fits perfectly (see Charles and Grusky 1995, p. 945).[5]

If a multiplicative shift model fails to fit the data, it is not necessary to resort immediately to a saturated model. Instead, segregation regimes may have a deep structure at the detailed occupational level, where the forces of male advantage ("patriarchy") may operate to predictably allocate men to the most desirable occupations. The latter queuing dynamic may, however, be obscured at the level of aggregate occupational groups because various macro-level forces (World War II, the rise of family-friendly employment) can generate aggregate patterns of labor supply that are idiosyncratic. This line of reasoning suggests a model that allows for distinct segregation profiles at the detailed and aggregate levels (see Table 2.2, line 6):

$$m_{ijk} = \alpha_k \beta_{ik} \gamma_{jk} e^{(Z_i \nu_j + Z_i \varphi_{ck})} \tag{2.9}$$

In equation 2.9, φ_{ck} refers to the scale values for major occupational categories (indexed by c), and ν_j refers to the scale values for detailed occupations nested in these major categories. As our multilevel hypothesis requires, the only outlet for cross-context variability is the shift effects defined at the level of major categories (φ_{ck}), given that the scale values for detailed occupations (ν_j) are constrained to be invariant. We can identify this model by forcing the major-category scale values to sum to zero within each context ($\sum_{c=1}^{C} \varphi_{ck} = 0$ for all k), by fixing all the major-category scale values in the first context to equal zero ($\varphi_{c1} = 0$), and by constraining the detailed scale values to sum to zero ($\sum_{j=1}^{J} \nu_j = 0$).[6]

If the preceding efforts to characterize segregation profiles all fail, we must fall back to a saturated model that allows profiles to freely vary across contexts. We can again represent this model in log-multiplicative terms:

$$m_{ijk} = \alpha_k \beta_{ik} \gamma_{jk} e^{Z_i \nu_{jk}} \tag{2.10}$$

Under this specification, the scale values (ν_{jk}) are now subscripted by k, implying that the segregation profile varies by context (country or historical period). The marginal effects for this model can be identified as before (see, e.g., equation 2.7), while the occupational scale values can be identified by forcing them to sum to zero within each context ($\sum_{j=1}^{J} \nu_{jk} = 0$ for all k).

The scale values from this saturated model may be used to calculate A. Although we previously provided a closed-form definition of A (see equation 2.3), it can also be rewritten in terms of occupational scale values (from equation 2.10):

$$A_k = \exp\left(1/J \times \sum_{j=1}^{J} \nu_{jk}^2 \right)^{1/2} \tag{2.11}$$

This formula implies that A indexes the dispersion in the occupational scale values. Moreover, by comparing equations 2.3 and 2.11, it becomes evident that the scale values (ν_j) can be rewritten in closed-form fashion:

$$\nu_j = \sum_{j=1}^{J} \left\{ \ln(F_j/M_j) - \left[1/J \times \sum_{j=1}^{J} \ln(F_j/M_j) \right] \right\} \tag{2.12}$$

where all terms are defined as in equation 2.1. This expression reveals that the occupational scale values are formed by deviating the ratio of females to males in the *j*th occupation (F_j/M_j) from the corresponding ratios averaged across all occupations. The exponent of ν_j may be interpreted as the multiplicative factor by which women are overrepresented or underrepresented in the *j*th occupation.

We can also reparameterize the saturated model (see equation 2.10) for the purpose of better revealing the structure of segregation at the aggregate and disaggregate levels (see Charles and Grusky 1995, pp. 952–53). This reparameterization may be expressed as follows:

$$m_{ijk} = \alpha_k \beta_{ik} \gamma_{jk} e^{(Z_i \nu_{jk} + Z_i \varphi_{ck})}, \tag{2.13}$$

with all symbols defined as before. Unlike the model of equation 2.9, the scale values for detailed occupations (ν_{jk}) are now subscripted by *k*, implying that cross-context variability in segregation is allowed at the detailed as well as aggregate levels. As before, the detailed scale values (ν_{jk}) can be identified by constraining them to sum to zero within each major occupational category (of each context), while the major-category scale values (φ_{ck}) can be identified by constraining them to sum to zero within each context.

The scale values from equation 2.13 allow us to construct summary indices that measure the extent of segregation within and between major occupational categories (see Grusky and Charles 1998, 2001). These indices take the following form:

$$A_w = \exp\left(1/J \times \sum_{j=1}^{J} \nu_{jk}^2 \right)^{1/2} \tag{2.14}$$

and

$$A_B = \exp\left(\frac{1}{C} \times \sum_{c=1}^{C} \varphi_{ck}^2 \right)^{1/2} \tag{2.15}$$

where all symbols are defined as before. Although some scholars have suggested that our approach is difficult to implement for detailed segregation arrays (e.g., Watts 1998), the model of equation 2.13 and the indices derived from it indicate, to the contrary, that log-multiplicative models will allow us to examine detailed arrays in innovative ways. We illustrate these methods in Chapter 3.

The foregoing review by no means provides an exhaustive introduction to the models and methods used in this book. Rather, our objective is merely to illustrate our general approach, leaving various elaborations to subsequent chapters. The main extensions to be developed subsequently involve (a) testing the extent to which segregation profiles follow a socioeconomic gradient (see Chapter 4), (b) incorporating individual-level covariates (such as citizenship status) that may affect segregation outcomes (see Chapter 7), and (c) distinguishing patterns of occupational and industrial segregation (see Chapter 8). These extensions are straightforward generalizations of the modeling approach discussed here.

CONCLUSIONS

We have single-mindedly pressed the case that conventional segregation indices are not faithful to the segregation concept. This concept pertains, after all, to the joint distribution of sex and occupation, yet conventional indices are sensitive to variability in the component (univariate) distributions. The modern analysis of labor markets should therefore distinguish between (a) rates of female labor force participation (the "gender margin"), (b) the occupational composition of the economy (the "occupation margin"), and (c) the extent to which occupations are differentially staffed by women and men ("sex segregation"). Indeed, because the forces affecting marginal distributions are distinct from those affecting the joint distribution, we would do well to avoid sex segregation indices that conflate these components. This understanding of the segregation concept appears to be accepted by most segregation scholars (see, e.g., Williams 1979; Blau and Hendricks 1979; England 1981; Bridges 1982; Handl 1984; Tienda and Ortiz 1987; Beller 1984; Bianchi and Rytina 1986; Abrahamson and Sigelman 1987; Jacobs 1989a, 1989b; Jacobs and Lim 1992; Presser and Kishor 1991; Brinton and Ngo 1993; Watts 1998).

Although segregation scholars have seemingly embraced a margin-free definition of segregation, they have nonetheless defaulted to indices (such as D) that fail to realize it. The continuing search for indices that correct for margin dependence suggests that such dependence is widely regarded as problematic. However, because this methodological work has typically proceeded by modifying or revising D, it has necessarily failed to generate a new index that eliminates margin dependence altogether. We have argued here and demonstrated elsewhere (esp. Grusky and Charles 1998) that A and its close cousins (such as A_M) not only solve the problem of margin dependence but are the *only* available solutions to it. Insofar as a margin-free conceptualization of segregation is insisted upon, there is no alternative but to use measures, such as A or A_M, that are functions of the odds ratios in a segregation array.

It follows that D or the usual revisions of it (such as D_s) cannot be defended without somehow minimizing the importance of a margin-free operationalization. This defense of D has been carried out on both conceptual and empirical fronts. On the conceptual front, sex segregation is often explicitly equated with whatever D measures, almost as if it is unnecessary to distinguish between a concept and its operationalization. We of course cannot dispute that D is best at measuring what D measures. However, some attempt should be made to understand precisely what D does measure, and any such effort leads inevitably to the conclusion that it reflects, in part, the mix of occupations in the economy. This marginal contamination is an inevitable by-product of operationalizing segregation as a function of the number of workers who are affected by it (Jacobs 2001, pp. 538–39). It is not our task here to understand the readiness with which U.S. researchers, in particular, have embraced this understanding of segregation, but no doubt it partly reflects their long-standing predilection for methodological individualism, as it is sometimes called (see Grusky and Charles 1998, p. 497). To be sure, we readily agree that D is of considerable interest and should continue to be reported, but it has to be appreciated that all D-based indices are conceptually complicated measures that conflate sex segregation with other features of the economy. This conflation may serve to answer questions of some interest, but conflation nonetheless it is.

To our mind, an intellectually more challenging attack on the margin-free approach rests on the claim that marginal distributions, far from being exogenous, are in fact partly generated by patterns of sex segregation. This is the "empirical" attack on A to which we alluded above. If, for example, the rise in female labor force participation is entirely attributable to a growth of female-demanding occupations (see Oppenheimer 1970), any change over time in rates of female labor force participation can be regarded as epiphenomenal; and indices, such as D_s, that are contaminated by variability in the marginal effect for gender can safely be used. The obvious irony here is that the foregoing case for index-based analysis cannot be made without carrying out the requisite modeling first. In the context of our modeling framework, arguments for endogeneity become testable hypotheses (about variability in marginal effects); and segregation analysts who seek to challenge the exogeneity assumption are accordingly obliged to resort to the very modeling framework that we advocate. Indeed, our main objective in this chapter is to demonstrate that log-multiplicative models are consistent with a wide range of segregation models, some of which explicitly allow for endogeneity of the margins (see, e.g., Table 2.2, lines 1–3).

The larger moral to our story is that index-based analysis of all kinds rests on strong assumptions about the structure of segregation data. This conclusion holds no less for A than for D or D_s. It is inappropriate, after all, to use A to summarize contextual variability when the multiplicative shift model fails to fit (and typically it does fail), because such lack of fit implies that segregation regimes vary in kind as well as degree. The frequently issued platitude that segregation indices should be selected on the basis of "research interests" makes no allowance for the possibility that the preferred measure fails to adequately characterize the data at hand. In virtually all segregation analysis, the preferred index is motivated and justified on the basis of research interests alone, and researchers are not held accountable, as they should be, for the data reduction that their measures imply. We have introduced here a modeling framework that allows segregation scholars to test the assumptions embodied in their preferred indices and to move beyond index-based analysis whenever the data require doing so.

The A Index under Multiplicative Transformation of Labor Force Sex Ratio

For each context k, when F_j is multiplied by the factor c for all j, A can be reexpressed as follows (see equation 2.1 for definition of terms):

$$A' = \exp\left(1/J \times \sum_{j=1}^{J} \left\{ \ln(cF_j/M_j) - \left[1/J \times \sum_{j=1}^{J} \ln(cF_j/M_j) \right] \right\}^2 \right)^{1/2}$$

$$= \exp\left(1/J \times \sum_{j=1}^{J} \left\{ \ln(c) + \ln(F_j/M_j) \right. \right.$$

$$\left. \left. - \left[1/J \times \sum_{j=1}^{J} \ln(c) + \ln(F_j/M_j) \right] \right\}^2 \right)^{1/2}$$

$$= \exp\left(1/J \times \sum_{j=1}^{J} \left\{ \ln(F_j/M_j) - \left[1/J \times \sum_{j=1}^{J} \ln(F_j/M_j) \right] \right\}^2 \right)^{1/2}$$

$$= A.$$

REVISITING CROSS-NATIONAL VARIABILITY IN SEX SEGREGATION

CHAPTER THREE

The Underlying Structure of Sex Segregation in Industrial Market Economies

In the growing subfield of gender stratification, the high-profile task of teasing out the underlying causes of segregation has been actively pursued, whereas the logically prior (but more prosaic) task of describing the structure of segregation has attracted a good deal less attention. Although there is a standing literature on descriptive issues (e.g., Anker 1998), much of it is based on flawed methods, excessively coarse data, and inadequate conceptual work. In this chapter, we overcome at least some of these problems with data, method, and conceptualization and develop a more accurate portrait of the structure of occupational sex segregation in industrial market economies. We proceed by applying the methodological approach described in Chapter 2 to a new archive of carefully harmonized occupational data from ten industrial market economies.

In the existing literature, three main strategies for carrying out descriptive segregation research can be distinguished, each of which has its own advantages and disadvantages. The dominant approach, at least among American scholars, has been to apply conventional indices to data available from international statistical sources, most notably the *Yearbook of Labour Statistics* published by the International Labour Office (see, e.g., Jacobs and Lim 1992; Anker 1998). This tradition has the virtue of representing a broad cross-section of countries, but it is also problematic because conventional index-based analysis can neither speak to cross-national differences in the qualitative contours of segregation nor eliminate the potentially confounding effects of variability in market supply or demand (see Chapter 2). We are left, then, with simple conclusions about cross-national variability in the extent of sex segregation, and even these conclusions are problematic to the extent that variability in marginal effects drives them.

At the other end of the methodological continuum, there is a long and distinguished tradition of case studies of sex segregation, most of which suggest that gender-typing can be highly variable and historically contingent (e.g., Boserup 1970; Tilly and Scott 1978; Sanday 1981; Scott 1986; Crompton, LeFeuvre, and Birkelund 1999). This line of research, while revealing, suffers from the usual limitations of case studies. As we have argued elsewhere, the seemingly idiosyncratic patterns identified in case studies may well disappear when more formal comparisons are carried out, not only because cross-national variation in labor supply and demand can create the (false) appearance of difference, but also because the extent of difference cannot be reliably gauged without explicitly assembling comparable data from multiple countries (see Grusky and Charles 2001). The conventional view, to which we subscribe, is that case studies can generate useful hypotheses about the structure of cross-national variability, but at some point these hypotheses should be subjected to broader testing than case studies allow.

In recent years, a third research tradition of log-multiplicative modeling has emerged, with the usual data source for such research again being the aggregate compilations of the International Labour Office (see, e.g., Charles 1992; Charles and Grusky 1995). For all its methodological rigor, this line of research has been vulnerable to the possibility that aggregate categories comprise widely different mixes of detailed occupations, thereby creating the appearance of cross-national variability in segregation when in fact all that varies is the occupational composition of the aggregate categories (cf. Chang 2000). This possibility, if borne out, undermines our long-standing interest in stripping away the potentially confounding effects of cross-national variability in the occupational structure. As we suggested in Chapter 2, it is altogether possible that a fundamental invariance in segregation patterns emerges at the aggregate level of major occupational categories, but only after more idiosyncratic patterns at the detailed level are controlled. We address this hypothesis by assembling an archive of cross-national data that are detailed enough to purge compositional differences at the disaggregate level.

The purpose of this chapter, then, is to overcome the shortcomings of conventional comparative research by fitting models that (a) control for cross-national variability in occupational supply and demand, (b) allow for cross-national idiosyncrasies in the qualitative contours of segregation, and (c) distinguish between the structure of segregation at the detailed and aggregate levels. To be sure, some of these shortcomings have been addressed in prior research (e.g., Chang 2000), but our analysis is unique in attending to all of them simultaneously. We hope that the resulting portrait of advanced industrial segregation will provide a useful benchmark for future studies of segregation in other countries and time periods (see also Grusky and Charles 1998, 2001).

RETURNING TO THE PUZZLES

Before turning to the analyses themselves, it is important to review two of the empirical puzzles outlined in Chapter 1, because our analyses are designed to speak directly to them. It may be recalled that Chapter 1 addressed (a) whether a worldwide segregation regime can be found, and (b) whether such a shared regime, insofar as it does exist, takes on a simple gradational form whereby men are disproportionately allocated to the best occupations. We elaborate on these two questions below.

Is There a Worldwide Segregation Regime?

In outlining some of the standing puzzles of segregation research in Chapter 1, we discussed cross-national variability in segregation regimes in relatively simple terms, as if cross-national analysis involved nothing more than inspecting segregation arrays from various countries and characterizing them as either similar or different. The discussion in Chapter 2 implies, however, that comparative analysis is complicated by the many different types of similarity and difference that may be distinguished. Although some forms of similarity may be directly observed in segregation data (Table 2.2, panel A), others are revealed only after applying controls for marginal effects and other obscuring noise (Table 2.2, panel B). The models discussed in Chapter 2 are summarized again in Table 3.1.

This modeling framework makes it possible to break down our initial global query about cross-national similarity into subquestions that distinguish between different forms of similarity. The analyses in this chapter address each of the four following subquestions.

TABLE 3.1
Cross-National Variability and Similarity in Sex-Segregation Regimes

Model	Forces Underlying Similarity or Variability	Examples of Relevant Scholars	Equation
A. Margin-Invariant Forms			
1. Complete similarity	None	None	2.4
2. Demand-side similarity	None	None	2.5
3. Supply-side similarity	Occupational labeling	Oppenheimer	2.6
B. Margin-Varying Forms			
4. Universal association	Universal sex roles, patriarchy	Chodorow; Firestone; Mincer and Polacheck	2.7
5. Multiplicative shift	Variability in egalitarianism	Parsons; Goode	2.8
6. Multilevel	Macro-institutional forces	Chang; Charles; Brinton	2.9
7. Saturated	Micro- and macro-institutional forces	Tilly and Scott; Bradley	2.10, 2.13

Are occupational sex-ratios identical in all countries? Although we have argued at length for margin-free analysis of segregation data, our argument is called into question by a long tradition of theorizing that represents the supply of female labor as endogenous to the segregation process (see Cotter et al. 1998; Cotter, Hermsen, and Vanneman 2001; Oppenheimer 1970, 1973). This alternative formulation implies that the ratio of women to men in each occupation (the "sex ratio") is cross-nationally invariant and that women are drawn into the labor force whenever occupations with female sex ratios ("female-demanding occupations") increase in size. We provide the first test of this formulation as well as closely related ones that similarly treat the forces of supply and demand as endogenous to the segregation process (see Table 3.1, lines 1–3).

Is the strength and patterning of sex-by-occupation association invariant? If rates of female labor force participation are exogenous (implying that the foregoing model of "supply-side similarity" is rejected), then cross-national variability in such rates will generate corresponding variability in occupational sex-ratios, and the search for invariance must accordingly focus on the sex-by-occupation association (see Table 3.1, line 4). We have noted elsewhere (see Chapter 2) that conventional segregation theories (such as theories of patriarchy) emphasize the cross-nationally generic forces generating segregation rather than ways in which these forces vary across countries. In this sense, these theories suggest that a family resemblance in segregation regimes may well emerge, albeit only after confounding differences in supply and demand are taken into account. This claim can be explicitly assessed by fitting our "universal association" model.

Is there a cross-nationally similar segregation profile? If the preceding model is rejected, it is still possible that the underlying association takes on a cross-nationally common form after all variability in the *strength* of association is purged. This hypothesis, represented by our "multiplicative shift model" (Table 3.1, line 5), is consistent with neo-functionalist and institutionalist accounts that represent labor markets as differing principally in the extent to which egalitarian practices have been institutionalized. Under such accounts, egalitarian forms and practices are presumed to be more deeply entrenched in "modern" labor markets than in traditional ones, suggesting that cross-national variability principally takes the form of across-the-board differences in the strength of segregation (Goode 1963; Ramirez 1987; see also Jackson 1998 for a less deterministic evolutionary account). These accounts, influential though they are, remain largely untested and may well prove to be empirically untenable. As we argued in Chapter 1, we suspect that cross-national variability takes on a more complicated form, with some types of inequality (horizontal segregation) likely to be especially resistant to egalitarian reform (see also Charles 1992, 1998).

Can a deep structure be found after filtering out "noise" at the detailed occupation level? Finally, an invariant segregation pattern may emerge at the level of aggregate occupational categories (such as "professional," "clerical"), but only after more idiosyncratic cross-national differences at the level of detailed occupational categories (such as "professor," "office clerk") are controlled. The sex-ratios for detailed occupations may be responsive to such country-specific effects as the types of labor that were available when the occupation expanded, the types of tasks that are assigned to the occupation, and the types of firms, industries, or occupations that served as models when the occupation was established. The structure of major-category segregation may be less variable because it is presumably driven by those deeper and less mutable forces generating horizontal and vertical inequality. We explore this possibility by fitting models that allow us to disentangle the structure of segregation at the detailed and aggregate levels (see Table 3.1, line 6).

If none of the foregoing models fits adequately, we must then rely on the saturated model (see Table 3.1, line 7) and conclude that cross-nationally idiosyncratic cultures, institutions, and organizational forms generate quite complicated forms of variability (Tilly and Scott 1978; Scott 1986; Bradley 1989; Crompton, LeFeuvre and Birkelund 1999). As always, there is much judgment involved in deciding whether difference or similarity should be stressed, especially because all conventional tests of model fit, including the widely used *BIC* (e.g., Raftery 1995), will inevitably reject almost any simplifying constraint in samples of our size. We therefore attempt to characterize our results with language that allows readers to reach their own conclusions about the extent of similarity or difference.

The Underlying Structure of Segregation Regimes

Insofar as a common segregation regime can be identified, we wish to characterize its shape and form not only by evaluating it against conventional representations, but also by developing alternatives to those conventions. The existing literature on the structure of segregation profiles is limited in this regard. Indeed, because index-based analysis has so dominated the field, one finds rather more discussion of the amount of segregation than its patterning. If nonetheless forced to identify a conventional wisdom here, it is undoubtedly the presumption that men crowd into the "best occupations," either because women have substantial domestic responsibilities that reduce their incentive to invest in demanding careers, or because employers exercise their tastes for discrimination through "glass ceiling" personnel policies and other forms of male-biased queuing in the labor market (see Chapter 1 for details). The resulting queuing model implies that labor markets should have a strongly "vertical" character to them in which men dominate the most desirable occupations (see Reskin and Roos 1990).

The question that then emerges is whether the vertical principle is as dominant as some commentators have assumed. We have suggested (see Chapter 1) that segregation regimes are also structured by a horizontal principle that allocates men into the manual sector and women into the nonmanual sector. This form of segregation is maintained and reproduced because (a) nonmanual occupations embody characteristics (service orientation) that are regarded as prototypically female, while (b) manual occupations embody characteristics (strenuousness, physicality) that are regarded as prototypically male. As we have put it elsewhere, segregation regimes are generated by the "interleaving" of horizontal and vertical principles, with both forms of segregation likely to be evident in all societies, albeit to varying degrees (Grusky and Charles 2001). The following analyses examine whether these two principles, taken together, can indeed provide an acceptable account of the contours of the segregation profile.

A NEW CROSS-NATIONAL DATA ARCHIVE

We apply these models to an archive of rigorously standardized data. In prior comparative research, segregation scholars have been hampered by the lack of high-quality data, and we have accordingly invested much time and effort in securing, coding, and harmonizing disaggregate data for a broad cross-section of industrial market economies. Because we have relied on data originally collected by national census bureaus, our pooled sample is large enough to support highly detailed analysis. The resulting segregation tables, which pertain to the occupationally active labor force, represent a diverse set of industrialized countries with market-based economies: Belgium, France, West Germany, Italy, Portugal, Sweden, Switzerland, the United Kingdom, the United States, and Japan (see Table 3.2 for sample details). Although some compromises naturally had to be made, our data are clearly superior in terms of occupational detail and cross-national comparability than those that have previously been available for comparative research.[1]

We have been aided in this regard by global trends toward economic and social integration and the consequent intensification of efforts to harmonize statistical collection methodologies and data classification procedures across nations. For our purposes, it is especially noteworthy that the National Statistical Institutes of the European Union agreed to establish a single harmonized variant of the 1988 International Standard Classification of Occupations (ISCO-88; see ILO 1990a), with the objective being to maintain maximal detail while also introducing, as necessary, modifications that smooth out cross-national inconsistencies in coding.[2] The resulting classi-

TABLE 3.2
Data and Sample Characteristics

Country	Census Year	Sample Size
Belgium	1991	3,418,512
France	1990	900,255
West Germany	1993	128,912
Italy	1991	21,071,282
Portugal	1991	4,037,130
Sweden	1990	4,059,813
Switzerland	1990	3,076,445
United Kingdom	1991	2,405,091
United States	1990	1,152,885
Japan	1990	12,220,974

fication, dubbed ISCO-88-COM, is now in place and appears to have garnered widespread support; however, given the obvious complexities involved in revising classificatory practices, many European countries had not completed their mapping protocols (into ISCO-88-COM) at the time of our initial data collection. We have relied heavily on the available national mappings, incomplete though they sometimes are, in constructing our own archive of data.

It goes without saying that ISCO-88-COM carries with it all the costs and benefits of the ISCO-88 scheme upon which it is based. By all accounts, ISCO-88 is superior to ISCO-68, largely because it distinguishes more rigorously between occupations with different skill and educational requirements. The major categories of ISCO-88 distinguish, for example, between "professionals" (such as medical doctors and university professors) and "associate professionals" (such as nurses and preschool teachers), whereas ISCO-68 obscures this distinction. The ISCO-88 classification is also superior to ISCO-68 in distinguishing between craft and operative work in the manual sector (see Elias and Birch 1993, 1994). The major categories of the resulting ISCO-88 classification (and its European Community variant) are (a) legislators, senior officials, and managers ("managers"); (b) professionals ("professional"); (c) technicians and associate professionals ("associate professional"); (d) clerks ("clerical"); (e) service workers and shop sales work-

ers ("sales/service"); (f) skilled agricultural and fishery workers ("agricultural"); (g) craft and related trades workers ("craft"); (h) plant and machine operators and assemblers ("operative"); and (i) elementary occupations ("laborers").[3]

Unfortunately, the necessary classifications were not available in ISCO-
88-COM categories at the time of our analyses, save in the case of Portugal.
We constructed tabulations for France, Germany, Sweden, Switzerland, and
the United Kingdom by commissioning national statistical agencies to process individual-level census data in accord with ISCO-88-COM protocol.
Fortunately, the translation keys mapping national occupational categories
into ISCO-88-COM have been made available in Belgium and Italy, and we
thus proceeded in those cases by securing the indigenous classifications and
then carrying out the recoding that the keys implied. In all remaining European countries, comparable tabulations could not be obtained before our
analyses, either because sufficient headway in the time-consuming ISCO
mapping process had not yet been made, or because the final mapping would
have required occupational information more detailed than that available in
the original census data.[4]

The two non-European countries in our archive, Japan and the United
States, were of course not party to European Union agreements on the establishment of ISCO-88-COM. In these countries, there are no official keys
for coding indigenous classifications into ISCO-88-COM, and the translation process is perforce less satisfactory. We proceeded by developing keys
of our own based, in part, on existing ISCO translation schemes devised
by Ganzeboom, Luijkx, and Treiman (1989). The resulting tabulations fall
short of the (extremely high) standards to which the other cases were held.
However, given that both Japan and the United States have long served as
benchmark comparative cases, we think that the classification error incurred
is well worth bearing.

The data sets in our sample also vary with respect to the number of "minor group" categories that were available in translating the national classifications into ISCO-88-COM. In this regard, the Italian case is perhaps
the most troubling, since here we were forced to work with only eighty-six
source categories. The coding rules for the indigenous Italian classification
often required more detail than the census bureau made available; consequently, we were obliged either (a) to aggregate some of the ISCO-88-COM
categories (thereby accommodating the equally broad indigenous categories)

or, (b) to force code broadly defined indigenous categories into ISCO-88-COM categories that were more narrowly defined. The Italian data are, by virtue of these compromises, arguably the most problematic among the European samples. Although some caution is therefore in order, there are surely no better Italian data available for purposes of carrying out comparative segregation research at the detailed level.

We do not mean to suggest that ISCO-88-COM protocol can be perfectly realized in the remaining European countries. Most notably, the ISCO-88-COM distinction between "professional" and "associate professional" nurses was available in only some of our indigenous national classifications, thus obliging us to assign all nurses to a single line in the associate professional category. In similar fashion, ISCO-88-COM distinguishes between religious "professionals" and religious "associate professionals," yet because of cross-national inconsistencies in implementing this distinction we had to abandon it altogether and create a merged line, which we then located in the "professional" major category. We opted, finally, to create a single agricultural class because many of our indigenous classifications failed to recognize the two-category skill distinction that ISCO-88-COM supports for this class. In all other respects, our classification closely resembles that of ISCO-88-COM; and we are accordingly in good position to carry out detailed comparative analyses. Appendix Table A3.1 lists the sixty-four occupations in our final classification and the component ISCO-88-COM categories that make up these occupations.

WHICH COUNTRIES ARE MOST SEGREGATED?

We begin our comparison by following conventional practice and carrying out an index-based analysis of sex segregation. In Table 3.3, the values of D, D_s, and A are listed in the first three columns, and the gender composition of the labor force is indicated in the final column. Consistent with previous studies, we find counterintuitive patterns of cross-national variability in D, with the lowest segregation scores occurring in countries, such as Japan and Italy, that are hardly bastions of gender egalitarianism. Obversely, Sweden has the highest value of D, a result that belies its reputation for progressive, woman-friendly social policy (see also Roos 1985; Charles 1992; Charles and Grusky 1995; Anker 1998; Jonung 1998). These anomalies partly resolve under indices that are not sensitive to the occupational composition of

TABLE 3.3
Standard Sex-Segregation Indices

Country	D	D_s	A	Labor Force % Female
Belgium	51.2	53.7	6.10	39.8
France	54.5	50.9	6.10	43.0
West Germany	50.9	45.9	4.50	41.2
Italy	43.0	40.9	3.31	35.7
Portugal	47.7	46.1	5.26	40.5
Sweden	60.2	49.4	5.47	48.6
Switzerland	55.5	50.4	5.52	38.0
United Kingdom	56.5	52.6	6.28	44.3
United States	45.1	45.8	4.39	45.7
Japan	44.8	49.3	5.87	39.8

NOTE: D = index of dissimilarity; D_s = size-standardized index of dissimilarity; A = association index. See Chapter 2 for index definitions.

the economy. Admittedly, neither A nor D_s reveals Japan as extremely segregated or Sweden as extremely integrated, but the indices do at least shift Japan and Sweden into middling positions in our sample of countries. We can conclude that D misled partly because the mix of occupations worked to suppress the index value in Japan and exaggerate it in Sweden.[5]

Although A resolves some of our counterintuitive results, there remain several puzzles that cannot be understood without formal modeling of the segregation data. It is surprising, for instance, that Italy and Portugal have relatively low values on A, because neither country is well known for its gender-egalitarian culture or family-friendly employment policies. We explore this puzzle in the following section (and in Chapter 4) by inspecting the segregation profiles for Italy and Portugal and identifying occupational sectors within these countries that are especially segregated or integrated.

Second, it is puzzling that D_s and A generate much the same rank-ordering of countries, even though A is margin-free and D_s is sensitive to variability in the marginal effects for gender. Given that D_s nonetheless tracks A well, it would appear that the marginal effects do not vary much across our sample of countries, even though the observed gender composition of the la-

TABLE 3.4
Sex-Segregation Models Applied to 10-Nation Data Set

Model[a]	L^2	d.f.	Δ	Explained Variability in Sex Segregation (%)	BIC[b]
A. Endogeneity Models					
1. Complete Similarity (N+O*S)	15,909,405	1143	21.2	—	15,889,087
2. Demand-Side Similarity (S*N+O*S)	15,596,832	1134	20.8	—	15,576,674
3. Supply-Side Similarity (O*N+O*S)	2,083,953	576	6.3	—	2,073,714
B. Country-Varying Marginal Effects					
4. Universal association model (S*N+O*N+O*S)	1,763,819	567	5.5	0.0	1,753,740
5. Multiplicative shift model (S*N+O*N+O*S+M*N)	1,517,231	558	5.1	14.0	1,507,312
6. Multilevel model (S*N+O*N+O*S+G*S*N)	957,588	495	3.6	45.7	948,789
7. Multilevel model with detailed-category shift effect (S*N+O*N+O*S+G*S*N+M*N)	858,281	486	3.4	51.3	849,642

[a] O = detailed occupation; G = major occupation; N = country; S = sex; M = global strength of association (multiplicative shift function). Delta (Δ) gives the percentage of cases that are misclassified under the respective model.

[b] Bayesian Information Criterion statistic (see Raftery 1986).

bor force is clearly quite variable (see Table 3.3, right-hand column). When we turn to formal modeling, we may accordingly find that the model of supply-side similarity, which imposes an equality constraint on the marginal effects for gender, fits better than is typically assumed.

Third, it is surprising that A reveals more cross-national variability in the overall level of segregation than do conventional indices, especially D. The models estimated in the following section (and in Chapter 4) cast light on the sources of this variability by revealing the types of occupations that generate it. The foregoing puzzles all suggest, then, that index-based analysis may provide a useful starting point for understanding segregation regimes, but only rarely is it an appropriate end point.

SIMPLE MODELS OF CROSS-NATIONAL VARIABILITY

We provide test statistics for our multiplicative and log-multiplicative models in Table 3.4. As expected, the data are wholly inconsistent with Models 1 and 2, both of which constrain the occupational marginal effects to be cross-nationally invariant. When these effects are allowed to vary (see Model 3), a sizable improvement in fit is secured, albeit at a cost of 567 degrees of freedom relative to Model 1. Under Model 3, a mere 6.3 percent of the respondents must be reclassified to bring about a perfect correspondence between the observed and expected values (see δ), a substantial improvement relative to what prevails for Models 1 or 2. By implication, we can conclude that the underlying rate of female labor force participation (the "marginal effect" for gender) does not vary dramatically by country, whereas the observed rate is affected by cross-national differences in occupational demand and consequent variability in the structural need for women. This result provides some support for treating the gender margins as partly endogenous (e.g., Oppenheimer 1970) and additionally explains why the values of D_s so closely track those of A (see Table 3.3). That is, while D_s is sensitive to variability in the marginal effects for gender (see Charles and Grusky 1995), the influence of such sensitivity is obviously dampened insofar as those effects tend not to vary much. Despite this result, one can hardly give blanket approval to the use of D_s, not only because we lack a conceptual rationale for allowing any margin dependence at all (no matter how small it may be), but also because there is no guarantee that Model 3 will fit equally well in other samples of countries.

Moreover, even within our own sample of ten countries, Model 3 fails to provide an entirely satisfactory fit, at least as indicated by conventional significance tests or *BIC*. This result motivates us to consider more complicated specifications that absorb all variability in marginal effects. If Model 3 is elaborated, then, to allow for cross-national variability in the marginal effects for gender, we arrive at a standard model of all two-way interactions that constrains the sex-by-occupation association to be constant (see Model 4 and equation 2.7). The contrast between Models 3 and 4 is obviously significant (at any typical α level), but the relatively minor reduction in δ might again be taken to imply that the marginal effects for gender are effectively invariant. We would caution against such an interpretation. Under Model 4, the marginal effects for gender in fact range from .23 for Italy to .42 for the United States, implying that the underlying propensity for female labor force participation (after controlling for the Oppenheimer "demand effect") is approximately 1.83 times stronger in the United States than in Italy (.42/.23 = 1.83). Likewise, the Swedish effect is also very strong (.41), while that for Japan (.25) is relatively weak. These estimates underline our conclusion that the model of supply-side similarity, though it performs better than other specifications in panel A, is nonetheless well off the mark in describing the structure of segregation data.

The main effects of interest under Model 4 are those pertaining to sex segregation. In Figure 3.1, we present the additive sex-by-occupation interaction terms from Model 4 ($ln[\delta_{ij}]$), with positive coefficients in this figure indicating female overrepresentation and negative coefficients indicating male overrepresentation.[6] The resulting graph, which depicts the pooled profile for our sample of ten countries, suggests that neither horizontal nor vertical accounts can by themselves provide an adequate description of the structure of sex segregation. The horizontal component to segregation is revealed in the characteristic crowding of women into nonmanual occupations, whereas a vertical logic is revealed in the tendency of men to dominate high-status positions (managerial, craft) within the manual as well as nonmanual sectors.

This interleaving of horizontal and vertical forces implies that a complete account of segregation requires joining together theories that typically emphasize only one of these forces. As we stressed in Chapter 1, two brands of theorizing are especially relevant in this regard, both of which are typically (but unconvincingly) represented as stand-alone accounts. Most obvi-

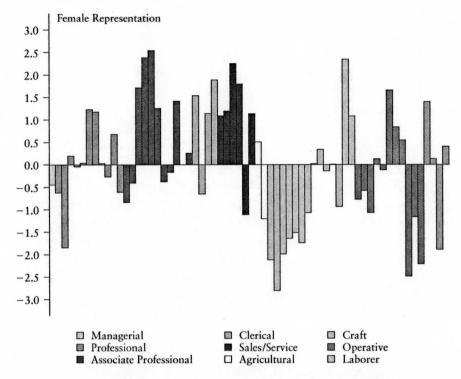

Figure 3.1   Pooled Profile of Sex Segregation for 10 Nations (Model 4)[a]

[a]Countries: Belgium, France, West Germany, Italy, Portugal, Sweden, Switzerland, United Kingdom, United States, Japan.

ously, "gender essentialist" theories are often represented as complete and full accounts of gender inequality, but in fact they principally explain why women crowd into service-oriented nonmanual occupations, thereby generating horizontal segregation (see, e.g., Gilligan 1982; Chodorow 1978; Fitzsimons 2002).

Likewise, queuing and other "male-dominance" models explain why men tend to dominate the most desirable jobs (within the manual and nonmanual sectors), but they cannot as readily explain the horizontal segregation of men and women into different sectors (see, e.g., Hartmann 1976; Reskin and Roos 1990). Although the contours of Figure 3.1 may not be altogether surprising, scholars of gender have not always appreciated that two types of segregative forces must be taken together to make sense of these contours. We are thus skeptical of grand descriptive theories that, for all their elegance, fail to recognize the fundamentally hybrid character of sex-segregation profiles.

The remaining models in Table 3.4 explore the extent to which this pooled segregation profile varies by country. Under our "multiplicative shift" specification (Model 5), the level of segregation is allowed to vary by country, while the underlying segregation curve is constrained to take on the same shape in each country (see equation 2.8). As noted in Chapter 2, this model is consistent with the practice of using a summary index, since it constrains all cross-national variability in segregation to take the form of differences in degree rather than kind. The multiplicative shift parameters estimated under this model (Φ_k) indicate whether the peaks and valleys of the segregation profile are compressed or expanded in each country. These shift parameters can be used to construct an index, A_M, that is closely related to A. As discussed in Chapter 2, these indices differ by virtue of the segregation profile that is presumed, with A_M conditioning on a shared segregation profile and A, by contrast, allowing the profile to freely vary.

The values of A_M in our ten-nation sample are reported in Table 3.5. For the most part, the country-specific shift parameters (A_M) do not vary much around the geometric mean (4.17), with the only obvious outlier being Italy (where $A_M = 2.91$).[7] In Figure 3.2, we apply these shift parameters to the underlying segregation profile (by multiplying v_j by Φ_k), because doing so allows us to represent graphically the extent of cross-national variability under Model 5. The resulting profiles, which cluster closely together, suggest that cross-national variability is quite limited.

In interpreting Figure 3.2, it is of course possible that Model 5 is correctly revealing a strong family resemblance in segregation regimes, but an obvious alternative interpretation is that the model suppresses variability by (improperly) conditioning on the same profile in all countries. The latter interpretation is in fact largely on the mark. In this regard, it bears recalling that more cross-national variability emerges under A, an index that does not condition on a common profile (see Table 3.3). Moreover, when we carry out an L^2 decomposition of the total cross-national variability in segregation (see Table 3.4), we find that only 14.0 percent of it can be attributed to differences in the level of sex segregation, whereas the remaining 86.0 percent arises from differences in the occupation-specific pattern of sex segre-

TABLE 3.5
Association Index under
Multiplicative Shift Model

Country	A_M
Belgium	3.95
France	4.82
West Germany	4.06
Italy	2.91
Portugal	4.22
Sweden	5.25
Switzerland	4.88
United Kingdom	5.13
United States	3.46
Japan	3.69

gation. We conclude that Model 5 is poorly suited for the purpose of capturing variability in sex segregation because such variability principally takes the form of differences in the profile itself rather than differences in the extent of segregation.

The preceding result implies that gender stratification systems are only weakly integrated and that pockets of extreme segregation and integration can therefore coexist in the same country. Although segregation scholars often characterize countries as more or less "egalitarian" or "woman-friendly," such characterizations cannot do justice to the multidimensionality of segregation regimes. In our earlier cross-national study, we likewise concluded that segregation regimes were "loosely coupled" (Charles and Grusky 1995), but we failed to identify the component pieces of segregation regimes that varied independently. The following analyses reveal that loose coupling takes on two main forms: (a) the parameters governing horizontal and vertical segregation vary independently, and (b) the parameters governing detailed and aggregate segregation vary independently. The former conclusion is pressed principally in Chapter 4, whereas the latter is pressed in the remainder of this chapter.

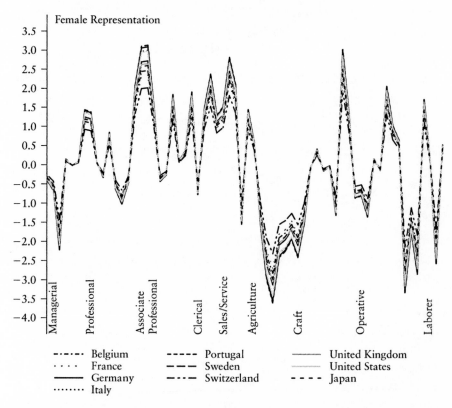

Figure 3.2   Sex-Segregation Profile with Scalar Multiplicative Shift (Model 5)

MULTILEVEL MODELS OF CROSS-NATIONAL VARIABILITY

We turn, then, to the task of developing simple multilevel models that distinguish between the structure of segregation within major occupational categories and the structure of segregation between those categories. In the "multilevel model" of line 6 (Table 3.4), the segregation profile at the major occupational level is allowed to vary across countries, while the corresponding profile at the detailed occupational level is constrained to be cross-nationally invariant (see equation 2.9). As described in Chapter 2, the rationale for this model is that major-category segregation is influenced by a host of macro-level forces, whereas detailed-category segregation is less mutable because the fundamental conditions of patriarchy guarantee that men in all countries consistently dominate the best occupations.

This argument, plausible though it may be, garners little empirical support in our ten-nation sample. When the total variability in sex segregation is decomposed, we find that only 45.7 percent is generated at the major occupational level, while the remaining 54.3 percent is generated at the detailed level. Moreover, the latter micro-level variability does not proceed from simple differences in the *extent* of segregation, because it proves impossible to summarize it with a simple multiplicative shift effect. In line 7 of Table 3.4, a shift effect is shown to explain only 10.4 percent of the total variability at the detailed occupational level ([957,588 − 858,281]/957,588 = 10.4), thus implying that almost all variability takes the form of more complicated differences in the segregation profile itself.

We must therefore turn to a saturated model that allows for cross-national variability at both levels. Under the model of equation 2.13, the structure of segregation is estimated at the major-category and detailed levels simultaneously, allowing us to compare how cross-national variability reveals itself at each of these levels. The major-category profiles from this model are graphed in Figure 3.3, and the detailed coefficients are graphed in Figure 3.4. In each figure, positive scale values refer to female overrepresentation, and negative scale values refer to male overrepresentation.

We consider first the structure of major-category segregation (Figure 3.3). As anticipated by the poor fit of Model 6 (Table 3.4), the major-category profiles do indeed vary nontrivially across countries, yet such variability is consistently expressed within the constraints of a stylized "leaning-N" profile. This profile reveals the simultaneous effect of horizontal and vertical processes, the former accounting for the crowding of women into the nonmanual sector, and the latter accounting for the tendency of men to dominate high-status occupations in both the manual and nonmanual sectors. The same conclusion was of course suggested by Figure 3.1. However, Figure 3.1 pertained to the "mean" pattern of segregation for the ten countries in our sample, whereas Figure 3.3 allows for variability around this mean.

The main conclusion from Figure 3.3, then, is that major-category variability is highly constrained because the same primitive segregating principles (horizontal and vertical effects) operate in all societies, albeit to varying degrees. The vertical effect is attenuated in the United States, while the horizontal effect is attenuated in Japan; and both vertical and horizontal effects are attenuated in Italy and Portugal (thereby accounting for their low

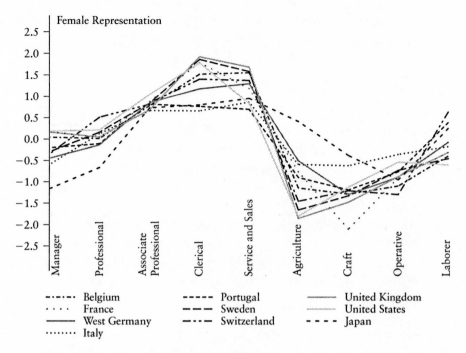

Figure 3.3   Aggregate Segregation Profile for 10 Nations

values on *A*). The macro-level segregation regimes of all modern industrial countries are accordingly built by mixing these two basic segregating processes in different proportions.

The micro-level parameter estimates (Figure 3.4) likewise reveal substantial cross-national variability. As again anticipated by Model 6, we find that the scale values for virtually all occupations are well scattered, thus suggesting that the forces of micro-level segregation manifest themselves in variable ways. We have suggested elsewhere that micro-level segregation is a deeply historical and cultural product that reflects such idiosyncratic forces as (a) the particular constellation of tasks assigned to an occupation (and the associated desirability of that occupation); (b) the closure strategies (such as unionization, credentialing) that occupational incumbents seized upon in attempting to monopolize skilled tasks; (c) the types of labor that were available when the occupation expanded and carried out its formative recruiting; (d) the types of firms, industries, or occupations that served as mod-

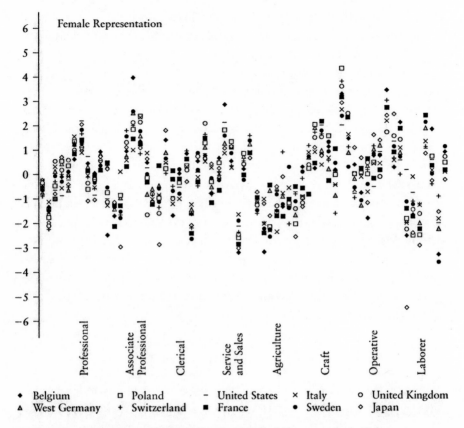

Figure 3.4　Cross-National Dispersion in Detailed-Category Scale Values

els for employment practices when the occupation was established or expanded (Stinchcombe 1965); and (e) the "woman-friendliness" of the owners, unions, and managers involved in occupational staffing and recruitment (Grusky and Charles 2001). These processes all suggest a form of path dependency whereby idiosyncratic local forces influenced the initial gender-typing of occupations and shaped their subsequent trajectory of development.

The imagery that emerges is that of loosely coupled segregation systems cobbled together from many occupation-specific "solutions" to the exigencies of modern industrial production and competing segregative and egalitarian cultural mandates. There is, to be sure, nearly as much variability at the major-category level as at the detailed level (see Model 6, Table 3.4); and hence our argument pertains to differences in the sources of variability rather than its extent. That is, macro-level variability has a simple and relatively lawful character to it, whereas micro-level variability does not. In Chapter 4, we pursue this argument more formally by demonstrating that (a) macro-level variability can be explained in large part by vertical and horizontal effects, whereas (b) micro-level variability is more chaotic and idiosyncratic.

The saturated model that we have been applying (equation 2.13) decomposes the association for each occupation into a micro-level (ν_{jk}) and macro-level (ϕ_{ck}) component. If these two components are combined, we can recover the total association for each occupation under the simpler saturated model (equation 2.10). We have listed these parameter estimates in Appendix Table A3.2. As anticipated, we find evidence of substantial cross-national variability, not merely in the extent of gender domination but also in its direction (male or female). In fact, thirty-one of our sixty-four occupations (48 percent) show cross-national inconsistency in the direction of gender domination, thus revealing how idiosyncratic segregative practices at the detailed level indeed are.

SEGREGATION INDICES REVISITED

We argue throughout this chapter that the viability of any index-based approach is an empirical matter. The foregoing results make it clear that all sex-segregation indices, conventional or otherwise, are empirically inadequate because the segregation profile itself is cross-nationally variable. If a summary measure is still insisted upon, A should be preferred because it relaxes the assumption that a common segregation profile holds. In this regard, it bears noting that A reveals more variability in the overall amount of segregation than conventional indices, such as D or D_s, have suggested. At the same time, even A is inadequate to the task, as the variability in sex-by-occupation arrays is fundamentally multidimensional in structure.

This variability may be better understood by abandoning the attempt to summarize all cross-national variability in a single index and instead allowing for distinct index values at the major-category and detailed levels. In Chapter 2, we used the parameter estimates from the model of equation 2.13 to define A_W and A_B (equations 2.14 and 2.15, respectively), with A_W referring to the amount of segregation within major categories and A_B referring

TABLE 3.6
Indices of Sex Segregation between and
within Major Occupational Categories

Country	A_B	A_W
Belgium	2.82	4.45
France	3.08	3.78
West Germany	2.38	3.29
Italy	1.76	2.92
Portugal	2.12	4.26
Sweden	3.18	3.77
Switzerland	2.92	3.89
United Kingdom	3.41	4.30
United States	2.91	3.12
Japan	2.13	5.12

NOTE: A_B = between-category association index; A_W = within-category association index. See equations 2.14 and 2.15 for index definitions.

to the amount of segregation between major categories. These index values are reported in Table 3.6.

The first, and perhaps most striking, feature of these two indices is that they correlate only weakly across countries ($r = .09$).[8] Although some countries in our sample have uniformly weak segregation at both levels (such as Italy), others combine strong within-category segregation with virtual integration at the macro-level (such as Japan). The latter results should give pause to scholars who have been emboldened to interpret the well-known "parallel lines" thesis as providing more general license for highly aggregate cross-national analysis (see, e.g., Jacobs and Lim 1992). To be sure, our results cannot speak directly to the thesis in its original form, since we lack the longitudinal data needed to determine whether A_B and A_W track over time. The present results suggest, however, that a cross-sectional analogue to the parallel lines thesis cannot be safely advanced, given that A_B and A_W are only weakly correlated and that inspection of either therefore conveys only limited information on the other. It follows that segregation systems are only "loosely coupled" at the detailed and major-category levels.

Why are segregation systems loosely coupled in this way? We have hypothesized that major-category segregation arises from fundamental segregating forces that are not equally relevant in generating detailed segregation. The deep structure of macro-level segregation reflects the interleaving of fundamental horizontal and vertical forces, whereas the chaos of micro-level segregation proceeds from the more haphazard effects of local union arrangements, the particular timing of expansionary pressures, and similar such context-specific institutional forces. There is of course much cross-national variability at both levels. However, because the sources of this variability differ, the correlation between major-category and detailed segregation is likely to be weak.

CONCLUSIONS

We led off this chapter suggesting that segregation analysts have turned prematurely to explanatory modeling without first establishing the most basic descriptive contours of sex segregation. In accounting for this state of affairs, it is surely relevant that the requisite data have until now been unavailable, but it is equally problematic that standard models and methods are inadequate. We have sought to make progress on both fronts by distinguishing between different types of similarity and difference, by developing models that correspond to these types, and by applying our models to a new archive of rigorously harmonized segregation data. This approach has allowed us to produce the first detailed mapping of sex segregation in industrial market economies. We then used the mapping to answer each of the four questions with which we led off this chapter, although some of our answers remain provisional and require additional analysis that is provided subsequently, principally in Chapter 4.

We began by asking whether the marginal distributions in a segregation array are the endogenous outcome of segregative processes. For the most part, proponents of index-based analysis have not sought to justify theoretically their use of margin-sensitive measures, yet we have shown that a potential justification can be found in models of the labor market that presume that the size of the female labor force is generated (endogenously) by (a) multiplying the sex ratio prevailing in each occupation by the size of that occupation, and (b) summing the resulting female counts across occupations

(Oppenheimer 1970, 1973; Cotter et al. 1998; Cotter, Hermsen, and Vanneman 2001). If this formulation is on the mark, our long-standing presumption that marginal effects must be controlled is called into question; and some types of margin-sensitive indices, such as D_s, may well be defensible. We have failed, however, to find much evidence in support of the endogeneity assumption. As was indicated in Table 3.4, the model of supply-side similarity comes closer to fitting than models implying other forms of endogeneity, but it nonetheless cannot be accepted under any conventional measure of model fit.

The search for cross-national similarities must therefore be carried out with models that control for marginal effects. In conventional segregation theories, the tendency has been to emphasize the generic forces generating segregation, implying that a family resemblance may emerge after purging cross-national differentials in female labor force participation and occupational demand. We were accordingly led to develop a model of "universal association" that presumes that a common structure to segregation emerges once these complications of market supply and demand are taken into account. This model again fails to fit well. As always, it is no easy task to judge whether a tolerable description of the data has been achieved, but we suspect that most scholars will agree that too much cross-national variability is concealed by the model of universal association.

Does such a model fail simply because of cross-national differences in the strength of segregation? This hypothesis is consistent with neo-functionalist and institutionalist accounts that represent labor markets as differing mainly in the extent to which egalitarian hiring, firing, and promotion has been institutionalized. Under such accounts, egalitarian forms and practices are presumed to be more deeply entrenched in "modern" labor markets than in traditional ones, suggesting that cross-national variability principally takes the form of across-the board differences in the strength of segregation (Goode 1963; Ramirez 1987; Jackson 1998). This "evolutionary" account, which undergirds the use of margin-free indices, again proves inconsistent with our cross-national data. As Table 3.4 reveals, a simple multiplicative shift model fails to explain much cross-national variability, indicating that the segregation profiles themselves are variable. The poor fit of this model motivates our (hardly subtle) theme that index-based analysis, even that based on A or A_M, cannot do justice to the complexity of cross-national variability.

This result does not force us to fall back on qualitative accounts emphasizing the wholly idiosyncratic sources of segregation. There is of course an idiosyncratic side to segregation outcomes; however, it plays out principally at the level of detailed occupations, where local and particularistic forces hold sway and determine the extent and direction of gender-typing. By contrast, a deep family resemblance can be teased out at the level of major-category segregation, with this shared profile revealing the simultaneous effects of vertical and horizontal forces. These effects, while differing in strength, nonetheless appear in all countries and lend a consistently hybrid form to the major-category profile.

The foregoing story mixes evidence with much speculation. The careful reader will appreciate that we have not demonstrated that vertical and horizontal effects can explain the core structure of macro-level segregation, nor have we shown that cross-national variability in this core structure can be attributed principally to variability in the strength of vertical and horizontal effects. Moreover, we have repeatedly referred to the "chaos" of micro-level segregation (and cross-national variability therein), yet it remains to be demonstrated that such segregation is indeed chaotic and cannot be explained in purely vertical terms. The purpose of the following chapter is to formally test these arguments about the horizontal and vertical components of segregation.

Recoding Rules for Translating ISCO-88
into 64-Category Classification

Occupation	ISCO-88 Codes
A. *Manager (MA)*	
Manager	111, 112, 114, 121–123, 131
B. *Professional (PR)*	
Physical science	211–213
Architect and engineer	214
Life science	221
Health	222
Professor	231
Secondary teacher	232
Other teacher	234, 235
Business professional	241
Lawyer and related	242
Social science and related	243–245, 247
Religious professional	246, 348
C. *Associate Professional (AP)*	
Physical science	311, 312
Inspector and related	313–315
Life science and health	321, 322
Nursing and midwife	223, 323
Primary teacher	233, 331, 332
Other teacher	333, 334
Finance and sales	341
Agent and broker	342
Admin. and social work	343, 346
Customs, tax, and related	344, 345
Art, entertaining, and sport	347

(*continued*)

APPENDIX TABLE A3.1
(*continued*)

Occupation	ISCO-88 Codes
D. *Clerical (CL)*	
Office clerk	411, 412, 414, 419
Material-recording	413
Cashier and teller	421
Client information	422
E. *Service and Sales (SS)*	
Travel attendant	511
Housekeeping and related	512
Personal care and related	513
Other personal service	514
Protective service	516
Salesperson and related	521, 522
F. *Agriculture and Fishery (AG)*	
Farmer	611–613, 921
Forestry and fishery	614, 615
G. *Craft (CR)*	
Miner and cutter	711, 712
Building finisher	713
Painter and related	714
Metal molder and related	721
Blacksmith and related	722
Machinery mechanic	723
Electrical mechanic	724
Metal precision	731
Handicraft	732, 733
Printing and related	734
Food processing	741
Cabinet-maker	742
Textile and garment	743
Pelt, leather, and shoe	744

APPENDIX TABLE A3.1
(*continued*)

Occupation	ISCO-88 Codes
H. *Operative (OP)*	
Wood processing	814
Other stationary-plant	811–813, 815–817
Metal and mineral	821
Chemical and related	822, 823
Wood product operative	824, 825
Textile and related	826
Food and related	827
Assembler	828, 829
Locomotive	831
Motor vehicle	832
Mobile plant operator	833, 834
I. *Laborer (LA)*	
Vendor and domestic	911–914, 916
Messenger and related	915
Mining and construction	931
Manufacturing and related	932, 933

APPENDIX TABLE A3.2

Occupation-Specific Segregation Parameters and Measures of Cross-National Dispersion in Segregation Parameters under Simple Saturated Model

| Occupation | COUNTRY[a] | | | | | | | | | | DISPERSION | |
	BE	FR	WG	IT	PO	SW	SZ	UK	US	JP	Variance	Uniform Typing
A. *Manager (MA)*												
Manager	0.20	0.45	−0.30	−0.60	−0.27	−0.23	−0.05	0.31	0.21	−1.07	0.19	No
B. *Professional (PR)*												
Physical science	−0.29	−0.29	−0.71	−0.13	0.20	−0.51	−0.79	−0.36	−0.08	−0.78	0.10	No
Architect and engineer	−1.12	−1.37	−1.51	−0.98	−0.80	−1.27	−2.11	−1.84	−1.27	−2.49	0.25	Yes
Life science	0.29	−0.64	0.09	0.44	0.28	0.26	−0.02	0.74	−0.28	−1.38	0.34	No
Health	0.34	0.71	0.26	−0.16	0.78	0.27	0.16	0.30	−0.56	0.13	0.13	No
Professor	0.31	0.71	−0.59	0.22	0.76	−0.04	−0.48	0.77	0.28	−0.23	0.22	No
Secondary teacher	1.32	1.38	0.90	1.65	1.85	0.89	1.11	1.22	0.92	0.38	0.16	Yes
Other teacher	1.26	1.51	1.08	1.01	1.51	1.83	1.59	1.22	2.28	1.39	0.13	Yes
Business professional	0.51	−0.24	−0.11	−0.04	0.73	0.39	0.22	−0.17	0.85	−1.60	0.44	No
Lawyer and related	0.31	0.34	−0.11	−0.34	0.24	−0.14	−0.53	0.05	0.09	−1.54	0.28	No
Social science and related	1.16	0.61	0.47	0.53	0.93	1.09	1.00	1.12	1.07	0.11	0.11	Yes
Religious professional	−2.24	0.78	0.35	−1.06	−0.20	−0.29	0.34	−0.92	−0.68	−0.38	0.67	No
C. *Associate Professional (AP)*												
Physical science	−0.68	−0.90	−0.51	−0.94	−0.22	−1.15	−0.09	−0.31	−0.02	−0.14	0.14	Yes
Inspector and related	−0.39	−0.14	0.09	0.78	0.06	−0.76	−0.60	0.02	−0.16	−2.04	0.49	No

Life science and health	1.82	1.49	1.80	1.24	1.36	2.46	2.79	2.14	1.74	1.85	0.21	Yes
Nursing and midwife	3.19	3.03	2.53	1.61	2.41	3.42	3.38	3.39	3.43	4.72	0.60	Yes
Primary teacher	2.36	2.28	2.73	2.95	3.25	2.82	1.86	2.86	2.09	1.84	0.21	Yes
Other teacher	1.61	0.87	0.26	1.54	0.69	0.85	1.51	−0.75	1.14	1.59	0.50	No
Finance and sales	−0.19	0.43	0.42	−0.42	−0.30	0.21	0.16	−0.08	0.38	−0.29	0.10	No
Agent and broker	−0.13	1.53	0.52	−0.15	−0.12	0.30	−0.27	−0.69	0.27	−1.95	0.71	No
Administrative and social work	2.36	1.77	1.63	1.27	1.36	1.70	1.09	1.77	1.97	2.62	0.20	Yes
Customs, tax, and related	−0.64	1.37	0.82	−0.50	0.69	−0.01	0.57	−0.21	0.40	0.31	0.35	No
Art, entertaining, and sport	0.99	0.99	0.70	−0.29	0.45	0.16	0.64	1.05	0.55	0.51	0.15	No
D. Clerical (CL)												
Office clerk	1.44	2.71	1.69	1.39	1.21	2.58	2.54	2.30	2.49	1.68	0.30	Yes
Material-recording	0.12	−0.23	0.07	−0.57	−0.58	−0.61	−0.61	−0.43	0.32	−1.03	0.16	No
Cashier and teller	2.49	2.23	1.07	0.56	0.53	2.80	1.15	2.28	1.93	1.42	0.59	Yes
Client information	2.64	3.56	2.47	1.18	2.14	2.94	3.14	4.13	2.48	1.48	0.72	Yes
E. Service and Sales (SS)												
Travel attendant	1.20	1.25	0.83	1.26	0.01	1.51	1.07	0.72	−0.28	1.53	0.34	No
Housekeeping and related	1.60	0.84	1.71	0.84	1.21	1.45	1.66	2.09	0.97	1.74	0.16	Yes
Personal care and related	4.50	3.26	2.63	1.69	2.48	3.24	3.20	3.61	2.88	2.04	0.58	Yes
Other personal service	2.33	2.52	2.56	1.11	2.07	2.47	1.86	3.00	1.84	1.67	0.27	Yes
Protective service	−1.60	−1.49	−1.38	−0.85	−2.01	−0.22	−0.83	−0.82	−1.15	−2.04	0.30	Yes
Salesperson and related	2.22	2.39	2.30	1.00	0.78	1.43	2.20	2.38	0.88	1.30	0.40	Yes

(*continued*)

APPENDIX TABLE A3.2
(*continued*)

| Occupation | COUNTRY[a] | | | | | | | | | | DISPERSION | |
	BE	FR	WG	IT	PO	SW	SZ	UK	US	JP	Variance	Uniform Typing
F. Agriculture and Fishery (AG)												
Farmer	0.16	0.40	0.49	0.54	0.48	−0.19	0.21	−0.47	−1.00	1.13	0.32	No
Forestry and fishery	−2.16	−1.39	−1.22	−1.78	−2.16	−3.01	−2.82	−2.96	−2.57	−0.14	0.75	Yes
G. Craft (CR)												
Miner and cutter	−3.46	−4.18	−3.07	−1.63	−3.42	−4.34	−4.11	−3.53	−3.02	−1.49	0.87	Yes
Building finisher	−3.48	−2.23	−1.76	−2.72	−3.17	−3.74	−3.45	−3.65	−3.26	−1.93	0.48	Yes
Painter and related	−2.52	−3.50	−1.74	−2.92	−2.66	−2.07	−1.76	−2.59	−1.52	−0.75	0.56	Yes
Metal molder and related	−1.18	−3.49	−2.02	−1.42	−2.77	−2.30	−0.15	−2.36	−2.06	−1.56	0.76	Yes
Blacksmith and related	−2.24	−2.77	−2.21	−1.17	−2.35	−0.95	−3.00	−2.65	−2.07	−1.32	0.45	Yes
Machinery mechanic	−2.48	−2.31	−2.77	−1.13	−3.05	−2.58	−2.12	−2.83	−1.85	−2.79	0.29	Yes
Electrical mechanic	−0.77	−2.35	−1.85	−0.63	−1.79	−1.21	−1.26	−2.39	−1.91	−1.59	0.33	Yes
Metal precision	−0.16	−2.61	−0.08	0.30	−0.91	−0.59	0.08	−0.97	−0.48	0.68	0.75	No
Handicraft	−0.84	−1.37	0.73	0.30	0.90	0.60	0.68	0.17	0.67	0.84	0.53	No
Printing and related	−0.22	0.29	−0.19	−0.22	−0.23	0.58	0.63	0.21	0.81	0.49	0.15	No
Food processing	−0.13	−2.04	−0.93	0.10	0.42	−0.46	−0.47	−0.08	−0.05	0.97	0.59	No
Cabinet-maker	−0.92	−0.82	−2.03	−1.03	−1.14	−0.85	−2.61	−1.26	−1.50	0.13	0.49	No
Textile and garment	2.15	1.25	1.93	2.05	3.14	1.14	2.69	2.14	0.99	2.74	0.47	Yes
Pelt, leather, and shoe	0.35	0.47	−0.15	1.07	1.19	−0.94	0.02	1.09	−0.17	1.45	0.52	No

H. Operative (OP)

Wood processing	-0.54	-0.69	-0.89	-0.94	-0.68	-1.15	-2.05	-0.70	-1.20	0.31	0.32	No
Other stationary-plant	-1.61	-0.42	-1.88	-0.49	-0.72	-1.58	-2.05	-1.37	-1.74	-0.17	0.42	Yes
Metal and mineral	-2.68	0.04	-0.39	-1.09	-0.68	-1.13	-0.97	-0.25	-0.52	-2.01	0.62	No
Chemical and related	-0.15	-0.75	0.23	0.08	-0.13	0.25	-0.02	0.02	-0.83	0.70	0.19	No
Wood product operative	-0.05	-0.50	0.58	0.12	0.19	-0.59	-0.27	-0.83	-0.31	0.55	0.20	No
Textile and related	2.44	2.06	1.82	1.79	1.44	1.71	1.79	0.97	1.82	1.49	0.14	Yes
Food and related	-0.68	0.27	-0.12	0.24	0.40	0.48	-0.43	0.79	0.78	1.57	0.38	No
Assembler	1.20	0.06	0.15	0.70	1.09	0.08	-1.22	0.67	0.33	0.95	0.45	No
Locomotive	-3.39	-1.94	-2.71	-2.44	-2.43	-1.79	-2.37	-2.99	-0.38	-6.16	1.95	Yes
Motor vehicle	-2.43	-2.24	-2.27	-0.51	-3.14	-1.71	-2.11	-1.97	-1.37	-3.13	0.55	Yes
Mobile plant operator	-2.52	-2.80	-2.70	-1.62	-3.11	-1.93	-2.91	-2.43	-2.27	-3.66	0.31	Yes

I. Laborer (LA)

Vendor and domestic	1.64	2.37	1.98	1.23	2.66	1.66	1.99	1.99	0.54	1.18	0.35	Yes
Messenger and related	1.62	0.40	0.02	0.01	1.21	-0.39	0.42	0.26	-0.01	0.16	0.33	No
Mining and construction	-3.74	-3.19	-2.08	-1.93	-2.98	-3.55	-0.10	-3.38	-2.52	-1.17	1.21	Yes
Manufacturing and related	-0.49	0.29	0.36	-0.09	0.90	0.72	0.84	0.46	-0.34	1.20	0.28	No

NOTES: Entries are scale values from the simple saturated model (equation 2.13). Values above zero indicate female overrepresentation; values below zero indicate female underrepresentation.

[a] BE = Belgium; FR = France; WG = Germany (West); IT = Italy; PO = Portugal; SW = Sweden; SZ = Switzerland; UK = United Kingdom; US = United States; JP = Japan.

93

CHAPTER FOUR

Revisiting Parsimony:
New Models of Vertical
and Horizontal Segregation

We have argued at length that conventional segregation analysis, which conceptualizes and measures segregation in unidimensional terms, cannot adequately represent the structure of sex segregation. Although most analysts have worked with simpler models of segregation than are empirically defensible, our objective in this book is somewhat more ambitious than merely discrediting standard practice as simplistic. After all, it is child's play to develop models that are more complicated than prevailing ones, but much more difficult to strike the proper balance between realism and parsimony. The purpose of this chapter, therefore, is to go beyond the obvious argument that sex segregation is "complicated" and to demonstrate wherein that complication resides, how it might be modeled, and why it matters in making sense of segregation.

To this end, we seek to show that segregation regimes take on a relatively parsimonious structure, albeit nothing so parsimonious as has been conventionally assumed. We argue in this chapter that the anatomy of segregation regimes can be captured in a small number of fundamental parameters ("parsimony of structure"), that cross-national variability in segregation regimes is expressed principally in terms of these parameters ("parsimony of variation"), and that the core explanatory forces generating such variability operate, in large part, via these parameters ("parsimony in causal dynamics"). We are thus suggesting that parsimonious models of segregation may be developed at three distinct but related levels. In the following sections, we discuss each type of parsimony in turn, reviewing its sources and the hypotheses that it implies. These hypotheses serve to formalize the core arguments of the book.

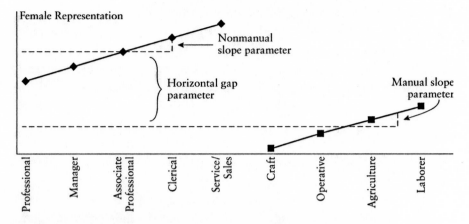

Figure 4.1   Anatomy of a Hypothetical Sex-Segregation Regime[a]

[a]In our models, the major occupational categories are coded in terms of a socioeconomic scale, thus allowing the intercategory distances to vary freely. For the purpose of simplifying the presentation, we have assumed here that intercategory distances are the same.

PARSIMONY OF STRUCTURE

We begin with the claim that the structure of segregation at the level of aggregate classes ("major occupational categories") may be described with no more than three parameters. These parameters are represented graphically in Figure 4.1: the "nonmanual slope parameter" governs the extent to which men dominate the most desirable classes in the nonmanual sector; the "manual slope parameter" governs the extent to which men dominate the most desirable classes in the manual sector; and the "horizontal gap parameter" governs the extent to which men are disproportionately allocated into the manual sector rather than the nonmanual one.

The horizontal axis of this figure arrays the nine major occupational categories defined by the International Labour Office on an approximate socioeconomic scale ranging from high (professional) to low (laborer). Following convention, the first five categories in this list may be characterized as nonmanual, and the second four may be characterized as manual. The vertical axis of this figure, labeled "female representation," indicates the extent to which women or men are overrepresented in each of these nine categories. In the interior of the figure, the slopes of the two lines reveal the strength of vertical segregation, with a steep positive slope indicating that men are much advantaged in the competition for desirable occupations, a moderate positive slope indicating that men are only weakly advantaged in this competition, and a negative slope (which is logically possible but empirically unlikely) indicating that women are advantaged. The extent of horizontal segregation (the "horizontal gap" parameter) is given by the vertical distance between the manual and nonmanual lines.[1] The foregoing three-parameter specification, which serves to summarize the aggregate structure of segregation, allows us to resolve long-standing empirical puzzles in the field that arose because most scholars have defaulted to a unidimensional view.

The two vertical slope parameters in Figure 4.1 are partly consistent with a unidimensional queuing formulation (whereby men secure better occupations than women), but our specification may be understood as a radical modification of this formulation because queuing theory does not allow for a "horizontal gap" expressing the tendency of women to be disproportionately allocated to the nonmanual sector (even though nonmanual occupations are, on average, more desirable than manual ones). Moreover, we allow the vertical principle to be stronger in some regions of the labor market (the manual sector) than in others,[2] and we also allow the vertical principle to be stronger at the aggregate level than at the level of detailed occupations (which are not represented in Figure 4.1). Finally, we have argued that vertical segregation is generated by the full array of micro-level processes summarized in Table 1.1, whereas conventional queuing theorists have tended to emphasize a smaller subset of these processes, especially employer discrimination. Although queuing theory thus motivates some aspects of our parameterization, it cannot provide a complete account of segregation (see Strober 1984; Reskin and Roos 1990).

The deficiencies of queuing theory and other unidimensional formulations arise in large part because the cultural underpinnings of segregation are fundamentally two-dimensional. The parameterization of Figure 4.1 rests on the premise, as elaborated in Chapter 1, that vertical segregation is undergirded by the cultural tenet of male primacy, whereas horizontal segregation is undergirded by the complementary cultural tenet of gender essentialism (see also Chapters 2–3). The tenet of male primacy represents men as more status worthy than women and better suited for positions of authority and domination, while the tenet of gender essentialism represents women as more competent than men in service, nurturance, and social interaction. In the modern context, these two cultural tenets tend to coexist with one another, thus giving segregation systems a hybrid character.

The resulting distinction between vertical and horizontal segregation has a distinguished history in the field and continues to be frequently invoked (see, e.g., Hakim 1996; Semyonov and Jones 1999; Blackburn, Brooks, and Jarman 2001). We wish to exploit the history underlying this distinction but also to recast it to better serve our analytic and explanatory ends. Unlike prior scholars, we explicitly operationalize horizontal segregation in terms of the manual-nonmanual distinction, thereby equating it with gender essentialism and defining it independently of vertical forms of segregation.[3] In conventional formulations, horizontal segregation has not been independently conceptualized. The long-standing tendency in the field has been to operationalize it as the residual association between occupation and sex after the effects of vertical segregation have been purged.[4] When horizontal segregation is independently conceptualized and operationalized, it becomes possible to theorize its sources, to develop hypotheses about the structure of cross-societal variability that correspond to such theories, and to test these hypotheses by examining whether vertical and horizontal effects, taken together, can account for sex segregation and can be explained by other macro-level forces.

The foregoing objectives, while constituting some of the themes of Chapter 3, have not yet been pursued with the formalism that distinguishes this chapter. That is, our informal inspection of segregation profiles in Chapter 3 suggested the interleaving of vertical and horizontal effects, but now we formally parameterize these effects and demonstrate that they indeed provide a comprehensive account of segregation at the aggregate level. Likewise, we wish to explicitly show that segregation at the disaggregate level cannot be explained in vertical terms, contrary to conventional queuing formulations. It follows that a parsimonious account of segregation can only be achieved at the aggregate level. Although we have rejected the standard indices that are routinely used to characterize segregation in one-dimensional terms, we demonstrate in this chapter that segregation scholars can adequately summarize the structure of aggregate segregation in a mere three dimensions, thus rendering the task of segregation analysis only marginally more complicated than prevailing practice.

PARSIMONY OF VARIATION

The implicit unidimensionalism of conventional segregation theorizing also reveals itself in prevailing stories about the structure of cross-national variability in segregation. The standard presumption in this regard is that such variability, while necessarily complicated and idiosyncratic, nonetheless mainly takes the form of differences in the extent to which egalitarian practices have been institutionalized. As egalitarianism diffuses, the proximate mechanisms underlying segregation (such as discrimination and gender-specific preferences) are expected to erode, thus reducing the overall amount of segregation. If this formulation were on the mark, we could characterize cross-national variability in entirely unidimensional terms, with countries differing principally in the extent to which egalitarian practices have diffused and undermined sex segregation.

The main conclusion of Chapter 3 was that unidimensional formulations of this sort fail spectacularly in representing the structure of cross-national variability. The multiplicative shift model, which allows for variation in the extent of segregation, explained only 14 percent of the total cross-national difference (see Table 3.4). Moreover, we found that conventional indices, such as D, generate strikingly counterintuitive results (see Table 3.3). The highest values of D were registered in gender-egalitarian countries (such as Sweden and France), while some of the lowest values were generated in countries that can hardly be regarded as bastions of gender equality (including Italy, Japan, and Portugal). These results imply that countries differ in more complicated ways than unidimensional theories suggest. The great failing of index-based analysis is not just that indices are margin-dependent but also that cross-national variability is too complicated to be summarized unidimensionally.

Although the radical data reduction of conventional comparative analysis must therefore be rejected, it remains unclear whether cross-national variability might still be summarized in some smaller number of parameters. We have suggested in prior chapters that indeed it can. In inspecting the segregation profiles of ten countries (see Chapter 3), we have concluded that aggregate segregation reliably assumes the basic shape of Figure 4.1, with cross-national variability thus taking the form of differences in the size of the horizontal gap and the strength of the manual or nonmanual slopes. The foregoing conclusion rested, however, on mere inspection of segregation profiles; and we have yet to more formally demonstrate that cross-national variability at the aggregate level can be captured with the three parameters of Figure 4.1. The careful critic of our work might reasonably point out that we have subjected conventional unidimensional formulations to explicit testing (via the multiplicative shift model) but have evaluated our own alternative formulation in more informal terms. We therefore provide in this chapter a formal test of our claim that aggregate segregation is generated in modern industrial countries by "mixing" vertical and horizontal principles in different proportions. In carrying out these analyses, we intend to show that variability at the aggregate level can be parsimoniously explained, whereas variability at the detailed level is a function of more idiosyncratic segregation practices that cannot be understood in entirely vertical terms.

As we further pointed out in Chapter 3, the poor fit of the multiplicative shift model implies that segregation regimes are "loosely coupled," where this means that segregative and integrative practices coexist in different sectors of the same labor market. We suggested that loose coupling potentially takes on two forms: (a) the parameters governing detailed and aggregate segregation may vary independently, and (b) the parameters governing horizontal and vertical segregation may vary independently. In Chapter 3, we presented evidence of the first form of loose coupling, but not the second. We develop models in this chapter that fit explicit parameters for vertical and horizontal segregation and accordingly allow us to test for loose coupling of the second type. In the following section, we argue that vertical and horizontal segregation are generated by different macro-level processes (see also Chapter 1), thus raising the possibility of "type 2" loose coupling.

PARSIMONY IN CAUSAL DYNAMICS

We ask, finally, whether our preferred three-parameter specification can be usefully applied in causal analyses of segregation. The causal tradition of gender scholarship is well developed; indeed, most segregation scholars eschew purely descriptive work, preferring to turn immediately to causal questions about the macro-level sources of segregation. In our view, the causal literature has developed prematurely, given that it has entailed explaining segregation without an adequate understanding of precisely what needs to be explained. We have therefore sought to make headway in describing the structure of sex segregation. In the concluding analyses of this chapter, we nonetheless develop an illustrative causal model that builds on our descriptive work by representing segregation in multidimensional terms.

We proceed by modeling cross-national variability in the parameters of horizontal and vertical segregation. Because these two dimensions of segregation reflect different cultural sources and dynamics, they cannot necessarily be expected to move in tandem as egalitarianism and modernization unfold. In fact, our core argument is that modern segregation, far from being a mere holdover from a less egalitarian past, is an organic feature of contemporary societies that is actively generated by processes that are part and parcel of modernization. To be sure, egalitarian reform does undermine some forms of vertical segregation, but this integrative effect is muted because (a) the logic of modern egalitarian ideology and policy is consistent with the persistence of horizontal forms of segregation, and (b) the associated rise of postindustrialism works to increase horizontal segregation as well as some forms of vertical segregation.

These arguments are summarized in Figure 4.2. As indicated in the subheadings of this figure, Graph A represents the basic parameters of sex segregation in a hypothetical baseline society that is unaffected by gender-egalitarian pressures and postindustrialism,[5] whereas Graphs B and C represent the respective effects of egalitarianism and postindustrialism on the

A. Baseline Regime: Low Egalitarianism and Low Postindustrialism

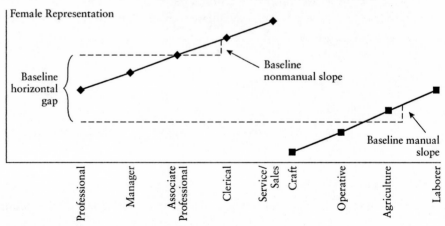

Figure 4.2   Variability in Sex-Segregation Regimes[a]

[a]On socioeconomic scaling of occupations, see note to Figure 4.1.

Figure 4.2   (*continued*)

B. Egalitarian Regime: Weakening the Nonmanual Vertical Effect

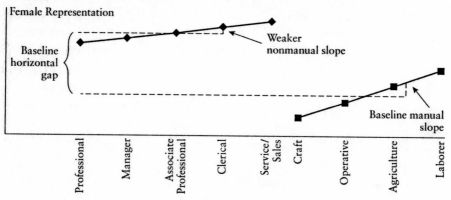

C. Postindustrial Regime: Increasing the Horizontal Gap and Strengthening the Nonmanual Vertical Effect.

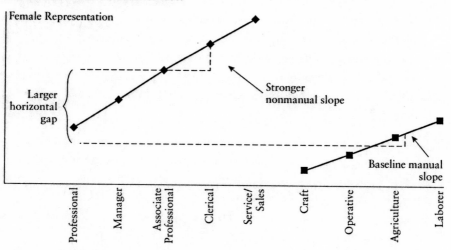

baseline parameters. The graphs of Figure 4.2 should be understood as representing ideal-typical societies rather than actual countries or time periods. In the following discussion, we wish merely to summarize the logic of our argument, ignoring for now the inevitable complications that emerge in real data.

How, then, do the twin forces of egalitarianism and postindustrialism operate? We have argued in Chapter 1 that gender egalitarianism renders norms of male primacy less consequential in the educational, familial, and labor market choices of workers and in the hiring, placement, and promotion decisions of employers. The logic of egalitarianism thus undermines the micro-level mechanisms that generate vertical segregation: We expect that women will increasingly evaluate themselves as capable of performing high-status tasks, that employers will shed their tastes for vertical discrimination against women, that associated forms of institutional discrimination will be delegitimated and gradually eliminated, and that women will, in turn, increasingly pursue high-status positions as their expectations of discrimination and other external sanctions recede (see Table 1.1). These effects should be strongest in the nonmanual sector, owing to the visibility of elite professional and managerial positions and the more formal, universalistic hiring and promotion practices that prevail at the top of the nonmanual hierarchy. As Graph B indicates, horizontal forms of segregation should be left largely unaffected, since the "different but equal" variant of egalitarianism that has diffused allows essentialist premises about female traits (such as nurturing) to persist and inform supply-side and demand-side processes.

The structural side of modernization is also consistent with the persistence and even deepening of sex segregation. The segregative effects of postindustrialism were elaborated in Chapter 1, but it may be useful to summarize them here.

Compositional effect. We have suggested, first, that nonmanual jobs are increasingly performed within service industries that tend to recruit or attract women (retail sales, communications, personal service), thus resulting in the feminization of the nonmanual sector and the consequent strengthening of horizontal segregation. This compositional effect arises because many service industries provide services that are functionally and symbolically similar to those traditionally provided by women in families (such as childcare, cleaning, personal support services) and because service-sector positions in the retail sales, commercial banking, and healthcare industries often demand emotional labor or interpersonal skills that are female-typed.

Adaptive effect. Second, service-sector expansion raises the demand for labor to the point where it can no longer be met by simply drawing further on the largely tapped supply of single women, meaning that employers must induce wives and mothers to enter the labor force, especially in the rapidly expanding routine nonmanual sector. This new labor force creates pressures for workplace adaptations (such as part-time work and flexible scheduling) that render the routine nonmanual sector a default "home" for female workers with extensive family responsibilities, low educational attainments, and more traditional gender-role ideals.[6]

Bureaucratizing effect. Finally, clerical and sales occupations are increasingly found in large bureaucratic firms rather than family-owned stores, and the associated jobs are therefore routinized and feminized. As independent entrepreneurs disappear, nonmanual clerical and sales jobs are deskilled, and employers characteristically turn to women to fill them.

The foregoing effects are all segregative and therefore counteract the effects of cultural egalitarianism. As Figure 4.2 indicates, the compositional effect of postindustrialism increases horizontal segregation, whereas the adaptive and bureaucratizing effects strengthen vertical segregation in the nonmanual sector.

Undoubtedly, other macro-level effects are also at work (see Chapter 1), only some of which may be regarded as secondary expressions or manifestations of the forces emphasized here. Although the macro-level sources of segregation are surely more complicated than we have allowed, our pared-down specification at least serves to reveal how modernity embodies forces for segregation as well as integration. This specification casts light on the persistence of hypersegregation in contemporary labor markets and thereby addresses one of the main puzzles with which we began this book.[7]

SEGREGATION DATA AND MEASURES

The analyses presented here are based on the same international data archive described in Chapter 3. We again apply a cross-nationally harmonized classification of sixty-four detailed and nine aggregate categories to segregation data from ten industrial market economies (see Table 3.2). As before, the data are organized in the form of a three-dimensional, 1,280-cell matrix with sixty-four occupations (see Appendix Table A3.1), two sexes, and ten countries. We report results based on "self-weighted" data in which the actual sample size in each country is preserved. Because large-sample countries (such as Italy and Japan) therefore have much leverage on our estimates, we have reestimated many of our models after standardizing sample sizes to an arbitrary constant ($N = 10,000$); and we accordingly note those few instances in which the self-weighted and standardized samples produce discrepant results.

We have measured horizontal inequality at the aggregate level by distinguishing the five nonmanual categories (managerial, professional, associate professional, clerical, service/sales) from the four manual categories (agriculture, craft, operative, laborer).[8] We measure vertical inequality with the internationally standardized socioeconomic index (SEI) published by Ganzeboom and Treiman (1996). This index, which is constructed as a weighted average of the educational attainment and income of occupational incumbents, is highly correlated with an international occupational prestige index (ibid.). We apply two variants of this scale in our analyses: (a) the aggregate variant (V1) assigns average SEI values to each of the nine major categories, and (b) the detailed variant (V2) assigns SEI values to each of the sixty-four detailed occupations. The former values, which range from twenty (laborers) to seventy (professionals), are listed in the stub of Table 4.1. The aggregate variant of this scale is used to examine the extent to which aggregate segregation is vertically organized, whereas the detailed variant is used to examine the extent to which detailed segregation is vertically organized.

We define "gender egalitarianism" as a commitment to gender-based equality of opportunity and operationalize it as the percentage of respondents in each country disagreeing with the statement that "men have greater rights to jobs during periods of high unemployment." This survey item, which comes out of the 1990 World Values Survey (WVS),[9] signals whether respondents accept the assumption of male economic dominance or reject it in favor of the norms of universalism and equal opportunity. We measure "postindustrialism" with a composite index that averages standardized scores on two variables: service-sector size, and economic rationalization. The first variable, service-sector size, is measured as the percentage of the 1990 labor force working in service-industry jobs (commercial, banking, service, transportation, communication), while the second variable, economic rationalization, is measured as the percentage of the active labor force that is employed rather than working as an employer, unpaid family worker, or own-account (self-employed) worker.[10] These data on service-sector size and economic rationalization were taken from the 1990, 1991, and 1992

Yearbook of Labour Statistics (ILO 1990, 1991, 1992). In Appendix Table A4.1, the values for each variable are provided, as is the zero-order correlation between the two macro-level variables (.50).

CAN THE STRUCTURE OF SEX SEGREGATION BE PARSIMONIOUSLY DESCRIBED?

We begin the analysis by asking whether our three-parameter specification suffices to describe segregation at the aggregate level (see Table 4.1). In addressing this question, it is useful to decompose the total sex-by-occupation association into a component occurring between major categories and a component occurring within them, because doing so allows us to establish how much association is available to be explained at each level. We find that 36.3 percent of the total association occurs between major categories while the remaining 63.7 percent occurs within them (see Table 4.1, panel A).

The key question that then arises is whether the between-category component may be explained in vertical terms. In its purest form, a queuing model implies that men are disproportionately allocated to the most desirable major occupations, thus suggesting the following specification:

$$m_{ijk} = \alpha_k \beta_{ik} \gamma_{jk} e^{\varepsilon(Z, V1_j)}, \tag{4.1}$$

where $V1_j$ refers to the aggregate version of our socioeconomic scale, ε refers to the effect of socioeconomic status on female representation (at the aggregate level), and the remaining terms are defined as in Chapter 2. The test statistic for this model, presented in line 4 of Table 4.1, indicates that only 2.5 percent of the total association at the aggregate level can be explained in vertical terms. Moreover, our estimate of ε under this model is .008, implying that female representation increases by a factor of 1.008 for each unit increase in socioeconomic status. The latter estimate, which indicates that women are (slightly) overrepresented in high-status occupations, is of course inconsistent with simple queuing perspectives (see Treiman and Terrell 1975; Roos 1985; Charles and Grusky 1995; see also Blackburn, Brooks, and Jarman 2001).

This result, while counterintuitive, is by no means unexpected. Indeed, there is a standing literature on the matter of why segregation does not take on a pure socioeconomic form (e.g., England 1979; Acker 1980), with some

TABLE 4.1
Pooled Models of Vertical and Horizontal Sex Segregation

Model[a]	L^2	d.f.	Total Segregation Explained (%)[b]	Aggregate Segregation Explained (%)[c]	Detailed Segregation Explained (%)[d]	BIC
A. Baseline Models						
1. No segregation S*N + O*N	16,211,858	630	0.0	0.0	0.0	16,200,659
2. Major-category segregation S*N + O*N + G*S	10,962,759	622	36.3	100.0	0.0	10,951,702
3. Universal association S*N + O*N + O*S	1,763,819	567	100.0	100.0	100.0	1,753,740
B. Models of Aggregate Segregation						
4. Vertical effect[e] S*N + O*N + S*V1	16,081,116	629	0.9	2.5	0.0	16,069,935
5. Horizontal effect S*N + O*N + S*H	13,874,529	629	16.2	44.5	0.0	13,863,348

6. Vertical and horizontal (additive) $S*N + O*N + S*V1 + S*H$	11,993,936	628	29.2	80.4	0.0	11,982,773
7. Vertical and horizontal (interactive) $S*N + O*N + S*V1*H$	11,734,173	627	31.0	85.3	0.0	11,723,028
C. Model of Detailed Segregation						
8. Vertical effect $S*N + O*N + G*S + S*V2$	10,659,649	621	—	—	3.3	10,648,610

[a] O = detailed occupation; G = major occupation; N = country (Belgium, France, West Germany, Italy, Japan, Portugal, Sweden, Switzerland, United Kingdom, and United States); S = sex; V1 = socioeconomic scale applied to aggregate categories; V2 = socioeconomic scale applied to detailed categories; H = manual-nonmanual distinction.

[b] The total association for segregation is given by the difference between the L^2 values for Models 1 and 3.

[c] The total association for aggregate segregation is given by the difference between the L^2 values for Models 1 and 2.

[d] The total association for detailed segregation is given by the difference between the L^2 values for Models 2 and 3.

[e] We assigned the following SEI scores at the major-category level: managers (55), professionals (70), associate professionals (54), clerical (45), sales/service (40), agricultural (23), craft (34), operative (31), laborer (20).

scholars arguing that socioeconomic scores overstate the desirability of routine nonmanual occupations and hence create the (misleading) appearance of female advantage. The latter account no doubt has some merit. However, our suspicion is that the queuing model fails not only because socioeconomic scales are flawed or because the vertical dynamic is weak, but also because this dynamic is obscured in the absence of controls for horizontal segregation. The structure of segregation is in this sense fundamentally multidimensional.

We can test this argument by fitting a multidimensional model and examining whether the vertical coefficient reverses sign and strengthens. When vertical and horizontal effects are simultaneously fit, the following model is generated:

$$m_{ijk} = \alpha_k \beta_{ik} \gamma_{jk} e^{\varepsilon(Z_i V1_j) + \omega(Z_i H_j)}, \tag{4.2}$$

where H_j is the horizontal term ($H_j = 1$ if j is a manual occupation and $H_j = 0$ otherwise), ω is the effect of horizontal status on female representation, and the remaining terms are defined as before. As shown in Table 4.1, the explained association under this specification increases dramatically from 2.5 to 80.4 percent (see line 6); and the vertical coefficient further assumes the expected negative sign and becomes quite strong $(-.050)$.[11] The horizontal coefficient is likewise very strong: The estimate of ω, -1.96, implies that female representation is 7.10 times greater in a nonmanual occupation than a corresponding manual occupation of the same socioeconomic status. This effect, which is equivalent to that associated with a downward shift in status of nearly forty points, is surely strong enough to suggest that scholars of gender stratification should move beyond their long-standing focus on vertical inequality and begin attending to horizontal forms of stratification. As we argue subsequently, horizontal segregation is a characteristically postmodern form of gender inequality, whereas vertical segregation is, by contrast, more vulnerable to the forces of gender egalitarianism.

The final model of panel B allows the strength of the vertical effect to differ across sectors. This model may be represented as follows:

$$m_{ijk} = \alpha_k \beta_{ik} \gamma_{jk} e^{\psi(Z_i N_j V1_j) + \varepsilon(Z_i M_j V1_j) + \omega(Z_i H_j)}, \tag{4.3}$$

where N_j is an indicator variable for nonmanual occupations ($N_j = 1$ if j is a nonmanual occupation and $N_j = 0$ otherwise), M_j is an indicator variable for manual occupations ($M_j = H_j$), and ψ and ε express the strength of vertical segregation within the nonmanual and manual sectors respectively.[12] With this specification, the explained association increases modestly (from 80.4 to 85.3 percent), and the vertical effect is revealed to be slightly weaker in the nonmanual sector ($-.040$) than in the manual sector ($-.047$). The modern segregation regime thus takes on the three-parameter form represented in Figure 4.1: The horizontal gap parameter captures the dramatic overrepresentation of women in the nonmanual sector, and the two slope parameters capture the tendency for men to dominate the best occupations within the manual and nonmanual sectors. To be sure, the two slope parameters under this specification are nearly equal in strength, but our subsequent analyses of country-specific segregation will reveal more substantial differences across sectors in the strength of the vertical principle.

It follows that our three-parameter specification effectively exhausts the structure of segregation at the aggregate level. Is disaggregate segregation equally amenable to a parsimonious account? Although we shall not attempt any elaborate modeling here, we can at least test the simple claim that segregation across detailed categories assumes a simple vertical form. This hypothesis can be tested with the following model:

$$m_{ijk} = \alpha_k \beta_{ik} \gamma_{jk} e^{\varepsilon(Z_i V2_j) + \varphi_c(Z_i)}, \tag{4.4}$$

where φ_c refers to the scale values for major occupational categories (indexed by c), and $V2_j$ refers to the detailed variant of our socioeconomic scale. As indicated in line 8, this model explains a mere 3.3 percent of the total disaggregate association; and the vertical coefficient, estimated at $-.034$, is only 68 percent as strong as the corresponding vertical coefficient ($-.050$) at the aggregate level (under the model of equation 4.2). We can conclude that the forces of patriarchy do not operate all that efficiently in allocating men to the most desirable occupations within each major category.

It is possible, of course, that the vertical coefficient is suppressed because various types of "essentialist effects" (such as a nurturing effect or service effect) have been improperly omitted from our model. It is surely worth exploring this possibility in future research. Absent explicit evidence of such bias, our provisional conclusion is nonetheless that disaggregate segregation does not have a clear vertical character to it, again calling conventional queuing models into question.

TABLE 4.2
Single-Country Models of Vertical
and Horizontal Sex Segregation[a]

Model	Aggregate Segregation Explained (%)	SEGREGATION COEFFICIENT	
		Vertical	Horizontal
A. *Vertical Effect* (S + O + S*V1)			
Belgium	3.66	0.01	
France	2.40	0.01	
West Germany	1.54	0.01	
Italy	12.78	0.01	
Portugal	0.52	0.00	
Sweden	1.02	0.01	
Switzerland	0.68	0.01	
United Kingdom	0.71	0.01	
United States	9.15	0.02	
Japan	0.61	0.00	
B. *Horizontal Effect* (S + O + S*H)			
Belgium	43.48		−1.10
France	40.41		−1.40
West Germany	42.34		−1.32
Italy	59.55		−0.83
Portugal	18.36		−0.49
Sweden	41.64		−1.53
Switzerland	42.01		−1.49
United Kingdom	39.34		−1.39
United States	55.44		−1.54
Japan	20.82		−0.65
C. *Vertical and Horizontal Effect (Additive)* (S + O + S*V1 + S*H)			
Belgium	75.08	−.053	−2.37
France	79.64	−.086	−3.45
West Germany	84.82	−.077	−3.14
Italy	75.73	−.027	−1.38
Portugal	39.02	−.034	−1.19
Sweden	79.95	−.080	−3.40
Switzerland	82.43	−.080	−3.23

TABLE 4.2
(*continued*)

Model	Aggregate Segregation Explained (%)	SEGREGATION COEFFICIENT	
		Vertical	Horizontal
United Kingdom	83.03	−.084	−3.34
United States	75.02	−.049	−2.69
Japan	77.63	−.075	−2.16

D. *Vertical and Horizontal Effect (Interactive)* (S + O + S*V1 + S*H + S*V1*H)

		Vertical, nonmanual	Vertical, manual	Horizontal
Belgium	85.84	−.039	−.085	−2.89
France	87.99	−.066	−.110	−4.09
West Germany	92.11	−.062	−.090	−3.61
Italy	83.84	−.017	−.046	−1.56
Portugal	71.93	−.004	−.089	−1.42
Sweden	87.84	−.065	−.114	−4.13
Switzerland	88.37	−.068	−.101	−3.86
United Kingdom	87.42	−.071	−.077	−3.80
United States	75.64	−.045	−.027	−2.86
Japan	77.94	−.078	−.013	−2.11

[a]Terms defined as in Table 4.1.

We conclude this section by asking whether our three-parameter specification suffices to describe the structure of aggregate segregation in *all* advanced industrial countries. We have estimated single-country models analogous to the pooled models of Table 4.1 and reported the relevant parameters and fit statistics in Table 4.2. The main conclusions that emerge are: (a) a simple unidimensional model explains only a small minority of the aggregate association in each country (see panel A); (b) the vertical segregation coefficient from this unidimensional model assumes the same positive (and counterintuitive) sign in each country; (c) our alternative multidimensional specification explains more than 70 percent of the aggregate association in each country (see panel D); (d) the vertical segregation coefficients from this model become strong and negative in each country; (e) the horizontal segregation effect is likewise strong in most countries (save Italy and Portugal) and may therefore be regarded as an important, if neglected, source of contemporary hypersegregation; and (f) the nonmanual slope coefficient is weaker than the corresponding manual coefficient in all but two countries (the United States and Japan).

In summary, our single-country and pooled analyses yield largely consistent conclusions about the underlying structure of aggregate segregation, with both sets of results suggesting that a three-parameter specification, which reveals a characteristic "leaning-N" profile, is descriptively adequate. Although we have emphasized that segregation data cannot be properly characterized with conventional indices, we have established here that the task of analyzing aggregate segregation data is quite tractable, requiring a mere three parameters. The objective of the following section is to explore in greater detail how these three parameters differ across countries and thereby produce characteristic variations on the "leaning-N" theme.

CAN VARIABILITY IN SEX SEGREGATION BE PARSIMONIOUSLY DESCRIBED?

The three-parameter specification becomes more attractive insofar as it captures much of the available cross-national variability in aggregate segregation. For the purposes of comparative analysis, the specification falls short if cross-national variability assumes a form that is not expressible as some mixture of vertical and horizontal effects, instead requiring additional parameters that express some more fundamental revision of the "leaning-N" profile of Figure 4.1 (see also Figure 3.3). It is possible, albeit unlikely, that cross-national variability is mainly expressed in that (small) portion of the sex-by-occupation association that is not captured by our three-parameter specification. If this were the case, our specification would obviously be less serviceable for cross-national comparison.

We address this issue in Table 4.3. The first panel in this table decomposes the total variability in segregation into a component occurring within major categories and a component occurring between them. As may be recalled from Chapter 3, these two components are approximately equal in size, with 45.7 percent of the total variability in segregation occurring between major categories and the remaining 54.3 percent occurring within them. The following model allows us to establish whether this between-category variability can be captured in our three fundamental parameters:

$$m_{ijk} = \alpha_k \beta_{ik} \gamma_{jk} \delta_{ij} e^{\psi_k(Z_i N_i V1_j) + \varepsilon_k(Z_i M_i V1_j) + \omega_k(Z_i H_i)} \tag{4.5}$$

With this specification (see Table 4.3, line 6), we freely fit the association between sex and occupation (δ_{ij}), but force all cross-national variability in that association to be captured in the three parameters of aggregate association (ψ_k, ε_k, ω_k). If this model is compared with one allowing aggregate association to vary freely (line 2), we can determine whether our three-parameter specification captures such aggregate variability as it obtains. We have also estimated trimmed versions of this model that allow cross-national variability in the vertical parameter (line 3), the horizontal parameter (line 4), and the vertical and horizontal parameters taken together (line 5).

The fit statistics in panel B indicate that our preferred model (line 6) accounts for 69.6 percent of the total variability in aggregate sex segregation. By contrast, the various trimmed versions of this model yield rather less impressive fit statistics, especially the model that eliminates cross-national variability in the horizontal effect (line 3). Although a two-parameter specification performs relatively well (see line 5), this model will be shown to obscure important cross-national differences in the extent to which the non-manual slope is attenuated. We conclude that comparative analysis should be carried out with our three-parameter model that allows for simultaneous cross-national variability in the size of the horizontal gap, the strength of the nonmanual slope, and the strength of the manual slope. The residual variability under this specification is not trivial (approximately 30 percent of total aggregate variability), but we demonstrate in the following section that such idiosyncrasies can be glossed over without concealing or distorting much of interest (see Table 4.6).

Is cross-national variability in disaggregate segregation equally "lawful"? In Chapter 3, we suggested that aggregate segregation varies in simple and lawful ways, whereas disaggregate segregation takes on idiosyncratic forms that can only be understood through careful historical study of the task content of occupations, the types of labor that were available when the occupation was expanding, the types of firms, industries, or occupations that were seized upon as models for employment practices, and similar such local and nation-specific forces (see Bielby and Baron 1986 for a related

TABLE 4.3
Cross-National Variability in Vertical and Horizontal Sex Segregation

Model[a]	L^2	d.f.	Total Variability Explained (%)[b]	Aggregate Variability Explained (%)[c]	Detailed Variability Explained (%)[d]	BIC
A. Baseline Models						
1. No cross-national variability (universal association) S*N + O*N + O*S	1,763,819	567	0.0	0.0	0.0	1,753,740
2. Variability in major-category effects S*N + O*N + O*S + G*S*N	957,588	495	45.7	100.0	0.0	948,789
B. Models of Aggregate Cross-National Variation						
3. Variability in vertical effect O*N + O*S + S*N*V1	1,639,619	558	7.0	15.4	0.0	1,629,700
4. Variability in horizontal effect O*N + O*S + S*N*H	1,441,636	558	18.3	40.0	0.0	1,431,717

Model						
5. Variability in vertical and horizontal effects (additive) $O*N + O*S + S*N*V1 + S*N*H$	1,284,361	549	27.2	59.5	0.0	1,274,602
6. Variability in vertical and horizontal effects (interactive) $O*N + O*S + S*N*V1*H$	1,202,807	540	31.8	69.6	0.0	1,193,208
C. Model of Detailed Cross-National Variation						
7. Variability in vertical effect $O*N + O*S + G*S*N + S*N*V2$	892,700	486	—	—	6.8	884,061

[a] O = detailed occupation; G = major occupation; N = country; S = sex; $V1$ = socioeconomic scale applied to aggregate categories; $V2$ = socioeconomic scale applied to detailed categories; H = manual-nonmanual distinction.

[b] The total variability in segregation is given by the L^2 value for Model 1.

[c] The variability in aggregate segregation is given by the difference between the L^2 values for Models 1 and 2.

[d] The variability in detailed segregation is given by the L^2 value for Model 2.

argument). This claim, plausible though it may be, has yet to be directly tested. Although we cannot provide a definitive test here, we can at least eliminate the hypothesis that disaggregate variability takes the form of simple differences in the strength of the vertical effect. To this end, we fit the following model:

$$m_{ijk} = \alpha_k \beta_{ik} \gamma_{jk} \delta_{ij} e^{\varepsilon_k(Z_i V2_j) + \varphi_{ck}(Z_i)}, \qquad (4.6)$$

where ε_k refers to country-specific values of the vertical coefficient, and φ_{ck} refers to country-specific scale values for major occupational categories. As shown in line 7 of Table 4.3, this model explains a mere 6.8 percent of the total disaggregate variability, a percentage substantially less than the explained aggregate variability under *any* of the models of panel B. It is always possible that a more complicated disaggregate model would generate a substantial improvement in fit.[13] However, the burden of proof now rests with those who would advance this counterargument, given that currently available evidence suggests that disaggregate segregation is indeed idiosyncratic and "unlawful."

The results presented to this point indicate that cross-national variability in aggregate segregation may be described in three parameters. However, a skeptic might suggest that these three parameters nonetheless tend to vary together, thus allowing for a more parsimonious specification in which cross-national variability is captured in a single "shift effect" that governs the *extent* of aggregate segregation (across all three parameters). In Chapter 3, we reported that segregation at the aggregate and disaggregate levels tended not to covary with one another, implying that segregation regimes are loosely coupled across levels. We are now asking whether the three aggregate parameters of segregation are also loosely coupled. Although a simple multiplicative shift model is not viable (see Chapter 3), we might still find that cross-national variability at the aggregate level assumes a relatively simple unidimensional form.

The estimates from panel C of Table 4.2 might lead one to suspect that a more parsimonious formulation of aggregate segregation is indeed possible. As revealed here, the two sets of segregation coefficients are strongly correlated ($r = .89$) because Portugal and Italy, our two postindustrialism laggards, have simultaneously low levels of horizontal and vertical inequality. The latter result is consistent with the causal hypotheses elaborated above; that is, because postindustrialism operates to increase both horizontal and vertical segregation, we should expect a stronger correlation between these forms of segregation in any sample of countries in which there is substantial variability on the postindustrialism dimension. The inter-coefficient correlation will tend to weaken in samples of countries that are more homogeneous on this dimension; for example, the correlation in our own sample drops to .67 when Portugal and Italy, which have the two lowest scores on postindustrialism, are excluded from the analysis.

The strongest evidence, however, of loose coupling emerges when the focus shifts to the vertical coefficients. As revealed in panel D, the vertical coefficients for the manual and nonmanual sectors tend not to covary ($r = .07$), with especially large sectoral differences appearing in Belgium, France, Portugal, Sweden, and Japan. Again, this result is consistent with our causal hypotheses, which specify that the negative effect of egalitarianism and the positive effect of postindustrialism (on vertical segregation) will only be found within the nonmanual sector. In both cases, the posited macro-level effect operates in the nonmanual sector alone, thereby weakening the correlation between the two sets of sector-specific coefficients as egalitarianism and postindustrialism take hold in some countries (but not in others).

The multiplicative shift model thus fails to fit because of loose coupling across sectors as well as across levels. These two forms of loose coupling require comparative segregation scholars to reject index-based analysis and recognize that segregation regimes are mixtures of several independent segregative principles.

CAN A PARSIMONIOUS CAUSAL MODEL BE DEVELOPED?

Although we have referred repeatedly to the effects of egalitarianism and postindustrialism on the structure of segregation, we have so far provided nothing more than informal evidence of the operation of these effects. We have found, for example, that horizontal segregation is especially strong in some countries with well-developed postindustrialism (Sweden) and especially weak in other countries with poorly developed postindustrialism (Italy, Portugal, and Japan). Likewise, nonmanual vertical segregation appears to be weaker in egalitarian countries (the United States) than in less egalitarian ones (Japan), but stronger in countries with postindustrial economies

(Sweden, the United Kingdom) than in those that have yet to become post-industrialized (Italy, Portugal). However, a skeptic might point to evidence that appears to contradict our hypotheses, including (a) the high levels of horizontal segregation in some countries (France, Switzerland) that are only weakly postindustrialized, and (b) the weakness of nonmanual vertical segregation in other countries (Belgium, the United States) in which postindustrialism is relatively well developed. Clearly, all such informal evaluations of the evidence can easily mislead (especially when the independent variables in question are highly correlated), and there is accordingly good reason to estimate models that formalize the argument. We fit such models in this section.

We carry out the analysis by estimating two models that constrain the parameters for vertical and horizontal segregation to be functions of egalitarianism and postindustrialism. The first model, which conditions on our additive specification of segregation (see Table 4.3, line 5), may be represented as follows:

$$m_{ijk} = \alpha_k \beta_{ik} \gamma_{jk} \delta_{ij} e^{\psi_k(Z_iV1_j) + \omega_k(Z_iH_j)}, \text{ where}$$
$$\psi_k = a_1 + b_{11}X_{1k} + b_{21}X_{2k}, \text{ and} \tag{4.7}$$
$$\omega_k = a_2 + b_{12}X_{1k} + b_{22}X_{2k},$$

with X_{1k} and X_{2k} referring to our country-level measures of gender egalitarianism and postindustrialism. Under this specification, the coefficient for vertical segregation (ψ_k) is constrained to be a function of the two country-level covariates (gender egalitarianism and postindustrialism), and the coefficient for horizontal segregation (ω_k) is likewise constrained to be a function of these two covariates. The intercepts in our macro-level equations, a_1 and a_2, are embedded in the sex-by-occupation association (δ_{ij}) and therefore are not identified. We have also estimated a second model that fits a separate vertical parameter for the manual and nonmanual sectors and constrains the resulting three segregation parameters (ψ_k, ε_k, ω_k) to be a function of our two macro-level variables. This model is identical to that of equation 4.5 except that three sets of side-constraints, one for each of the three segregation parameters, are now imposed.[14]

The fit statistics for these two models are reported in Table 4.4, and the relevant coefficients are reported in Table 4.5. As indicated in the former table, the macro-level variables in the additive model explain 45.4 percent of the total aggregate variability, while those in the interactive model explain

TABLE 4.4

Cross-National Variability in Vertical and Horizontal Sex Segregation: Models with Covariates

Model	L^2	d.f.	Aggregate Variability Explained[a]	BIC
1. Universal association (S*N + O*N + O*S)	1,763,819	567	0.0%	1,753,740
2. Vertical and horizontal effects (MODEL 1) + (S*V1*GENDER EGALITARIANISM) + (S*H*GENDER EGALITARIANISM) + (S*V1*POSTINDUSTRIALISM) + (S*H*POSTINDUSTRIALISM)	1,397,827	563	45.4%	1,387,819
3. Vertical and horizontal effects with interactions (Model 2) + (S*V1*H*GENDER EGALITARIANISM) + (S*V1*H*POSTINDUSTRIALISM)	1,371,614	561	48.6%	1,361,642

[a]The variability in aggregate segregation is given by the difference between the L^2 values for Models 1 and 2 in Table 4.3.

TABLE 4.5
Effects of Covariates on Vertical and Horizontal Segregation

Model and Parameter	Estimate	Consistent with Hypotheses?
A. *Additive Specification* (Model 2, Table 4.4)		
1. Egalitarianism effects		
Vertical segregation	.0001	Yes
Horizontal segregation	−.0118	No
2. Postindustrialism effects		
Vertical segregation	−.0156	Yes
Horizontal segregation	−.7074	Yes
B. *Interactive Specification* (Model 3, Table 4.4)		
1. Egalitarianism effects		
Vertical segregation, nonmanual sector	.0003	Yes
Vertical segregation, manual sector	−.0008	No
Horizontal segregation	−.0165	No
2. Postindustrialism effects		
Vertical segregation, nonmanual sector	−.0196	Yes
Vertical segregation, manual sector	.0138	No
Horizontal segregation	−.6284	Yes

48.6 percent of this variability.[15] The coefficients reported in the latter table are largely consistent with our hypotheses. We find that a one-unit increase in postindustrialism, which is roughly equal to the difference between France ($X_2 = 0.11$) and the United States ($X_2 = 1.04$), increases horizontal segregation by a factor of 2.03 (exp[.7074] = 2.03). At the same time, a one-unit increase in postindustrialism strengthens the nonmanual socioeconomic effect by .0196, whereas a one-unit increase in gender-egalitarianism weakens this nonmanual vertical effect by .0003. The latter coefficient appears small partly because the metrics on the socioeconomic and egalitarianism variables are so small. This coefficient implies, for example, that the nonmanual socioeconomic effect for Germany, which was earlier estimated at −.062 (see Table 4.2, panel D), would decrease by about 14.2 percent were Germany ($X_1 = 58.46$) to become as egalitarian as Sweden ($X_1 = 87.93$).[16] While an effect of this size is perhaps modest, it is surely not trivial.

This is not to suggest that the coefficients of Table 4.5 are completely consistent with our hypotheses. Most obviously, we did not anticipate any effect of egalitarianism on horizontal segregation, yet our models indicate a nontrivial segregative effect (under both specifications). This effect may arise because egalitarianism draws an increasingly broad and heterogeneous cross-section of women into the burgeoning lower nonmanual sector. Although our hypotheses emphasized that egalitarianism creates an enlarged "female elite" by opening up new female professional and managerial opportunities, it also operates to increase the normative acceptability of female employment and thereby encourages labor force participation among women who treat their domestic roles as primary and who are neither interested in nor qualified for elite occupations. These nonelite entrants may regard the growing clerical and associate-professional sectors as attractive employment options that allow them to balance work and family demands.[17] The elite and nonelite effects of egalitarianism, when taken together, serve to raise female representation in the nonmanual sector as a whole and thus increase horizontal segregation. If this interpretation is on the mark, it again suggests that segregation is an organic and continuously regenerated feature of contemporary labor markets rather than an ascriptive residue.

The second unexpected finding revealed in Table 4.5 pertains to the effects of egalitarianism and postindustrialism on vertical segregation in the manual sector. Although we had not developed any hypotheses for these relationships, we find that the relevant coefficients are, for each macro-level variable, the opposite of the corresponding coefficients in the nonmanual sector (see Table 4.5, panel B). The unexpected effect of egalitarianism may well arise from the same dynamic that we advanced in explaining the negative coefficient for horizontal segregation. That is, egalitarianism creates higher rates of labor force participation among less career-committed women, with the new family-oriented labor force tending to opt for employment in less demanding occupations that may be combined with domestic obligations. The increase in horizontal segregation implies, of course, that most such women will locate in the nonmanual sector, as was previously discussed (see also note 17). However, among those women who do locate in the manual sector, heavy domestic obligations preclude moving into career-oriented occupations at the top of the manual hierarchy (such as craft occupations), meaning that the less demanding manual occupations (such as operative occupations) will, by default, receive much of the influx. The resulting increase in vertical segregation within the manual sector may therefore arise from the same heterogeneity-inducing processes that account for the increase in horizontal segregation.

In the final model of this chapter, we permit our two macro-level variables to directly affect segregation in each of the nine major occupations, thereby allowing us to translate the foregoing effects on horizontal and vertical segregation into corresponding effects on the underlying categories themselves. We adopt a specification that allows such effects to be estimated after purging the data of any cross-national variability in the distribution of detailed occupations that comprise the major categories. This multi-level explanatory model may be represented as follows:

$$m_{ijk} = \alpha_k \beta_{ik} \gamma_{jk} \delta_{ij} e^{Z_i \nu_{jk} + Z_i \varphi_{ck}}, \quad \text{where}$$
$$\varphi_{ck} = \alpha_c + b_{1c} X_{1k} + b_{2c} X_{2k}$$

(4.8)

Under this specification, ν_{jk} refers to country-specific scale values for detailed occupations, φ_{ck} refers to country-specific scale values for major occupational categories, α_c is the intercept for the cth major occupational category,[18] b_{1c} is the effect of gender egalitarianism on segregation in the cth major occupational category, and b_{2c} is the effect of postindustrialism on segregation in the cth major occupational category. The two slope coefficients (b_{1c}, b_{2c}) specify the relationship between the independent variables and female representation in each major occupational category after cross-national differences in the detailed composition of these categories have been purged. Although cross-national variability in detailed-category segregation is freely fit in equation 4.8, the specification is not saturated because major-category scale values (φ_{ck}) are constrained to be a function of the macro-level variables (see equation 2.13 for the saturated version of this model). As before, the detailed scale values in this model (ν_{jk}) can be identified by constraining them to sum to zero within each major occupational category (in each country), while the major-category scale values (φ_{ck}) can be identified by constraining them to sum to zero within each country.

This model yields a likelihood-ratio test statistic of 68,614 with 56 degrees of freedom. The coefficients for the model, displayed in Table 4.6, provide insights into the occupation-specific mechanisms by which our macro-level covariates affect vertical and horizontal segregation. The first coefficient, for example, implies that a one-unit increase in egalitarianism yields a 2 percent increase in female representation among managers (exp[.018] =

TABLE 4.6
Effects of Covariates on
Major-Category Segregation

Occupation	Gender Egalitarianism	Post-industrialism
Manager	.018	.096
Professional	.023	−.301
Associate professional	.015	−.062
Clerical	.017	.379
Service/Sales	.007	.296
Agriculture	−.046	.044
Craft	−.030	−.177
Operative	.013	−.235
Laborer	−.019	−.041

NOTE: Coefficients are estimates of b_{1c} and b_{2c} (Equation 4.8).

1.02). The remaining coefficients in the first column reveal that the positive effect on horizontal segregation is generated by strengthened female representation in the five nonmanual occupations and weakened female representation in three of the four manual occupations. Likewise, the decline in nonmanual vertical segregation is generated by slightly stronger coefficients in the high-status occupations (managers, professionals) than in the low-status ones (associate professional, clerical, service/sales), and the increase in manual vertical segregation is generated by a negative coefficient in the high-status category (craft) and positive or weakly negative coefficients in the lower-status ones (operatives, laborers).[19]

As for the postindustrialism variable, the coefficients in Table 4.6 indicate that the increase in horizontal segregation is generated by (a) strengthened female representation in managerial, clerical, service, and sales occupations, and (b) weakened female representation in craft, operative, and laborer occupations. Moreover, the patterning of effects within each sector imply that postindustrialism strengthens nonmanual vertical segregation and weakens manual vertical segregation, just as Table 4.5 indicated.[20]

The principal conclusion, then, from this closing exercise is that it was ultimately superfluous. For the most part, the effects of our macro-level variables can be successfully represented by characterizing segregation in terms of horizontal and vertical parameters, meaning that there is no need to fall back to a more detailed description of occupation-specific outcomes. To be sure, there are minor occupation-specific deviations from the story that our more parsimonious specification tells (see, especially, notes 19 and 20), but none that raises doubts about the main dynamics underlying the effects of egalitarianism or postindustrialism.[21]

CONCLUSIONS

We began this chapter by asking whether a parsimonious account of segregation is still feasible in the context of a model-based approach. The analyses that we have assembled on this question are complicated and cannot be exhaustively recounted here; however, the theme running throughout is that a relatively parsimonious model of segregation can indeed be developed, albeit nothing as simple as the one-parameter specification that is implied by standard index-based approaches. This chapter takes us beyond the obvious point that conventional approaches oversimplify by developing models that explicitly parameterize the complexity of segregation data in ways that we think are compelling.

We have distinguished between three types of parsimony and estimated models that test for each type in turn. The results from these analyses suggest that contemporary segregation regimes have a shared anatomy that takes on different forms by dint of combining horizontal and vertical processes in different proportions. The following are our main conclusions.

Parsimony of structure. We first showed that the seemingly complicated profiles of contemporary segregation can be reproduced in three parameters: (a) a horizontal gap parameter capturing the dramatic overrepresentation of women in the nonmanual sector; (b) a manual slope parameter capturing the strong tendency for men to dominate the best manual occupations; and (c) a nonmanual slope parameter suggesting that male advantage at the top of the class structure persists but has weakened in at least some industrial countries. The resulting "leaning-N" model, which constitutes the shared anatomy of modern segregation, cannot be reconciled with queuing accounts in their simplest form. These accounts fall short not only because the horizontal gap parameter cannot be understood in simple vertical terms, but also because the forces of vertical advantage do not operate very power-fully at the level of detailed occupations. At the detailed level, we find that a mere 3 percent of the available association can be explained in vertical terms, thus implying that forces other than patriarchy are at work.

Parsimony of variability. In the second round of analyses, we showed that our three-parameter specification serves not merely to characterize the structure of segregation, but also to capture common forms of cross-national variability in that structure. It is misleading to resort to standard index-based analysis because the two vertical parameters are "loosely coupled," meaning that the strength of one parameter does not well predict the strength of the other. We also showed that variability in detailed segregation cannot be explained in vertical terms; that is, while aggregate variability can be summarized in three parameters, detailed variability appears to be a func-tion of more idiosyncratic labor market processes.

Parsimony in causal modeling. We concluded our analyses by model-ing the twin effects of egalitarianism and postindustrialism on our three seg-regation parameters. This macro-level causal specification casts light on the persistence of hypersegregation in contemporary labor markets and thus speaks to one of the puzzles with which we began this book. Although egal-itarianism undermines vertical segregation in the nonmanual sector, the as-sociated rise of postindustrialism works to increase horizontal segregation as well as to counteract the effects of egalitarianism on nonmanual vertical seg-regation. These countervailing processes imply that segregation, far from be-ing an ascriptive vestige of preindustrialism, is actively generated by con-temporary market processes.

We hope that the foregoing summary will convince any remaining skep-tics that model-based analyses can generate results that move well beyond those secured through more conventional approaches. The skeptical view of modeling (e.g., Jacobs 2001), which we regard as wildly off the mark, will no doubt become less credible as our analytic approach diffuses into related subfields. We suspect, for example, that new and important insights will be secured by applying models of this general type to other forms of sex segre-gation (such as segregation by college major),[22] to data arrays that cross-classify sex, race, and occupation and thereby make it possible to analyze sex and race segregation simultaneously, and to multi-level data that incorporate measures of human capital (such as education) into conventional segregation arrays and therefore allow analysts to bridge the long-standing divide between descriptive and explanatory models.

Likewise, we could easily incorporate additional covariates into our cross-national causal models, thus allowing us to explore the effects of such macro-level variables as (a) the structure of families and government "family policy" (Hakim 2000; Trappe and Rosenfeld 2001), (b) the type of welfare regime (Chang 2000; Daly 2000), (c) the distribution of full-time, part-time, or marginal employment (e.g., Brinton 2001; Tijdens 2001; Yu 2001), and (d) the distribution of female and male education (e.g., Hanson, Schaub, and Baker 1996). The existing literatures on these macro-level effects typically treat segregation in unidimensional fashion (cf. Chang 2000) and therefore fail to appreciate that its vertical and horizontal forms develop in fundamentally different ways.

We realize that such extensions would likely go unappreciated by scholars who regard models of this general type as excessively formal. Inevitably, tastes for formal model-building vary, with some scholars appreciating the rigor and explicitness of such models and others bemoaning the "fetishism of method" (e.g., Coser 1975) that can distract from the substance of the argument. We thought it useful to include at least one chapter that rendered our arguments in explicit terms that leave little room for misunderstanding. For scholars with less taste or patience for formalism, we hasten to note that the following three chapters on long-term trend in segregation revert to a less formal and more descriptive approach, with the horizontal and vertical dimensions of segregation left implicit in the analysis rather than formally parameterized. Although it might well be useful to recast these models in formal terms, we shall not do so here; and the resulting chapters are less model-intensive and more readable as a consequence. It should nonetheless be emphasized that these analyses could readily have been carried out with the three-parameter model featured here.

This chapter concludes our extended discussion of cross-national variability in segregation and moves us to the next section on long-term trends in segregation. The following three chapters examine the historical dynamics of vertical and horizontal sex segregation in the United States, Japan, and Switzerland. These case studies allow us to explore the evolution of segregation at the aggregate and disaggregate occupational levels in the context of diverse cultural traditions, institutional forms, and economic forces.

While our main objective is to provide a rich, qualitative description of trends in sex segregation, our results also provide preliminary insights into how these trends relate to international secular pressures (such as egalitarianism and postindustrialism) and particularistic national events and circumstances. We will therefore refer frequently to the macro-level forces that have been more explicitly examined in this chapter and the preceding one.

Descriptive Statistics for Explanatory Variables

	1. Gender- Egalitarianism	2. Post- industrialism
Belgium	51.52	0.47
France	58.95	0.13
West Germany	58.46	0.11
Italy	47.66	−1.06
Portugal	54.27	−1.94
Sweden	87.93	0.87
Switzerland	54.70	0.09
United Kingdom	58.62	0.49
United States	71.06	1.04
Japan	25.71	−0.21
Mean	56.89	0.00
(Standard Deviation)	(15.89)	(0.90)
Zero-order Correlation		
1.	1.00	
2.	0.50	1.00

THE EVOLUTION
OF SEX SEGREGATION

CHAPTER FIVE

Profiles of Change: Sex Segregation in the United States, 1910–2000

Kim A. Weeden, Cornell University

INTRODUCTION

This chapter examines occupational sex segregation in the United States between 1910 and 2000. It differs from previous studies in three ways. First, it articulates, formally models, and assesses the empirical validity of three conventional accounts of the trajectory of sex segregation: reproductive accounts, which emphasize temporal stability in sex segregation; evolutionary accounts, which suggest a gradual integration of the occupational structure; and "punctuated-equilibrium" accounts, which predict long periods of stability punctuated by periods of radical change. The images of change, or lack thereof, that these accounts imply often guide the interpretation of empirical findings in the field. Nevertheless, they do not appear in the literature as coherent entities, are rarely clarified, and have never been pitted against one another in the context of formal empirical models.

The second major contribution of this chapter lies in its attention to the occupation-specific contours, or pattern, of sex segregation. Most prior analyses focus exclusively on trends in the *level* of segregation, seemingly implying that the *pattern* of gender distribution (that is, the specific occupations in which women are over- or underrepresented) is stable. This chapter, in contrast, examines whether and how trajectories of segregation vary across occupations. This difference in emphasis reflects more than merely methodological taste. As discussed below, each conventional account of historical variability in the level of segregation has at least one variant that implies that the underlying pattern of sex segregation will fluctuate over time.

Without methodologies that explicitly attend to changes in the pattern of segregation, these variants cannot be evaluated adequately.

The chapter's third contribution stems from its use of data that are unique in their historical range and level of detail. The data on which most of the analysis relies contain information about the sex composition of 237 detailed occupations in each decade between 1910 and 1990. Although pieces of this time series have been analyzed elsewhere, data from all nine censuses have not been assembled and reconciled into a historically comparable classification scheme.[1] This allows the timing of shifts in segregation to be pinpointed more accurately than has previously been possible. A secondary data set incorporates preliminary data from the 2000 Census, thereby offering an early glimpse of contemporary trends in sex segregation.

HISTORICAL TRENDS IN SEX SEGREGATION: PREVAILING EXPLANATORY MODELS

Occupational segregation is most often viewed as a unidimensional, scalar entity that rises or falls with the level of gender equality in a given historical context (see Chapter 1). Scholars who focus on the cultural entrenchment of the sexual division of labor and the continual reproduction of gender inequality that arises out of this division of labor characterize the historical trajectory of sex segregation as stable and persistent. Those who emphasize gradual replacement of ascriptive criteria with universalistic criteria as the basis for allocating persons to positions, by contrast, characterize segregation as declining in strength. Still others, most notably historians and economic historians, emphasize idiosyncratic events and circumstances (World War II and the rise of modern feminism, for example) that shaped the national sex-segregation profile. These three characterizations of gender inequality and of the trajectory of segregation—the reproductive, evolutionary, and punctuated-equilibrium accounts, respectively—are summarized in Table 5.1 and elaborated below.

Reproductive Accounts

Conventional wisdom holds that levels of sex segregation were remarkably stable in the United States until the 1970s, when integration began to occur, albeit at a snail's pace (e.g., Gross 1968; Jacobs 1989a, 2001; Reskin and Roos 1990; King 1992; Reskin 1993; Jacobsen 1994; Cotter et al. 1995;

TABLE 5.1

Predicted Historical Trends in the Level and Pattern of Occupational Sex Segregation

Model and Variant	Predicted Change in Level	Forces Affecting Pattern	Implied Modeling Outcome
A. Reproduction			
1. Stable pattern	None	Sex-role stereotyping, sex-linked traits	Universal association model fits; A is constant
2. Varying pattern	None	Occupational change, labor-control strategies	Universal association model rejected; A is constant
B. Evolutionary			
3. Stable pattern	Monotonic decline	Uniform diffusion of egalitarian norms	Multiplicative shift model fits; shift-effect parameters decline monotonically
4. Varying pattern	Monotonic decline	Occupation- or sector-specific egalitarianism	Multiplicative shift model rejected; A declines monotonically
C. Punctuated Equilibrium			
5. Stable pattern	Nonmonotonic change	Marketwide shocks (World War II, feminism)	Multiplicative shift model fits; shift-effect parameters vary across periods
6. Varying pattern	Nonmonotonic change	Occupation- or sector-specific shocks	Universal association model fits within each posited period

NOTE: See text for model descriptions.

F. Blau, Simpson, and Anderson 1998; Baunach 2002). A number of now familiar arguments have been proposed to account for this long-term stability. These arguments are explicated in detail in Chapter 1 and elsewhere, and hence it suffices to give only a cursory review here.

On the supply side, the persistence of occupational segregation has been linked to role divisions within the family (Parsons and Bales 1955; Polachek 1979; G. Becker 1985), biological, psychological, or psychoanalytic differences between men and women (e.g., Baron-Cohen 2003; Chodorow 1978; Ellis 1993; Rosaldo and Lamphere 1974; Stockard and Johnson 1980); sex-specific socialization during childhood (e.g., Marini and Brinton 1984); lifelong reminders and admonitions about gender-appropriate behavior (Jacobs 1989b; see also Chan 1999); gendered job information and sponsorship networks (see Granovetter 1995, p. 169; Petersen, Saporta, and Seidel 2000, pp. 768–72; also Roos and Reskin 1984; Straits 1998); and the adjustment of expectations to compensate for perceived opportunities (Roos 1985, p. 72; Xie and Shauman 1997; Jacobs 2001).

On the demand side, the intransigence of employer behavior, organizational structures, state regulations, and wider economic and cultural institutions facilitate the reproduction of segregation. Some employers may simply exercise a taste for discrimination, while others unintentionally replicate the status quo through their recruitment practices, as when their perceptions of the characteristics of desirable job applicants are colored by the prevailing gender composition of an occupation and by the social valuation and compensation of the occupation (Reskin and Roos 1990; Tomaskovic-Devey 1993). Organizational structures such as seniority systems, internal labor markets, and apprenticeship and job-training requirements may also perpetuate sex segregation (Roos and Reskin 1984; Bielby and Baron 1984, 1986; Yamagata et al. 1997; Nelson and Bridges 1999; Reskin and McBrier 2000; for reviews, see Reskin, McBrier, and Kmec 1999; Kaufman 2002). Finally, segregation may also persist insofar as it reinforces more fundamental institutional arrangements. For example, segregation may serve capitalists' interests, by reducing men's resistance to deskilling and providing a reserve army of cheap labor, or male workers' interests, by supporting existing systems of patriarchy, restricting the labor supply, and maintaining high wages (Firestone 1970; Hartmann 1976; R. Edwards 1979; Burris and Wharton 1982; Walby 1986; H. Bradley 1989; Cohn 2000).

It bears emphasizing that although these arguments are intended to account for stability in the level of segregation, many of the social processes they identify will also create stability in the pattern of segregation (Model 1, Table 5.1). If segregation is indeed generated by sex-linked biological traits, deeply entrenched cultural stereotypes, gendered work cultures, or intrinsic differences in the nature of occupational tasks, the sex type of particular occupations is also likely to be relatively constant. Consider, for example, the claim that some occupations are disproportionately filled by women because these occupations require less human capital, impose smaller wage penalties for labor force interruptions, and are otherwise more compatible with women's childbearing and domestic responsibilities (G. Becker 1985, 1991; Polachek and Siebert 1993). In the absence of exogenous forces that alter the human-capital requirements of particular occupations, the sex composition of those occupations is not likely to change. Likewise, if sex segregation emerges out of differences between the sexes in their abilities and attitudes, the sex type of any given occupation will be stable, again barring exogenous shifts in the task niche of that occupation. More generally, explanations of segregation that posit either (a) a causal relationship between the tasks of an occupation and its gender composition or (b) an institutionally generated path dependence in this composition imply that the pattern of segregation will be stable.

At the same time, it is possible to construct reproduction scenarios in which the overall level of segregation remains constant, but not the particular pattern of segregation (Model 2, Table 5.1). Queuing theorists, for example, attribute the "feminization" of some occupations to their declining desirability (Thurow 1975; Reskin and Roos 1990; see also Kuhn and Bluestone 1987), which in turn may occur, for example, when technological developments strip those occupations of their high skill levels. Despite the feminization (or, in theory, masculinization) of particular occupations, the overall level of segregation would presumably remain much the same because the most attractive occupations, whichever they might be, would always be reserved for (white) men. Similarly, the logic of class-conflict arguments does not preclude fluctuations in the sex composition of specific occupations. That is, as long as employers consistently promote segregation as a labor-control strategy, levels of segregation will remain high; however, the particular occupations in which they deploy this strategy can vary in response to changes in the economic or social context of production (Burris and Wharton 1982). Thus, although both the queuing and class-conflict arguments predict stability in the level of segregation, they do not rule out shifts in the occupation-specific pattern of segregation.

Evolutionary Accounts

In contrast to the stasis of reproduction accounts, evolutionary models posit a gradual and continuous reorganization of the stratification system, driven by the spread of meritocracy and cultural egalitarianism (see Chapter 1). Structural-functional versions of this argument assert that pressures for merit-based occupational allocation grow as technology becomes more complex (Kerr et al. 1960; D. Bell 1973), while cultural versions treat the rise of egalitarian values as exogenous to structural changes in the economy (Goode 1963; Parsons 1970; Meyer and Rowan 1977; Meyer 2001; Berkovitch 1999). In either case, the argument predicts gradual and continuous integration of the occupational structure, such that the overall level of sex segregation declines each decade.

Egalitarian pressures operate through a variety of more proximate causal forces, including (a) the erosion of discriminatory tastes among employers, (b) the decline of gender-specific socialization in the home and at school, (c) the equalization of occupational aspirations and human capital accumulation, (d) the shift from a family- to an individual-based labor market, (e) the creation of legislation designed to promote women's educational or employment opportunities, and (f) the rise of bureaucratic organizational forms (also, see Table 1.1 in Chapter 1).[2] Presumably, most of these forces operate incrementally, at least in the aggregate, through organizational death and cohort replacement. Organizations that sustain discriminatory labor practices eventually die out because they are disadvantaged in competitive markets (G. Becker 1975), and cohorts whose members conform to outdated notions of gender-appropriate behavior eventually leave the labor market and are replaced by younger workers who have benefited from more education, advances in birth control, and revised expectations (Goldin 1990, p. 214).[3]

These processes imply not only a slow and steady decline in the level of segregation, but also a relatively uniform decline across occupations. Egalitarian pressures play out in ways that increase women's representation in "men's" occupations and men's representation in "women's" occupations (Model 3, Table 5.1). This logic is consistent with segregation scholars' long-standing reliance on summary sex-segregation indices, which make no distinction between changes brought about by women's entry into traditionally male occupations or men's entry into traditionally female occupations.

Conventional logic notwithstanding, the integrative pressures accompanying the rise of egalitarianism need not affect all occupations with the same strength (Model 4, Table 5.1). Chapter 1 suggested that elite occupations (for example, professions, government administration) will integrate most rapidly and extensively because their visibility, desirability, and meritocratic cultures make them more susceptible to legislative and normative pressures for gender equality (see also Charles 1998). This implies a decline in vertical segregation within the nonmanual sector, but little integration elsewhere in the occupational structure. Likewise, horizontal forms of segregation may be especially resistant to change, given that they are rooted in essentialist beliefs that are largely compatible with gender egalitarianism.

These are by no means the only arguments suggesting occupation-specific variability in the timing and extent of integration. As Chapter 8 implies, the uneven distribution of occupations across industries may also lead to uneven integration. That is, mandates for universalistic hiring and promotion standards may be stronger in the organizations and industries that depend heavily on the goodwill of their institutional environments (such as public-sector firms, or firms that rely on government contracts), thereby implying that the occupations that draw heavily from these industries will integrate more rapidly than others (DiMaggio and Powell 1983; Beggs 1995). Furthermore, achievement-based job allocation, as opposed to ascriptive allocation, may be more deeply institutionalized in newer and technologically more advanced industries than it is in declining sectors (G. Williams 1979; Erikson and Goldthorpe 1992). And finally, economic restructuring in particular industries (such as the routinization of retail sales) can exacerbate segregation in occupations that dominate in those industries (Bluestone et al. 1981; Charles 1992, 1998), thereby offsetting broader integrative pressures. As with the reproduction accounts, then, one can distinguish between evolutionary accounts that posit a relatively constant pattern of segregation and those that predict variability in such patterns.

Punctuated-Equilibrium Accounts

In the preceding accounts, the forces for stasis and change are, with a few exceptions, identified independent of specific historical events and developments. By contrast, many historical accounts of trends in segregation emphasize the proximate impact of specific economic crises, political movements, or legislative developments (Kessler-Harris 1982; Milkman 1987; Goldin 1990). Work in this tradition characterizes the trajectory of segregation as subject to long periods of stasis interrupted by bursts of relatively rapid change whenever exogenous shocks to the system upset the equilibrium. This punctuated-equilibrium model thus represents an alternative to evolutionary accounts, which emphasize segregation's slow but steady decline, and reproduction accounts, which emphasize its relative permanence.[4]

Two historical periods are typically offered as examples of cultural or economic shocks to the gender-stratification system: the World War II era and the modern "gender-egalitarian" era. Wartime labor shortages and economic expansion during World War II drew women into paid labor, particularly in traditionally male-dominated sectors. Many of these women entered manufacturing occupations in heavy industry and professional occupations in the public sector (see, e.g., Chafe 1970; Kessler-Harris 1982; Milkman 1987), although they were often segregated within occupations by department, job classification, or task (Milkman 1987). Women's success in these jobs challenged stereotypes about women's ability to perform male-typed tasks, thereby leading to broader integrative pressures throughout the occupational structure.

According to conventional wisdom, this integrative shift was only temporary. Many of the women who were called into the work force returned to the home immediately after the war, accompanied by a new, family-centered ideology. Although women continued to work in the paid economy in the 1950s, their work roles were seen as supplementary to their functions as wives, mothers, and homemakers. Employed women were again concentrated in occupations that were compatible with this primary role, and it was not until the 1960s and 1970s that tensions between economic need and family roles again came to the fore (Chafe 1972; Kessler-Harris 1982). The wartime mobilization story thus predicts constant patterns of occupational sex segregation until World War II, a temporary integration, and then resumption of prewar patterns.

The second historical period often singled out in historicist accounts of segregation is the modern period, here defined as 1970 to the present, when women's career aspirations were again transformed. The reemergence of feminist ideologies and the accompanying changes in the legal environment and shifts in gender relations encouraged women to seek the education and skills they needed to enter traditionally male occupations (Kessler-Harris 1990; Beller 1984). At the same time, the reduction of overt discrimination against women was likely hastened by the implementation and enforcement of Equal Employment Opportunity (EEO) legislation, although the extent of the reduction is unknown (see, e.g., Beller 1982).

It is exceedingly difficult in practice to disentangle the effects of the resurgence of feminism, EEO laws, and broader shifts in the cultural value system. For my purposes, the key feature of the historicist account of change in segregation is merely that egalitarianism, whether it takes the form of feminist ideologies or EEO legislation, exerts itself as a period effect, thereby implying an identifiable discontinuity in occupational gender distributions. This model thus predicts the trajectory of change most often depicted in previous American segregation studies: stability in occupational gender distributions until 1970, followed by pronounced integration.

As with the reproductive and evolutionary accounts, the shocks to the stratification system associated with the rise of feminism, and to a lesser extent wartime labor shortages, are often discussed as if they affect all occupations (Model 5, Table 5.1). It is reasonable to suspect, though, that these shocks also had occupation-specific effects (Model 6). World War II may have promoted the temporary integration of unskilled or semiskilled manufacturing occupations (where labor demand was greatest) and jobs in public-sector administration, health, and education, but the breakdown of gendered stereotypes about competency in these occupations may have produced relatively little integration in other occupations (Kessler-Harris 1982, p. 286). Furthermore, the arguments in the preceding section, which pointed to occupation-specific integration associated with egalitarianism, apply whether such egalitarianism is conceptualized as a long-term secular trend or as a post-1970 phenomenon.

The three conventional accounts of the sources of segregation thus lead to different predictions about the timing and extent of changes in the level of sex segregation. Reproduction theories imply virtually no change, evolutionary accounts imply gradual and monotonic integration, and punctuated-equilibrium models imply long periods of stasis broken by periods of rapid integration and, in the case of the World War II period, resegregation. Variants of these theories imply instability in the underlying pattern of segregation that may not be reflected in a global measure. Each thus suggests a particular modeling outcome (Table 5.1, column 4). By applying the modeling techniques discussed in Chapter 2, with some elaborations, the empirical validity of each account can be assessed formally. First, though, it is necessary to introduce the data, and to tackle the issues of comparability and aggregation that inevitably arise in historical segregation research.

DATA

Most analyses in this chapter are based on occupation-by-sex tables derived from the decennial United States censuses from 1910 to 1990 (U.S. Bureau of the Census 1958, 1961, 1973, 1982, 1993b).[5] Over this period, the Census Bureau frequently revised the occupational classification schemes, making comparative analyses difficult. Fortunately, it also published a series of special reports that provide keys for translating data between classification schemes (U.S. Census Bureau 1958, 1968, 1972, 1989, 1993a), and, in more recent decennial censuses, it reported data from the prior decade in the contemporary classification scheme (U.S. Census Bureau 1961, 1973, 1982).

These sources were used to create a data set with comparable occupation codes. The general procedure was to combine occupations that split from a single code in an earlier scheme ("backward aggregation") or, alternatively, contributed to a single code in a later scheme ("forward aggregation"), using the aforementioned technical papers to guide aggregation decisions. Reconciling occupation schemes from 1970, 1980, and 1990 with earlier industry-based schemes also required supplementary data on the industrial distribution of managerial, operative, and labor occupations. Finally, because the Census Bureau made major changes to the classification scheme between 1970 and 1980, simple one-to-one matches between a 1980 occupation code and a 1970 code are scarce. Rather than assigning the 1970 code that contributed the plurality of persons to a given 1980 code (e.g., Ruggles and Sobek 2003), the 1980-in-1970 counts were instead generated by multiplying the number of men (women) in a 1980 occupation by the percentage of men (women) who entered that occupation from a given 1970 category (see U.S. Census Bureau 1989, table 2).

The resulting data set contains 237 comparable occupations for each decade from 1910 to 1990 (see Appendix Table A5.1), making it unusually comprehensive in the level of detail and temporal range represented. Forward-backward aggregation (e.g., G. Williams 1979; Carlson 1992) nonetheless has its costs. Because it reduces the level of detail in the occupational scheme, forward-backward aggregation underestimates the degree of segregation in any one decade. It may also overestimate change in segregation if the lost detail "reflects a real job differentiation rather than simply a change in labeling" (England 1981, p. 278; King 1992). It bears emphasizing, though, that the consequences of forward-backward aggregation will vary depending on the extent of segregation in the aggregated occupations and the measure of segregation that is used. The association index (A), for example, will decline when highly segregated occupations are combined, but increase when relatively integrated occupations are combined.

To determine the extent to which aggregation affects the observed trajectory of segregation, three segregation indices (D, D_s, and the log of A; see below) were regressed on dummy variables indexing the decade and the classification scheme using the five overlapping-year data sets from the Census Bureau's technical papers. In these regression models, the constant term represents the level of sex segregation in 1910 (the omitted category). Each decade effect represents the deviations from the 1910 level, net of the effects of the classification scheme. These purged coefficients suggest trends that are quite similar to, or if anything more pronounced than, those calculated from the forward-backward data set. To simplify interpretation, the forward-backward aggregated data are used throughout the chapter.

Whereas the pitfalls of aggregation thus appear to underestimate change, two potential sources of bias in the early census data may lead to inflated estimates of change. First, as late as 1930, census enumerators may have systematically recoded women in sex-atypical occupations into sex-typical occupations under the assumption that the atypical reports were errors (Conk 1978; Bose 2001). Such gender-based coding may have been especially prevalent in the farm sector, where enumerators may have arbitrarily assigned men to "farmer" and women to "farm worker" regardless of the work actually performed (Jacobs 1989a).

It is nearly impossible to know how much of this "cleaning" took place during the census interview (see Abel and Folbre 1990). It is feasible, though, to assess how much took place during processing by comparing the original census returns—available in the 1910 Public Use Microdata Sample (PUMS) (Preston 1989)—with the original published data. If cleaning introduced substantial bias, the level of segregation in the PUMS data should be lower than in the original 1910 tables. This is not the case.[6] Moreover, the published tables contain some occupations in which the counts of women are extremely low; if truly systematic recoding had occurred, one would expect zero counts. Nevertheless, if occupation codes were altered for any women (or men) because of their sex, the following analyses will overestimate segregation in the first decades of the study period (cf. Goldin 1990), implying that some of the observed integration is due to modifications in census procedures.

Second, changes in the Census Bureau's definition of the labor force may affect the observed trends. Before 1940, this definition included any individual who chose to report a gainful occupation, meaning one for which monetary compensation was received (A. Edwards 1943; Moen 1988). In later censuses, enumerators, rather than the respondents themselves, determined whether a person was working or looking for work during the week of the census, then recorded the individual's self-reported occupation or unemployment status (Moen 1988). The earlier definition of the labor force may have excluded women whose primary social identity was "housewife," even if they worked in the paid labor force (Abel and Folbre 1990). This would affect segregation trends if women in certain occupations (farm, boardinghouse, or manufacturing, for example) were particularly unlikely to report that their work was "gainful" or to be coded by enumerators as gainfully employed (Abel and Folbre 1990; see also Bose 2001).[7] Although it is again difficult to know how many women chose not to report an occupation, it is notable that the substantive results reported here do not differ when the six farm occupations, where one might expect underreporting to be the greatest, are excluded.[8]

The final data issue pertains to the treatment of empty occupation-by-sex cells, which are problematic for some of the log-linear models used in the analysis. Rather than add an arbitrary constant to these cells (Agresti 1990), zero counts are replaced with expected values from a log-linear model that constrained segregation to be equal across adjacent decades. For example, values imputed for empty cells in the 1920 data are based on the average of the sex ratios in those occupations in 1910 and 1930, adjusted for variations in the gender composition of the labor force. This procedure generates a conservative estimate of change over the relevant decades because occupations with empty cells cannot, by definition, contribute to observed trends. Although the indices of segregation are unaffected by zero cells, the data set with imputed values is used throughout the chapter for the sake of consistency. After imputing and weighting by the inverse of the sample size on which the Census Bureau based the published occupation-by-sex tables, the primary data contain 267,685,466 cases.

These data are supplemented with a secondary cross-classified array that incorporates data from the 2000 Census. At the time this chapter was written, the Census Bureau had not released tables providing the sex distribution in detailed occupations; nor had it released a "crosswalk" that would allow the 2000 Census occupational classification scheme to be reconciled with earlier schemes. It has, however, released preliminary counts of the sex distribution in twenty-one aggregate occupations, taken from the Census 2000 Supplemental Survey (U.S. Census Bureau 2002a; for details on the survey methodology and accuracy, see U.S. Census Bureau 2002b, 2002c). Without information on the industrial distribution of laborer and operative occupations, it was not possible to reconcile these data with data collected before 1970. It was feasible, however, to aggregate data from 1970, 1980, and 1990 into the twenty-one-category scheme by matching the detailed occupation titles from earlier schemes to a list of the detailed titles constituting each of the twenty-one aggregate occupations.[9] Given the unavoidable guesswork this matching process entailed, results based on these data should be interpreted cautiously. Nevertheless, they provide a useful "first cut" at recent trends.

CHANGES IN THE LEVEL OF SEGREGATION

Using the disaggregate data from 1910 to 1990, three summary measures of segregation were calculated—the index of dissimilarity (D), the size-standardized index (D_s), and the association index (A) (see Chapter 2 for index definitions). These values are presented in Table 5.2 and plotted (as a percentage of the 1910 value) in Figure 5.1. All three measures show a decline in segregation in the modern period, but show that this decline began in the 1960s, not in the 1970s as much previous research has suggested (Jacobs 1989a; Reskin and Roos 1990; Reskin 1993; Jacobsen 1994, 1997; cf. F. Blau and Hendricks 1979). In spite of this decline, segregation at century's

TABLE 5.2
Sex-Segregation Indices
in the United States, 1910–1990

| Year | A | | D | | D$_s$ | | L.F. % |
	Value	% of 1910	Value	% of 1910	Value	% of 1910	Female
1910	23.4	100.0	66.0	100.0	70.0	100.0	20.0
1920	23.6	100.2	65.2	98.8	68.1	97.4	20.5
1930	26.7	104.2	68.2	103.3	69.7	99.6	22.1
1940	9.9	72.8	68.1	103.2	67.0	95.8	24.3
1950	7.1	62.3	64.5	97.7	61.9	88.5	27.9
1960	9.0	69.6	65.1	98.6	63.6	90.9	32.5
1970	6.3	58.3	61.4	93.0	57.8	82.6	37.7
1980	5.5	54.2	54.3	82.2	53.3	76.2	42.5
1990	4.9	50.4	48.2	73.0	50.3	71.8	45.7

NOTES: Indices are calculated based on data for 237 occupations. Percentages in column 2 are based on the natural log of A.

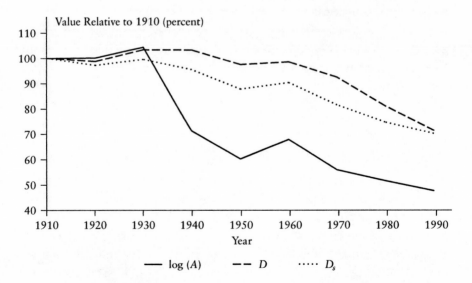

Figure 5.1 Historical Trends in the Level of Sex Segregation in the United States, 1910–1990

TABLE 5.3

Sex-Segregation Indices
in the United States, 1970–2000

Year	A		D		D_s		L.F. %
	Value	% of 1970	Value	% of 1970	Value	% of 1970	Female
1970	5.3	100.0	47.9	100.0	53.5	100.0	38.0
1980	4.9	95.5	45.0	94.0	48.8	91.4	42.5
1990	4.7	92.5	41.0	85.6	47.8	89.5	45.7
2000	4.3	88.2	39.6	82.7	47.1	88.1	46.4

NOTES: Indices are calculated based on data for 21 aggregate occupations. Percentages in column 2 are based on the natural log of A.

end remained substantial. In 1990, A, for example, shows that women were still over- or underrepresented in the average occupation by a factor of nearly five.

Analogous statistics calculated from the aggregate data, covering the period from 1970 to 2000, are presented in Table 5.3 and plotted in Figure 5.2. Not surprisingly, all three indices show lower levels of segregation in the aggregate data than in the disaggregate data. Even so, segregation remains a salient feature of the contemporary labor market, with the average underrepresentation factor in 2000 hovering above 4. Of more interest, however, are trends in the indices. They show that integrative shifts beginning in the latter part of the twentieth century continued through the turn of the twenty-first, at least at the level of aggregate occupations. By the 2000 Census, the segregation indices were between 82.7 percent (D) and 88 percent (A, D_s) of their 1970 values.

The three segregation indices are generally consistent with respect to the direction, but not the rate, of change. Consider Table 5.2, where A shows the most dramatic integration, dropping by 50 percent between 1910 and 1990, compared with roughly 30 percent for D and D_s. The greatest disparities across indices appear between 1930 and 1950, when A, and to a lesser extent D_s, decline sharply. D, in contrast, shows little change until 1960, after which it loses approximately 10 percent (of its 1960 value) in each subsequent decade. Similarly, in the most recent data (see Table 5.3), A implies a

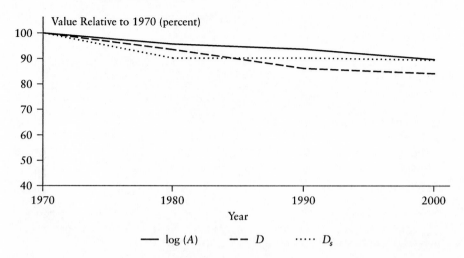

Figure 5.2   Historical Trends in the Level of Sex Segregation in the United States, 1970–2000

relatively consistent decline of between 3 and 4.5 percentage points (relative to the 1970 value) in each decade, D indicates that the largest decline occurred between 1980 and 1990, and D_s suggests that the most dramatic decline took place between 1970 and 1980, with very little action thereafter.

What accounts for these interindex disparities? They do not seem to be driven solely by sampling error. When occupations with sparse cell counts are reclassified into functionally similar occupations, the disparity between A and D_s is reduced but not eliminated (see Weeden 1998).[10] Moreover, sparse cell counts are nonexistent in the aggregate data, where similar disparities in the rate of change appear.

Instead, the observed disparities in trends across indices stem from the properties of these indices. The first such property is the compositional sensitivities of D and D_s—specifically the well-known sensitivity of D to changes in the occupational structure and the less well known sensitivity of D_s to changes in the rate of female labor force participation (see Chapter 2). Obviously, both the occupational structure and the gender composition of the labor force changed dramatically over the century. For example, in 1910 slightly less than a third of the labor force worked in farm occupations, 12 percent were laborers, and 5 percent were found in each of the professional, managerial, and clerical sectors. By 1990 less than 2 percent of the labor force worked in farm occupations, 4 percent were laborers, 21 percent were professionals, 12 percent were managers, and 19 percent were clerks (see Appendix Figure A5.1). As is evident from the last columns of Table 5.2 and 5.3, rates of female labor force participation also varied substantially. It should come as little surprise, then, that indices that are sensitive to changes in these margins would indicate different trends than an index that is not sensitive to those changes (e.g., F. Blau, Simpson, and Anderson 1998; Wells 1999; cf. Jacobs 2001, p. 539).

The second source of interindex disparities stems from the greater weight A, compared with D or D_s, attaches to integration that occurs in highly segregated occupations (see Weeden 1998). This weighting, in turn, is a consequence of its underlying logic. That is, A is an occupation-based measure constructed to determine the extent of overrepresentation in the average occupation, not an individual-centered measure designed to capture, for example, the proportion of women who would have to change occupations to reach full integration.

The dramatic integration evinced by A between 1930 and 1940, when the indices differ most (see Table 5.2), thus offers an important and meaningful substantive insight—it implies that occupations that experienced the greatest integration in this period are those that were highly segregated in 1930. Indeed, the list of occupations that integrated most substantially during this period is headed by operative and craft occupations (including plumbers and pipe fitters, telegraph and telephone linemen, stationary firemen, metal heaters, stone cutters and carvers, plasterers, brick masons and stonemasons, cabinet makers, tinsmiths and coppersmiths, and carpenters) in which men were extremely overrepresented in the early decades of the century (see Appendix Table A5.1). The entry of relatively few women into these occupations could thus effect dramatic changes in their sex ratios, which would of course influence the average level of overrepresentation or underrepresentation. As discussed below, the integration of manual occupations in this period is entirely consistent with the growing prevalence of "marriage bars," which prohibited married women from holding particular jobs; with the mechanization and deskilling of blue-collar jobs during the Depression; and with the early mobilization of women in anticipation of World War II.

The most important feature of Figures 5.1 and 5.2, at least for my purposes, is not the interindex disparities, but rather the lack of convincing support the indices provide for the historical models of change discussed in the preceding section (see also Table 5.1). Neither stability nor monotonic integration is apparent. And, although both the World War II and the post-1970 periods were characterized by substantial change in the level of segregation, they do not stand out as dramatic punctuation points. At the same time, it may be misleading to evaluate trajectories of change based on any summary index: all three indices make underlying assumptions about the global character of segregative or integrative shifts, and these assumptions may simply not be warranted in the context of the United States. The models in the next section evaluate these assumptions, thereby offering formal tests of the predictions of the reproduction, evolutionary, and punctuated-equilibrium accounts.

FORMAL MODELS OF TRENDS

Table 5.4 provides fit statistics, calculated from the disaggregate data, of the log-multiplicative models implied by these three stories of change. Generic forms of the models featured here are introduced in Chapter 2 (see Table 2.2 and equations 2.7 and 2.8), while the elaborations used in Models 5 and 6 are formally specified in Weeden 1998. In Table 5.4, model numbers correspond to those in Table 5.1.

Model 1, the universal association model, evaluates versions of the reproduction argument that imply historical stability in both the level and the pattern of segregation. It allows for change in women's share of the labor force and in the occupational structure, and it allows occupations to vary in their sex composition. The level and pattern of segregation, however, is constrained to be the same in all nine decades. Given the downward trend in A observed in Figure 5.1, it is hardly surprising that this model fails to fit according to a conventional chi-square test and leaves a nontrivial percentage of the cases misallocated.[11] The association it leaves unexplained represents historical variability in either the level of segregation alone or in both the level of segregation and its pattern.

Model 3, the multiplicative shift model, addresses whether global shifts in the level of segregation can account for the inability of Model 1 to fit the data. This model is consistent with the evolutionary claim that segregation

TABLE 5.4
Fit Statistics from Log-Linear and Log-Multiplicative Models of Sex
Segregation in the United States, 1910–1990 (237 Occupations)

Model	L^2	df	L^2_H/L^2_T	Δ
1. Universal association (S*T + O*T + O*S)	4,669,953	1,888	—	3.1
3. Multiplicative shift (S*T + O*T + O*S + A*T)	3,793,048	1,880	18.8	2.9
5. Multiplicative shift, level varying between periods (S*T + O*T + O*S + A*P)				
a. World War II	4,199,803	1,886	10.1	3.0
b. Modern (1970–90)	3,896,831	1,886	16.6	2.9
c. Combined	3,866,044	1,884	17.2	2.9
6. Universal association, pattern varying between periods (S*T + O*T + O*S*P)				
a. World War II	1,925,934	1,416	58.8	1.9
b. Modern (1970–90)	2,322,929	1,416	50.3	1.8
c. Combined	1,231,715	944	73.6	1.2

NOTES: O = occupation; S = sex; T = time; P = period effects (see text); A = global association
parameter (ϕ). Delta (Δ) represents the percentage of cases that is misclassified under the relevant model.
Model numbers correspond to those in Table 5.1.

decreased gradually and monotonically, but that the pattern of segregation
was stable over time. That is, it assumes that all occupations integrate or segregate by the same multiplicative factor, but allows this factor to vary across
decades. The resulting decade-specific shift effects (denoted Φ_k, or A_M in
Chapters 2 and 3) are measures of the level of segregation that have been
purged of all compositional effects. If this model provides an adequate fit of
the data, and if the estimated shift-effect parameters decreased monotonically over the course of the twentieth century, support would be found for
the stable-profile version of the evolutionary account (see Table 5.1). If only
the second condition is met, the results would be consistent with the varying-
profile version.

As shown in Table 5.4, neither condition is met. Model 3 fails to fit the
data, reduces Δ by very little, and leaves over 80 percent of the change in sex

segregation unexplained. This indicates considerable historical variability in the underlying pattern of segregation. Moreover, the shift-effect parameters—as much as they can be believed, given that the model does not fit the data—do not show a monotonic decline over time (estimates available upon request). Similar conclusions can be drawn from the aggregate data, where neither the universal association model nor the multiplicative shift effect model provide adequate fits.[12] Moreover, in these data, the shift effect model captures only 16.5 percent of the residual association from the more constrained model, suggesting that changes in segregation between 1970 and 2000 also occurred largely in the underlying pattern rather than in the overall level. The evidence from both data sets, then, indicates that the evolutionary account, like the reproduction account, can be rejected in the context of the twentieth-century United States.

The next task is to evaluate the punctuated-equilibrium family of models, and more specifically, the claim that World War II and the 1970s and 1980s represent historical periods in which economic or cultural "shocks" led to sudden changes in the level of sex segregation. Only the disaggregated data cover the relevant time periods, and even here imperfectly: the timing of the census data is not ideal for assessing World War II effects. They cannot recapture the minimum of the segregation curve—the bulk of the war mobilization effort took place after the 1940 census, and men had largely reentered the labor force by the 1950 census. Industry surveys nonetheless show that women's presence in manufacturing was stronger in 1950 than in 1940 (Milkman 1987, table 3), suggesting that there will be some residual effect of World War II in the 1950 data.

Model 5 assesses whether sudden shifts in the level of segregation during the World War II and the modern periods provide an adequate account of change. Three variants are fit, each of which is consistent with a different permutation of period effects. Model 5a evaluates the impact of World War II by distinguishing between the pre–World War II era (1910–40), the immediate postwar decade (1950), and the contemporary era (1960–90). Model 5b assumes stability up to 1970, when the American feminist movement regained momentum, and allows for declines in segregation in each decade thereafter. Model 5c is consistent with the claim that both World War II and the post-1970 era were periods of substantial change. It assumes stability before World War II, decline in the immediate postwar era, and then continuous decline between 1970 and 1990. Each of these models constrains the shift effect parameters to be constant within the decade or decades constituting the period in question. For example, in Model 5a, the multipliers that expand or contract the pattern of segregation are constrained to be equal for the first four decades.

The results indicate that none of these period-effect models explains more than 17.2 percent of the historical variability in segregation, nor do they reduce Δ substantially relative to Model 1 (see Table 5.4). This relatively poor performance implies that either (a) global integrative and segregative shifts occurred, but the periods are misspecified, or (b) the underlying pattern of segregation changed significantly within one or more of the specified periods. Explanation (a) can be rejected because Model 3, which allowed the segregation curve to expand or contract freely in all decades, failed to fit. Explanation (b) can be evaluated by fitting a set of models (6a through 6c) that constrain the pattern of segregation to be constant within periods, but allow the pattern to vary across periods. Model 6a assumes that the pattern of segregation varied between the prewar period (1910–40), the immediate postwar period (1950), and the modern period (1960–90), but not within the prewar and modern periods; Model 6b allows the pattern of segregation to differ between 1970, 1980, and 1990, but constrains it to be identical in the decades up to 1970; and Model 6c is consistent with the claim that both the World War II and postfeminist eras were periods of significant change in the pattern of segregation.

Models 6a, 6b, and 6c perform quite well, accounting for 59, 50, and 74 percent, respectively, of the variance left unexplained by Model 1 (see Table 5.4). Model 6a expends the fewest degrees of freedom relative to the variability explained, although Model 6c generates the lowest Δ and BIC scores. Not surprisingly, none of the three models fits by conventional log-likelihood standards. These results indicate that the pattern, not merely the level, of sex segregation changed substantially between the periods specified by the punctuated-equilibrium account. Of the models identified in Table 5.1, then, the varying-profile punctuated-equilibrium story provides the most accurate description of trends in segregation in the United States. Even so, the pattern of segregation varied considerably in periods other than World War II and the modern era.

Two general conclusions can be drawn from these analyses. First, although the evolutionary and punctuated-equilibrium stories of change accurately predict variability in the overall level of sex segregation over the twentieth century, neither adequately accounts for the timing or character of these changes. Second, and more fundamentally, the underlying pattern of occupational sex segregation has changed substantially since 1910. The methodological implication of this result is that no segregation index, including A, can adequately characterize change in the sexual division of paid labor in the United States. Indeed, interest in occupational case studies suggests an awareness that aggregate-level analyses may obscure important developments at the level of specific occupations (Reskin and Roos 1990; Jacobs 1992, 1995; Cohn 1985; Wright and Jacobs 1994; see also Burris and Wharton 1982, p. 43). The substantive implication of these results is that, insofar as reproductive forces, economic crises, or cultural shifts have affected segregation over this period, these pressures operated in occupation-specific ways.

OCCUPATION-SPECIFIC SHIFTS IN SEX SEGREGATION

The preceding results beg additional questions. Which occupations experienced the most integration over the course of the twentieth century? Which experienced the least? Do patterns emerge in the location of integrative or segregative shifts in the occupational structure and, if so, how can these patterns be understood? The remainder of this chapter explores trends in the overrepresentation or underrepresentation of women and men in particular occupations. The goal is to identify (a) the major sectors of the occupational structure where segregative or integrative shifts were concentrated, (b) the critical decades, or turning points, when such shifts occurred, and (c) the social forces or historical exigencies that might account for these occupation-specific changes.

To this end, Figure 5.3 presents trends in female representation in nine major occupational categories, calculated from the primary (1910 to 1990) data. The values it graphs are sex-segregation parameters taken from a saturated, multilevel model (see equation 2.13) fit to the disaggregate data, where positive values indicate female overrepresentation and negative values indicate male overrepresentation.[13] The nine major occupation categories correspond to those often used in historical studies, Census Bureau documents, and stratification scholarship: professional, managerial, clerical, sales, craft, operative, service, farm, and labor.

Analyzing segregation at the level of the major category gives us considerable leverage to identify the sectors of the occupational structure in which integrative or segregative shifts were concentrated. It is nonetheless the case that the detailed occupations constituting these major categories differ considerably in the extent and direction of integration or segregation, thereby suggesting that segregative processes at the micro and macro levels may differ substantially (see also Chapter 3). Readers interested in micro-level integrative shifts are referred to Appendix Table A5.1, which provides parameter estimates that index segregation in each of the 237 occupations in all nine decades, and Appendix Table A5.2, which provides parameter estimates of segregation in twenty-one aggregate occupations from 1970 to 2000. (These estimates are from a saturated model; see equation 2.10.) The following discussion concentrates on changes in segregation that took place at the macro-level, but refers to the detailed occupation estimates wherever they facilitate interpretation of the major-category trends.

Consistent with the cross-national results presented in Chapters 3 and 4, Figure 5.3 reveals high levels of both horizontal and vertical sex segregation throughout the twentieth century. The former is manifested as female overrepresentation in nonmanual occupations, and the latter as male domination of the highest-status occupations (such as craft and managerial occupations) within both the manual and nonmanual sectors. Furthermore, the occupation-specific trends are partly consistent with the argument that vertical segregation is more susceptible to egalitarian pressure than horizontal segregation. That is, the gap between upper and lower nonmanual occupations has closed somewhat in the past several decades, whereas the gap between manual and nonmanual occupations remained largely unchanged over the same period. Although there is some evidence, then, of the processes discussed in Chapter 1, this simple account fails to do justice to the complexity of change in segregation, as elaborated below.

In examining Figure 5.3, the first and most obvious conclusion is that across-the-board shifts in segregation were largely lacking in any decade. Some occupations evince period-specific integration followed by stability, others experienced periods of integration followed by resegregation, and still others reached full integration early in the century but continued to feminize (that is, become more segregated) thereafter.[14] During the 1970s and 1980s, an era often characterized as one in which women first made slow but steady progress throughout the occupational structure, some occupations (operative and craft, for example, especially in the building trades) were be-

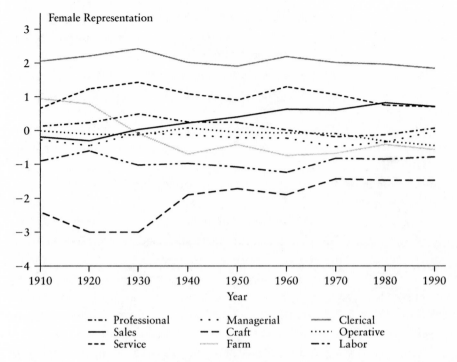

Figure 5.3   Trends in U.S. Sex Segregation by Major Occupation Category, 1910–1990: Scale Values from Multilevel Model Fit to Detailed Data (237 Occupations)

coming increasingly segregated. In the decade bracketing World War II, women at least temporarily increased their relative representation in some male-dominated occupations but not in others, a finding that belies the claim that wartime demand broke down barriers to women's employment throughout the occupational structure. In the 1930s and 1940s, the dramatic decline in the overall level of segregation (see Figure 5.1) was largely driven by pronounced integration of professional, clerical, service, and craft occupations, but was offset by segregation or stagnation in other occupational categories.

In unpacking these occupation-specific trends in segregation, it is useful to begin with the professions, if only because these occupations are often the focus of women's equality claims. Women's relative representation in the professions increased substantially between 1970 and 1990, a finding largely consistent with other American studies (Beller 1984; Reskin and Roos 1990; cf. Carter and Carter 1981). Integration was especially pronounced in elite male-dominated professions such as architecture, engineering, law, and medicine (see Appendix Table A5.1). This trend commenced after the enactment of the 1964 Civil Rights Act, which outlawed discrimination in hiring, job assignment, promotion, and pay, and the proliferation of more specific antidiscrimination measures at the national, state, and local levels of government. Legal mandates such as these undoubtedly reflected and reinforced other concomitant mechanisms for change, including a resurging feminist movement in America, rising educational attainment of women, growing political demands for labor market equality, changing gender roles and stereotypes, and diminishing tastes for discrimination among employers.

The much-vaunted integration of elite nonmanual occupations after 1970 represented an important shift in the segregation regime. It is important to recognize, however, that this occurred after four decades in which women's representation in these occupations actually declined. Indeed, between 1910 and 1960, women were overrepresented in the professional category (which includes the semiprofessions of nursing and teaching), relative to other occupations, although their representation diminished rapidly after 1930.

Women's initially high level of representation in the professions, and their declining representation thereafter, likely reflects the changing nature of the female labor force. In the early twentieth century, a relatively small proportion of women worked at paid labor, and few remained in the labor force throughout their adult years. Those in the paid labor force were either women from poor or working-class households or the career-oriented, highly educated, and single daughters of the middle and upper classes (Kessler-Harris 1982; Goldin 1990). These women were particularly likely to be found in either the low-status service and clerical occupations or in the semiprofessions, respectively (Etzioni 1969; Blitz 1974; Fuchs 1975). In the decades that followed, this selection effect weakened as a far broader spectrum of women entered and remained in paid labor, thereby driving down the human capital of the "average" female worker and, at the same time, reducing women's overrepresentation in the professions relative to other occupations (see also Chapter 1 on this compositional effect).

In the 1930s and 1940s, the effects of changes in the composition of the female labor force were likely supplemented by changes in the legal and social climate surrounding women's participation in the professions. As is often noted, high rates of unemployment during the Depression motivated public sentiment against hiring married women and delegitimized women's participation in paid employment. The political and social rhetoric of the day encouraged employers to offer high-paying, stable jobs to men, who were presumed to be the primary breadwinners for their families (Kessler-Harris 1982).

What has not been sufficiently appreciated, however, is that these marriage bars were more formalized and strictly enforced in some employment sectors than in others, and are therefore likely to have affected occupations unevenly.[15] In the private sector, employers could choose between bowing to public or personal sentiment and hiring women at substantially lower wages. Presumably some employers, particularly those hardest hit by the Depression, chose the latter option. In the public sector, the negative sentiment toward women's employment was reflected in laws that required officials to lay off civil-service workers whose spouses were also employed by the federal government (such as 1932's National Economy Act, Section 213), a provision that almost exclusively affected women, or that severely restricted the employment of married women regardless of their husbands' employment status (Goldin 1990, pp. 165–66). These informal and formal marriage bars were disproportionately applied to professional and clerical workers, in part because the public sector employed a large share of such workers. As a result, their proliferation in the 1930s and 1940s undoubtedly contributed to the steep decline in women's relative levels of representation in professional (and clerical) occupations.

Like the professions, managerial occupations show evidence of integration between 1970 and 1990. Indeed, by the later decade, women were no longer substantially underrepresented in management, although of course some of the women who are categorized as managers may have been the "beneficiaries" of purely nominal changes in the way their employers labeled clerical and sales jobs (Smith and Welch 1984; see also Jacobs 1992). As in the professions, the post-1970 integrative shifts came on the heels of four decades in which men's overrepresentation in managerial occupations was actually increasing. This increase in segregation likely reflects not only the same changes in the composition of the female labor force that affected professional occupations, but also qualitative transformations of managerial work as it shifted from family-run businesses to large bureaucratic enterprises.

Lower-status nonmanual occupations in the clerical, sales, and service categories receive far less public attention than do professions or managerial occupations, but the timing of their integrative or segregative shifts are nonetheless worth noting. Throughout the century, women were overrepresented in these occupations, albeit to greater or lesser degrees. Clerical occupations, for example, underwent considerable growth and feminization between 1910 and 1930. Although this is earlier than in other countries (see results for Japan in Chapter 6, for example), the timing supports historical accounts that point to the dramatic expansion of secondary education and growing labor demand in white-collar sectors. Clerical occupations appear to have reached a female saturation point early in the study period, such that since 1930, women's representation in this sector has declined relative to other sectors, albeit nonmonotonically. Women were, for example, eleven times more likely than men to be clerks in 1930, but "only" seven times more likely in 1990.[16] Sales occupations, by contrast, feminized steadily between 1920 and 1980. This timing is entirely consistent with the claim that feminization in this sector had its roots in the rationalization and bureaucratization of the retail industry (Bluestone et al. 1981; Goldin 1990; Charles 1992).

Historical patterns of segregation in service occupations are marked by two periods in which women's relative overrepresentation shows evidence of decline: the decades between 1930 and 1950, and those after 1960. Integrative shifts in the first period may reflect the geographical and occupational redistribution of black agricultural laborers in the 1930s. In these years, demand for cotton and tobacco fell sharply, natural disasters decimated crops, and federal subsidies were offered to those who mechanized their farms. These changes disproportionately hurt black sharecroppers and tenant farmers and spurred their migration from the rural South to urban centers in the North (e.g., G. Davis and Donaldson 1975; Wilson 1980; Johnson and Campbell 1981). Because positions in "men's" occupations were scarce, and often reserved for whites, black men were forced to disproportionately enter the low-paying and low-status service jobs that were formerly the domain of working-class and immigrant women.[17] Similarly, the integration of service occupations after 1960 likely reflects another influx of men, this time immigrants and native workers displaced from manufacturing occupations (see Lorence 1992), as well as the expanding opportunities for women in higher-status occupations.

In the manual sector, World War II is often identified as the first contemporary period in which women were able to break down barriers to heavily male-dominated occupations. Note, though, that the timing and extent of changes in segregation in the craft, labor, and operative categories do not support this argument. Women increased their representation in craft occupations between 1940 and 1950, as the "Rosie the Riveter" hypothesis predicts, but the extent of this integration is relatively modest, particularly when compared with changes that occurred in the 1930s and again in the 1960s. Women's representation in operative occupations, which was roughly proportional in 1930, became slightly greater relative to other occupations, but their representation in labor occupations was constant over the war years. It is possible, of course, that wartime integration of these occupations occurred, but began before the 1940 census or had largely reversed by the 1950 census.

If the World War II years were characterized by modest integration or even stagnation in the manual sector, the prior decade was characterized by dramatic declines in the extent of male overrepresentation in craft and operative occupations. These integrative shifts may have occurred in response to period-specific disruptions to traditional labor and job queues (Reskin and Roos 1990). As noted earlier, Depression-era marriage bars affected professional and clerical occupations more than blue-collar occupations, and many of the women displaced from white-collar occupations may have been forced to take their chances in the manual sector. At the same time, the employers who were hardest hit by the Depression, who were concentrated in manufacturing, may have chosen to ignore public sentiment and hire women at wages well below the market rate for male labor. Finally, the rapid mechanization and deskilling of skilled blue-collar jobs in this period, spurred in part by federal incentive programs, may also have contributed to this trend (Kessler-Harris 1982).

Farming occupations likewise show a dramatic shift in segregation in the early decades of the century. In 1910 and 1920, women were overrepresented in farming, whereas by 1930 men were overrepresented.[18] Segregation in these occupations vacillated somewhat after 1940, but male overrepresentation in farming continued through 1990. The shift toward male overrepresentation in farming in the early decades is likely the result of several macro-level trends. Most obvious is the replacement of family farms with large-scale industrial enterprises. In addition, consecutive drought years during the 1930s forced at least one member of farming families to seek outside work. Evidence suggests that during the Depression "women's" jobs, though low-status and low-wage, were more readily available than "men's" jobs (Wandersee 1981; Kessler-Harris 1982), and hence wives could anticipate slightly more success in the cash economy than their husbands.

Many of these explanations for occupation-specific trends are necessarily speculative, although they are in line with evidence emerging from historical studies of women's employment. Such explanations deserve to be evaluated more comprehensively than is possible in this chapter. The broader point to be made, though, is that historical trends in sex segregation in the United States are likely far more complex than has previously been appreciated. Attempts to explain change in segregation's overall level are in many ways doomed to failure because occupational developments do not follow a common historical trajectory. The forces that led to reproduction and change in sex segregation between 1910 and 1990 appear to have operated in local, not global, ways.

What about more recent trends? To offer a preliminary answer to this question, Figure 5.4 presents trends in eight major occupation categories be-

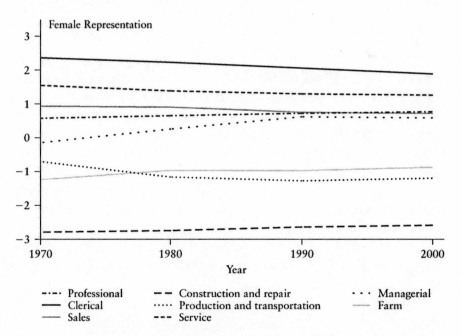

Figure 5.4   Trends in U.S. Sex Segregation by Major Occupation Category, 1970–2000: Scale Values from Multilevel Model Fit to Aggregate Data (21 Occupations)

tween 1970 and 2000, again calculated from a saturated multilevel model.[19] It reveals some evidence of occupation-specific trajectories. For example, production and transportation occupations became increasingly segregated in the 1970s, whereas managerial, sales, clerical, service, and construction and repair occupations became, if anything, less segregated. Nevertheless, these category-specific differences in segregation trajectories are not as prominent as in Figure 5.3. Indeed, between 1990 and 2000 the trend lines are nearly parallel, thus suggesting a global, albeit modest, integration at the level of the major occupation group over this decade.

CONCLUSION

The foregoing analysis points to the inadequacy of conventional accounts in understanding sex segregation and its historical evolution in the United States. When subjected to formal evaluation, standard reproductive and evolutionary accounts, which posit constant or steadily declining overall levels of sex segregation, are found wanting. The punctuated-equilibrium story, which treats occupational gender distributions as the product of macro-level events and circumstances (in this case wartime labor shortages and a changing ideological climate), fares slightly better.

This historicist account only fits the data if we allow for historical variability in the pattern, not just the level, of occupational sex segregation, particularly before the 2000 Census. So, the economic shock to the segregation system represented by the World War II labor crisis influenced patterns of segregation, but only in the manual sector. Likewise, the resurgence of feminism and the associated rise in egalitarian cultural and legal practices in the post–civil rights era may have reduced vertical segregation after 1970, but here too integrative trends did not permeate all occupations until the 1990s. Instead, reductions in vertical segregation were manifested primarily in the nonmanual sector in the form of increasing female representation in elite managerial and professional occupations. Within the manual sector, male overrepresentation in the highest-status occupations (especially in the building trades) actually intensified between 1970 and 1990.

Although changes in the levels of sex segregation are not easily reconciled with common evolutionary, reproductive, or historicist accounts, some of these occupation-specific developments lend themselves to such interpretations. For example, although vertical inequality is delegitimized in some areas of the economy, horizontal segregation has shown little sign of abating as American women and men continue to be separated across the manual-nonmanual divide. This persistent overrepresentation of women in nonmanual occupations throughout the twentieth century provides some support for reproductive arguments. Integrative trends in the professions and management in recent decades are consistent with popular notions of growing egalitarianism. And the integration of craft, clerical, and service occupations during the 1930s supports historicist accounts that point to discrimination against married women during the Depression era, the forced urban migration of black farm laborers, and technological changes within the manufacturing sector.

The broader lesson to be learned is that there is a mismatch between the level at which accounts of segregation trends are pitched and the level at which such trends are found. The forces that drive change or stasis in sex segregation—such as gender-specific socialization or sex-linked traits, egalitarianism, and historical or cultural shocks to the system—are often discussed as if they operate uniformly across the occupational structure. The results presented in this chapter, by contrast, suggest that analysts would do better to consider the occupation- or sector-specific impact of their favored explanatory variables.

Additional evidence of the importance of occupation-specific developments, and of the secular pressures or contextual shocks that may have given rise to these developments, are provided in Chapters 6 and 7, which consider the evolution of Japanese and Swiss sex-segregation regimes.

APPENDIX TABLE A5.1

Detailed Classification Scheme and Saturated Scale Values for the United States, 1910–1990 (237 Occupations)

Category and Component Detailed Occupations	1910	1920	1930	1940	1950	1960	1970	1980	1990
Professional									
1. Accountants and auditors	1.33	1.41	1.18	0.36	0.50	0.70	0.74	0.98	1.32
2. Actors, athletes, dancers, and other entertainers	2.76	3.00	2.91	2.05	1.51	1.83	1.16	0.90	0.94
3. Airplane pilots and navigators	−1.67	−1.62	−1.01	−1.73	−1.99	−2.77	−2.48	−3.06	−2.31
4. Architects	−0.34	−1.35	−0.45	−0.97	−0.97	−1.31	−1.53	−1.14	−0.67
5. Artists and art teachers	3.44	3.12	3.01	2.16	1.78	1.70	1.24	1.21	1.14
6. Authors	3.51	3.27	3.26	2.10	1.79	1.22	0.88	1.10	1.08
7. Chemists	0.36	0.73	0.39	−0.68	0.07	−0.05	−0.21	0.00	0.21
8. Clergy	−1.51	−0.78	−0.28	−0.94	−0.90	−1.44	−1.75	−1.46	−1.05
9. Religious, group, and social welfare workers	3.91	4.08	4.36	3.54	2.91	2.65	2.11	1.90	1.83
10. College presidents, deans, and professors	2.17	2.63	2.78	1.76	1.06	1.02	0.83	0.74	0.72
11. Dentists	0.20	0.08	−0.49	−1.40	−1.30	−1.44	−1.55	−1.31	−0.82
12. Designers and draftspersons	0.98	1.42	1.24	0.52	0.24	−0.05	−0.18	0.12	0.22
13. Editors and reporters	1.69	1.97	2.37	1.67	1.50	1.63	1.19	1.33	1.32
14. Civil engineers	−5.35	−4.57	−4.50	−3.21	−1.89	−2.85	−2.54	−2.15	−1.47
15. Chemical, metallurgical, and mining engineers	−5.48	−5.41	−4.65	−2.45	−1.70	−2.45	−2.55	−1.58	−1.03
16. Electrical engineers	−4.21	−4.25	−3.33	−2.83	−2.17	−2.52	−2.30	−1.62	−1.10
17. Industrial, aeronautical, mechanical, and other engineers	−5.09	−4.71	−4.57	−3.08	−2.37	−2.34	−2.26	−1.32	−0.74

18. Farm and home management advisors	1.56	1.82	2.39	2.68	2.23	2.18	1.76	1.25	1.06
19. Funeral directors and embalmers	0.43	0.44	0.70	-0.07	-0.38	-0.44	-0.85	-1.13	-1.04
20. Lawyers and judges	-1.69	-0.77	-0.33	-0.89	-1.06	-1.01	-1.20	-0.49	-0.02
21. Librarians	4.93	5.49	5.87	4.96	4.30	4.07	3.34	2.92	2.73
22. Musicians and music teachers	4.06	3.70	3.44	2.42	2.22	2.55	1.97	1.42	1.57
23. Nurses, professional and student professional	6.20	6.74	7.48	6.56	5.96	6.00	5.36	4.53	4.01
24. Optometrists	1.55	0.73	0.24	-0.27	-0.54	-0.82	-1.39	-1.08	-0.65
25. Pharmacists	-0.14	-0.08	0.07	-0.38	-0.15	-0.18	-0.22	0.17	0.56
26. Photographers	1.85	1.71	1.80	0.95	0.69	0.32	-0.03	0.07	0.18
27. Physicians and osteopaths	0.86	0.70	0.60	-0.15	-0.43	-0.30	-0.59	-0.67	-0.38
28. Chiropractors and therapists not elsewhere classified	4.03	3.32	2.89	2.11	1.74	1.97	1.88	1.91	1.89
29. Radio operators	-2.10	-2.04	-1.16	-1.24	-0.04	0.14	0.14	0.74	-0.05
30. Surveyors	-2.77	-2.55	-2.72	-2.33	-0.97	-0.88	-1.67	-1.28	-1.11
31. Teachers, not elsewhere classified	5.02	5.17	5.01	3.88	3.33	3.22	2.51	2.09	2.09
32. Technicians, medical, dental, and testing, not elsewhere classified	2.53	3.76	3.45	2.00	1.67	1.31	1.12	1.06	1.01
33. Veterinarian	-6.67	-6.04	-3.47	-1.88	-0.43	-1.57	-1.13	-0.55	0.09
34. Professional, technical, and kindred workers, not elsewhere classified	2.08	2.11	2.46	1.62	1.22	1.14	0.99	0.94	0.90
Managerial									
35. Buyers, department heads, and floor managers, store	2.23	2.42	2.49	1.71	1.28	1.16	0.76	0.94	1.33
36. Buyers and shippers, farm products	-1.47	-2.92	-2.52	-1.54	-1.30	-1.54	-1.86	-1.05	-0.40

(continued)

163

Category and Component *Detailed Occupations*	*1910*	*1920*	*1930*	*1940*	*1950*	*1960*	*1970*	*1980*	*1990*
37. Conductors, railroad	-3.45	-3.23	-3.42	-4.24	-2.78	-3.54	-2.74	-2.53	-1.31
38. Credit managers	-0.08	0.88	1.12	0.79	0.98	1.20	0.84	1.00	1.33
39. Inspectors and officials, public administration	0.67	0.77	1.19	0.68	0.41	0.56	0.24	0.58	1.36
40. Managers and superintendents, building	0.94	1.77	2.66	2.42	1.59	1.77	1.37	1.16	1.13
41. Ship's officers, pilots, pursers, and engineers	-7.09	-6.63	-5.89	-2.89	-1.30	-3.02	-2.24	-2.65	-2.60
42. Officials of lodges, societies, and unions	2.48	1.98	2.17	1.17	0.16	0.12	0.12	0.41	0.53
43. Postmasters	2.98	2.99	3.09	2.48	1.98	1.92	1.00	1.06	0.93
44. Purchasing agents and buyers, not elsewhere classified	0.39	0.69	0.94	0.36	-0.04	0.04	-0.07	0.38	0.62
45. Managers: construction	-1.73	-3.25	-2.31	-2.11	-1.86	-1.54	-1.82	-1.14	-1.00
46. Managers: manufacturing	-0.45	0.02	0.07	-0.33	-0.44	-0.33	-1.02	-0.93	-0.50
47. Managers: transportation	-1.55	-1.72	-1.32	-0.94	-0.93	-0.68	-0.93	-1.36	-0.87
48. Managers: communications, utilities, and sanitary services	1.09	-0.06	1.08	0.22	-0.02	0.19	-0.26	-0.02	0.04
49. Managers: wholesale trade	-0.44	-1.20	-0.54	-0.65	-0.71	-0.41	-1.13	-0.99	-0.41
50. Retail managers: eating and drinking places	1.35	1.76	2.37	1.59	1.23	1.50	1.11	0.98	1.04
51. Retail managers: food and dairy product stores	1.18	1.06	1.13	0.90	0.64	0.64	0.29	0.08	0.43

52. Retail managers: general merchandise	1.14	1.07	1.46	0.97	0.98	1.17	0.72	0.82	1.10
53. Retail managers: apparel and accessories	2.73	2.35	2.28	1.57	1.46	1.61	1.21	1.36	0.21
54. Retail managers: motor vehicles and accessories	-0.84	-1.83	-1.26	-1.15	-1.23	-0.95	-1.11	-0.27	-0.04
55. Retail managers: gasoline service stations	-0.34	-0.28	-0.22	-0.82	-1.12	-1.44	-1.62	-0.53	0.89
56. Retail managers: furniture, hardware, and other goods	0.54	0.60	0.81	0.52	0.31	0.46	0.23	0.19	0.49
57. Managers: banking, finance, insurance, and real estate	-0.04	0.22	0.62	0.10	0.27	0.48	0.20	0.43	0.68
58. Managers: personal services	2.13	2.18	2.17	1.67	1.37	1.62	0.98	0.97	1.09
59. Managers: all other industries	0.81	0.52	0.65	0.50	0.53	1.06	0.52	0.62	0.77
Clerical									
60. Clerical agents, not elsewhere classified	0.31	0.59	0.84	0.61	0.57	0.79	0.89	1.23	1.54
61. Collectors, bill and account	0.75	1.14	0.89	0.33	0.50	0.99	1.20	1.88	1.90
62. Library attendants and assistants	5.34	3.60	4.51	4.44	3.32	3.51	3.07	2.78	2.41
63. Physicians' and dentists' attendants and assistants	5.02	5.02	6.40	5.86	5.20	5.99	5.13	4.65	4.20
64. Bookkeepers and cashiers	3.27	3.72	4.05	3.41	3.52	3.81	3.33	3.21	2.72
65. Mail carriers	-0.74	-0.75	-1.16	-1.59	-1.55	-1.51	-0.68	-0.58	0.09
66. Stenographers, typists, and secretaries	5.04	5.65	6.26	5.41	5.08	5.62	5.12	5.09	4.67
67. Messengers, office runners, and telegraph messengers	1.08	1.32	0.59	-0.34	0.66	0.70	0.36	0.26	0.00

(continued)

APPENDIX TABLE A5.1
(*continued*)

Category and Component Detailed Occupations	1910	1920	1930	1940	1950	1960	1970	1980	1990
68. Telegraph operators	1.67	2.23	2.34	1.41	0.98	1.08	0.89	1.84	1.59
69. Telephone operators	5.85	6.19	6.36	5.64	5.31	5.43	4.61	3.73	3.06
70. Ticket, station and express agents	0.37	0.80	0.54	-0.22	0.36	1.04	1.22	1.26	1.65
71. Clerical, not elsewhere classified	1.56	2.35	2.46	2.11	2.11	2.44	2.12	2.00	1.88
Sales									
72. Advertising agents and salesmen	0.39	0.68	0.94	0.15	0.50	0.48	0.39	0.99	1.17
73. Auctioneers	-3.05	-3.95	-3.47	-0.10	-0.02	-1.48	-0.97	-0.44	-0.72
74. Demonstrator	4.55	4.13	4.67	4.23	3.76	4.80	4.10	3.69	3.02
75. Hucksters and peddlers	0.62	0.24	0.09	-0.26	0.46	2.60	3.08	2.57	1.73
76. Insurance agents, brokers, and adjusters	0.11	0.36	0.57	-0.11	-0.11	0.10	0.03	0.62	1.00
77. Newspaper vendors	-1.05	-0.96	-1.02	-1.16	-0.93	-0.80	-0.76	0.57	0.60
78. Real estate agents and brokers	-1.03	-0.16	0.79	0.48	0.48	1.14	1.02	1.22	1.21
79. Stock and bonds salespersons	-1.07	-1.55	-1.04	-0.96	0.09	-0.38	-0.51	-0.14	0.15
80. Salespersons and sales clerks, not elsewhere classified	2.55	2.65	2.58	1.94	1.78	1.93	1.47	1.18	0.93
Craft									
81. Bakers	0.75	0.46	0.81	0.23	0.24	0.67	0.92	1.17	1.14
82. Boilermakers	-4.52	-4.30	-4.47	-3.34	-2.40	-4.09	-2.63	-2.76	-2.46
83. Bookbinders	4.10	3.90	3.69	2.17	2.50	2.56	2.09	1.76	1.42
84. Brickmasons, stonemasons, and tile setters	-5.65	-6.40	-6.59	-2.74	-2.89	-3.28	-2.61	-3.05	-3.13

85. Cabinetmakers	-3.30	-5.26	-5.60	-1.98	-1.95	-1.95	-1.09	-1.17	-1.59
86. Carpenters, including apprentices	-6.16	-5.04	-6.22	-2.91	-2.98	-3.43	-2.53	-2.64	-2.79
87. Cement and concrete finishers	-2.53	-2.32	-2.48	-2.46	-2.76	-3.55	-2.50	-3.11	-3.15
88. Electrotypers and stereotypers	-0.13	-2.84	-2.51	-1.88	-0.93	-2.55	-1.37	-1.52	-1.70
89. Engravers, photoengravers, and lithographers	0.60	0.05	0.11	-0.47	-0.47	0.02	0.06	0.33	0.24
90. Compositors and typesetters	1.54	1.04	0.68	-0.27	-0.44	-0.06	0.06	0.65	0.68
91. Press operators and plate printers, including apprentices	0.31	0.32	-1.26	-1.29	-0.94	-0.86	-0.57	-0.62	-0.68
92. Decorators and window dressers	1.22	1.58	2.71	1.55	1.40	2.15	2.08	2.23	2.24
93. Electricians, including apprentices	-3.52	-5.56	-5.14	-2.78	-2.64	-2.57	-2.16	-2.61	-2.71
94. Crane and derrick operators, stationary engineers	-6.47	-5.20	-6.04	-2.90	-2.77	-3.03	-2.56	-2.48	-2.35
95. Blacksmiths, forge workers, and hammer workers	-5.32	-7.17	-6.12	-3.05	-2.54	-1.79	-1.44	-1.64	-1.81
96. Craft supervisors: all industries	1.10	0.92	0.83	0.27	-0.17	-0.32	-0.65	-0.69	-0.78
97. Furriers	1.68	1.58	1.61	0.96	0.43	0.54	0.24	0.62	0.32
98. Painters, construction and maintenance, and glaziers	-2.96	-4.12	-4.37	-2.04	-1.63	-1.59	-1.35	-1.38	-1.43
99. Heat treaters, annealers, and temperers	-1.97	-3.40	-2.11	-2.21	-1.94	-1.84	-1.71	-1.49	-1.54
100. Inspectors, scalers and graders: log and lumber	0.04	0.34	0.07	-0.92	-0.81	-0.81	-0.27	-0.69	-1.08
101. Inspectors, other industries	0.30	-0.76	0.48	-0.03	-0.29	-0.38	-0.67	-0.92	-1.28
102. Jewelers, watchmakers, goldsmiths, and tinsmiths	1.16	0.36	0.12	-0.31	-0.55	-0.39	-0.21	0.03	0.04

(continued)

Category and Component Detailed Occupations	1910	1920	1930	1940	1950	1960	1970	1980	1990
103. Line and service workers, telegraph, telephone, and power	-5.74	-4.88	-8.06	-1.94	-1.49	-1.59	-1.82	-1.09	-1.17
104. Locomotive engineer	-3.60	-3.39	-3.57	-4.38	-2.84	-4.22	-3.05	-3.00	-2.76
105. Locomotive fireperson	-4.07	-3.86	-4.04	-4.86	-3.34	-3.50	-2.72	-2.66	-2.41
106. Loom fixers	-5.72	-5.11	-2.80	-2.80	-2.18	-2.41	-2.09	-1.81	-1.72
107. Machinists, mechanics, and job setters, inc. apprentices	-4.49	-6.23	-6.22	-2.25	-2.09	-2.11	-2.00	-2.17	-2.17
108. Millers of grain, flour, and feed	-2.34	-4.64	-2.47	-2.49	-2.73	-2.68	-2.01	-0.80	-0.09
109. Millwrights	-6.16	-6.09	-5.34	-2.68	-3.20	-4.40	-2.67	-1.93	-2.14
110. Molders, metal	-3.31	-5.69	-5.11	-2.42	-2.22	-1.15	-0.29	-0.54	-0.93
111. Motion picture projectionists	-2.03	-1.82	-1.99	-1.76	-1.72	-1.46	-1.29	-0.97	-0.64
112. Opticians and lens grinders and polishers	1.27	1.45	1.36	0.43	0.39	0.59	0.57	0.86	1.25
113. Paperhangers	0.19	-0.37	0.59	-0.02	0.38	0.46	-0.36	-0.12	0.10
114. Pattern and model makers, except paper	-0.10	-2.71	-3.13	-1.83	-1.11	-1.73	-1.21	-1.10	-1.40
115. Piano and organ tuners and repairers	-0.50	-1.69	-2.13	-1.97	-1.12	-1.21	-1.21	-1.25	-1.45
116. Plasterers	-5.35	-5.29	-6.55	-2.61	-2.53	-3.35	-2.44	-2.41	-1.80
117. Plumbers and pipefitters, including apprentices	-6.96	-7.70	-8.89	-2.71	-2.48	-3.46	-2.75	-3.02	-3.08
118. Rollers and roll hands, metal	-3.05	-2.78	-2.94	-2.58	-1.53	-1.18	-0.87	-0.60	-0.55
119. Roofers and slaters	-2.99	-2.78	-2.94	-2.70	-2.96	-3.70	-2.59	-3.22	-3.05

120. Shoemakers and repairers, except factory	−0.85	−2.24	−2.17	−1.85	−0.87	−0.97	0.45	0.19	−0.23
121. Stone cutters and stone carvers	−5.24	−5.49	−6.53	−2.33	−1.35	−1.49	−0.81	−1.05	−1.47
122. Structural metal workers	−2.74	−2.52	−2.69	−2.34	−2.88	−3.17	−2.62	−3.06	−2.90
123. Tailors	2.24	1.85	1.60	0.93	0.82	1.03	1.00	0.93	1.10
124. Tinsmiths, coppersmiths, and sheet metal workers	−4.19	−5.36	−6.03	−2.57	−2.36	−2.12	−2.05	−1.64	−1.51
125. Upholsterers	0.95	0.94	0.44	−0.22	−0.11	0.10	0.08	0.02	−0.16
126. Craft workers and apprentices, not elsewhere classified	1.52	0.80	0.60	−0.96	−1.37	−1.35	−1.82	−2.40	−2.68
Operative									
127. Asbestos and insulation workers	−1.61	−1.40	−1.56	−1.61	−1.34	−1.01	−2.06	−1.82	−2.08
128. Attendants, auto service and parking	−0.19	−0.05	−0.75	−1.30	−1.32	−1.59	−1.73	−1.12	−1.03
129. Blasters and powderers	−3.03	−2.82	−2.98	−2.49	−2.50	−2.16	−1.22	−1.71	−1.35
130. Boat operators, canal and lock keepers	−2.24	−1.78	−1.43	−1.34	−1.45	−1.92	−0.94	−1.36	−1.29
131. Brake and switch operators, railroad	−5.06	−3.03	−3.62	−3.92	−2.91	−3.51	−2.49	−2.77	−2.63
132. Chain, rod, and axe crew, surveying	−2.04	−1.82	−1.99	−2.00	−1.50	−0.86	−2.27	−1.28	−1.13
133. Conductors and motorcar operators, street rail	−3.31	−2.67	−4.86	−2.14	−1.90	−1.83	−1.88	−2.31	−2.47
134. Delivery and route drivers	−3.70	−3.29	−3.75	−1.81	−1.74	−1.31	−1.62	−1.26	−1.08
135. Dressmakers, except factory	9.31	10.12	9.59	6.85	5.80	5.64	4.72	4.33	4.09
136. Dyers	0.61	−1.27	−0.57	−0.76	−0.84	−0.82	−0.53	−0.49	−0.62

(continued)

169

Category and Component Detailed Occupations	1910	1920	1930	1940	1950	1960	1970	1980	1990
137. Filers, grinders, and polishers, metal	0.83	0.33	0.03	-0.60	-0.77	-0.53	-0.61	-0.83	-1.19
138. Fruit, nut, vegetable graders and packers, except factory	3.35	2.99	3.99	3.07	2.74	3.18	2.44	1.96	1.63
139. Furnace and smelter operators and pourers	-3.66	-5.25	-2.32	-1.91	-1.53	-1.71	-1.32	-2.04	-2.02
140. Heaters, metal	-3.39	-5.55	-6.10	-1.31	-0.79	-1.42	-1.58	-1.33	-1.39
141. Laundry and dry cleaning operatives	4.20	4.03	4.28	3.43	2.96	3.24	2.69	2.16	1.75
142. Meat cutters, except slaughter and packing houses	-2.71	-2.17	-2.78	-2.17	-1.62	-1.15	-1.09	-1.23	-1.09
143. Milliners	9.10	9.31	9.15	5.79	4.39	4.57	3.90	4.57	4.27
144. Mining operatives and laborers, not elsewhere classified	-3.62	-2.64	-4.90	-2.95	-2.54	-3.21	-2.22	-2.52	-2.69
145. Motorcar operators: mine, factory, and logging camp	-3.79	-3.58	-3.74	-3.43	-2.39	-2.93	-2.37	-2.34	-2.14
146. Oilers and greasers, except auto	-2.78	-2.86	-3.13	-2.32	-1.87	-2.22	-1.57	-1.73	-1.79
147. Painters, except construction and maintenance	0.54	0.58	0.67	0.33	0.21	0.10	0.09	-0.21	-0.48
148. Photographic process workers	2.84	3.04	3.18	2.19	2.04	2.04	1.65	1.39	1.12
149. Power station operators	-2.74	-1.25	-1.42	-0.76	-0.95	-0.56	-1.68	-1.52	-1.51
150. Sailors and deck hands	-4.63	-3.97	-5.49	-2.52	-1.84	-2.72	-2.26	-2.32	-2.27
151. Sawyers	-4.10	-4.76	-2.60	-1.70	-1.61	-1.35	-0.55	-0.72	-0.82

152. Spinners, textile	4.14	3.92	3.88	3.94	3.32	3.64	2.35	1.96	1.58
153. Stationary fire operators	−6.42	−5.84	−8.25	−2.56	−2.43	−2.82	−1.11	−1.81	−1.80
154. Bus, taxi, and truck drivers and chauffeurs	−3.61	−2.23	−2.96	−2.53	−2.37	−1.84	−1.14	−0.91	−0.94
155. Weavers, textile	3.58	3.29	3.22	2.19	1.81	1.97	1.91	1.81	1.58
156. Welders and flame-cutters	−1.27	−1.06	−1.22	−1.30	−1.03	−0.71	−0.96	−1.46	−1.92
157. Operatives: sawmills, misc. wood products	1.20	1.21	1.38	0.43	−0.11	0.13	0.18	0.00	−0.34
158. Operatives: furniture and fixtures	1.24	1.59	1.57	1.06	0.95	1.11	1.31	0.82	0.43
159. Operatives: stone, clay, and glass products	1.51	1.77	1.87	1.47	1.20	1.21	0.93	0.67	0.60
160. Operatives: motor vehicles and equipment	0.46	1.34	1.47	0.93	0.65	0.51	0.22	0.17	0.19
161. Operatives: iron and steel	1.32	1.49	1.52	0.87	0.64	0.77	0.51	0.32	0.19
162. Operatives: nonferrous metals	1.99	2.20	2.34	1.35	1.03	0.52	0.29	0.25	−0.29
163. Operatives: electrical machinery, equipment, supplies	3.42	3.16	3.05	2.66	2.40	2.53	2.25	1.95	1.55
164. Operatives: misc. manufacturing, inc. tobacco and leather	3.02	3.03	3.16	2.66	2.34	2.53	2.20	1.76	1.19
165. Operatives: food, dairy, and beverages	2.81	2.93	3.11	2.28	1.83	1.93	1.50	1.05	0.90
166. Operatives: textile mills	3.87	3.75	3.71	2.74	2.39	2.61	2.20	2.73	2.53
167. Operatives: apparel, accessories	4.15	4.08	4.37	4.15	3.64	4.01	4.01	2.51	1.93
168. Operatives: pulp, paper, and paperboard products	3.51	3.05	2.88	2.11	1.54	1.44	0.90	0.28	0.18
169. Operatives: printing, publishing, and allied industries	3.44	3.24	3.04	2.65	2.04	2.08	1.76	1.40	1.09

(continued)

APPENDIX TABLE A5.1
(*continued*)

Category and Component Detailed Occupations	1910	1920	1930	1940	1950	1960	1970	1980	1990
170. Operatives: chemicals and allied products	3.14	2.76	2.89	1.76	1.05	1.03	0.86	0.83	0.75
171. Operatives: petroleum refining, petrol and coal products	0.08	0.39	−0.51	−1.12	−1.29	−1.64	−1.58	−1.08	−1.01
172. Operatives: rubber and plastic products	2.92	2.20	2.48	1.83	1.44	1.70	1.46	0.87	0.91
173. Operatives: not specified manufacturing	3.42	3.12	3.35	2.65	2.16	2.23	1.45	1.43	0.98
174. Operatives: construction	2.26	−1.83	−2.97	−1.92	−1.58	−2.13	−1.50	−1.70	−1.67
175. Operatives: transport, communications, utilities	−0.82	−0.57	−0.20	−1.03	−0.65	−0.75	−0.50	−0.39	−0.40
176. Operatives: wholesale and retail trade	2.98	2.98	3.02	2.14	1.77	1.85	1.60	1.28	0.86
177. Operatives: business and repair services	−1.37	−2.61	−0.56	0.22	0.38	0.63	0.54	0.92	0.77
178. Operatives: public administration	0.98	0.89	1.33	0.77	0.33	0.16	0.20	0.12	0.00
179. Operatives: all other industries	1.04	0.25	2.02	2.04	1.62	1.73	1.69	1.37	1.00
Service									
180. Private household launderers	8.59	8.41	9.27	6.76	5.68	6.31	4.67	2.49	2.67
181. Private household housekeepers and other workers	6.63	6.49	6.39	5.53	5.14	5.58	5.10	4.49	4.16
182. Midwives, practical nurses, and hospital attendants	5.63	5.43	5.01	3.65	3.31	3.76	3.73	3.44	3.06

Occupation									
183. Attendants, professional and personal services, n.e.c.	3.38	4.31	4.05	3.50	2.95	3.16	3.19	3.14	3.28
184. Attendants and ushers, recreation and amusement	-0.13	1.99	1.46	1.00	0.52	0.65	0.65	0.81	0.64
185. Barbers, beauticians, manicurists	1.58	1.77	2.68	2.76	2.25	2.57	2.52	2.47	2.64
186. Bartenders	-2.37	-2.00	-0.79	-0.89	-0.39	0.22	0.45	1.10	1.09
187. Boarding house and lodge keepers	5.45	5.29	5.52	4.52	3.24	4.33	2.71	2.46	2.08
188. Bootblacks	-2.92	-2.66	-2.72	-0.88	-1.10	-0.86	-0.57	-0.66	-1.04
189. Charpersons and cleaners	4.97	4.24	4.21	2.93	2.65	3.04	3.11	2.39	2.39
190. Cooks, except private household	3.16	3.08	3.06	2.36	2.41	2.86	2.26	1.54	1.01
191. Elevator operators	-3.28	1.96	2.01	1.15	1.42	1.56	0.81	0.13	-0.62
192. Firefighters	-3.43	-3.22	-3.40	-4.21	-3.23	-3.71	-2.68	-2.96	-1.98
193. Guards, watchpersons, and doorkeepers	-3.00	-2.19	-1.48	-1.28	-1.57	-1.19	-1.14	-0.65	-0.61
194. Police officers and detectives, public and private	-2.27	-1.53	-1.03	-1.70	-1.71	-1.28	-1.53	-1.18	-0.60
195. Marshals and constables	-4.79	-2.53	-1.50	-1.41	-1.30	-0.91	-1.43	-1.55	-1.27
196. Housekeepers and stewards, except private household	4.39	4.31	4.33	3.90	3.50	3.70	3.38	3.28	3.25
197. Janitors and sextons	2.17	1.83	1.48	0.64	0.22	0.39	-0.16	0.11	0.27
198. Porters	-2.55	-1.45	-2.61	-1.64	-1.52	-1.64	-1.57	-2.19	-2.18
199. Sheriffs and bailiffs	-4.15	-1.78	-0.50	-0.95	-0.90	-0.65	-0.96	-1.08	-0.80
200. Wait staff and counter workers	3.41	3.47	3.83	3.50	3.54	3.97	3.68	3.26	2.51
201. Crossing watchers and bridge tenders	0.29	-0.11	-0.66	-1.51	-0.92	2.11	2.06	1.99	1.71

(continued)

Category and Component Detailed Occupations	1910	1920	1930	1940	1950	1960	1970	1980	1990
202. Service workers, except private household, not elsewhere classified	3.89	3.75	3.91	2.96	2.67	2.88	2.25	1.70	1.35
Farm									
203. Farmers (owners and tenants)	0.56	0.34	0.42	−0.74	−1.33	−0.70	−1.21	−0.81	−0.57
204. Farm managers	2.19	2.04	−0.46	−1.01	−0.44	−1.21	−1.32	−0.86	−0.74
205. Farm supervisors	1.34	1.19	−1.34	−1.23	−1.06	−1.53	−0.93	−0.32	−0.74
206. Farm laborers—wage workers	1.67	1.26	0.84	−0.18	−0.01	0.26	−0.06	−0.04	−0.19
207. Farm laborers—unpaid family	2.34	2.38	2.60	1.32	1.63	2.06	1.20	1.32	0.97
208. Farm service workers, self-employed	−0.02	0.18	0.01	−0.81	0.37	−1.44	−0.13	0.17	−0.23
Labor									
209. Fishers and oysterers	−1.33	−1.46	−2.35	−2.18	−1.99	−2.06	−1.37	−1.29	−1.50
210. Garage laborers, car washers, and greasers	−2.98	−2.23	−2.68	−2.14	−1.09	−1.12	−0.88	−0.87	−1.32
211. Gardeners and groundskeepers, except farm	−0.58	−0.50	−0.86	−1.61	−1.47	−1.85	−1.76	−1.22	−1.45
212. Longshore workers and stevedores	−3.64	−2.11	−5.40	−2.31	−2.27	−2.91	−2.31	−1.57	−1.21
213. Lumber workers, raft workers, and wood choppers	−3.88	−3.00	−3.85	−2.83	−2.46	−2.56	−1.99	−2.45	−2.49
214. Teamsters	−4.67	−2.92	−4.34	−2.41	−1.90	−3.25	−1.39	−1.70	−1.79

No.	Occupation								
215.	Laborers: sawmills, mill work, misc. wood products	-0.89	-0.15	-0.37	-1.59	-1.40	-1.29	-0.64	-0.63	-0.66
216.	Laborers: furniture and fixtures	-0.15	0.97	0.26	-0.45	-0.32	-0.14	0.18	0.07	-0.06
217.	Laborers: stone, clay, and glass	-0.53	0.15	-0.17	-0.72	-0.95	-1.06	-0.81	-0.70	-0.13
218.	Laborers: motor vehicles and equipment	-1.09	-0.02	-0.01	-0.43	-0.74	-1.13	-1.14	-0.58	-0.36
219.	Laborers: iron and steel	-0.52	-0.45	-0.61	-1.23	-1.21	-1.45	-0.65	-0.65	-0.43
220.	Laborers: nonferrous metals	-0.04	0.06	-0.22	-0.83	-1.07	0.78	-0.83	-0.78	-0.75
221.	Laborers: electrical machinery, equipment, and supplies	1.65	1.48	1.26	1.06	0.64	-1.05	0.76	0.77	0.77
222.	Laborers: misc. manufacturing, inc. tobacco and leather	1.71	1.79	1.64	1.31	0.99	1.00	0.93	0.77	0.31
223.	Laborers: food, dairy, and beverages	1.01	1.23	1.49	0.51	-0.19	-0.23	-0.42	-0.02	0.06
224.	Laborers: textile mill	2.13	2.17	1.88	1.00	0.41	0.59	0.77	0.40	0.49
225.	Laborers: apparel, accessories, and fabricated textiles	3.69	3.47	3.25	2.31	1.69	1.84	1.88	1.45	1.14
226.	Laborers: pulp, paper, and paperboard products	1.09	0.92	0.84	0.26	-0.32	-0.43	-0.30	-0.28	-0.08
227.	Laborers: printing, publishing, and allied industries	2.52	2.19	1.59	0.72	0.11	0.37	0.57	0.59	0.61
228.	Laborers: chemicals and allied products	0.53	0.31	0.22	-0.30	-0.78	-1.09	-0.52	-0.30	-0.04
229.	Laborers: petroleum refining and products	-2.02	-1.59	-2.01	-2.28	-2.23	-2.28	-2.04	-1.40	-1.19
230.	Laborers: rubber and plastic products	1.40	0.98	1.40	0.87	0.38	0.34	0.19	0.00	0.23

(continued)

APPENDIX TABLE A5.1
(*continued*)

Category and Component Detailed Occupations	1910	1920	1930	1940	1950	1960	1970	1980	1990
231. Laborers: not specified manufacturing	1.30	1.35	1.38	0.57	0.22	0.11	0.08	0.23	0.32
232. Laborers: construction, including carpenters' helpers	−4.29	−3.60	−4.81	−2.30	−2.59	−2.71	−2.24	−2.15	−2.13
233. Laborers: transportation, communication, and utilities	−1.50	−0.98	−1.64	−2.22	−1.61	−1.88	−1.62	−1.41	−1.12
234. Laborers: wholesale and retail trade	0.03	0.43	0.24	−0.54	−0.61	−0.98	−0.26	−0.28	−0.20
235. Laborers: business and repair services	−2.66	−2.60	−2.53	−0.39	−0.88	−0.81	−0.52	−0.62	−0.55
236. Laborers: public administration	−0.61	−0.60	−1.27	−1.85	−1.29	−1.33	−0.44	−0.60	−0.35
237. Laborers: all other industries	0.27	0.49	0.08	−0.80	−0.41	−0.08	0.39	−0.18	−0.10

NOTE: Positive values indicate female overrepresentation; negative values indicate male overrepresentation.

Aggregate Classification Scheme and Saturated Scale Values
for the United States, 1970–2000 (21 Occupations)

Major Category and Component Occupations	1970	1980	1990	2000
Managerial				
1. Management occupations	−0.47	−0.13	0.15	0.09
2. Farmers and farm managers	−1.81	−1.39	−1.17	−1.21
3. Business and financial operations occupations	−0.04	0.42	0.80	0.76
Professional				
4. Computer and mathematical occupations	−0.25	−0.10	−0.03	−0.22
5. Architects, engineers, and scientists	−1.38	−0.91	−0.74	−0.64
6. Community, social services, and legal occupations	0.25	0.36	0.51	0.77
7. Education, training, and library occupations	1.79	1.55	1.52	1.59
8. Arts, design, entertainment, sports and media occupations	0.38	0.50	0.54	0.52
9. Healthcare practitioner and technical occupations	1.83	1.71	1.64	1.59
Service				
10. Healthcare support occupations	3.09	2.82	2.56	2.62
11. Protective service occupations	−1.52	−1.19	−1.03	−0.79
12. Food preparation, building, grounds maintenance occupations	1.34	1.01	0.73	0.59
13. Personal care and service occupations	2.57	2.27	2.25	1.87
14. Sales	0.78	0.77	0.60	0.55
15. Clerical (office and administrative support)	2.15	2.03	1.85	1.67
16. Farming, forestry, and fishing	−0.78	−0.65	−0.91	−0.72
Construction and repair				
17. Construction trades occupations	−3.01	−2.92	−2.82	−2.87
18. Extraction occupations	−1.81	−2.79	−2.93	−2.63
19. Installation, maintenance, and repair occupations	−2.56	−2.53	−2.46	−2.34
Production and transportation				
20. Production occupations	0.36	0.12	−0.02	−0.14
21. Transportation and material moving occupations	−0.91	−0.97	−1.05	−1.06

NOTE: Positive values indicate female overrepresentation; negative values indicate male overrepresentation.

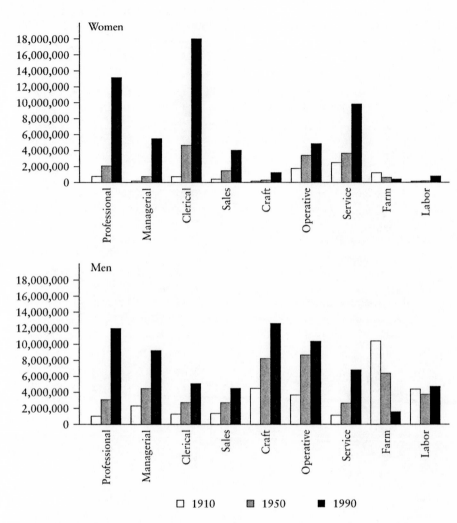

Appendix Figure A5.1 Absolute Occupational Distributions of Men and Women in the United States, 1910, 1950, and 1990

CHAPTER SIX

Gender and Age in the Japanese Labor Market, 1950–1995

Maria Charles, University of California, San Diego; Mariko Chang, Harvard University; and Joon Han, Yonsei University

With regard to gender equity in employment, Japan is commonly regarded as a laggard. Some scholars have therefore been surprised by cross-national comparisons of summary sex-segregation indices, which have placed Japan, at worst, near the center of the international distribution (see, e.g., Roos 1985; Charles 1992; Jacobs and Lim 1992; Brinton and Ngo 1993; Shirahase and Ishida 1994; see also Chapter 3, this volume). This seemingly counter-intuitive finding has been attributed to distinctive features of Japan's sex-segregation profile, especially its relatively integrated clerical and manufacturing work forces.

In this chapter we examine the evolution of Japan's distinctive pattern of sex segregation between 1950 and 1995, and we explore how specific macro-level structures and micro-level processes may have contributed to the development of the Japanese sex-segregation regime. In particular, we consider the influence of specific organizational and institutional features, including rigid divisions of household labor, strongly age-graded employment structures, and lifetime employment practices. We suggest that these factors may have worked to moderate the segregative impact of postindustrial economic restructuring and to promote feminization of some unskilled manual occupations.

This chapter includes a first-ever analysis of trends in occupational sex segregation by age cohort. Although the relationship between age and occupational gender distributions in Japan has been examined by some researchers (Brinton and Ngo 1993; Shirahase and Ishida 1994), very little is known

179

about *trends* in this relationship. As is discussed in the following section, many general models of change in sex segregation suggest age-specific dynamics. By bringing age explicitly into the analysis, we may be able to gain some insights into the causal mechanisms underlying change in Japanese sex segregation.

Japan is an especially interesting case for analyzing aggregate-level cohort effects because of the strong age dependence that has historically characterized individual work and family biographies there. Most notably, the appropriate timing of school, work, and family transitions are subject to strong normative pressures in Japan. Nearly all Japanese men and women marry, and do so between the ages of 20 and 30. Births are strongly concentrated between the ages of 25 and 29 (Coleman 1983; Brinton 1993, figure 2.4; Lee and Hirata 2001). Female employment rates depend heavily on age and have followed an M-shaped curve in urban areas throughout the postwar period (see, e.g., Brinton 2001). Age is a central determinant of workplace mobility as well: firm-internal labor markets are important in large Japanese firms, and strict rules of seniority govern promotion decisions (Kumazawa 1996). Strong age dependence of familial and labor market transitions means that any cultural, social, or economic shifts are likely to have clear age-specific manifestations.[1]

CATALYSTS FOR CHANGE IN
JAPANESE SEX SEGREGATION

In Japan, as in the United States, historical trends in sex segregation have been shaped by global processes of change, as well as by social and economic developments at the national level. Table 6.1 shows some occupation- and age-specific relationships that can be derived from the sociological literature. Specifically, we consider the possible influence of three macro-level processes on historical trends in sex segregation: changes in Japanese employment practices, postindustrial economic restructuring, and the rise and diffusion of gender-egalitarian cultural principles. These three factors are discussed in detail in the following sections.

Changing Employment Practices

Japanese employment practices have undergone several significant transformations since World War II (see Kumazawa 1996 for an excellent review).

TABLE 6.1
Pressures for Change in Japanese Sex Segregation, 1950–1995

	IMPLIED TREND IN FEMALE REPRESENTATION			
	Occupations[a]	*Direction*[b]	*Timing*	*Ages*
1. Partial Breakdown of Permanent-Employment System	Clerical/ manufacturing	+	Post-1970	Reentering
2. Postindustrial Economic Restructuring	Nonmanual, especially sales/ service/clerical	+	Continuous	Reentering
3. Rise of Gender-Egalitarian Cultural Norms				
a. Global variant	All	+/−	Continuous	All
b. Elite variant	Professional/ manager	+	Post-1960	All
c. Family-based variant	All	+/−	Post-1980	Child-rearing

[a]Based on Japanese major-group categories; see occupational classification in Appendix Table A6.1.

[b]+/− denotes increasing female representation in occupations with a disproportionate share of men, and decreasing female representation in occupations with a disproportionate share of women.

Most important to the development of occupational sex segregation is the weakening commitment to lifetime employment since the economic slow-down of the early 1970s. As indicated in Table 6.1, the literature suggests that this development has increased the representation of older women in clerical and manufacturing occupations in Japan.

The Japanese "permanent employment" system was in its heyday during the economic boom of the 1950s and early 1960s, when large firms sought to recruit and retain qualified workers by offering security of employment and possibilities for firm-internal career advancement. In this employment model, male college graduates start out alongside unmarried women in low-level clerical ("administrative support") positions and are then trained for management through a series of firm-internal promotions.[2] Men with man-agement aspirations are expected to work very long hours, often at the expense of their health and personal lives; women face strong social pressure to exit the labor force upon marriage (Kiyoko 1995; Ogasawara 1998).

Employers' commitment to lifetime employment began to wane in the early 1970s, when slow economic growth and an aging workforce began to inflate wage bills unsustainably. Following the oil shock and recession, large employers sought to increase flexibility through increased reliance on contingent workers. By the mid-1970s, older women—often with grown or school-aged children—had become a significant labor pool for temporary and part-time work, especially for low-level clerical jobs. In addition, employers in manufacturing firms attempted to reduce labor costs and increase flexibility by stepping up recruitment of older female reentrants for home-based piecework (McLendon 1983; Sakuma 1988; Brinton 1993). This suggests growing female representation among older clerical and manufacturing workers in the post-1970 period, with acceleration in the 1990s as a new period of slow (or negative) economic growth commenced.

Economic Restructuring

As discussed in Chapter 1, the Western literature on gender stratification links postindustrial structural shifts (that is, economic rationalization and service-sector expansion) to increasing labor force participation of wives and mothers and to feminization of nonmanual occupations, especially lower- and mid-level ones. Postindustrial economic restructuring commenced later in Japan than in most Western economies, and the proportion of the Japanese work force that works in the manufacturing industry and in the informal sector (in self-employment and family enterprises) is still relatively large. Nonetheless, substantial expansions of the salaried class and the service sector are evident in the postwar period. The share of the labor force that is self-employed or family workers dropped from 61 to 24 percent between 1950 and 1993, and the share working in the service sector (defined as commerce, transportation, communication, finance, and service industries) increased steadily from 30 to 60 percent during the same period (ILO 1990, 1995; see also Shimada and Higuchi 1985).[3] According to the "postindustrialism" thesis, represented in Table 6.1, these structural shifts increase female representation among nonmanual workers, especially in sales, service, and clerical occupations (see Chapter 1 for details).

This effect is predicated in part on pronounced growth in the employment of wives and mothers; that is, employers must successfully recruit older, nonemployed women into the paid labor force and into the nonmanual sector. Structural and cultural incompatibilities between work and family roles in Japanese society may thus be expected to weaken any demand-driven expansion of the female labor force (see, e.g., Buchmann and Charles 1995; Brinton 2001).

Growing Gender Egalitarianism

The emergence and global diffusion of legal and popular mandates for gender equality has also been widely discussed in connection with trends in American and European sex segregation. To what extent might we expect ideologically driven shifts in Japan? On one hand, there is little question that the sexual division of labor remains deeply entrenched in Japanese culture and society. McLendon once described the Japanese ideal of a desirable marriage as "a strong husband who guides and takes care of his wife, [and a wife] who supports her husband and is obedient" (1986: 161). Japanese women still feel intense normative pressure to quit their paid jobs upon marriage or childbirth, and parents' educational aspirations and educational investments are accordingly lower for daughters than for sons (Brinton 1993; Lee and Hirata 2001).[4]

On the other hand, there are some indications that Western-style debates about women's roles and general trends toward greater gender equality have played out in Japan as well. The gender gap in educational attainment has shrunk in recent decades (Ishida 1998), as it has throughout the industrialized world.[5] International and domestic pressures have also led to some legal concessions at the national level (Kumazawa 1996). During the 1960s and 1970s, Japanese women filed some successful lawsuits protesting forced retirement upon marriage and discrimination in wage and layoff policies (Upham 1987). In 1980 the Japanese government ratified the United Nations Convention on the Elimination of All Forms of Discrimination against Women, and in 1985 it passed a national Equal Employment Opportunity (EEO) law. In its original formulation, the EEO legislation was designed to encourage, rather than require, employers to refrain from gender discrimination (Kiyoko 1995). Amendments passed in 1998 that took effect in 1999 strengthened the law by including prohibitions against sex discrimination in hiring and in assignment to promotion tracks. Although the law lacked any real enforcement mechanisms during the period considered here, the passage of any equal protection law suggests at least symbolic commitment to gender-egalitarian principles at the state level. Even symbolic gestures may influence the behavior of firms and the aspirations of young women (see Lam 1992; Kumazawa 1996; Strober and Chan 1999 on the legal context of female employment in Japan).

Table 6.1 shows three ways in which normative pressures for gender equality may be manifested. The first involves uniformly integrative trends across all occupations and age cohorts (that is, increasing female representation in "male" occupations, decreasing female representation in "female" occupations), and the second and third involve occupation- and age-specific effects, respectively. Arguments underlying each of these empirical predictions are described below. While we cannot definitively adjudicate among these arguments, we can assess their consistency with observed Japanese trends.

The "global" variant of the gender-egalitarianism thesis (line 3a) is the conceptual model that underlies much contemporary American gender-stratification research (see Chapter 1). This model can be derived from modernization theories, which posit increasingly meritocratic hiring practices and decreasing attention to ascriptive traits, including gender, as industrialization advances (Kerr et al. 1960; Goode 1963; Parsons 1970; see also Jackson 1998). Neoinstitutionalist analysts provide a more culture-centered model, but also suggest a generalized process of gender equalization (e.g., Ramirez 1987; Berkovitch 1999). By either account, we would expect a continuous, marketwide trend toward occupational integration in Japan's rapidly modernizing postwar economy. In other words, women's presence should increase in male-dominated occupations and decrease in female-dominated occupations.

A second model of egalitarianism posits uneven (instead of across-the-board) trends, with integrative pressures most directly manifested in the elite professional and managerial occupations. By this argument (Table 6.1, line 3b), international and domestic equal-opportunity advocates focus on elite academic and managerial positions owing to their high levels of pay, prestige, and autonomy, their intrinsic rewards, and their relatively meritocratic occupational cultures. Furthermore, given the national and international visibility of these positions, conformity to equal-opportunity laws and to globally emergent norms of gender equality are likely to be closely scrutinized (see Brinton and Kariya 1998 for a similar argument). In the parlance of Chapters 1 and 4, universalism would thus be said to reduce "vertical" sex segregation within the nonmanual sector, but not "horizontal" segregation (that is, segregation across the manual-nonmanual divide). This process should be evident by the 1960s, when gender equality was established as an international policy objective and when feminist movements and discourse had emerged in even the most traditional of national contexts (see Upham 1987; Kumazawa 1996, chapter 7 on Japan; see Pietilä and Vickers 1990; K. Bradley and Ramirez 1996; Bradley and Charles 2003 on the global context).

Egalitarianism may also be manifested as age-specific trends—reflecting a weakening of the sexual division of labor in the family (line 3c). Neoclassical economic theory holds that women choose female-typed occupations because these are more compatible with childrearing obligations and because the requisite skills are portable and do not deteriorate during lengthy labor force withdrawals (Polachek 1981; Becker 1991; Estévez-Abe, Iversen, and Soskice 2003). To the extent that the diffusion of universalistic cultural principles undermines gender distinctions in the family, these arguments suggest increasing labor force attachment of young mothers, and a convergence of male and female occupational distributions within the corresponding age range. This shift would require not only declining gender discrimination in the labor market, but also fundamental attitudinal and behavioral shifts in the private sphere. The latter are likely to occur only through cohort replacement. Any family-based egalitarian trends will therefore appear relatively late (after 1980, for example, when the first "postfeminism" cohort of men and women reached childrearing age in Japan).[6]

DATA AND METHODS

We examine these accounts with data drawn from population censuses conducted by the Japanese Bureau of Statistics between 1950 and 1995 at five-year intervals. These data are weighted to reflect actual sample sizes. Occupation-by-sex tables for the years 1975 through 1995 were taken from the respective census reports (Japanese Bureau of Statistics 1976, 1982, 1986, 1994, 1998). For the period between 1950 and 1970, we relied upon a government compilation of occupational data that were extracted from the 1930 through 1970 censuses and standardized to the 1970 occupational classification (Japanese Bureau of Statistics 1974). Because of comparability problems, we decided against using pre-1950 data.[7]

For the age-specific analyses, breakdowns of occupation by sex and five-year age group were taken from the 1970 through 1995 census reports. (Cross-classifications by age and sex were not available before 1970.) In order to consistently exclude individuals who had reached retirement age, we limited the age-specific analyses to economically active persons between the ages of 20 and 49.[8] Analyses thus cover trends in the occupational distributions of six five-year age groups: 20–24, 25–29, 30–34, 35–39, 40–44, and 45–49. Pooled analyses include workers of all ages.[9] The Japanese Bureau of Statistics defines the economically active population as those engaged in any work for wages, salaries, or profits during the survey week (including part-time work and home handicraft), those working without pay on a family-managed farm or in a family-run business during the survey week, and those temporarily absent from their jobs (Japanese Bureau of Statistics 1998).

A historically uniform set of occupational categories was created by mapping 1975 through 1995 data onto the 1970 Japanese occupational classification. Some 1970 categories were subsequently collapsed into related categories to reduce the number of zero cells in the age-specific data matrix.[10] The resultant classification consists of 141 detailed occupations, which fall into the following nine major-group categories: (1) professional and technical workers, (2) managers and officials, (3) clerical workers, (4) sales workers, (5) agricultural workers, (6) workers in transport and communications, (7) craft and manufacturing workers, (8) protective service workers, and (9) service workers (see Appendix Table A6.1 for a list of the detailed occupations constituting these categories).

As in the previous chapter, trends in overall levels of sex segregation are assessed at the detailed occupational level by computing three summary indices, A, D, and D_s (defined in Chapter 2). We then examine changes in the pattern of sex segregation across our nine aggregated occupational categories by presenting a series of saturated "multilevel" models (equation 2.13), one for each time point. These analyses are carried out first for the labor force as a whole, and then for each of our six age cohorts separately. In addition, we explore trends in sex segregation across detailed occupational categories by computing a simple saturated model (equation 2.10) for each time point using the pooled sample.

TRENDS IN THE LEVEL OF SEX SEGREGATION

Panel A of Table 6.2 shows 1950–95 trends in the overall level of occupational sex segregation across the 141 occupations. Values are presented for the A, D, and D_s indices. The last column of Table 6.2 gives women's share of the labor force. Historical trends in the three segregation indices are graphed in Figure 6.1.

We begin by noting that, consistent with findings from earlier research on Japan, women's share of the labor force fell between 1970 and 1975. This may be attributed to contraction of the agricultural sector and declining overall rates of self- and family employment at early stages of Japanese industrialization. The reduction in female employment between 1970 and

TABLE 6.2
Trends in Occupational Sex Segregation in Japan,
by Age (141 Occupations)

Year	Association Index (A)	Dissimilarity Index (D)	Size-Standardized Index (D_s)	Labor Force % Female
A. All Ages				
1950	6.98	40.52	51.89	38.61
1955	7.82	41.15	50.95	39.14
1960	6.23	42.77	49.93	39.15
1965	6.11	43.11	48.93	39.05
1970	5.55	45.84	46.76	39.13
1975	5.37	46.62	46.41	37.00
1980	5.07	48.23	45.93	37.90
1985	5.00	48.34	45.94	38.84
1990	4.49	48.94	44.86	39.61
1995	4.31	50.06	44.44	39.91
B. Age Groups				
Age 20–24				
1970	6.96	55.28	51.55	45.82
1975	7.27	57.98	51.82	45.32
1980	6.72	60.39	51.44	48.39
1985	6.52	59.56	51.40	48.27
1990	5.42	57.71	47.74	49.50
1995	4.95	56.95	48.29	48.65

(*continued*)

TABLE 6.2
(*continued*)

Year	Association Index (A)	Dissimilarity Index (D)	Size-Standardized Index (D_s)	Labor Force % Female
Age 25–29				
1970	6.20	51.02	49.25	31.46
1975	6.38	51.81	49.80	30.10
1980	5.74	53.02	48.91	33.22
1985	6.24	54.45	49.75	34.75
1990	4.98	53.91	46.46	37.93
1995	4.80	55.57	45.79	39.94
Age 30–34				
1970	6.07	51.67	49.26	32.21
1975	6.16	50.82	49.72	30.15
1980	5.66	51.03	48.36	32.00
1985	5.81	51.77	49.08	32.96
1990	5.21	51.03	47.29	33.46
1995	4.83	51.58	45.99	34.42
Age 35–39				
1970	5.81	50.57	47.91	36.11
1975	5.69	49.37	48.61	34.81
1980	5.64	51.75	48.75	36.11
1985	5.76	52.41	49.40	36.77
1990	5.14	51.25	48.49	37.48
1995	4.92	51.76	46.79	37.18
Age 40–44				
1970	5.83	49.25	46.97	39.27
1975	5.56	48.84	47.93	37.57
1980	5.40	50.96	47.25	38.78
1985	5.77	52.37	48.96	40.23
1990	5.14	52.52	47.79	40.36
1995	4.91	52.86	47.71	40.64
Age 45–49				
1970	5.94	48.19	46.65	44.13
1975	5.68	48.46	46.86	39.03
1980	5.26	49.84	46.12	39.10
1985	5.66	51.14	48.18	40.55
1990	5.05	53.18	47.44	41.50
1995	5.08	54.46	47.59	41.46

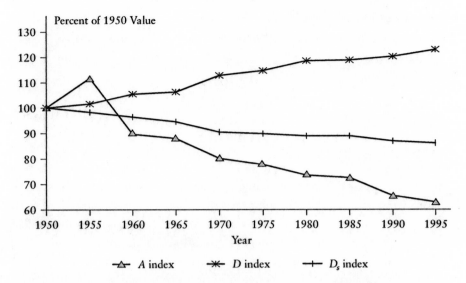

Figure 6.1   Indices of Occupational Sex Segregation, Japan 1950–1995

1975 may also reflect widespread layoffs of "noncore" workers during the recession and oil crisis. Since 1975 the size of the female labor force has grown steadily in Japan.[11] As in the West, this trend has coincided with a variety of supply- and demand-side changes, including service-sector expansion, falling fertility rates, and growing educational opportunities.

Trends in A suggest growing sex segregation between 1950 and 1955, but a steady decline since 1955, with the most pronounced declines occurring from 1955 to 1960 and from 1985 to 1995. In 1995, women or men are overrepresented by a factor of 4.31 in the average occupation, compared with a factor of 6.98 in 1950.

Also noteworthy in Figure 6.1 are the divergent trends implied by the different segregation indices. While both A and D_s show downward tendencies (since 1955 for A, since 1950 for D_s), the dissimilarity index (D) *increases* steadily from 1950 to 1990. According to D, about 50 percent of Japanese women (or men) would have had to be removed from the labor force in 1995 to arrive at a gender-neutral distribution; the corresponding figure was about 41 percent in 1950. The segregative trend suggested by D reflects its sensitivity to historical shifts in the occupational structure: contraction of the relatively integrated agricultural sector, and corresponding

increases in the sizes of the more sex-segregated service and managerial occupations, underlie this upward trend. The divergence between A and D_s, although less substantial, reflects in part the sensitivity of D_s to the gender
margin.[12]

OCCUPATIONAL PROFILES OF SEX SEGREGATION

As we have repeatedly suggested, summary segregation-index scores conceal
occupation-specific trends. Figure 6.2 shows trends in female representation
in the nine major occupational categories, measured at five-year intervals between 1950 and 1995. As in the previous chapter, census years are ordered
along the horizontal axis, and the vertical axis represents scale values taken
from our saturated multilevel model (equation 2.13), which allows us to
chart major-category trends net of compositional shifts at the level of the 141
detailed occupations. Values above zero indicate female overrepresentation
(relative to the average occupation); values below zero indicate female underrepresentation. A flat line is thus indicative of stability in occupational gender ratios, a downward-sloping line indicates declining female representation, and an upward-sloping line indicates increasing female representation.

In addition, we present in Appendix Table A6.1 scale values for each of
the 141 detailed occupations. These values are taken from a series of simple
saturated models, one for each time point. Again, positive values indicate an
overrepresentation of women; negative values indicate female underrepresentation. The exponents of these values give the factor by which women
are under- or overrepresented in the respective occupation. These detailed-
category scale values are useful for interpreting the trends shown in Figure 6.2.

Throughout the period under investigation, Japanese patterns of sex
segregation show important similarities to the generic international profile
presented in Chapter 3 (Figure 3.1). Horizontal segregation is manifested in
women's overrepresentation in nonmanual occupations (save management),
and vertical segregation of nonmanual occupations is manifested in men's
strong domination of managerial work, and in the strongly negative scale
values shown in Appendix Table A6.1 for the most elite professional occupations (scientific researchers, engineers and technicians, physicians, judicial
workers, and university professors, for example). Service occupations are the

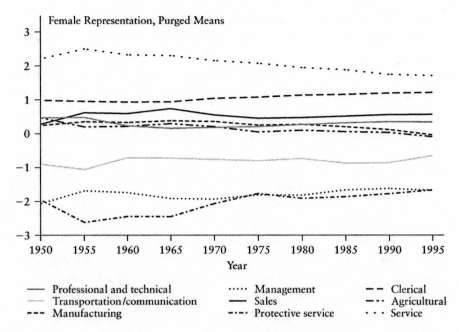

Figure 6.2   Trends in Japanese Sex Segregation by Major Occupational Group

most heavily female-dominated, with women overrepresented by a factor of more than 5 to 1 over the entire period.[13]

But, in contrast to patterns found in the West, women were *over-represented* in manufacturing occupations during most of the postwar period in Japan (between 1950 and 1990).[14] This particularity may be partly attributable to firms' historical reliance on noncareer factory employees and low-wage contract workers ("pieceworkers") for routine production labor (Brinton 1993; Kumazawa 1996). Also somewhat unusual from a Western perspective is the relative integration of sales work in Japan. Although scale values for the aggregate sales category are consistently above zero, such work has historically not been as overwhelmingly female in Japan as in the United States and many European countries. This can be attributed to the persistence of self-employment and family-run enterprise in Japan, especially in small wholesale and retail sales establishments (Brinton 1993; Cheng 1997).[15] Moreover, firm-internal job rotations for (predominantly male) career employees may include stints in sales departments of large firms (Brinton 1993).

Regarding historical trends, Figure 6.2 shows convergence in the trend lines since 1955, which is consistent with the downward historical trajectory of *A* shown in Figure 6.1. In particular, we see integration of "female" service and "male" managerial and protective service occupations since 1955. The detailed scale values shown in Appendix Table A6.1 suggest that the gender-integration of protective services is supported by trends in all detailed occupations, especially police and firefighters. Occupation-specific trends within the service category vary across occupations, however, and many are strongly nonlinear. Some of the most substantial integrative shifts between 1950 and 1995 are found for restaurant waiters, hotel workers, and caretakers.

Particularly noteworthy is the finding that female representation in professional occupations increased between 1965 and 1990, and women's representation in management increased between 1970 and 1990, albeit modestly in both cases. This development is consistent with trends observed in the United States (see Chapter 5) and elsewhere during the same time period. Contributing to the professional-category trend are strong increases in female representation among engineers and technicians, judicial workers and accountants, authors, and artists since 1970.[16] Changes in the major managerial category reflect a growing female presence among company directors and among other types of managers and government officials. Female inroads into the professions and management show no signs of acceleration in the wake of the 1985 EEO legislation. Indeed, trends are virtually flat for these two categories after 1990. We consider more recent developments further on.

Consistent with structuralist arguments, which posit increasing female representation in nonmanual occupations in postindustrial economies, results suggest steady feminization of clerical occupations since 1960, and of sales occupations since 1975. As noted, female representation in the professions and management increased during this time as well, although modest reversals of this trend are in both cases evident between 1990 and 1995. Although trends within detailed occupational categories are neither uniform nor monotonic, women's presence did grow significantly in many specific nonmanual occupations (including pharmacist, author, director, key puncher, accounting clerk, retail sales). As in the United States, we find *decreasing* scale values in the major service category after 1955, suggesting that a "female saturation point" may have been reached in many of these occupations. We consider these results in greater detail as we examine results of the age-specific models.

AGE-SPECIFIC TRENDS

Panel B of Table 6.2 shows trends between 1970 and 1995 in summary sex-segregation indices and in rates of female labor force participation, broken down by age cohort.

The A and D indices again follow distinct historical trajectories, with D increasing (nonlinearly) for most age groups between 1970 and 1995 and A declining gradually. Although overall levels of sex segregation have generally been higher among younger than older workers during this period, age-specific dispersion in sex-segregation scores has decreased over time, with steeper declines in A among younger than older cohorts.[17]

Consistent with past research, we find that age-specific levels of female employment have followed an M-shaped profile throughout this period, with greatest participation among women in their early twenties and the lowest participation among those in their prime childbearing and childrear-ing years (ages 25–40). This pattern is indicative of the strong structural and cultural incompatibility of work and maternal roles in Japan, in particular the weak public- and private-sector provisions for child care, strong norms of intensive mothering, long and inflexible work hours, and long commute times (see, e.g., Kumazawa 1996; Brinton 2001; Hirao 2001).

Female labor force participation decreased for all age groups between 1970 and 1975, but has risen across the board since 1975. Particularly large increases are evident between 1985 and 1995 for women aged 25 to 29. This age-specific trend may be due to increasing employment of young wives and mothers, delays in family formation, or both.

Occupation-specific trends in sex segregation are again examined based on scale values from a series of multilevel models. Results are shown in Figure 6.3, where each line pertains to an age group and each panel shows trends in female representation for one major occupational category (again net of lower-level compositional effects). To aid in the interpretation of these figures, men's and women's absolute occupational distributions for 1970 and 1995 are graphed in Appendix Figure A6.1.

Results confirm the strong age-dependence of Japanese gender distribu-tions. For each occupational category, our estimates of female representation

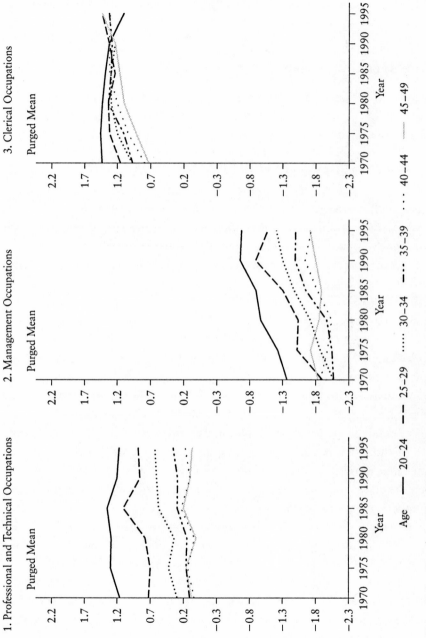

Figure 6.3   Trends in Female Representation in Japan, by Age

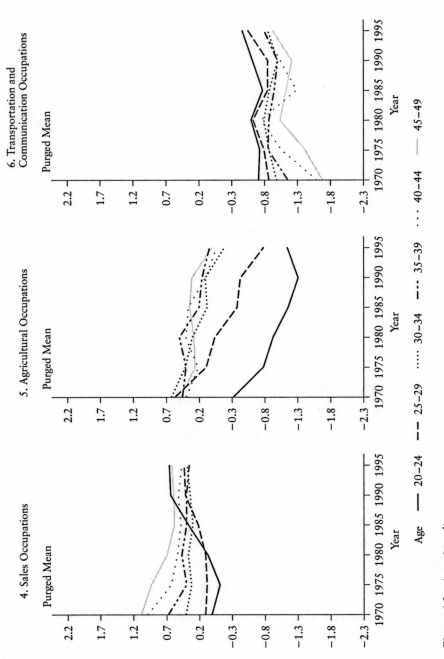

Figure 6.3 (continued)

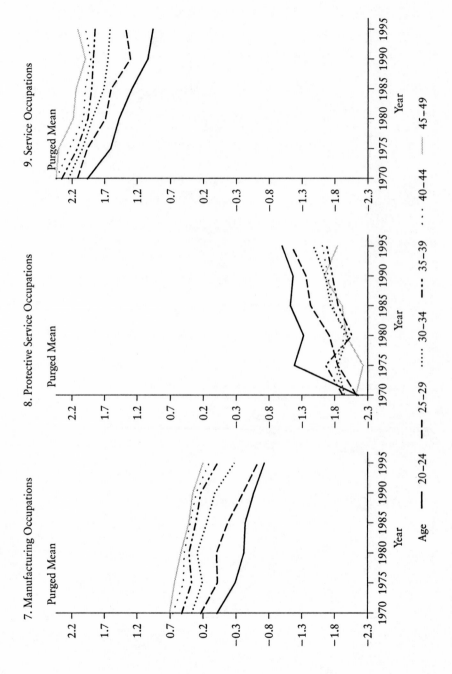

Figure 6.3 (continued)

(the "purged scale values") vary widely across age groups. Generally speaking, scale values for professional, managerial, transportation/communication, and protective services workers are higher for *younger* than for older workers, and scale values for sales, agricultural, manufacturing, and service workers are higher for *older* workers. Within the professional category in 1995, for example, female representation was nearly three times greater for the youngest than for the oldest cohort.[18] This is consistent with previous research suggesting strong pressure for even highly educated women to exit the labor market with marriage or the birth of a first child (see Hirao 2001 for a review of this literature). In contrast, women's representation in both service and manufacturing occupations was approximately three times stronger for the *oldest* than for the youngest cohort in 1995, a pattern of age-dependence that may reflect the unique organization of some manufacturing and service occupations in Japan, in particular the heavy reliance on married family workers and informal pieceworkers in service and manufacturing industries. The positive age-dependence of female agricultural representation no doubt reflects the gradual replacement of small family-run farms by larger agricultural enterprises (which are less likely to engage women).

How have age-specific occupational gender distributions evolved over time?

Turning first to the professional occupations, we can see that female representation increased modestly for four of our six age cohorts. Change between 1970 and 1995 was most pronounced for workers in their thirties, with female representation increasing by a factor of 1.34 for the cohort aged 30 to 34, and by a factor of 1.42 for the cohort aged 35 to 39.[19] Among workers in their early twenties and late forties, however, scale values show virtually no change between 1970 and 1995, despite substantial increases in the absolute numbers of professional women in those age groups (see Appendix Figure A6.1). This stability reflects, among other things, growing female representation among workers aged 20 to 25 in sales occupations, and growing female representation among workers aged 45 to 49 in clerical occupations.[20] In addition, it should be noted that women who pursue elite professional credentials may not enter the labor force until their mid-twenties (and their occupational outcomes are therefore not reflected in the trend line for workers aged 20 to 24).[21] Again we find no evidence of a post-1985 "EEO effect."

Since the "professional" group defined by the Japanese Census Bureau includes both professions (medical doctor and university professor, for example) and semiprofessions (nurse, primary school teacher),[22] trends in the (less heterogeneous) managerial category may provide a better gauge of change in women's access to elite, traditionally male-dominated positions. These are shown in the second panel of Figure 6.3. The general upward trajectory of these lines is far more striking than for the professions. While the absolute number of women in management remains very small (Appendix Figure A6.1), all cohorts show stronger female representation in 1995 than in 1970. The trend has been most pronounced among young workers, especially those aged 25–35.[23]

As in Figure 6.2, however, a general flattening (and for some cohorts, a pronounced downward bend) can be seen in the professional and managerial trend lines after 1990 (Figure 6.3, panels 1 and 2). We attribute this unexpected result to Japan's most recent economic slowdown, which commenced in the early 1990s as unemployment began to climb and growth slowed. We suspect that some Japanese employers excluded women from full-time positions and from internal labor markets during the 1990s in order to reserve "core" jobs for men (see Brinton 2001).[24]

As can be seen in the third panel of Figure 6.3, women's presence in clerical work has increased since 1970 for all but the youngest age cohort. Among workers aged 20–24, female clerical representation was initially very high, but it has declined significantly over time.[25] Slopes differ significantly by age, with the most pronounced upward trend evident among workers in their forties. Consistent with both the first and second hypotheses in Table 6.1, results suggest that employers have been relying increasingly upon reentering wives and mothers (that is, women in their forties) to fill entry-level clerical positions.[26] Many of these positions are likely temporary, part-time, or both.

The gender composition of sales occupations also shows decreasing age dependence. In 1970 and 1975 female representation in the sales category was considerably weaker among younger than among older workers. After 1975 it increased dramatically among workers aged 20 to 29, and by 1995 it was strongest among workers in their early twenties (see Figure 6.3, panel 4). Although the *overall* upward trend is consistent with the postindustrialism thesis, age-specific results indicate that this increasing feminization is not achieved through increased representation of older, "reentering" women. As small family-run enterprises are replaced by large retail organizations, younger women may be filling many of the restructured sales jobs in Japan. Moreover, the absolute occupational distributions shown in Appendix Figure A6.1 suggest that *men* have been absorbing much of the growth in the Japanese sales category since 1970.

Female representation in service occupations decreased for all age groups between 1970 and 1995 (see panel 9). This is consistent with the overall trend line shown in Figure 6.2 and is attributable, we believe, to growing opportunities in other nonmanual occupations. In contrast to trends in the sales and clerical occupations, we find *increasing* age-dependence in this category, with the steepest declines among younger workers, who showed the lowest scale values in 1970.[27] Growing age dispersion is also found for the agricultural and manufacturing occupations (panels 5 and 7), where female representation has been falling for all age groups, but most steeply among workers in their twenties. The more pronounced declines among young women in these categories may be attributable to growing opportunities for single (childless) women in more desirable white-collar occupations.

Trends in the "transportation and communications" category vary by age and are very uneven. For most age groups, however, we see a tendency for increasing female representation after 1985, as suggested by the overall trends presented earlier.

How do the results of these analyses square with the hypotheses presented in Table 6.1?

Consistent with the first hypothesis, we find that among workers in their forties, female representation in clerical occupations has grown steadily since 1970. Although the *relative* representation of older (reentering) women has not increased among manufacturing workers, we do note that their absolute numerical presence in this major category has increased substantially (see Appendix Figure A6.1). As suggested in the first line of Table 6.1, these trends may be partly attributable to the partial breakdown of the permanent employment system and the replacement of permanent with temporary and part-time positions. Kumazawa suggests that increasing reliance on middle-aged housewives (working part-time) reflects efforts by managers to find people "willing to perform dull work uncomplainingly" (1996, p. 177).

Overall increases in female representation in most nonmanual occupations since the 1970s are consistent with the "postindustrialism" thesis (Table 6.1, item 2), but age-specific trends provide mixed support. As predicted, female representation in clerical occupations has increased most markedly among workers aged 40 to 49.[28] In the sales category, however, it is women in their twenties, and not older reentrants, who have shown the steepest increases. In addition, absolute occupational distributions (shown in Appendix Figure A6.1) suggest that *men* are relatively well represented among sales employees in Japan.

In service occupations, we in fact find *downward* trends since 1955, as was the case in the United States (Chapter 4). As opportunities for women grew elsewhere in the nonmanual sector, women's relative representation in strongly feminized service occupations could almost only decline.[29]

Overall, then, we find only partial support for the postindustrialism thesis in the Japanese context. We attribute the observed inconsistencies to the relatively low rates of formal employment among Japanese wives and mothers, heavy reliance on firm-internal promotion into management, and a tradition of drawing upon female reentrants for manufacturing work. Structural models of occupational sex segregation are predicated in part upon increased labor force participation among older women (Oppenheimer 1970), and such growth has been relatively modest in Japan. Moreover, the manufacturing sector, which remains large, absorbs a large number of relatively unskilled reentrants, further reducing the supply of women available for routine sales and service jobs.

Evidence consistent with the operation of gender-egalitarian cultural pressures can be found in women's increasing professional and managerial representation between 1970 and 1990 (Figure 6.2). Results are most consistent with the "elite" variant of this argument (item 3b). Japanese women's presence is considerably stronger today than in 1970 in all historically male-dominated professional occupations except religious workers, and in public- and private-sector managerial occupations. These trends may reflect practical pressures relating to labor supply and demand, grassroots consciousness-raising activities, efforts by politicians and businessmen to maintain legitimacy in a changing normative environment, or all of the above. Consistent with neoinstitutionalist accounts, Kumazawa accounts for improvements in women's economic opportunities with reference to a "tide of external pressures that swept into Japan beginning in 1975 in the form of calls by the United Nations and the International Labor Organization for the elimination of gender-based discrimination" (1996, p. 187). He suggests, though, that more fundamental change requires stronger commitment to the labor force by women.

The flattening of the professional and managerial trend lines after 1990 was unexpected, and may be indicative of an economically induced backlash. The effect of gender-role ideology on women's occupational opportunities is certainly not a determinate one. Organizational, institutional, and economic factors (including economic cycles) condition the impact of any attitudinal shift on women's labor market role (see also Yu 2001). Studies conducted in a variety of national contexts have suggested that opportunities for women contract in tight labor markets (e.g., Pyle 1990; Reskin and Roos 1990; Charles 2000; Brinton 2001). We suspect that Japanese employers are especially reluctant to hire women for elite positions when these women are competing with unemployed or underemployed men for a shrinking pool of good jobs.

Consistent with the "family-based" version (Table 6.1, line 3c) of the egalitarianism argument, we found that it was women of prime childbearing age (those aged 30 to 39) who made some of the most significant gains in professional occupations between 1970 and 1995. Further study, at the individual level of analysis, is necessary in order to determine whether this trend reflects increased compatibility between career and family roles or simply declining fertility rates among women with professional aspirations. Meanwhile, though, two findings cast doubt on the notion that democratization of the Japanese family has been an important catalyst for gender integration of the labor market. First, female representation in professional and managerial occupations remains considerably lower for women who have reached the normative age of marriage and childbearing than for women in their early twenties. And second, rates of labor force participation have remained relatively low among women in their thirties.

Finally, trends toward increasing feminization of clerical and sales occupations are inconsistent with the "global" variant (Table 6.1, line 3a) of the egalitarianism argument, which posits an across-the-board integration of occupations. This result supports our argument that simple index-based analysis is inadequate in analyzing segregation trends (see Chapter 2).

CONCLUSION

Our results are consistent with those from previous studies, which have attributed Japan's relatively low overall level of sex segregation to strong female representation in unskilled manual work. These findings should again serve to caution researchers and policy makers against treating summary sex-segregation statistics as generic gauges of "women's economic status." Occupation-specific descriptions offer a far more accurate portrait of female labor market opportunities.

The pattern of Japanese sex segregation that we have uncovered exhibits many familiar features. Horizontal segregation has long been evident in Japan, in the form of persistent female overrepresentation in nonmanual (service, associate professional, and to a lesser extent, clerical) occupations. Within the nonmanual sector, vertical segregation is evident in men's ongoing dominance of management and the elite professions; within the manual sector, it is evident in the segregation of male craft workers from female production workers in the major "manufacturing" category.

But important Japanese particularities are observed as well, most notably women's strong presence in manufacturing occupations and the relative integration of sales and clerical work during much of this period. We have emphasized a variety of social and economic factors that may have helped generate and maintain these uniquely Japanese patterns. These include the "permanent employment system," the importance of seniority in governing promotions and employee relations, the relative prevalence of self-employment, and persistent normative pressures in families and in many large firms for wives and mothers to give up their jobs.

Our historical analyses revealed modest declines in vertical sex segregation since about 1970. This result is consistent with arguments citing a growing influence of gender-egalitarian norms and institutions in industrial nations. But once again, integrative shifts do not affect all occupations equally, as would be implied by evolutionary accounts. Rather than across-the-board equalization, gender egalitarianism in Japan, as in the United States, takes the form of increasing female representation at the top of the nonmanual hierarchy. Also consistent with results for the United States, horizontal segregation is not abating in Japan. Although Japanese service occupations have become somewhat less female-dominated, the feminization of clerical, sales, and some associate professional occupations has intensified in recent decades. We attribute these trends to the partial breakdown of the Japanese permanent employment system since 1970, to the postindustrial restructuring of the economy (specifically, service-sector expansion and rationalization of the work process), and to the durability of essentialist definitions of female attributes and tasks (see Chapter 1).

Our age-specific analyses do not provide much evidence of fundamental shifts in the division of labor in Japanese families. The pattern of female labor force participation still follows a clear M-shaped profile over the life course, with rates markedly lower among women in prime childbearing and childrearing years. And although female representation in the professions and management has increased among workers in their late twenties and thirties, women who have not yet reached the normative age of family formation are clearly better represented in these occupations.

Persistent normative and structural constraints on maternal employment undoubtedly underlie these age-specific patterns. While such constraints exist in all industrialized nations, they are unusually strong in Japan.

The site of our next historical study, Switzerland, is an equally revealing test case in which the forces for egalitarianism again confront persistent normative and structural constraints on maternal employment.

APPENDIX TABLE A6.1

Japanese Occupational Classification and Results of Saturated Models (141 Occupations)

	1950	1955	1960	1965	1970	1975	1980	1985	1990	1995
1. Professional and Technical Workers										
Scientific researchers	-0.72	-0.86	-1.45	-1.85	-2.00	-1.95	-1.88	-1.52	-1.21	-1.11
Engineers and technicians	-2.91	-4.42	-3.80	-4.10	-3.36	-2.98	-2.89	-2.34	-1.92	-1.97
Physicians	-0.86	-0.90	-1.12	-1.24	-1.36	-1.25	-1.27	-1.27	-1.21	-1.03
Dentists	-0.74	-0.80	-0.82	-1.09	-1.18	-1.10	-1.05	-1.02	-1.07	-0.95
Pharmacists	0.57	0.61	0.70	0.72	0.83	0.97	1.10	1.21	1.29	1.46
Nurses and midwives	7.21	7.10	5.34	4.93	4.71	4.73	4.58	4.37	4.28	4.13
Chiropractors, masseurs, related	0.41	0.42	0.37	0.23	0.25	0.24	0.01	-0.10	-0.24	-0.31
Other medical and public health technicians	1.94	2.14	1.96	2.03	1.77	1.67	1.62	1.65	1.72	1.82
Judicial workers and registered accountants	-2.44	-2.73	-2.53	-2.43	-2.19	-2.03	-1.98	-1.90	-1.70	-1.51
Kindergarten, primary, secondary teachers	0.93	0.81	0.51	0.49	0.48	0.66	0.68	0.62	0.65	0.75
Professors (college and university)	-0.94	-0.90	-1.03	-0.98	-0.83	-0.75	-0.82	-0.72	-0.67	-0.65
Other teachers	1.78	1.75	1.41	0.94	0.73	0.67	0.41	0.28	0.32	0.35
Religious workers	-0.06	-0.03	-0.30	-0.38	-0.51	-0.43	-0.60	-0.71	-0.82	-0.84
Authors, reporters, and editors	-1.42	-1.31	-1.47	-1.38	-1.04	-1.00	-0.76	-0.53	-0.30	-0.12
Sculptors, artists	-1.35	-1.24	-1.72	-1.41	-1.01	-0.85	-0.39	-0.21	0.02	0.14
Designers	-0.80	0.45	0.44	0.45	0.39	0.37	0.34	0.43	0.55	0.52
Photographers and cameramen	-0.84	-1.07	-1.67	-1.99	-1.76	-1.71	-1.38	-1.31	-1.17	-0.91
Musicians	0.95	0.97	0.61	0.87	1.15	1.38	1.75	2.16	2.19	2.26

Actors and professional athletes	0.46	0.42	0.31	0.11	0.02	0.02	0.15	0.41	0.70	0.82
Other professional and technical workers	1.34	1.27	1.44	1.45	1.49	1.26	1.30	1.40	0.72	1.13
2. Managers and Officials										
Directors of company	-1.06	-1.09	-1.09	-1.14	-1.36	-1.48	-1.35	-1.69	-1.84	-2.88
Government officials, other managers and directors	-2.61	-2.66	-2.81	-3.15	-2.88	-3.15	-3.28	-2.55	-2.37	-1.95
3. Clerical Workers										
General clerical, key punchers, etc.	1.13	1.07	0.92	0.84	0.75	0.71	0.60	0.40	0.52	0.40
Accounting clerks	1.94	1.95	1.86	1.67	1.59	1.48	1.34	1.10	1.07	0.92
Clerical workers in post and communication	0.39	0.12	-0.12	-0.18	-0.25	-0.44	-0.58	-0.47	0.04	0.44
Bill and account collectors	1.09	0.83	0.67	0.44	0.34	0.02	-0.19	-0.16	-0.01	-0.04
Clerical workers in transportation	-1.18	-1.47	-1.86	-1.98	-2.01	-2.03	-2.35	-1.74	-1.94	-1.51
Stenographers and typists	3.01	3.29	3.82	4.13	4.26	4.35	4.49	4.28	3.57	3.70
4. Sales Workers										
Retail dealers	-0.29	-0.22	-0.16	-0.21	-0.05	0.02	0.16	0.34	0.41	0.32
Restaurant operators	0.92	0.97	0.91	0.65	0.67	0.74	1.22	1.30	1.42	1.32
Wholesale, retail sales	1.38	1.21	1.16	1.14	0.99	1.09	1.26	1.22	1.36	1.47
Peddlers and street vendors	1.25	1.18	1.19	1.19	1.03	0.86	0.86	0.78	0.92	0.88
Junk dealers, other sales-related workers	-1.57	0.14	-0.18	-0.26	-0.48	-0.37	-0.30	-0.42	-0.17	-1.19
Traveling salespeople (except insurance)	1.51	-1.71	-2.03	-2.23	-2.21	-2.09	-1.78	-1.48	-1.61	-1.90

(continued)

	1950	1955	1960	1965	1970	1975	1980	1985	1990	1995
Insurance agents	-0.67	0.38	0.99	1.52	1.43	1.56	1.50	1.50	1.64	-0.40
Commodity, real estate agents and brokers	-0.67	-1.04	-0.92	-0.17	-0.21	-0.27	-0.52	-0.46	-0.58	0.53
5. Agricultural Workers										
Farmers and sericulturalists	1.53	1.53	1.32	1.19	1.14	1.04	0.91	0.81	0.75	0.66
Livestock raisers	1.14	0.98	0.94	0.75	0.67	0.65	0.59	0.53	0.52	0.42
Forest rearers, other agricultural	-0.53	-0.68	-0.85	-0.83	-0.78	-0.69	-0.75	-0.87	-0.94	-1.29
Gardeners and landscape gardeners	-1.61	-3.86	-2.09	-1.76	-1.76	-1.56	-1.43	-1.43	-1.28	-1.08
Fishermen	-1.21	-1.10	-1.36	-0.81	-0.97	-1.03	-0.88	-0.82	-0.77	-0.64
Seaweed and shell gatherers	0.95	0.73	0.39	0.10	0.09	-0.51	-0.26	-0.06	0.08	0.02
Aquiculture workers	0.66	0.92	0.58	0.67	0.47	0.34	0.30	0.29	0.24	0.21
6. Transport, Communications Workers										
Automobile drivers	-4.50	-5.92	-4.78	-4.30	-4.01	-4.06	-4.01	-3.90	-3.57	-2.94
Conductors	0.21	1.10	1.34	1.25	0.94	0.33	0.29	0.49	0.63	0.60
Sea, air, rail, other transport operators	-2.86	-2.79	-3.06	-3.10	-3.43	-3.65	-3.79	-4.10	-3.91	-3.75
Radiotelegraphists, other communication workers	-2.96	-3.57	-2.17	-2.58	-2.67	-2.20	-1.83	-2.33	-2.10	-1.78
Wire telegraphists	-0.80	-1.10	-0.38	-0.02	0.23	0.10	-0.42	-0.72	-0.83	-0.65
Telephone operators	4.60	4.96	4.05	4.37	4.38	4.72	5.02	4.72	3.92	4.26
Mail and telegram deliverers	-2.44	-3.02	-2.59	-3.43	-3.39	-2.97	-2.67	-2.28	-1.87	-1.40

7. Crafts, Manufacturing Workers

Mining workers	-0.87	-1.16	-1.40	-1.70	-2.02	-2.15	-2.45	-2.66	-2.60	-2.57
Iron, steel furnacemen, pourers, related	-3.55	-5.43	-3.07	-3.36	-3.31	-3.12	-3.06	-3.13	-2.97	-2.83
Molders, forgers and hammermen	-2.68	-1.79	-1.63	-1.54	-1.43	-1.50	-1.54	-1.66	-1.59	-1.70
Metal rolling mill, drawing operators	-3.70	-2.44	-2.43	-2.64	-2.71	-2.80	-2.85	-2.62	-2.54	-2.37
Metal cutting machine operators	-2.26	-2.03	-1.83	-1.67	-1.40	-1.28	-1.07	-1.11	-1.13	-1.25
Metal press machine operators	-0.58	-0.45	-0.57	-0.57	-0.43	-0.42	-0.30	-0.33	-0.45	-0.48
Welders and framecutters	-3.15	-3.38	-2.73	-2.53	-2.22	-2.21	-1.92	-1.87	-1.81	-2.00
Tin-, coppersmiths, sheet metal workers	-2.23	-2.45	-2.41	-2.11	-1.92	-2.16	-1.87	-1.88	-1.72	-1.71
Galvanizers	-0.82	-0.64	-0.55	-0.57	-0.61	-0.64	-0.56	-0.77	-0.92	-1.05
Other metal material and processing workers	-0.56	-0.50	-0.52	-0.56	-0.45	-0.48	-0.45	-0.45	-0.48	-0.61
General machine assemblers and repairmen	-1.40	-0.71	-0.35	-0.52	-0.40	-0.62	-0.40	-0.17	-0.20	-0.43
Electric, semiconductor assembly, repair	0.53	-0.02	0.59	0.70	1.03	0.75	0.93	0.99	0.74	0.44
Electric wire and cable makers	0.93	0.92	0.40	0.07	-0.17	-0.14	0.03	0.08	0.13	0.07
Auto, rail, ship assembly, repair	-3.90	-3.83	-3.11	-3.04	-2.57	-2.76	-2.65	-3.18	-2.98	-2.99
Bicycle assembly, other transportation repair	-0.72	-1.49	-1.80	-1.67	-1.69	-1.76	-1.68	-1.66	-1.38	-1.58
Watch assemblers and repairmen	-1.59	-0.88	-0.48	0.04	0.20	0.26	0.79	0.69	0.35	0.10
Lens grinders and adjusters	0.09	0.24	0.32	0.49	0.51	0.56	0.55	0.49	0.39	0.25
Other meter, optic instrument assembly, repair	0.39	0.63	0.55	0.79	0.66	0.47	0.63	0.76	0.73	0.61

(continued)

APPENDIX TABLE A6.1
(*continued*)

	1950	1955	1960	1965	1970	1975	1980	1985	1990	1995
Silk reelers	4.38	4.73	3.78	3.80	3.42	3.02	2.41	2.42	2.17	1.52
Spinners	3.51	3.36	3.56	3.16	2.58	2.51	2.05	1.79	1.57	1.42
Doublers, thread, yarn twisters, winders	2.97	3.12	2.87	2.47	1.95	1.78	1.41	1.33	1.23	1.21
Weavers	3.02	3.24	2.92	2.53	2.19	2.01	1.77	1.65	1.36	1.16
Knitters	2.14	2.10	2.01	1.96	2.02	1.73	1.39	1.35	1.08	0.86
Net, rope makers (except metal and straw)	2.02	2.42	2.06	1.86	1.74	1.68	1.56	1.51	1.30	1.18
Textile and yarn washers and bleachers	1.67	0.76	0.53	0.50	0.36	0.22	0.11	0.06	−0.12	−0.20
Textile dyers	0.23	0.08	−0.15	−0.06	0.02	−0.03	0.01	−0.02	−0.04	−0.11
Other silk reel and textile workers	2.23	2.22	2.21	2.04	1.82	1.62	1.51	1.49	1.33	1.22
Tailors	−0.61	0.20	0.26	−0.02	0.28	0.33	0.26	0.15	0.03	−0.10
Dressmakers for ladies and children	4.00	3.26	3.46	3.70	3.68	3.32	3.03	3.03	2.61	2.47
Other garment, textile fabrics workers	2.23	2.65	2.41	2.47	2.55	2.57	2.56	2.53	2.47	2.37
Sawyers	−1.84	−1.68	−1.19	−0.94	−0.74	−0.71	−0.60	−0.71	−0.80	−0.85
Veneer makers	0.24	0.60	0.36	0.40	0.29	0.29	0.21	0.08	0.01	−0.21
Wood workers	−1.91	−1.22	−1.21	−0.80	−0.63	−0.52	−0.36	−0.41	−0.35	−0.45
Wood furniture makers and related workers	−3.18	−2.61	−1.94	−1.11	−0.73	−0.52	−0.39	−0.49	−0.51	−0.55
Other wood, bamboo, grass workers	0.04	0.97	0.74	0.61	0.62	0.59	0.56	0.40	0.34	0.19

Pulp makers, paper makers, paper millers	0.79	0.57	-0.13	-0.89	-1.11	-0.96	-1.03	-0.98	-1.09	-1.06
Other pulp, paper, paper products workers	1.45	1.42	1.24	1.10	0.97	0.78	0.75	0.69	0.57	0.48
General stereotypers	-0.96	-1.22	-1.57	-1.54	-1.31	-1.21	-1.08	-0.87	-0.52	-0.48
Type-pickers and type-setters, pressmen	-0.56	-0.57	-0.69	-0.58	-0.58	-0.57	-0.49	-0.44	-0.41	-0.46
Bookbinders	0.96	1.17	0.96	1.07	0.91	0.87	0.85	0.81	0.80	0.68
Other printing and binding workers	1.18	0.95	0.53	0.90	0.77	0.63	0.62	0.67	0.65	0.68
Rubber and plastic products workers	1.39	0.49	0.90	0.43	0.14	-0.11	-0.19	-0.25	-0.41	-0.46
Leather tanners	-0.76	-0.71	-0.55	-0.11	-0.08	0.09	0.07	0.09	-0.03	-0.19
Shoemakers and shoe repairmen	-1.29	-1.29	-0.84	-0.14	0.38	0.62	0.75	0.80	0.81	0.73
Other leather and leather products makers	-0.07	0.74	0.80	0.81	0.94	0.93	1.07	1.11	1.03	0.91
Glass formers	0.13	-0.99	-0.53	-0.78	-1.13	-1.07	-1.04	-1.19	-1.03	-0.96
Potters	0.70	0.97	0.67	0.72	0.71	0.60	0.67	0.55	0.37	0.23
Ceramic decorators	1.25	1.55	1.64	1.46	1.66	1.77	1.88	1.93	1.96	1.79
Brick, tile and earthen pipe makers	0.33	0.34	0.01	0.10	0.06	0.07	-0.02	-0.12	-0.31	-0.37
Cement products makers	-0.28	-0.08	-0.45	-0.22	-0.28	-0.21	-0.32	-0.58	-0.82	-1.05
Stone cutters	-2.80	-2.37	-1.73	-1.47	-1.23	-1.14	-1.04	-1.14	-1.19	-1.39
Other ceramic, clay, stone products workers	0.62	0.69	0.61	0.27	0.27	0.12	0.06	0.04	-0.02	-0.12
Grain polishers and millers	0.27	0.24	0.08	0.12	0.01	-0.15	-0.21	-0.50	-0.44	-0.67
Bakers and confectioners	0.60	0.16	-0.03	0.29	0.30	0.42	0.49	0.50	0.53	0.68

(continued)

	1950	1955	1960	1965	1970	1975	1980	1985	1990	1995
Macaroni and other noodle makers	0.86	0.82	0.63	0.88	0.87	0.99	1.01	0.93	0.98	0.93
Tofu, arum root, related products makers	1.13	0.94	0.72	0.85	0.77	0.78	0.81	0.84	0.84	0.81
Alcoholic beverage makers	0.38	-1.23	-0.72	-0.68	-0.72	-0.49	-0.59	-0.62	-0.57	-0.56
Aquatic products processing workers	1.73	1.57	1.60	1.57	1.55	1.70	1.67	1.66	1.55	1.51
Other food and beverage manufacturing workers	0.45	0.51	0.98	1.03	1.00	1.10	1.25	1.30	1.33	1.44
Chemical operatives	-0.31	-1.19	-1.41	-1.61	-1.63	-1.72	-1.68	-1.59	-1.44	-1.49
Oil and fat processing workers	0.09	-0.21	-0.74	-0.62	-0.64	-0.57	-0.49	-0.64	-0.71	-0.53
Other chemical products workers	1.06	0.65	0.39	0.19	0.17	0.03	0.01	0.06	0.03	0.02
Construction, stationary engine machinery	-1.79	-1.60	-1.51	-1.62	-1.81	-2.08	-2.05	-2.36	-2.38	-2.43
Electrical workers	-4.95	-4.91	-4.23	-4.26	-3.84	-4.32	-3.98	-4.04	-3.66	-3.42
Tobacco workers	2.09	2.31	2.01	1.61	1.18	0.93	0.78	0.78	0.71	0.64
Painters	-0.85	-0.32	-0.45	-0.56	-0.73	-0.95	-1.03	-1.19	-1.21	-1.30
Lacquerers	-0.30	0.10	0.03	0.27	0.37	0.46	0.48	0.42	0.42	0.38
Upholsterers	-1.32	-1.21	-0.55	-0.09	0.09	0.37	0.15	-0.01	-0.12	-0.23
Paperhangers	-1.72	-1.01	-1.08	-0.56	-0.49	-0.56	-0.59	-0.81	-1.07	-1.27
Jewelers, gold-, silversmiths, related	0.30	0.45	0.60	0.44	0.17	0.11	0.09	0.22	0.24	0.13
Metal engravers, stamp engravers	-1.27	-0.90	-0.85	-0.57	-0.56	-0.60	-0.43	-0.45	-0.36	-0.33
Luggage and handbag makers	0.15	0.51	0.77	0.88	0.99	1.12	1.24	1.32	1.27	1.12

Drawingmen	−0.11	−0.19	−0.48	−1.11	−1.40	−1.06	−1.43	−1.33	−0.71	−0.81
Miscellaneous craft, production workers	0.78	0.84	0.82	0.69	0.53	0.63	0.74	0.67	0.71	0.86
Ship and land stevedores	−1.20	−1.52	−1.57	−1.61	−1.53	−1.56	−1.34	−1.02	−0.95	−1.21
Deliverymen	−0.08	−0.28	−0.17	−0.36	−0.15	−0.32	−0.53	−0.53	−0.45	−0.16
Other laborers	0.86	0.96	1.02	0.97	1.15	1.09	0.91	0.67	0.95	0.28
8. Protective Service Workers										
Self-defense forces, police, fire fighters	−2.44	−2.81	−3.00	−3.15	−2.95	−3.85	−4.51	−4.58	−4.84	−3.33
Guards, watchmen and janitors	−2.40	−2.77	−3.12	−3.22	−3.37	−3.53	−3.58	−3.33	−3.12	−2.89
Other protective service workers	−0.63	−0.48	−0.34	−0.34	0.08	0.04	−0.47	−0.58	−1.18	−0.71
9. Service Workers										
Domestic service workers	4.78	4.52	4.71	4.45	4.95	4.98	5.03	5.88	5.23	4.71
Barbers, beauticians	1.61	1.64	1.69	1.71	1.75	1.78	1.87	1.75	1.87	1.62
Bathhouse workers	0.97	1.00	1.02	1.04	1.19	1.19	1.22	1.20	1.42	1.41
Laundry-men and dry cleaners	1.04	0.92	0.82	0.74	0.59	0.50	0.36	−0.01	0.22	0.54
Cooks, bartenders	0.93	0.87	0.90	0.94	1.01	1.04	1.29	1.39	1.73	1.01
Waiters, servants, geisha girls, related	2.23	2.28	2.41	2.64	2.94	3.25	3.60	3.65	4.21	4.27
Recreation and amusement place workers	1.08	1.22	1.25	1.48	1.53	1.35	1.59	2.09	2.20	1.94
Temporary keepers, caretakers, lessors	0.47	0.42	0.58	0.88	1.16	1.42	1.49	1.59	1.70	1.72
Masters, attendants of hotel, geisha-house	0.03	0.14	0.36	0.49	0.68	0.77	0.90	1.18	1.51	1.59
Fashion models, advertising	3.01	2.70	2.96	2.57	2.59	2.08	1.87	1.19	0.89	−0.32
Other personal, miscellaneous service	1.12	1.05	1.06	1.12	1.28	1.40	1.94	1.77	2.14	2.26

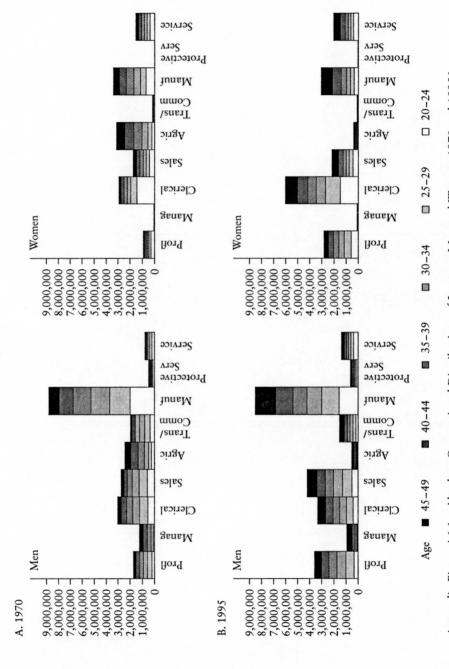

Appendix Figure A6.1 Absolute Occupational Distributions of Japanese Men and Women, 1970 and 1995[a]

[a]Figures are population estimates, based on 20 percent samples.

CHAPTER SEVEN

Gender, Nativity, and Occupational Segregation in Switzerland, 1970–2000

In our earlier work, we identified the Swiss occupational structure of 1980 as one of the most sex segregated in the industrialized world. This distinction was in large part attributable to the extraordinarily strong segregation of (male) managerial and (female) service occupations (Charles 1992; Charles and Grusky 1995). Results presented in Chapter 3, based on data collected one decade later, in 1990, suggest a significant decline in segregation, thus making Switzerland an especially intriguing case study in understanding the sources of egalitarian change. Switzerland now appears to occupy a middle-of-the-road position among advanced industrial nations with respect to both level and pattern of sex segregation.

In this case study, we examine historical developments in occupational sex segregation using detailed data from Swiss national censuses of 1970, 1980, and 1990, supplemented by preliminary, more aggregated data from newly released 2000 census tables. In interpreting trends we once again consider the possible influence of gender-egalitarian cultural shifts and postindustrial economic restructuring. We also explore some unique institutional features of the Swiss economy and society that may have mediated the impact of these cultural and structural pressures. Two important such features are Switzerland's heavy reliance on immigrant labor and its strong tradition of occupation-specific (that is, vocational) education.

Switzerland presents an excellent case for examining the role of immigrant labor in the development of occupational sex segregation. Swiss employers have long relied upon immigrants, especially men from the Mediterranean countries of southern Europe, to fill labor shortages. As a result, foreign nationals today make up a larger share of the work force in Switzerland than in any other Western European country. Previous research suggests that the availability of a large pool of immigrant labor has strongly affected the structure of labor demand and the process of occupational allocation in Switzerland (Charles 2000). In this chapter, we extend our modeling approach to examine the historical interaction of gender with citizenship status in the Swiss occupational structure.

A Swiss case study also presents an opportunity to consider the role of vocational education in the process of occupational allocation and sex segregation. Since 1970, postsecondary education has undergone an unprecedented expansion in Switzerland, resulting in a proliferation of occupation-specific credentials and a tightening of the link between the educational system and the labor market. Today, most associate professional, clerical, craft, and skilled manufacturing occupations and some retail sales and service jobs are allocated on the basis of occupation-specific vocational credentials (see Buchmann and Sacchi 1998 on the Swiss educational system). This state of affairs stands in contrast to the stronger emphasis on on-the-job training in the United States, United Kingdom, Japan, and elsewhere (see Estévez-Abe, Iversen, and Soskice 2003 on general- versus specific-training regimes). As elaborated in the next section, some sociological accounts would predict an equalizing effect of this growing reliance on occupation-specific training, while others would suggest that it legitimates, or even intensifies, existing patterns of gender stratification. While we cannot hope to adjudicate among these competing accounts definitively, it is possible to speak to such matters indirectly by comparing our Swiss results to those secured in the preceding chapters and in earlier analyses of other countries.

THE CONTEXT OF GENDER STRATIFICATION IN SWITZERLAND

In the following paragraphs, we provide some background information on the Swiss economy and society, and we consider how changing cultural and legal norms, structural shifts in the economy, and Switzerland's distinctive immigration and education policies may have affected the development of occupational sex segregation between 1970 and 2000.

Family sociologist David Popenoe once described Switzerland as an "outpost of the traditional family" (1988). This may seem to be at odds with

Switzerland's 700-year democratic tradition and its exceptionally high level of economic and social development.[1] But it is indeed true that legal provisions for gender equality emerged later in Switzerland than in other Western nations at comparable levels of economic development. Most notable in this regard is, of course, the late extension of the national franchise to women, which occurred in 1971. The importance of sexual equality as a political issue has grown steadily since the early 1970s, however. A constitutional amendment was passed guaranteeing women and men equal rights in 1981, and Swiss voters narrowly approved a new marriage and family law in 1985. The latter granted married women the right to engage in paid work (without obtaining their husbands' permission), and it overturned men's rights to choose the family place of residence and to manage their wives' savings and inheritance. Final restrictions on women's participation in local elections were overturned by the Swiss Supreme Court in 1990 (on female employment in Switzerland, see also Simona 1985; Calonder Gerster 1990; Bundesamt für Statistik 1994a; Levy et al. 1997; and Buchmann et al. 2002).

Women's political and social mobilization resulted in some significant gains, especially during the 1980s. The persistent gender gaps in educational attainment and in university attendance have shrunk, and the Swiss government has made a well-publicized effort to increase female representation within the ranks of its own bureaucracy. Although the ideology of domestic motherhood and the sexual division of labor remain firmly entrenched in the Swiss family, those women who do pursue a career (often at the expense of motherhood) may today legitimately assert their rights to equal opportunity within the labor market.

The Swiss economy has undergone structural shifts similar to those occurring in other industrial nations. Between 1970 and 1990, service-sector employment expanded from 45 percent to 64 percent of the labor force (and more than 76 percent of the female labor force) (Bundesamt für Statistik 1993). By 1981, when Switzerland's "equal rights" amendment was ratified, a sizable majority of the labor force was already employed in service-industry jobs. Women's postindustrial market role was thus institutionalized in the absence of major national pressures for gender equality. This sequence of events is relevant to the extent that the existence of comfortable service-sector niches (for example, in semiprofessional and clerical occupations) reduces women's inclination to seek access to traditionally male-dominated occupations. As we show, however, no such diversionary effect is apparent. Like their American and Japanese counterparts, Swiss women greatly increased their presence in elite managerial and professional occupations between 1980 and 1990.

Another noteworthy Swiss development is the increasing importance of occupation-specific credentialing (as opposed to the general certification that predominates in the American and Japanese contexts).[2] Today, following a massive twenty-year expansion of postcompulsory education, formal vocational or academic credentials govern access to all but the least desirable occupations in Switzerland.[3] This growing reliance on occupation-specific certification may have affected the historical development of occupational sex segregation in two ways. On one hand, it may increase gender inequality by translating the sex-typed occupational aspirations of young adolescents directly into vocational choices with long-term career consequences (Stockard and McGee 1990; Baker and Jones 1993; Buchmann and Charles 1995). On the other hand, increasing availability of clear meritocratic standards of occupational qualification may weaken employer reliance on statistical discrimination and thus promote higher rates of gender-atypical employment (Becker 1975; Sewell, Hauser, and Wolf 1980; Hout 1996; Meyer 2001). Moreover, women may be more inclined to pursue male-dominated work when they have a means of formally demonstrating their qualification (Milkman and Townsley 1994). The most convincing evidence of an equalizing effect of vocational credentials would be increased access of Swiss women to skilled craft and production occupations, which have been exceptionally resistant to gender integration in other national economies.

The present study also presents an opportunity to consider the role of alternative "secondary" labor pools in the process of occupational sex segregation. Owing to its small native population, Switzerland had to rely heavily on immigrant labor to sustain high rates of economic growth during the postwar decades. Huge numbers of low-skilled guest workers from southern Europe were admitted between 1950 and 1970, as were thousands of professionals and academics from other northern European countries (especially Germany) (Soysal 1994). In 2000, more than 20 percent of the Swiss labor force was made up of foreign workers. Because many men come alone to work in Switzerland, the immigrant labor force is disproportionately male.[4]

The distinctive legal status and undifferentiated public image of "foreigners," combined with the relative ethnic homogeneity of the native population, means that the process of labor market stratification in Switzerland can be captured quite well with respect to just two dichotomous distinctions—sex and citizenship status (see Charles 2000).[5] The Swiss labor market therefore provides an excellent context for examining the relationship of crosscutting distinctions (including ethnicity, race, or national origin) to patterns of occupational sex segregation.

The tradition of relying on (male) immigrants to relieve labor shortages may have influenced patterns of sex segregation by providing employers with an alternative strategy for filling positions in low-level service occupations and in the expanding male-dominated professions (which were characterized by extreme labor shortages into the early 1970s). To examine these effects, we extend our modeling approach to chart occupation-specific trends in segregation by gender and citizenship status simultaneously.

DATA AND METHODS

The primary data used for these analyses are taken from the Swiss decennial censuses of 1970, 1980, and 1990. These data are supplemented with some newly available figures from the 2000 Census. In Switzerland, as in most other countries, the national classification of occupations has undergone substantial change over the decades. To facilitate historical comparisons, the Swiss Census Bureau collaborated with private-sector labor consultants to construct from its 1970, 1980, and 1990 occupational classifications a historically harmonized set of occupational categories, which were then mapped onto the European Community version of the International Labour Office's "International Standard Classification of Occupations," ISCO-88 (COM) (Bundesamt für Statistik 1994b). Although a comparable breakdown from the 2000 Swiss census is not available at this time, the Swiss Statistical Office recently provided an unpublished data table that allows historical comparison at a more aggregated level. These 1990–2000 trends in occupational composition are examined in the concluding empirical section of this chapter.

Because of some substantial differences between the 1970 and 1980 national coding schemes, comparability across the 1970 to 1990 period is best at the level of twenty-five "submajor" categories (see Appendix Table A7.1). These can be aggregated into the following nine "major" occupational categories:

1. Senior officials and managers (e.g., innkeeper, bank director);
2. Professionals (e.g., doctor, lawyer);
3. Associate professionals and technicians (e.g., nurse, engineering technician);
4. Clerical workers (e.g., secretary, bank teller);
5. Service workers and shop sales workers (e.g., waiter, salesperson);
6. Skilled agricultural and fishery workers (e.g., farmer);[6]
7. Craft and related trades workers (e.g., carpenter, butcher);
8. Machine operators and assemblers (e.g., lathe operator, printing press operator);
9. Unskilled laborers (e.g., building cleaner, hand packer).

For the primary 1970–90 analyses, data are in the form of a three-way, 150-cell table that breaks down the employed labor force by occupation (into twenty-five categories), sex, and year (1970, 1980, 1990). Because of historical shifts in the definition of labor force participation, men and women working fewer than six hours per week were omitted from the analysis,[7] as were members of the armed forces and individuals for whom occupational information was missing. Where instructive, we interpret results with reference to trends in the composition of more detailed national occupational titles. Although historical consistency in occupational definitions cannot be ensured at this level of detail, some insights can be garnered from informal examination of developments in more detailed and deeply institutionalized occupational categories (for example, restaurant waiter, medical doctor).

Data used for the 1990–2000 trend analyses include men and women employed at least one hour per week (again, members of the armed forces and individuals with missing occupational information were omitted). Owing to changes in the Swiss occupational classification, some of the occupational categories used for the 2000 census could not be mapped into a single two-digit ISCO category (that is, they spanned multiple categories). We dealt with this problem by collapsing some of our submajor groups, thus arriving at a nineteen-category classification for the 1990–2000 comparisons. These nineteen categories can be aggregated into the nine major ISCO groups listed above.

As in the two previous chapters, trends in the overall level of sex segregation are assessed using the dissimilarity index (D), the size-standardized index (D_s), and the margin-free association index (A). For the 1970–90 analyses, occupation-specific trends are examined at the level of nine aggregate-level categories by computing a saturated "multilevel" model, which constrains the major-category effects and the minor-category effects within them to sum to zero at each time point (equation 2.13). The virtue of this model is that it purges the data of compositional effects generated at the detailed occupational level. We also explore trends at the disaggregate level by computing simple saturated models (equation 2.10) for each time point.

To explore the relationship between sex segregation and trends in the distribution of immigrant labor, a four-way cross-classification of occupation, gender, year, and citizenship status (native versus foreign) is employed. For each census year, we compute three sets of occupation-specific scale values based on the logged ratios of native women to native men, foreign men to native men, and foreign women to native men, respectively. We carry out analyses for the 1970–90 period, supplemented with analyses for 1990–2000, as data allow.

AGGREGATE-LEVEL TRENDS IN THE
SEXUAL DIVISION OF LABOR

Values of the three summary sex segregation indices are shown in Table 7.1, first for the 1970–90 period, and then for the 1990–2000 period. In Panel A, we again find discrepant developments for the three measures, with A and D_s declining, but D remaining relatively constant.[8] This discrepancy reflects the sensitivity of D to historical shifts in the occupational structure. In the computation of D, the expansion of the highly segregated associate professional and clerical occupations has likely offset any integrative trends. Values in Panel B suggest relative stability in all index values between 1990 and 2000.

Demographic trends in the Swiss labor force are summarized in Table 7.2. Here we see evidence of steady growth in female labor force participation, with women's share of the labor force climbing from 34 to 44 percent between 1970 and 2000. Notably, Swiss women make up a smaller share of the labor force than do their counterparts in either the United States or

TABLE 7.1

Trends in Summary Sex-Segregation Indices for Switzerland,
1970–1990 and 1990–2000

A. 1970–1990

	1970	1980	1990
Association index (A)	5.90	5.49	4.37
Index of dissimilarity (D)	48.34	49.97	48.41
Size-standardized index (D_s)	52.01	50.79	44.90

B. 1990–2000

	1990	2000
Association index (A)	4.09	4.02
Index of dissimilarity (D)	44.22	46.18
Size-standardized index (D_s)	42.74	42.88

NOTE: Values in panel A are based on twenty-five two-digit ISCO categories, with the active labor force defined as individuals working at least six hours per week (Bundesamt für Statistik 1994b). Values in panel B are based on distributions across nineteen occupational categories, with the active labor force defined as individuals working at least one hour per week (Bundesamt für Statistik 2003).

TABLE 7.2

Labor Force Composition in Switzerland, 1970–2000 (percent)

	1970	1980	1990	2000
Female	34.14	36.15	39.18	43.70
Swiss	26.73	30.08	31.94	35.20
Foreign	7.41	6.07	7.24	8.50
Men	65.86	63.85	60.82	56.31
Swiss	51.31	51.51	46.00	43.14
Foreign	14.56	12.34	14.82	13.17
Foreign	21.96	18.41	22.06	21.67
Total	2,987,523	3,064,846	3,578,655	3,787,175

NOTE: Values are the percentage share of the total labor force (Bundesamt für Statistik 2003).

Japan, at least through 1990 (see Tables 5.2 and 6.2, respectively; see also Charles 2002). This has been due largely to low labor force participation rates of mothers, even those with older children (Buchmann et al. 2002).[9] Maternal market activity has long been inhibited by a number of ideological, economic, and institutional factors in Switzerland. One is women's relative economic security during the period in question. In 1990 a remarkable 97 percent of all children were born into a two-parent household in this country (Bundesamt für Statistik 1994a), and it was generally possible to comfortably support a family on a single male income. As a result, Swiss women have historically been freer to choose the role of full-time homemaker than have their counterparts in most other industrial societies.[10]

Also discouraging maternal labor force participation is the structural incompatibility of market and family roles. Public and private child-care arrangements are scarce in Switzerland, and school schedules are difficult to reconcile with the demands of even part-time work. Many children return home daily for two-hour lunch breaks, and school hours vary widely from day to day and from child to child (Buchmann and Charles 1995; Charles et al. 2001). Finally, a long historical tradition of addressing labor shortages through immigration may reduce demand-side pressures on women to join the paid labor force. We consider labor force participation of foreign-born men and women in a subsequent section.

The remainder of this chapter explores historical shifts in the composition of *particular* occupational categories. We examine trends first by gender alone, and then in interaction with citizenship status.

OCCUPATION-SPECIFIC TRENDS IN THE SEXUAL DIVISION OF LABOR

Figure 7.1 gives the absolute distributions of male and female workers over the nine major occupational categories for 1970, 1980, and 1990. Results suggest patterns of horizontal and vertical segregation similar to those found elsewhere in the industrial world (Chapter 3): women are strongly concentrated in nonmanual occupations, especially in the associate professional, clerical, and service/sales categories, and men dominate the highest-status categories within both the manual and nonmanual sectors (managerial and skilled craft occupations). Also apparent in Figure 7.1 are the structural

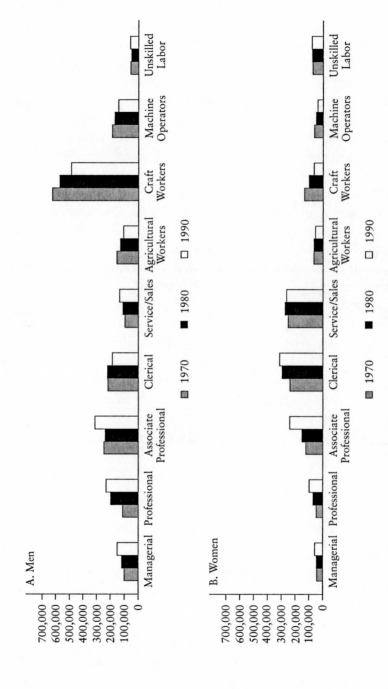

Figure 7.1 Trends in Absolute Occupational Distributions, Switzerland, 1970–1990

trends discussed above: service-sector expansion, contraction of the manu-facturing sector, and moderate growth of the female labor force.[11]

Of course, such absolute frequency distributions are themselves strongly influenced by major structural transformations since 1970, and they there-fore provide only a hazy view of trends in segregation per se. Through ex-amination of major-category scale values from our saturated multilevel model, it is possible to disentangle 1970–90 shifts in the economic structure and in the size of the female labor force from actual changes in the interac-tion between sex and occupation. Results are shown in Figure 7.2. Appen-dix Table A7.1 gives scale values for each of the twenty-five detailed occu-pations, taken from a series of simple saturated models. In both cases, values above zero indicate female overrepresentation (relative to the average cate-gory); values below zero indicate female underrepresentation.

As in the two previous chapters, we find decreasing vertical segregation in the nonmanual sector (in the form of pronounced integration of elite

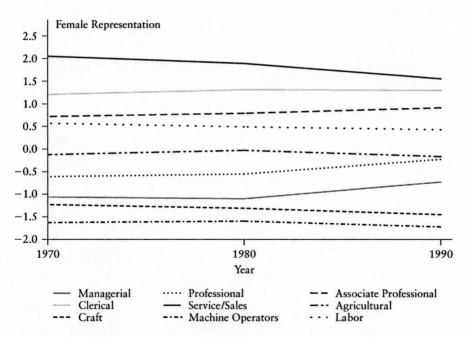

Figure 7.2   Trends in Sex Segregation, 1970–1990: Multilevel Model Fit to 25 Submajor Categories

white-collar occupations), but a striking resilience of horizontal segregation. While one traditionally female-dominated category (sales and service occupations) has become more integrated, others (clerical and associate professional) have become increasingly sex-typed. Moreover, women's relative representation in skilled blue-collar work (craft and machine operative) declined, contributing to increased vertical segregation within the nonmanual sector as well.

The most striking changes displayed in Figure 7.2 are steep increases in female professional and managerial representation since 1980. As can be seen in Appendix Table A7.1, women's relative presence grew in all four disaggregate professional categories and in government administration. In two detailed categories (life sciences and health, and other professionals), micro-level scale values indicate near gender parity by 1990. In the teaching professions (tertiary and secondary education), women's initial overrepresentation increased slightly over this twenty-year period, and in the strongly male-dominated physical and engineering sciences occupations, men's overrepresentation fell from a factor of 7.39 to a factor of 4.57.[12] The integrative trends in these academic occupations are reminiscent of those documented for the United States and Japan. Their relatively late commencement in Switzerland may reflect the concurrence of late-emerging gender-egalitarian pressures and an abundance of relatively attractive clerical and associate-professional opportunities.

Female gains in managerial occupations were more significant in the public than in the private sector, perhaps owing to the greater legal constraints and stronger legitimacy pressures affecting public organizations (W. Scott and Meyer 1987; Beggs 1995; see also Lieberson 1980). Women's presence among high-level government administrators increased sharply between 1980 and 1990, while female representation among corporate and general managers remained virtually unchanged (and actually decreased from 1970 to 1980). Since a disproportionate share of female managers work in small, family-owned businesses, economic restructuring (the replacement of independent enterprises with large corporate chains) likely contributed to women's declining presence in this category.[13]

Trends in mid- and lower-level nonmanual categories are mixed, with associate professional and clerical occupations showing increasing feminization, but sales and service occupations becoming somewhat more integrated since 1970. Within the associate-professional group, the most substantial change occurred in physical and engineering sciences, where men's overrepresentation decreased from a factor of 2.69 to a factor of 1.55 between 1970 and 1990.[14] The increasing segregation of the aggregate clerical group can be attributed to massive inflows of women into the secretarial category.[15] Indeed, more than 28 percent of the female labor force worked in clerical occupations by 1990. In contrast, Figure 7.2 shows a downward-sloping trend for the sales and service category. Underlying this decline is increasing male representation in both the personal and protective services and the salespersons and demonstrators categories. Examination of the original (nonstandardized) data suggests that much of this change reflects trends in two categories: women's share of restaurant waiters dropped from 80 to 74 percent between 1970 to 1990, and their share of retail sales workers fell during the same period from 81 to 75 percent. Men's growing representation in the service and sales categories may be attributable to Switzerland's relatively restricted female labor supply and its unusually large pool of (male) immigrant labor. This is discussed in greater detail later in the text. In any case, it is clear that the expansion of the Swiss service sector during this period did not coincide with a uniform feminization of mid-level nonmanual occupations. Increases in female participation, it would seem, have been most substantial in the categories that require higher-level qualifications.

Trends in craft and machine operating occupations do not lend much support to the notion that occupation-specific educational credentialing translates into increased female access to skilled blue-collar positions. Within the craft group, for example, the only detailed category to show increasing female representation over this period is building trades, where the absolute numbers of women remain very small.[16] Segregative shifts are also evident within the major machine operator group.[17]

We thus find little to suggest that occupation-specific credentialing promotes gender neutrality in the allocation of nonacademic positions. In fact, we find *increasing* sex segregation in all four major occupational categories that are governed by nonacademic vocational credentialing (i.e., clerical, associate professional, craft, machine operating). Continued male dominance of these occupations is tied to gender differences in choice of vocational program, which undoubtedly reflect adolescents' understandings of gender-appropriate work.

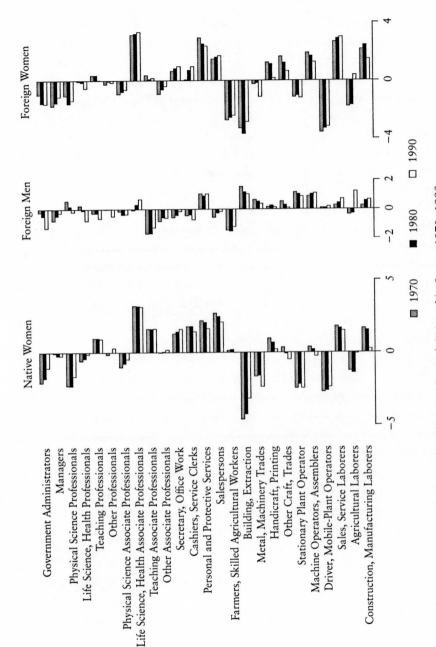

Figure 7.3 Occupational Representation by Gender and Citizenship Status, 1970–1990

In the following section we examine how trends in the size and distribution of the foreign labor force may have helped shape the trends described above.

Trends in Segregation by Gender and Citizenship Status

Trends in the composition of the Swiss labor market were presented in Table 7.2. Foreign-nationals (men and women) made up 22 percent of the labor force in 1970, 18 percent in 1980, and 22 percent in 1990 and 2000.[18] Underlying the reduced foreign presence between 1970 and 1980 was a sharp economic downturn and a tightening of national immigration quotas. Foreign labor recruitment increased again in the 1980s, with growing demand for labor. Since then, annual quotas for admission of foreigners have been set by the federal government in close consultation with business associations and trade unions (Hoffmann-Nowotny 1986; Schmitter Heisler 1988).

Shifts in the overall size of the immigrant labor force have been accompanied by marked changes in the occupational distribution of foreign workers. Trends in the representation of native women, foreign men, and foreign women are displayed in Figure 7.3. Values contrast the occupational representation of the respective gender-citizenship group to that of native men. As with the previous figures, values above zero indicate overrepresentation of the respective group; values below zero indicate underrepresentation. Movement toward group parity is thus revealed by a shortening of the bars between 1970 and 1990. To aid in the interpretation of these values, trends in the absolute occupational distributions of each of the four groups—Swiss men, Swiss women, foreign men, foreign women—are shown in Appendix Figure A7.1.

Foreign men's occupational distribution conforms to expectations in many respects: throughout the period under consideration, they are underrepresented among managerial, clerical, and associate professional workers, and they are strongly overrepresented in blue-collar occupations, especially in construction, manufacturing, and manual labor. More surprising is the overrepresentation of foreign men in the personal and protective service category, and their strong presence in some professions (physical sciences, life sciences), especially in 1970. The latter reflects labor shortages during the late 1960s and early 1970s. When economic growth outpaced the supply of university-credentialed native workers, Swiss employers were forced to recruit large numbers of professional men from neighboring Northern European countries (Soysal 1994).

Both foreign and native women are strongly overrepresented in sales, service, and clerical work, and underrepresented in management, the professions, and blue-collar occupations. The main differences between foreign women and their native counterparts is the former group's weaker presence in the highly skilled professional categories and their stronger representation among blue-collar workers and unskilled laborers.

Historical trends in the distribution of native women (relative to native men) are very similar to those displayed in the simple gender-by-occupation graph (Figure 7.2): native-female representation is increasing among government administrators, professionals, associate professionals, and clerical workers, and it is decreasing in sales and service jobs. This implies that the changes in occupational gender representation reflect distributional shifts within the native population, and not just changes in the size or distribution of the immigrant labor force.

We hasten to add that immigrant workers experienced distributional change as well. Particularly illuminating in this regard are the divergent trends found for native women and nonnative men. While the relative representation of foreign men has decreased markedly in government administration and in the male-typed professions (physical science, life science, other professionals), that of Swiss women has grown substantially. This may be due in part to a growing grassroots fear of *Überfremdung* (overforeignization), which prompted conscious policy efforts to increase representation of native Swiss (including women) in the professions during the 1980s.[19] Nativist sentiments, changing gender norms, expansion of Swiss tertiary education, and the proliferation of professional and managerial positions combined to enhance opportunities for native Swiss women at the top of the occupational structure between 1980 and 1990. Trends among foreign women were mixed in these categories, perhaps reflecting the conflicting normative mandates to promote gender equality and to avoid *Überfremdung*.

Foreign-male representation also declined in skilled craft and operative jobs. This likely reflects competitive pressures associated with contraction of the industrial sector: given widespread nativist sentiment during the 1970s and 1980s in Switzerland, national citizens were in a better position to hold on to the shrinking number of skilled nonmanual jobs.

Figure 7.3 also shows a growing representation of foreigners—both male and female—among corporate and general managers. Contributing to these gains is, no doubt, the recent growth of immigrant self-employment (Charles 2000). Foreigners may attempt to buffer themselves from discrimination and gain some competitive advantage through the development of ethnic enclave economies. Most common in Switzerland are family-run restaurants and import shops. Since 1970, the representation of immigrant men and women has also increased in most associate professional, clerical, and sales occupations.

To what extent can the gender integration of sales and service occupations (Figure 7.2) be attributed to trends in the distribution of foreign men? It bears reiterating here that the representation of women in sales and service occupations is declining even within the native labor force (Figure 7.3). At the same time, the absolute trends in Appendix Figure A7.1 suggest considerable flows of nonnative men into sales and personal and protective service occupations following the most recent wave of immigration. Between 1980 and 1990 more than 17,000 foreign men were added to these two categories, and the number of native women decreased by approximately 23,000. According to the unstandardized national data (not shown), the most pronounced absolute growth in foreign men's service presence was in restaurant food service and food-preparation occupations.[20] The trends shown in Appendix Figure A7.1 are consistent with the notion that foreign men are absorbing growth in some low-wage, relatively undesirable female-dominated occupations. But this is clearly not the only factor underlying the observed gender integration of sales and service occupations: Substantial (but smaller) numbers of *native* men also moved into these categories, especially into sales jobs, during this period.

Trends in the more aggregated categories used for our historical modeling (Figure 7.3) support the preceding interpretation. For example, the representation of foreign men (relative to native men) increased steadily in the "salespersons" category between 1970 and 1990. Representation of native women fell during the same period.

Because Swiss labor policy is targeted and immigrant work visas are often issued for specific occupations, it is unlikely that foreigners actually displaced native workers in service jobs between 1970 and 1990. A more plausible story is that middle-class Swiss women could afford to reject low-status service employment, especially restaurant and domestic service work. As growing numbers of native women obtain credentials in the more attractive clerical and associate professional occupations, foreign nationals (and in particular foreign men) may serve as reserve labor supply for some growing, relatively unattractive service jobs.[21]

Results once again point to the contextual dependence of demand-driven processes. Cultural and institutional constraints on female labor force participation, and the availability of alternative labor pools (e.g., immigrants, ethnic minorities) to work in an expanding service sector likely moderated the segregative impact of postindustrial economic restructuring in Switzerland. As described in the previous chapter, cultural constraints on female labor force participation were also operative in Japan, although they played out rather differently.

In sum, results for the 1970–1990 period indicate declining vertical segregation in the Swiss nonmanual sector. As in Japan and the United States, this decline came in the form of increasing female representation in prestigious male-dominated positions in the professions and in government administration. Amplifying this effect in Switzerland was the growing presence of foreign men in low-level service work. Also consistent with results in the foregoing chapters, horizontal segregation shows little sign of abating. Although male representation did increase in some service and sales occupations, these integrative tendencies were partially offset by women's growing concentration in secretarial and associate professional work, and by native men's continued dominance of skilled blue-collar occupations.

In the following section we use new (albeit somewhat more aggregated) occupational data for the 1990 and 2000 census years to investigate trends in Swiss sex segregation during the 1990s.

CONTINUITY AND CHANGE, 1990–2000

Figure 7.4 presents trends in female representation across nine major occupational categories between 1970 and 2000. Given limitations on the historical comparability of the two-digit occupational categories across this period, the parameter estimates graphed here, unlike those in Figure 7.2, were not computed from "multilevel" models. This means that we cannot rule out the possibility that historical shifts reflect changes in the relative sizes of the detailed occupations comprising these nine categories. Nonetheless, it is reassuring that the 1970–1990 trends represented in Figure 7.4 are generally consistent with those shown in Figure 7.2 for the same period.[22]

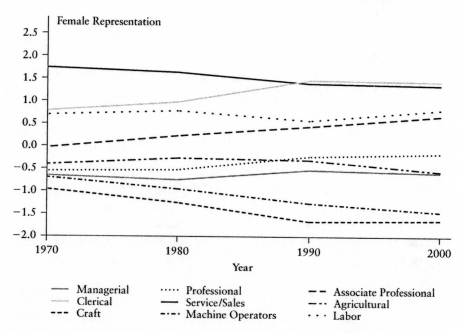

Figure 7.4 Sex Segregation across 9 Major Categories, 1970–2000

Changes between 1990 and 2000 in many cases represent a continuation of earlier trends. Professional and associate professional occupations continued to feminize; male dominance of agriculture and machine operating occupations increased; and women's representation in the managerial, clerical, sales/service, and craft categories was relatively stable. One noteworthy change, however, was growing feminization of unskilled laborer occupations since 1990.

What do these results tell us about trends in vertical and horizontal sex segregation during the 1990s? Strong increases in female professional representation provide further evidence of declining vertical segregation in the nonmanual sector. In the manual sector, we see no such decline; indeed, trends in the laborer category suggest a departure from the skill upgrading of female employment between 1970 and 1990. Sex segregation across the manual-nonmanual divide has, if anything, intensified since 1990, most notably due to segregative trends in the associate professions, machine operator, and agriculture categories. We next examine recent trends separately for foreign and native men and women.

Changes between 1990 and 2000 in the representation of native women, foreign men, and foreign women are displayed in Figure 7.5. As before (see Figure 7.3), values contrast the occupational representation of the respective gender-citizenship group to that of native men.

With regard to the distribution of foreign workers, results again suggest continuation of some earlier trends as well as some significant shifts. Continuity can be found in foreign men's ongoing movement into mid-level nonmanual work. Noteworthy changes include a reversal of trends in the professions, where foreign-male presence began to grow during the 1990s. We also see new trends in the unskilled laborer category, with increasing representation of foreign and native women and decreasing representation of foreign men (all relative to native men). Native women also lost some ground in management, although we suspect that analysis of more detailed occupational data would reveal continued progress for this group in government administration.

Taken together, these trends suggest skill upgrading of the foreign-male labor force between 1990 and 2000 (after significant deterioration during the 1970s and 1980s), and growing bifurcation of the female labor force. Growing representation of women in the least skilled manual occupations may be attributable to decreasing economic security of Swiss families and growing rates of single motherhood during the 1990s (Budowski, Tillman, and Bergman 2002). Uncredentialed, relatively unskilled women who might have otherwise chosen to work as full-time homemakers may increasingly seek employment at the bottom of the occupational hierarchy.

Although native men's dominance is weakening at the top of the nonmanual hierarchy, results suggest that Swiss men are consolidating control over the shrinking pool of skilled manual jobs. We thus see decreasing vertical segregation within the nonmanual sector between 1990 and 2000, but increasing vertical segregation within the manual sector. These divergent trends support arguments, elaborated in Chapter 1, suggesting greater salience of universalistic cultural pressures in elite nonmanual labor markets. They are also consistent with previous research findings that suggest a positive effect of occupational growth on opportunities of marginal social groups (Charles 2000).

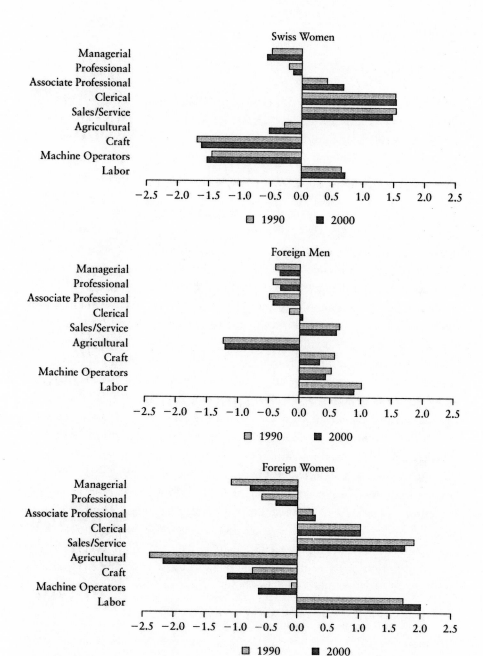

Figure 7.5 Occupational Representation by Gender and Citizenship Status, 1990–2000

NOTE: Classification across nine major ISCO categories (Bundesamt für Statistik 2003).

CONCLUSIONS

Increased female presence in professional and managerial occupations, combined with substantial flows of foreign men into low-level service work in Switzerland contributed to a marked decline in overall levels of sex segregation between 1980 and 1990. The striking integration of elite professional occupations during this time period suggests that gender-egalitarian ideals may contribute to delegitimation and erosion of vertical inequalities even in an established postindustrial labor market that offers a wide range of relatively attractive "female" jobs in the clerical and associate-professional sectors. Increasing rates of female university attendance as well as growing public pressure to reduce the representation of foreign nationals in visible professional and managerial positions likely contributed to the observed decline in vertical segregation within the nonmanual sector. We found, for example, that the growing presence of native women in academic occupations since 1980 was accompanied by equally pronounced declines in foreign male representation. At least in the case of Switzerland, the spread of universalistic discourse appears to have effected a more pronounced erosion of boundaries based on gender than of those based on national origin.

Structural constraints on wives' market activity and a long-standing tradition of addressing labor shortages through immigration have likely moderated the impact of postindustrial structural shifts on horizontal segregation in the Swiss context. Indeed, results suggest that Swiss employers increasingly relied upon immigrant men to fill lower-level sales and service positions, especially in the restaurant industry (see also Chapter 5 on the possible effects of black urban migration on patterns of sex segregation in the United States during the 1930s). This trend was, however, offset by growing feminization of mid-level clerical and associate professional occupations, as well as increasing masculinization of blue-collar occupations. Consistent with results of our U.S. and Japanese case studies, we thus find that horizontal segregation (i.e., the sorting of men into manual, women into nonmanual work) remains largely intact in the Swiss occupational structure.

These results suggest an overall improvement in the occupational status of the native female labor force in Switzerland since 1970. As increasing numbers of young native women obtained educational credentials required for work in the expanding white-collar segment of the economy, their presence in unskilled (generally low-paying) service and manufacturing jobs declined. At the same time, it seems likely that the growing specialization of educational credentials and the formidable structural barriers to combining family and market roles contributed to a growing bifurcation of the female labor force in Switzerland—into a small group of university-educated professional women (many of whom are childless) and a large group of vocationally credentialed white-collar workers (who are primarily young and single).

These findings have a number of important implications. First, they cast doubt on simple notions of education as a gender-neutral allocating mechanism. The growth of certification requirements in Switzerland undoubtedly has *mixed* effects—sometimes integrative, sometimes segregative. On one hand, the increasing representation of Swiss women in the professions and in government administration suggests that academic credentialing may improve female access to some elite male-dominated occupations. At the same time, occupation-specific credentialing at the nonelite level may effectively transform adolescents' gendered career ambitions into tangible and permanent market distinctions (Calonder Gerster 1990; Stockard and McGee 1990; Baker and Jones 1993; Buchmann and Sacchi 1998; Charles et al. 2001).[23] Vocational education thus may contribute to the reproduction and legitimation of sex segregation in many manual and nonmanual jobs in Switzerland.

Second, demand-driven models, which link sex segregation to service-sector expansion and increasing female labor force participation (e.g., Oppenheimer 1970; K. Davis 1984; Charles 1992), are more applicable in contexts conducive to expanded female labor force participation. Where structural or ideological factors constrain female labor force participation, or where an alternative supply of cheap, flexible labor is available, employers will undoubtedly feel less compelled to actively recruit nonemployed women to fill service-sector jobs. It is important for researchers to consider how the segregative impact of economic restructuring may be mediated by cultural practices, by social histories, and by policies that determine the relative availability for market work of wives, mothers, and "alternative" pools of labor.

Finally, results are once again inconsistent with evolutionary accounts of historical change in sex segregation. Rather than across-the-board integrative tendencies, all three of our historical cases (i.e., United States, Japan, Switzerland) show complex patterns of aggregate-level change, with some major categories becoming more integrated, others becoming less integrated. At the disaggregate level, trends are even less systematic, seemingly reflecting the idiosyncratic institutional and cultural forces playing out in the respective national and historical contexts.

In the following chapter, Kim Weeden and Jesper Sørensen illustrate how our structural modeling approach can be generalized to allow two dimensions of sex segregation—occupational and industrial—to be modeled simultaneously. Among other things, this allows more explicit empirical tests of arguments (made here and elsewhere) that attribute historical or cross-national variability in occupational sex segregation to variability in industrial structure—in particular to variability in the size of the service sector.

Occupational Sex Segregation in Switzerland: Female Representation
and Absolute Counts, 1970, 1980, 1990

Code	Occupation	1970 Scale Value[a] (N)^Men (N)^Women	1980 Scale Value[a] (N)^Men (N)^Women	1990 Scale Value[a] (N)^Men (N)^Women
1	Managerial occupations	(102,231) (25,721)	(123,296) (29,122)	(158,686) (43,977)
11	Government officials	−1.70 (7,542) (438)	−1.65 (9,098) (599)	−0.95 (11,954) (1,793)
12	Corporate and general managers	−0.18 (94,689) (25,283)	−0.31 (114,198) (28,523)	−0.30 (146,732) (42,184)
2	Professional occupations	(115,058) (31,954)	(195,340) (57,362)	(231,715) (88,852)
21	Physical, mathematical, and engineering science professionals	−2.00 (38,017) (1,635)	−2.14 (82,367) (3,317)	−1.52 (100,320) (8,496)
22	Life science and health professionals	−0.53 (16,236) (3,032)	−0.37 (22,178) (5,213)	−0.08 (24,226) (8,630)
23	Teaching professionals	0.83 (24,540) (18,019)	0.86 (39,497) (31,967)	0.86 (41,581) (38,079)
24	Other professionals	−0.22 (36,265) (9,268)	−0.04 (51,298) (16,865)	0.28 (65,588) (33,647)
3	Associate professional occupations	(253,094) (116,497)	(242,609) (147,458)	(327,285) (248,009)

(*continued*)

(*continued*)

Code	Occupation	1970 Scale Value[a] $(N)^{Men}$ $(N)^{Women}$	1980 Scale Value[a] $(N)^{Men}$ $(N)^{Women}$	1990 Scale Value[a] $(N)^{Men}$ $(N)^{Women}$
31	Physical, mathematical, and engineering science associate professionals	−0.99	−0.72	−0.44
		(122,401)	(111,348)	(107,419)
		(14,563)	(18,470)	(26,804)
32	Life science and health associate professionals	3.04	2.99	2.87
		(7,299)	(9,514)	(14,123)
		(48,580)	(64,590)	(96,577)
33	Teaching associate professionals	1.50	1.52	1.56
		(15,282)	(19,212)	(21,674)
		(21,892)	(29,860)	(40,089)
34	Other associate professionals	−0.09	−0.01	0.17
		(108,112)	(102,535)	(184,069)
		(31,462)	(34,538)	(84,539)
4	Clerical occupations	(233,824)	(238,340)	(198,884)
		(247,443)	(311,078)	(332,107)
41	Secretarial, skilled office work	1.16	1.31	1.47
		(216,463)	(218,210)	(170,216)
		(221,091)	(275,976)	(287,501)
42	Cashiers, tellers, and customer service clerks	1.56	1.63	1.39
		(17,361)	(20,130)	(28,668)
		(26,352)	(35,102)	(44,606)
5	Service and sales occupations	(96,462)	(113,929)	(140,316)
		(262,281)	(286,903)	(275,340)
51	Personal and protective service workers	1.96	1.83	1.41
		(67,719)	(77,775)	(96,021)
		(152,979)	(166,208)	(152,436)
52	Salespersons and demonstrators	2.48	2.28	1.97
		(28,743)	(36,154)	(44,295)
		(109,302)	(120,695)	(122,904)

APPENDIX TABLE A7.1
(*continued*)

Code	Occupation	1970 Scale Value[a] (N)[Men] (N)[Women]	1980 Scale Value[a] (N)[Men] (N)[Women]	1990 Scale Value[a] (N)[Men] (N)[Women]
6	Agricultural occupations	(162,769)	(135,345)	(107,948)
		(52,563)	(51,596)	(39,622)
61	Farmers and skilled agricultural workers	0.01	0.11	−0.05
		(162,769)	(135,345)	(107,948)
		(52,563)	(51,596)	(39,622)
7	Craft and related trades occupations	(696,412)	(636,177)	(540,211)
		(129,792)	(90,676)	(51,181)
71	Building trades, extraction workers	−4.53	−4.30	−3.30
		(237,179)	(246,179)	(234,607)
		(819)	(1,144)	(3,347)
72	Metal, machinery, and related trades workers	−1.35	−1.28	−2.05
		(289,828)	(251,423)	(195,515)
		(23,953)	(23,883)	(9,714)
73	Precision, handicraft, printing, and related trades workers	0.89	0.65	0.15
		(53,113)	(39,706)	(28,904)
		(41,401)	(26,013)	(13,029)
74	Other craft and related trades workers	0.54	0.16	−0.22
		(116,292)	(98,869)	(81,185)
		(63,619)	(39,636)	(25,091)
8	Machine operation and assembly occupations	(199,140)	(180,460)	(149,296)
		(48,302)	(34,727)	(21,099)
81	Stationary plant and related operators	−2.32	−2.10	−2.28
		(12,849)	(11,129)	(6,346)
		(403)	(466)	(251)
82	Machine operators and assemblers	0.58	0.32	−0.16
		(80,871)	(67,794)	(54,171)
		(45,853)	(31,846)	(17,891)

(*continued*)

APPENDIX TABLE A7.1
(*continued*)

Code	Occupation	1970 Scale Value[a] (N)Men (N)Women	1980 Scale Value[a] (N)Men (N)Women	1990 Scale Value[a] (N)Men (N)Women
83	Drivers and mobile-plant operators	−2.80	−2.66	−2.45
		(105,420)	(101,537)	(88,779)
		(2,046)	(2,415)	(2,957)
9	Unskilled laborers	(51,269)	(44,437)	(53,561)
		(61,931)	(65,511)	(68,356)
91	Sales and service elementary occupations	1.83	1.78	1.65
		(22,467)	(24,125)	(27,625)
		(44,660)	(48,790)	(55,621)
92	Agricultural laborers	−1.29	−1.39	−0.37
		(18,962)	(10,082)	(5,997)
		(1,659)	(,860)	(1,600)
93	Mining, construction, manufacturing, and transport labor	1.61	1.51	0.37
		(9,840)	(10,230)	(19,939)
		(15,612)	(15,861)	(11,135)
Total		(1,910,259)	(1,909,933)	(1,907,902)
		(976,484)	(1,074,433)	(1,168,543)

[a]Parameter estimates from a simple saturated model. Values above zero indicate female overrepresentation; values below zero indicate female underrepresentation. Data source: Bundesamt für Statistik 1994b.

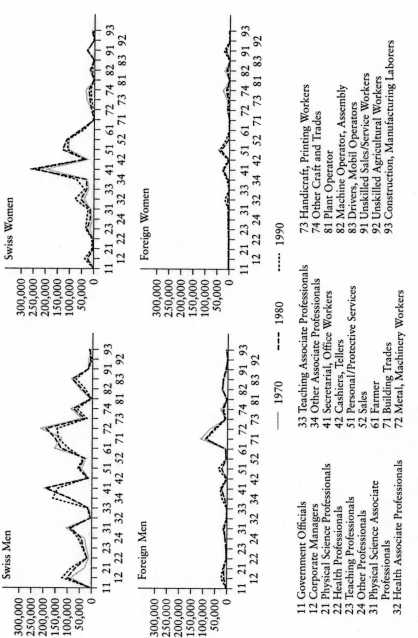

Appendix Figure A7.1   Trends in Absolute Occupational Distribution by Sex and Citizenship Status, 1970, 1980, and 1990

THE INDUSTRIAL CONTEXT
OF SEX SEGREGATION

CHAPTER EIGHT

A Framework for Analyzing Industrial and Occupational Sex Segregation in the United States

Kim A. Weeden, Cornell University, and Jesper B. Sørensen, Massachusettes Institute of Technology

INTRODUCTION

Sociological analyses of segregation have traditionally focused on the distribution of men and women across occupational boundaries, perhaps reflecting the long-standing disciplinary belief that occupations represent the "backbone of the reward structure" (Parkin 1971, p. 18). Nevertheless, contemporary sociologists of gender and work are increasingly turning their attention to the distribution of the sexes across labor market structures other than occupations. Job-level analyses, for example, have burgeoned in popularity, spurred in part by research demonstrating that the more fine-grained the unit of analysis, the more extreme the segregation of men and women at work (e.g., Bielby and Baron 1984; Reskin and Roos 1990; Tomaskovic-Devey 1993, 1995; Huffman and Velasco 1997; Bayard et al 1999; for a review, see Reskin, McBrier, and Kmec 1999). Likewise, analyses of firm-level data demonstrate the importance of interfirm segregation in shaping earnings, opportunities for promotion, and other labor market outcomes (e.g., Petersen and Morgan 1995; Tomaskovic-Devey 1993; England, Reid, and Kilbourne 1996; Tomaskovic-Devey, Kalleberg, and Marsden 1996; Carrington and Troske 1998; Bayard et al. 1999; Kaufman 2002; Tomaskovic-Devey et al. 2003). And industries and economic sectors, long the staples of scholarship in labor economics, continue to play a role in sociological studies of sex segregation (e.g., Jacobs 1989; see also Reskin 1993).

In spite of growing recognition of the importance of these manifold, often cross-cutting labor market structures, most empirical research in the segregation literature still privileges one labor market dimension, thereby ignoring the complex interplay of segregation across labor market structures. Part of the problem, we think, is that theoretical interest in the multiple "dimensions" of sex segregation has not been accompanied by the development of methods suitable for analyzing them. This chapter begins to fill this gap by providing a new framework for the analysis of segregation in contexts in which more than one labor market structure is salient.

We demonstrate the usefulness of this framework by analyzing industrial and occupational segregation in the U.S. labor market. Our choice of industries and occupations for this illustrative analysis is driven, in part, by the ready availability of data. However, it also reflects our belief that although the theoretical literature provides ample evidence of the relevance of industries to sociological analyses of segregation, sociologists lack answers to many fundamental empirical questions about the sexual division of labor across industries and occupations.

One set of unanswered questions pertains to the strength and pattern of gender segregation in industries (or, conversely, occupations) after controlling for differences in the distribution and gender composition of occupations (or industries). To what extent does the well-documented segregation of men and women into different occupations reflect industrial segregation and differences in the industrial composition of occupations? Conversely, does industrial sex segregation exist at all, net of occupational segregation? If so, what is its typical pattern? The models we develop below allow us to estimate the cost of ignoring industry in studies of occupational segregation, assess the net association between industry and gender, and compare the relative strength of sex segregation across these two dimensions.[1]

A second set of questions pertains to the three-way interaction among industry, occupation, and sex, and in particular, to the variation in occupational segregation across industries. This variation can take two forms: first, industries may differ in the *strength* of occupational segregation, where "strength" refers to the extent to which women are under- or overrepresented in occupations within those industries; and second, industries may differ in their *pattern* of occupational sex segregation, where "pattern" refers to the direction and relative degree of sex-typing of individual occupations. For example, an occupation (such as sales clerk) that is predominantly male in one industry (say, retail automotive) may be predominantly female in another (retail apparel). Alternatively, an occupation may be female-typed in all industries but be among the most segregated occupations in one industry and among the least segregated in another.

Although a smattering of studies attend to differences in the strength of occupational segregation across industries (e.g., Bridges 1980, 1982; Stearns and Coleman 1988; Cartwright and Edwards 2002; Tomaskovic-Devey et al. 2003), industry differences in the pattern of segregation have not been sufficiently appreciated in prior theoretical or empirical work. This state of affairs arises, we argue, because of the field's nearly universal reliance on index-based methodologies. As noted in Chapter 2, these methods can measure variability in the strength of segregation, but are not equipped to capture variability in its patterns. Association models, by contrast, allow us to distinguish the two components of interindustrial variability in occupational segregation and to quantify the relative contribution of each to the association in the data.

Before we develop the log-multiplicative framework for analyzing segregation across multiple labor market structures, it is useful to review, if only briefly, why industries constitute a relevant second dimension for sociological analyses of segregation. To make our case, we outline extant theoretical accounts of segregation that either rely on industry distinctions or can logically be extended to an industry-level analysis. We note at the outset that our illustrative analysis does not attempt to adjudicate among these theoretical accounts, although our models could be elaborated to do so.[2]

WHY STUDY INDUSTRY?

In empirical analyses of segregation, industries, which aggregate organizations operating within a common product market, are most often (a) ignored altogether (see Chapter 5), (b) used as a proxy for occupations where the information on the latter are lacking (see, e.g., Jacobs and Lim 1992), or (c) cross-classified with occupations to define labor market positions that approximate jobs (see, for example, Kaufman 2002). The first procedure is tantamount to aggregating across the industry dimension of a three-way cross-classification of industry, occupation, and sex, while the second is equivalent to aggregating across the occupation dimension. Both are likely to underestimate the extent to which men and women occupy different positions in the opportunity structure if, for example, male overrepresentation in a given occupation in one industry is partially or fully offset by female overrepresentation in that same occupation in another industry. If the purpose of segregation research is to reveal the "true" extent of sex segregation in a given labor market, the third procedure, in which one analyzes the industry-occupation nexus, serves as a useful corrective to either form of aggregation.

Our interest in industries extends beyond these descriptive concerns. Many of the supply-side theories that have been proposed to account for segregation across occupations (such as sex-differentiated investments in skills and training, gender-specific job choices, sex-typed socialization) can logically be applied to industries, and demand-side explanations of segregation have long incorporated industrial distinctions. We review some of these conceptualizations in this chapter, paying particular attention to arguments relevant to (a) the strength and pattern of industrial segregation (independent of occupational segregation), (b) variability across industries in the strength of occupational segregation, and (c) variability across industries in the pattern of occupational segregation.

Strength and Pattern of Industrial Segregation

We begin with four theoretical accounts that predict a sexual division of labor differentiated along industrial lines. These arguments, which we discuss in turn, locate the source of industrial segregation in processes of labor market segmentation, imprinting and the institutionalization of gender labels, the translation of household gender roles to the market, and balkanization.

Perhaps the best-known of these arguments emerges from the segmented labor market literature. Proponents of this approach have suggested that women are disproportionately relegated to the peripheral sector, which is made up of competitive firms in industries that use labor-intensive production methods, have fewer economic resources, and offer low-wage, unstable, dead-end jobs (see, e.g., Beck, Horan, and Tolbert 1978; Blankenship 1983). Employers in peripheral industries benefit from segregation, it is argued, because crowding creates a labor surplus, lowers wages, and maintains a pool of expendable labor, thereby increasing profits. Employers in the core, which consists of monopolistic firms in industries that use technologically advanced and capital-intensive production methods, support segregation out of a desire to create internal divisions in the working class, a belief that women will have rapid turnover in highly skilled positions, or immunity from the need to economize on labor costs by hiring women.[3]

Whereas segmented labor market approaches emphasize the link between the current economic environment and hiring practices, imprinting arguments point to the lasting impact of an industry's developmental history (see, e.g., Stinchcombe 1965; Milkman 1987). More specifically, the characteristic sex ratio in an industry "reflects the economic, political, and social constraints that are operative when that industry's labor market initially forms" (Milkman 1987, p. 7). These constraints involve such variables as core or periphery location, principal mode of control (piecework or assembly line, for example), supply and cost of male and female labor, and the actual or anticipated political impact of recruiting male versus female labor. According to the imprinting argument, firms that enter early in an industry's development model their structures on firms operating in related industries or in the wider environment. Once a particular social arrangement is in place, there are tendencies for inertia, with existing organizations retaining their structures and new organizations modeling themselves after successes within their industries (Stinchcombe 1965; Hannan and Freeman 1989). Ultimately, sex-role stereotyping gathers the force of an ideology and is reproduced by employers, even during periods of major economic crises and labor shortages (Milkman 1987).[4]

Imprinting may be seen, then, as an industry-level analogue to occupational sex-typing. Both arguments rest on the assumption that the gender type of a position is established early and becomes institutionalized in hiring practices. It should be recognized, however, that according to the imprinting argument, the sex type of an industry emerges from a complex set of environmental contingencies. This sex-typing may match stereotypes about domestic gender roles, but the correspondence is neither necessary nor universal. Indeed, in the early stages of sex-typing, employers may attempt to recast the gender image of a task or product rather than choose workers that match its existing image (Milkman 1987; see also Reskin and Roos 1990).

A related argument also emphasizes the institutionalization of sex stereotypes, but links these stereotypes more directly to broader cultural forces ("gender essentialism"; see Chapter 1), and in particular to the domestic division of labor (e.g., Caplow 1954; Oppenheimer 1970; but see Cohn 1985). According to this line of thought, stereotypes about the "sex-type" of an industry are generalized from the gendered nature of its product and, in turn, affect both workers' job choices and employers' hiring preferences. As a result, women are better represented in industries that produce goods or services that are functionally or symbolically similar to women's traditional domestic roles, such as personal service industries, or traditionally purchased by women, such as apparel and food. Although existing theories about gender roles usually address the tasks that are performed (that is, the occupation) rather than the context in which those tasks are performed, we believe that they are equally applicable at the latter, the industry level. Indeed, the commodification of tasks traditionally performed within the family may have created or enlarged particular industries, with changes in the occupational structure occurring as a byproduct of these industrial shifts. For an example, we need look no further than the historical case studies featured in this volume, which emphasize the link between the expansion of female-typed service industries and the subsequent feminization of white-collar occupations.

The fourth and final plausible source of industrial segregation points not to the sex stereotype of the entire industry, but to the sex stereotype of key occupations within it. If an industry forms a relatively self-contained labor market, with most promotion and recruitment proceeding internally, the exclusion of women (or men) from port-of-entry occupations will greatly reduce overall female representation in that industry (for a related argument at the occupation level, see England 1992). Consider, for example, metal-working occupations in heavy manufacturing industries. The workers who originate in these highly male-typed occupations will, over time, disperse into other occupations (such as personnel officer) within the industry, some of which may be relatively integrated or even female-typed in other industries. The end result is that the industry itself, rather than just metal-working occupations, becomes disproportionately male. Such balkanization will of course occur only to the extent that port-of-entry occupations are sex-typed and industrial labor markets are self-contained.

The foregoing arguments provide clues about which industries are likely to be female-typed: those that are peripheral, those formed in historical periods in which female labor was particularly cheap or prevalent (relative to male labor), those in which products are consistent with traditional female household roles, and those with insular labor markets and female-typed entry occupations. These theories offer a useful corrective to explanations of the sexual division of labor that focus exclusively on the level or pattern of occupational segregation. More important, at least for our purposes, they offer sufficient reason to believe that men and women will be differentially distributed across industries, even independent of occupational segregation in the labor market and of the occupational mix in various industries.

Industry Differences in the Strength of Occupational Segregation

Apart from its utilitarian role as a substitute for occupational or job-level data, industry most often enters sociological analyses of segregation in the role of an explanatory variable in models of the level of occupational sex segregation (e.g., Semyonov and Scott 1983; Charles 1992, 1998; Lorence 1992). The theoretical links between industries and the level of occupational sex segregation emerge from three lines of research: segmented labor market theories, institutional models, and social movement (unionization) research.

Segmented labor market approaches predict that occupational sex segregation will be stronger in core than in peripheral industries. According to this line of thought, the labor market in peripheral industries operates much like the competitive markets of neoclassical economics. Peripheral employers have little margin to indulge in their tastes for discrimination (G. Becker 1975), and, because labor comprises a large fraction of their costs, they have strong incentives to hire the least expensive workers available, even if doing so violates stereotypes or generates opposition from dominant-group workers (see, e.g., Cohn 1985, 2000; Reskin and Roos 1990; Kaufman 2002). Presumably, core employers have greater economic leeway to discriminate. Moreover, although segmented labor market theorists routinely argue that employment practices in the core are more bureaucratic and universalistic, thereby implying less occupational segregation, these purportedly bureaucratic hiring practices may merely institutionalize sex segregation by closing off port-of-entry occupations to women or by legitimating seniority-based promotion systems that favor long-time (male) workers (see, e.g., Roos 1984; Bielby and Baron 1986; Nelson and Bridges 1999).

Institutional theorists have been quick to note that employers' hiring practices are shaped by their normative and institutional as well as economic environments. According to these theorists, firms compete not only for market share and profits, but also for political power and legitimacy, and in this competition firms are under pressure to adopt personnel practices that are sanctioned in the wider institutional environment (see, e.g., Meyer and Rowan 1977; Tomaskovic-Devey and Skaggs 1999). As society becomes increasingly rationalized and bureaucratized, these legitimated practices come to include gender-egalitarian hiring and promotion standards (for a related argument, see Charles 1992, 1998). Industries vary, however, in the extent to which organizations are subject to institutional pressures, government regulation, and enforcement of equal employment laws (Hodson 1983; Beggs 1995; see also Guthrie and Roth 1999). The pressures to conform to the spirit of equal employment laws, for example, may be greater in industries that are highly visible, employ a large proportion of state workers, or are heavily dependent on government contracts (see, for example, Chapter 6 on growing female representation in elite Swiss civil service occupations). Levels of occupational sex segregation may also be lower in industries that experienced their greatest period of expansion in more recent decades, when gender-egalitarian norms were stronger.

Finally, a number of scholars have sought to untangle the relationship between unionization and occupational segregation by sex (see, e.g., Bridges 1982; Milkman 1987; Wallace and Chang 1990; Kaufman 2002). Because unions act to protect the interests of their typically male memberships, they may advocate practices that exclude women from the best occupations in their industries. This would suggest higher levels of occupational sex segregation in more heavily unionized industries (Wallace and Chang 1990; cf. Bridges 1982). However, not all unions are male-dominated, and not all male-dominated unions resist gender equality (Kessler-Harris 1982; Milkman 1987). Indeed, in the face of declining union membership, contemporary unions have made explicit overtures to women, racial and ethnic minorities, and other groups that historically have been underserved by collective bargaining. The strength and even the direction of the association between industrial unionization and occupational sex segregation thus remains an open empirical question.

Industry Differences in Patterns of Occupational Sex Segregation

The preceding arguments pertain to industry differences in the strength of occupational segregation, but, at least as they are currently formulated, do not make clear predictions regarding cross-industry variability in the pattern of occupational segregation. However, the logic of two of these approaches, the imprinting and institutional arguments, suggest possible sources of such industry-specific patterns.

As previously noted, the imprinting argument claims that new organizations base their hiring practices, and in particular their preferences for male or female labor, on the practices adopted by successful firms in the same or related industries. It is likewise possible that new firms will mimic either the precise pattern of occupational segregation prevailing in related industries or the institutional features—for example, systems of job differentiation and job ladders, authority structures, and strength requirements— that contribute to a particular pattern of occupational sex segregation (see, e.g., Bielby and Baron 1984). Either process is likely to lead to similar patterns of occupational segregation in industries whose products are closely related and in industries that share founding conditions.

A second plausible source of interindustry variation in patterns of occupational segregation emerges from the logic of institutional theory. We have already noted that industries may vary in the extent to which they are subject to gender-egalitarian norms and legal mandates. Pressure to conform to these norms may also vary across occupations. Prestigious professional and managerial occupations, for example, have long been the focus of the most vociferous demands for equality and hence are more likely to manifest legal and normative egalitarianism than blue-collar occupations (see Chapter 1 for details; also see Charles 1998). To the extent that industries are differentially exposed to gender-egalitarian norms, pressures to conform to these norms can be expected to be strongest in a few highly visible occupations. This would then lead to variation in the pattern of occupational segregation across industries.

While far from a truly comprehensive analysis of the relationship between industrial and occupational segregation, the preceding sections nonetheless serve their main purpose, which is to demonstrate that the conceptual importance of industries is well grounded in the gender-stratification and labor market literatures. Using relatively familiar theories, one can generate predictions about (a) the existence of industrial segregation (net of occupational segregation), (b) industry-level variation in the strength of occupational segregation, and (c) industry-level variation in the pattern of occupational segregation. In the next section, we develop log-multiplicative models that overcome the methodological complexities that arise when one conceptualizes industries and occupations as distinct but intersecting dimensions of the sexual division of labor.

A LOG-LINEAR MODELING APPROACH

The few analysts who have attempted the simultaneous analysis of segregation across industries and occupations (e.g., Bridges 1980; Lorence 1992) have found it extremely difficult to separate these two dimensions. At the root of the problem lie the marginal dependencies of index-based methodologies (see, e.g., Chapter 2), and in particular the dependence of D on the occupational composition of the country, time period, industry, or other social unit being studied. Indeed, because industries are likely to be more heterogeneous in their occupational composition than are nations or time periods, the marginal dependencies of D may make it even more misleading for examining interindustry variability.

Log-linear and log-multiplicative techniques resolve these problems by allowing us to model sex segregation across two labor market dimensions without introducing the marginal dependencies that characterize conventional scalar indices. The starting point for our discussion of the log-multiplicative framework is the multiplicative shift effect model originally developed in the context of cross-national research (Charles and Grusky 1995; see also Chapter 2):[5]

$$m_{ijk} = \alpha_k \beta_{ik} \gamma_{jk} e^{\phi_k(Z_j \mu_i)}, \qquad (8.1)$$

where k indexes country (or time period in Chapters 5–7), i indexes occupation, j indexes sex, m_{ijk} is the frequency in cell (i, j, k), α_k is the grand mean in the kth country (time period), β_{ik} is the marginal effect for the ith occupation in the kth country (time period), γ_{jk} is the marginal effect for the jth sex in the kth country (time period), and Z_j is an indicator variable of gender ($Z_1 = 0 = $ men, and $Z_2 = 1 = $ women). The μ_i are the scale values for the ith occupation; in order to identify the model, μ_i are normalized to have zero mean and unit variance. The ϕ_k are "multiplicative shift effects" that allow the strength of association to vary across nations or any other comparative units. In its original cross-national form, the model assumes that the structure of occupational sex segregation (given by the μ_i) is the same across nations, but the strength of the association between occupation and gender differs.

One could adapt this cross-national model to a three-dimensional array of industry by occupation by sex in a straightforward way by simply replacing nations with industries as the third dimension, k, in the model. However, while the nation-by-sex interaction is typically (but not always) regarded as a nuisance term, the industry-by-sex interaction is, for our purposes, an important object of inquiry in its own right. Thus, where Charles and Grusky (1995) allow the marginal effect for sex (that is, the overall sex ratio) to vary freely across countries (see also Chapter 3 of this volume), we wish to explicitly model the two-way industry-by-sex association, in the same way that we model the occupation-by-sex association.

With this in mind, we can develop a set of models for the three-dimensional, industry-by-occupation-by-sex array. In the subsequent discussion, rows refer to occupation, columns refer to sex, and layers refer to industry. We note where the models correspond with one or more of the perspectives on industrial and occupational segregation outlined in the introductory section.

The first model, that of conditional independence, assumes that there is no sex segregation by occupation or industry. Model 1 is given by:

$$m_{ijk} = \alpha \beta_i \gamma_j \delta_k \lambda_{ik}, \tag{8.2}$$

where the λ_{ik} allow the occupational distributions to vary freely by industry, δ_k is the marginal effect of the kth industry, and other terms are defined as above. It is exceedingly unlikely that this model will fit the data, but Model 1 is useful insofar as it quantifies the total association between sex and the two labor market structures in the data, and thereby serves as a baseline against which we can compare the less constrained models that follow.

Model 2 assumes that there is constant occupational sex segregation across industries, but no industrial sex segregation. This simple "row effects" model is given by:

$$m_{ijk} = \alpha \beta_i \gamma_j \delta_k \lambda_{ik} e^{\phi(Z_j \mu_i)}. \tag{8.3}$$

The scale values (μ_i) generated under Model 2 define the pattern of segregation; that is, they identify the occupations in which women are over- or underrepresented. The ϕ parameter measures the strength of the occupation-by-sex association, with large values indicating more extreme levels of occupational sex segregation. This model assumes that segregation is constant across industries. In ignoring industrial segregation, it is consistent with the majority of sex-segregation research that implicitly aggregates across industries, but improves upon such analyses by purging all cross-occupational variability in industrial composition.

The "layer effects" (Clogg 1982) model (Model 3) assumes constant industrial sex segregation across occupations, with no occupational segregation:

$$m_{ijk} = \alpha\beta_i\gamma_j\delta_k\lambda_{ik}e^{\psi(Z_j\nu_k)}. \tag{8.4}$$

The interpretation of the parameters under this model is similar to that for Model 2. Scale values ν_k reflect the sex ratios of the different industries (net of marginal effects), while the association parameter ψ indicates the strength of industrial sex segregation. This model is consistent with studies in which researchers consider the extent of industrial sex segregation without controlling for occupational segregation (e.g., Jacobs and Lim 1992).

Combining Models 2 and 3, we can also allow for occupational segregation (constant across industries) and industrial segregation (constant across occupations):

$$m_{ijk} = \alpha\beta_i\gamma_j\delta_k\lambda_{ik}e^{\phi(Z_j\mu_i)}e^{\psi(Z_j\nu_k)}. \tag{8.5}$$

This model implies that the distribution of men and women is due both to occupational sex segregation, the pattern and strength of which is invariant across industries, and to industrial sex segregation, the pattern and strength of which is invariant across occupations. The parameters are interpreted as before, although the μ_i now reflect occupational sex segregation *net* of industrial sex segregation, and the ν_k measure the extent of industrial sex segregation net of occupational sex segregation. For example, a positive μ value for the occupation "inspectors and compliance officers" would indicate that women are overrepresented in this occupation, after we take into consideration the fact that most of these inspectors are located in the heavily male construction industry.

Model 5 allows us to test whether any industrial variations in occupational segregation reflect differences in the level of occupational segregation, pattern of occupational segregation, or both. This model fits industrial and occupational sex segregation, as in Model 4. However, although it assumes a generic pattern of occupational sex segregation common to all industries, it allows the level of occupational segregation to vary across industries:

$$m_{ijk} = \alpha\beta_i\gamma_j\delta_k\lambda_{ik}e^{\phi_k(Z_j\mu_i)}e^{\psi(Z_j\nu_k)}. \tag{8.6}$$

Under this model, the ϕ_k track variations in the degree of sex segregation across industries. Relative to those with high values of ϕ_k, industries with low values have more compressed common scale values, the μ_i. In other words, occupational sex segregation is less extreme in industries with low values of ϕ_k. So, for example, women may be overrepresented in the occupation "secretary" and men may be overrepresented in the occupation "purchasing agents and buyers" in all industries, but the extent of overrepresentation may be greater in trucking and warehousing than in entertainment and recreation services. As suggested earlier, such interindustry variability in the strength of sex segregation may reflect differences in industries' institutional environments, rates of unionization, or economic competitiveness.

If Model 5 fails to adequately characterize the data, the next step is a saturated model:

$$m_{ijk} = \alpha\beta_i\gamma_j\delta_k\lambda_{ik}e^{\phi_k(Z_j\mu_{ik})}. \tag{8.7}$$

Model 6 fits a unique scale value for each industry-occupation cell, thus allowing the pattern of occupational segregation to vary freely across industries. It also fits a set of industry-specific ϕ values, which capture industry variations in the strength of occupational segregation.[6] The saturated model is consistent with research that examines the industry-occupation nexus as a proxy for more detailed, job-level information (e.g., Kaufman 2002).

DATA

To illustrate the utility of these models, we apply them to a data set generated from the 1990 Equal Employment Opportunity (EEO) Supplemental Tabulations File (U.S. Census Bureau 1993b, 1993c).[7] The EEO file presents data for the entire U.S. civilian labor force that has been extrapolated from the information given by a "long-form" subsample of the population. To approximate the actual sample size on which the EEO tabulations are based, we weighted the data by 15 percent.

The EEO file cross-tabulates detailed occupation (511 categories) by industry (98 categories) by sex. We would have preferred to use this highly detailed matrix of 100,156 cells, but it proved to be computationally intractable (see Clogg 1982). We therefore aggregated the published table into an array containing 44 industries and 125 occupations. Because industrial segregation is the principal substantive focus of this chapter, we chose to retain as much detail in the industry classification as possible even at the expense of reducing the number of occupations. We note, however, that our industry effects may capture omitted occupational effects and hence should be considered upper-bound estimates.

Appendix Tables A8.1 and A8.2 present our industrial and occupational classification schemes, respectively. To determine which occupations and industries to combine, we applied five rules sequentially. First, we eliminated six farm and five private household service occupations, as well as all individuals in the agricultural production and private household industries. These sectors contained a high proportion of structural zeros, here defined as industry-occupation locations with neither male nor female incumbents. Second, we aggregated occupations that were defined in the EEO file by their industrial locations. For example, we combined the categories of "laborers, construction," "laborers, nondurable goods manufacturing," and "laborers, durable goods manufacturing" into a single "laborer" occupation. Third, we aggregated occupational categories that were defined by employment situation. For example, we combined "self-employed managers and administrators" with "salaried managers and administrators." Fourth, we followed fairly standard Census Bureau schemes to group the remaining occupational and industrial categories into less-detailed categories (e.g., U.S. Bureau of the Census 1989, Appendix B [occupation] and Appendix D [industry]).

Finally, we identified the remaining occupations that generated structural zeros. On a case-by-case basis, we combined each of these occupations with a functionally similar occupation in the classification scheme. The final matrix is thus free of empty cells in the industry-by-occupation array generated by collapsing over sex. However, some of the industry-occupation cells contain only male or only female workers. Because these "sampling" zeros are problematic in models that saturate the three-way association, we added a small constant, 0.1, to the 192 empty cells in the three-way array (Agresti 1990).[8] After weighting, eliminating the farm and private household workers, and adding 0.1 to the empty cells, our data array contains 17,923,371 individuals in 11,000 cells (125 occupations by 2 sexes by 44 industries).

RESULTS

The central empirical issues of this chapter pertain to industrial segregation and inter-industry variations in occupational segregation. More specifically, what is the strength of industrial segregation, net of industry variation in occupational composition and the differential distribution of men and women across occupations? What is the pattern of industrial segregation? Does the strength or pattern of occupational sex segregation vary by industry? We address each of these questions in turn.

To this end, Table 8.1 presents the fit statistics for the log-multiplicative association models described previously. Because of the sample size, the likelihood-ratio test statistics (L^2) are extremely large by the standards of conventional log-linear studies. This means that including additional parameters that capture what might substantively be considered trivial differences will nonetheless effect large absolute declines in L^2. For this reason, we pay greater attention than usual to Δ, which measures the percentage of cases misallocated under the given model and is insensitive to sample size. We would, however, reach the same substantive conclusions regarding model selection if we were to use conventional comparisons of L^2 or BIC (Raftery 1986).

The Strength of Industrial Segregation

As one would expect, the model of conditional independence (no industrial or occupational sex segregation) fits poorly, misclassifying over a quarter of the cases. This lack of fit can be attributed to sex segregation across industries, across occupations, or both. The model of constant occupational segregation with no industrial segregation (Model 2) fits considerably better, misclassifying only 7.3 percent of cases and accounting for a large share (86.3 percent) of the variability unexplained by the independence model (see Table 8.1, line B2). Model 3, which specifies constant industrial segregation with no occupational segregation, misallocates 17.0 percent of the cases and reduces L^2 by 40.4 percent relative to the conditional independence model. These figures suggest stronger segregation across occupations than across industries (see also OECD 1985), particularly in light of the fact that we were

TABLE 8.1

Fit Statistics for Log-Linear and Log-Multiplicative Models
of Occupational and Industrial Sex Segregation

	L^2	d.f.	L_H^2/L_T^2	Δ
A. Model				
1. Conditional independence (null association)	7,882,738	5,499	100.0	26.4
2. Constant occupational sex segregation (homogeneous row effects)	1,081,627	5,375	86.3	7.3
3. Constant industrial sex segregation (homogeneous layer effects)	4,700,680	5,456	40.4	17.0
4. Independent industrial and occupational segregation	575,953	5,332	92.7	5.0
5. Multiplicative shift effect for occupational segregation in each industry (constant industrial segregation)	526,685	5,289	93.3	4.7
B. Contrast				
1. Total variability (Model 1)	7,882,738	5,499	100.0	
2. Variability explained by occupational segregation (Model 2 vs. Model 1)	6,801,111	124	86.3	
3. Variability explained by industrial segregation (Model 3 vs. Model 1)	3,182,058	43	40.4	
4. Variability explained by differing levels of occupational segregation across industries (Model 5 vs. Model 4)	49,268	43	8.6	

NOTE: Delta (Δ) represents the percentage of cases misclassified under the relevant model.

forced to aggregate occupations as well as industries. Nonetheless, industry emerges as an important dimension of sex segregation in its own right. In fact, the reduction in L^2 per degree of freedom is greater for Model 3 than for Model 2.

We should be cautious of making too much of these results, though, because the strength and pattern of industrial segregation emerging from Model 3 may be merely an artifact of not controlling for occupational sex segregation. Because of compositional effects, industrial sex segregation may indeed be negligible once we purge the association between gender and occupation from the data. We address this possibility by fitting Model 4, which allows for both occupational and industrial sex segregation. This specification accounts for 92.7 percent of the total association in the data, and misclassifies 5 percent of the cases. The parameter estimates from Model 4 confirm that occupational segregation is stronger than industrial segregation; the parameter Ψ pertaining to the strength of the association between occupation and sex is estimated to be 17.3, whereas the industry-by-sex analogue is only 3.8. However, industrial sex segregation has independent explanatory power. In fact, industrial sex segregation cuts the unexplained association from the occupational segregation model in half (see Table 8.1, line B4).[9] We draw two conclusions from these results: (1) both occupational and industrial sex segregation have substantial, independent effects; but (2) occupational sex segregation is stronger than industrial sex segregation.

The Pattern of Industrial Segregation

The occupational and industrial scale values estimated in Model 4 serve two substantive purposes. First, they allow us to determine whether prevailing notions regarding patterns of occupational sex segregation still hold when the effects of industrial sex segregation are purged from the data. Our results suggest that sex-segregation researchers can breathe a sigh of relief: the correlation between the unpurged occupational scale values (from Model 2) and the purged scale values (from Model 4) is 0.99. Indeed, the correlation between the occupation scale values from a standard occupation-by-sex array (collapsing over industry) and the purged values from Model 4 is almost unity. Second, the industry scale values (ν) describe the pattern of industrial sex segregation. It is worth examining these scale values in some detail, given the relative lack of information in the empirical literature regarding the (net) segregation of men and women across industries. To this end, Figure 8.1 graphs the industry scale values, which are defined so that negative values indicate male overrepresentation and positive values indicate female overrepresentation.

For purposes of discussion, we can group the industries in Figure 8.1 into three clusters based on the extent and direction of segregation. The first cluster contains industries in which men are strongly overrepresented. This cluster is dominated by classic heavy industries such as iron and steel manufacturing (where men are overrepresented by a factor of 2.63),[10] mining, and automotive production. It also contains the construction industry, where net of other effects, men are overrepresented by a factor of 2.43.[11]

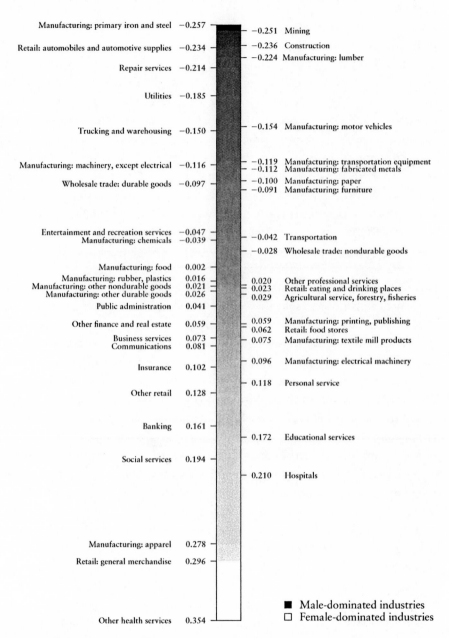

Figure 8.1   Industrial Sex Segregation: Purged Scale Values from Model 4

Finally, it includes industries involving automobiles and trucks (retail automotive dealers and gasoline stations, trucking and warehousing, and repair services), utilities, and the wholesale trade of durable goods. The second cluster consists of industries that are relatively integrated by sex. It contains a mix of "light" manufacturing and service industries. Within this cluster, female representation varies widely, from a factor of .84 in the entertainment and recreation industry to 1.43 in electrical machinery manufacturing.[12] The third and final cluster contains industries in which women are strongly overrepresented. Although there is no clear boundary between this cluster and the relatively integrated industries, the best cutoff point seems to lie between electrical machinery manufacturing and insurance, where female overrepresentation reaches 1.5 times the overall sex ratio (see Figure 8.1). Based on this cutoff point, women are strongly overrepresented in ten industries, with the multiplier ranging from 1.47 in insurance to an astonishing 3.78 in other health services, which includes offices and clinics of health practitioners, nursing, and personal care facilities.[13] With one exception (apparel manufacturing), these industries depend upon customer service (retail industries, insurance, banking) or interpersonal and nurturing skills (educational services, social services, health care).

The pattern of industrial segregation in Figure 8.1 has several plausible explanations. Segmented labor market approaches find some corroboration in the fact that men are overrepresented in many of the most capital-intensive industries. On balance, however, the evidence seems mixed—some capital-intensive industries are not male-typed, and some heavily male industries are not capital-intensive.[14] Moreover, the observed patterns are also consistent with several other interpretations. Male overrepresentation in manufacturing industries, for example, may arise because these are relatively insular labor markets and men are overrepresented in key port-of-entry occupations. Furthermore, most of the industries in the male-dominated cluster experienced their initial expansion in the late nineteenth and early twentieth centuries, well before the recent rise in female labor force participation. Conversely, the dramatic overrepresentation of women in service industries may reflect the timing of women's entry into the labor force, which coincided with, and was in part caused by, the expansion of the service sector (Oppenheimer 1973). Both of these results are consistent with the claim that the social organization of an industry reflects the legacy of its founding conditions, although of course the evidence from this cross-sectional analysis is far from definitive. Finally, the observed patterns of industrial segregation can also be interpreted as demonstrating a functional or symbolic association between industry and women's household roles. The overrepresentation of women in service-sector industries, for example, may arise because these industries sell services similar to those for which women have traditionally been responsible in the home; likewise, in manufacturing industries, there is a notable tendency for the sex of workers who produce particular goods to match the sex of those who are most likely to consume or purchase them (see Caplow 1954, p. 232; A. Scott 1994; Charles 1998; Chapter 1 herein).

Industry Variation in Occupational Segregation

Under Model 4, almost 5 percent of cases are still misclassified. The remaining association in the table hails from two sources: differences in the strength of occupational segregation across industries, and differences in the pattern of occupational segregation across industries. To evaluate the relative size of each component, we fit Model 5, which allows the strength of occupational sex segregation to vary across industries but constrains the pattern of segregation (defined by the scale values) to be the same across industries. The model also allows for constant industrial segregation across occupations. As the fit statistics suggest, interindustry variation in the strength of occupational segregation is negligible. Model 5 still misclassifies 4.7 percent of the cases, and the improvement in L^2 is modest considering the sample size. In fact, differences in the strength of occupational segregation account for only 8.6 percent of the unexplained association in Model 4 (see Table 8.1, Model Contrast 4). Stated differently, over 91 percent of the remaining association is due to industry differences in the pattern of association. These differences can only be accounted for by fitting the saturated model—that is, by estimating a unique set of scale values for each industry.

The action—or what remains of it—thus appears to lie in industry differences in the pattern of occupational sex segregation. Although occupational scale values correlate rather highly across industries, some variability is clearly evident.[15] To get a sense of this variability, we tallied, for each of our 125 occupations, the number of industries in which men were overrepresented and the number of industries in which women were overrepresented (see Table 8.2, page 268).[16] About one-third of the occupations are uniformly sex-typed across industries: in twenty-four occupations, most of which are office management, clerical, or administrative support occupations, women are overrepresented in all forty-four industries; and in seventeen occupations, most of which are in engineering, repair, or construction crafts, men are overrepresented in all industries.

The majority of occupations, however, are not consistently typed across industries. For example, the occupation of marketing manager evinces female overrepresentation in sixteen industries (most strongly in personal service) and male overrepresentation in twenty-three industries (most strongly in motor vehicle manufacturing), and is virtually gender-neutral in the remaining five industries. Only one occupation, freight and stock handlers, is integrated in more than a quarter of the industries, and most occupations are integrated in fewer than five industries.[17] We thus find evidence of strong interindustry variability in patterns of occupational sex segregation, as one would expect based on arguments citing industry-specific historical developments and industrial differences in susceptibility to gender-egalitarian pressures.

CONCLUSION

The multidimensional nature of sex segregation is widely recognized in the theoretical literature, but to date, methodological limitations have thwarted corresponding empirical analyses. The two-dimensional models of sex segregation introduced in this chapter will, we hope, help remedy this situation. To demonstrate the potential of our multidimensional modeling approach, we applied it to industrial and occupational sex segregation data for the contemporary United States. Three substantive conclusions can be drawn from this analysis.

First, men and women are segregated across industries, and not merely because industries differ in their occupational composition. Even if they share the same occupation, women are concentrated in service industries and men are concentrated in manufacturing industries. Although both groups are represented in retail, men are overrepresented where the product is stereotypically male (in automobile sales, for example) and women are overrepresented where the product is stereotypically female. Evidence of a net effect of industry provides support for arguments attributing historical or cross-national differences in occupational sex segregation to differences in the industrial structure, and in particular to variability in the relative size of the service sector.

Second, our analysis suggests that interindustry variability in occupational sex segregation cannot be understood solely by examining the overall level within each industry. Rather, there are fundamental differences across industries in the sex composition of particular occupations. This finding poses a challenge to segregation theories: how and why do patterns of occupational sex segregation vary across industries? In our view, the most promising explanations emerge from theories that attend to the historical contingencies surrounding industry formation and development or that focus on interindustrial variability in gender-egalitarian pressures. Cross-national or historical analysis of sex segregation across industry-occupation categories may help adjudicate among these, and other, theoretical perspectives outlined in this chapter.

We note, however, that some or all of the observed effect of industries on occupational segregation stems not from characteristics of the industry per se, but from relatively low variance in the characteristics of the organizations comprising industries. As critics of the dual labor market approach pointed out long ago, organizations, not industries, define the distribution of occupations and allocate workers to those occupations (Granovetter 1981; Baron 1984; see also Reskin, McBrier, and Kmec 1999). Even within an industry, organizations may vary along a number of dimensions potentially relevant to occupational segregation, including size, founding conditions, competitive environment, supply of qualified workers, organizational culture, and the like (e.g., Baron and Bielby 1980). Nevertheless, these organizations share a product market and, as a result, may share not only production technologies and a common position within the economy, but also political interests, collective bargaining activities, regulations, patterns of exchange and dependence on suppliers and buyers, and legal limits on their behavior, including employment practices (Kalleberg and Berg 1987, pp. 102–7; Burt 1983; Hannan and Freeman 1989).

By choosing industry as the second dimension for our illustrative analysis, we assumed that organizations vary less within industries than they do between them (for similar approaches, see Hodson 1983; Beggs 1995). It remains an open question, though, whether product markets shape the pattern of sex segregation (as, for example, the household division-of-labor argument suggests), whether industrial variations in these patterns merely capture the aggregate effect of organization-level characteristics, or whether, as seems most likely, both industrial and organizational contexts matter.

Third, our results indicate that occupational segregation is considerably stronger than industrial segregation, however one interprets the latter. If, for methodological or substantive reasons, one wishes to characterize the opportunity structure with one dimension, as much previous research has done, then occupation is a good choice, at least relative to industry. This suggests two practical implications. Researchers who insist on scalar indices of segregation can safely ignore industries, given that the strength of occupational segregation varies little across industries. On the other hand, our findings recommend a modeling approach that can account for differences in the pattern of occupational segregation across industries. Index-based approaches ignore such differences and thus miss the true character of industrial variations in occupational sex segregation.

The utility of the log-multiplicative modeling framework is not limited to the analysis of industrial and occupational segregation. The models we propose could be used to evaluate hypotheses about sex (or racial group) segregation in a variety of cross-cutting labor market structures, including employment situation (public versus private), work status (full-time versus part-time; self-employed versus salaried), job title, and establishment. The latter two applications might be especially fruitful in light of the mounting evidence that segregation and wage inequality occur at the job-title and establishment level (Bielby and Baron 1984; Petersen and Morgan 1995; Carrington and Troske 1998; Bayard et al. 1999; see also Reskin, McBrier, and Kmec 1999). By adopting methods that recognize and reflect the multidimensional character of sex segregation, scholars can continue to make progress toward understanding gender inequality in all its complexity.

TABLE 8.2
Interindustry Variability in Occupational Sex Typing[a]

Occupation	# OF INDUSTRIES IN WHICH OCCUPATION SHOWS:		
	Female Over-representation	Male Over-representation	Gender Neutrality
Financial managers	32	5	7
Managers, marketing, advertising, and public relations	16	23	5
Administrators, education, and related fields	32	9	3
Other specified managers	37	2	5
Managers, executives, and administrators, not elsewhere classified	19	21	4
Accountants and auditors	44	0	0
Personnel, training, and labor relations specialists	44	0	0
Purchasing agents and buyers	42	1	1
Inspectors and compliance officers	19	22	3
Other management related occupations	44	0	0
Engineers, architects	8	31	5
Engineers, civil	0	44	0
Engineers, electrical and electronic	1	43	0
Engineers, industrial	0	42	2
Engineers, mechanical	0	44	0
Engineers, not elsewhere classified	0	44	0
Computer systems analysts and scientists	28	12	4
Operations and systems researchers and analysts	41	0	3
Actuaries, statisticians, and mathematical scientists	40	2	2
Chemists, except biochemists	12	26	6
Physicists, biologists, and other natural scientists	13	24	7
Health diagnosing occupations	8	31	5
Registered nurses	44	0	0
Other health assessment and treatment occupations	37	7	0
Teachers	37	5	2
Social scientists and urban planners	40	3	1
Social and recreation workers	39	5	0

TABLE 8.2
(*continued*)

Occupation	# OF INDUSTRIES IN WHICH OCCUPATION SHOWS:		
	Female Over-representation	*Male Over-representation*	*Gender Neutrality*
Lawyers and judges	14	26	4
Writers, artists, entertainers, and athletes	38	3	3
Other professional specialty occupations	40	3	1
Licensed practical nurses	43	1	0
Health technologists and technicians	40	2	2
Electrical and electronic technicians	0	42	2
Industrial and mechanical engineering technicians	3	39	2
Drafting and surveying technicians	3	39	2
Other engineering and science technicians	15	20	9
Airplane pilots and navigators	0	44	0
Computer programmers	27	8	9
Technicians, not elsewhere classified	19	21	4
Supervisors and proprietors	19	23	2
Finance and other business services sales occupations	41	2	1
Sales representatives, commodities, except retail	5	33	6
Cashiers and counter clerks	44	0	0
Retail and personal service sales workers	39	3	2
Other sales-related occupations	35	7	2
Supervisors, administrative support occupations	43	0	1
Computer and peripheral equipment operators	44	0	0
Secretaries	44	0	0
Stenographers and typists	44	0	0
Receptionists	44	0	0
Other information clerks	44	0	0
File clerks	44	0	0
Records processing occupations, except financial	44	0	0

(*continued*)

TABLE 8.2
(*continued*)

Occupation	# OF INDUSTRIES IN WHICH OCCUPATION SHOWS:		
	Female Over-representation	Male Over-representation	Gender Neutrality
Bookkeepers, accounting, and auditing clerks	44	0	0
Payroll and timekeeping clerks	44	0	0
Other financial records processing occupations	44	0	0
Telephone operators	44	0	0
Mail and message distributing occupations	36	5	3
Production coordinators, expediters, and dispatchers	44	0	0
Traffic, shipping, and receiving clerks	17	21	6
Stock and inventory clerks	37	2	5
Other material recording and distributing clerks	43	1	0
Adjusters and investigators	44	0	0
Data-entry keyers	44	0	0
Other administrative support occupations	44	0	0
Guards and protective service occupations, not elsewhere classified	3	38	3
Police, sheriffs, firefighters, and related occupations	4	40	0
Food preparation and service occupations	44	0	0
Dental assistants, health aides, and nursing aides	44	0	0
Cleaning and building service occupations	8	27	9
Recreation attendants, guides, ushers, and bellhops	30	12	2
Other personal service occupations	44	0	0
Agricultural service occupations, fishers, and hunters	2	41	1
Supervisors, mechanics, and repairers	0	44	0
Automobile mechanics, except automobile body	0	43	1
Industrial machinery repairs	2	42	0

TABLE 8.2
(*continued*)

Occupation	# OF INDUSTRIES IN WHICH OCCUPATION SHOWS:		
	Female Over-representation	*Male Over-representation*	*Gender Neutrality*
Electronic and communication equipment repairs	1	43	0
Heating, air-conditioning, and refrigeration mechanics	0	44	0
Other mechanics and repairers	0	44	0
Supervisors, construction occupations	0	44	0
Carpenters	0	44	0
Electricians	0	44	0
Painters, construction and maintenance	1	40	3
Plumbers, pipefitters, and steamfitters	0	44	0
Other construction trades	0	44	0
Extractive occupations	7	36	1
Supervisors, production occupations	5	35	4
Tool and die makers	3	41	0
Machinists	0	44	0
Sheet metal workers	2	42	0
Other precision metal workers	11	30	3
Precision textile, apparel, and furnishings occupations	37	3	4
Precision food production occupations	21	19	4
Precision inspectors, testers, and related workers	19	23	2
Plant and systems operators	0	44	0
Other precision production occupations	20	15	9
Metalworking and plastic working machine operators	4	34	6
Fabricating machine operators	27	13	4
Metal, plastic, and wood-processing machine operators	10	33	1
Printing machine operators	32	7	5
Textile machine operators, except sewing	21	18	5
Textile sewing machine operators	41	3	0

(*continued*)

TABLE 8.2
(*continued*)

Occupation	# OF INDUSTRIES IN WHICH OCCUPATION SHOWS:		
	Female Over-representation	*Male Over-representation*	*Gender Neutrality*
Packaging and filling machine operators	41	3	0
Furnace, kiln, and oven operators, except food	1	42	1
Other specified machine operators	18	19	7
Miscellaneous and not specified machine operators	25	15	4
Welders, cutters, solderers, and brazers	1	43	0
Assemblers	38	4	2
Hand-working occupations	26	13	5
Graders and sorters, except agricultural	42	1	1
Production inspectors, testers, and weighers	33	9	2
Truck drivers	0	44	0
Driver-sales workers	8	32	4
Other motor vehicle operators	4	38	2
Rail and water transportation occupations	6	36	2
Supervisors, material moving equipment operators	0	43	1
Crane, hoist, and winch operators	0	44	0
Excavating, grading, and dozer machine operators	2	42	0
Other material moving equipment operators	0	44	0
Supervisors, handlers and laborers, not elsewhere classified	4	40	0
Helpers, craft and production	4	40	0
Laborers	5	34	5
Freight, stock, and material handlers	4	29	11
Service station occupations and vehicle washers	6	34	4
Hand packers and packagers	44	0	0

[a]See note 16 for definition of male and female "overrepresentation" and "gender neutrality."

Industry Recoding Scheme, United States

WS #[a]	Title	EEO #	EEO Title (1990 Census Codes)
1	Agricultural service, forestry, and fisheries	2	Agriculture services (012–030)
		3	Forestry and fisheries (031–039)
2	Mining	4	Coal mining (041)
		5	Oil and gas extraction (042)
		6	Mining, except fuels (040, 043–059)
3	Construction	7	Construction (060–099)
4	Manufacturing: food	8	Food and kindred products (100–129)
5	Manufacturing: textile mill products	9	Textile mill products (132–150)
6	Manufacturing: apparel	10	Apparel and other finished textile products (151–159)
7	Manufacturing: paper	11	Pulp, paper, and paperboard mills (160)
		12	Miscellaneous paper and pulp products (161)
		13	Paperboard containers and boxes (162–170)
8	Manufacturing: printing and publishing	14	Printing, publishing, and allied industries (171–179)
9	Manufacturing: chemicals	15	Plastics, synthetics, and resins (180)
		16	Drugs (181)
		17	Chemicals and allied products except drugs and plastics (182–199)
10	Manufacturing: rubber and plastics	19	Rubber products, plastics footwear, and belting (210, 211, 213–219)
		20	Miscellaneous plastic products (212)
11	Manufacturing: other nondurable goods	18	Petroleum and coal products (200–209)
		21	Other nondurable goods (130–131, 220–229)
12	Manufacturing: lumber	22	Logging (230)
		23	Sawmills, planing mills, millwork (231)
		24	Wood buildings, mobile homes, and miscellaneous wood products (232, 241)
13	Manufacturing: furniture	25	Furniture and fixtures (242–249)

(continued)

WS #[a]	Title	EEO #	EEO Title (1990 Census Codes)
14	Manufacturing: iron and steel	27	Primary metal industries, except aluminum (270, 271, 280)
		28	Primary aluminum industries (272–279)
15	Manufacturing: fabricated metals	29	Metal forgings and stampings (291)
		30	Fabricated metal industries, except metal forgings (281–290, 292–309)
16	Manufacturing: machinery, except electrical	31	Computers and related equipment (322–330)
		32	Machinery, except electrical, not elsewhere classified (331)
		33	Other specified and not specified machinery (310–321, 332–339)
17	Manufacturing: electrical machinery	34	Radio, TV, and communication equipment (341)
		35	Electrical machinery, equipment, and supplies, not elsewhere classified (342–349)
		36	Household appliances and not specified electrical machinery, equipment, and supplies (340, 350)
18	Manufacturing: motor vehicles	37	Motor vehicles and motor vehicle equipment (351)
19	Manufacturing: transportation equipment	38	Other transportation equipment (352–370)
20	Manufacturing: other durable goods	26	Glass and glass products (250)
		39	Other durable goods (251–269, 371–391)
		40	Not specified manufacturing (392–399)
21	Trucking and warehousing	42	Trucking service and warehousing (410–411)
22	Transportation	41	Railroads (400)
		44	Water transportation (420)
		45	Air transportation (421)
		46	Other transportation (401–409, 422–439)
23	Communications	47	Telephone communications (441)
		48	Other communications (440, 442–439)
24	Utilities	49	Electric light and power (450)
		50	Gas and steam supply systems (451)
		51	Electric and gas and other combinations (452–469)
		52	Other utilities and sanitary services (470–499)
25	Wholesale trade: durable goods	53	Wholesale trade, lumber and construction materials (502–509)

WS #[a]	Title	EEO #	EEO Title (1990 Census Codes)
		54	Wholesale trade, scrap and waste materials (531)
		55	Wholesale trade, other durable goods (500, 501, 510–530, 532–539)
26	Wholesale trade: non-durable goods	56	Wholesale trade, paper and paper products (540)
		57	Wholesale trade, petroleum products (552–559)
		58	Wholesale trade, other nondurable goods (541–551, 560–579)
27	Retail: general merchandise	60	Retail trade, general merchandise stores (591–600)
28	Retail: food stores	61	Retail trade, food, bakery, and dairy stores (601–611)
29	Retail: automobiles and automotive supplies	62	Retail trade, motor vehicle dealers (612–619)
		63	Retail trade, gasoline service stations (621)
		64	Retail trade, automotive and home supply stores and miscellaneous vehicle dealers (620, 622)
30	Retail: eating and drinking places	67	Retail trade, eating and drinking places (641)
31	Other retail	59	Retail trade, building materials and hardware and garden stores (580–589)
		65	Retail trade, apparel and accessories, including shoes (623–630)
		66	Retail trade, home furnishings and equipment stores (631–640)
		68	Retail trade, other (590, 642–699)
32	Banking	69	Banking and other savings institutions (700–701)
33	Insurance	70	Insurance (711)
34	Other finance and real estate	71	Real estate, including real estate insurance offices (712–720)
		72	Other finance (702–710)
35	Business services	73	Personnel supply services (731)
		74	Computer and data processing services (732–739)
		75	Other business services (721–730, 740–741)

(continued)

WS #[a]	Title	EEO #	EEO Title (1990 Census Codes)
36	Repair services	76	Automotive repair and related services (751)
		77	Other repair services and automotive services (742, 750, 752–760)
37	Personal service	79	Hotels and motels (762–769)
		80	Beauty and barber shops (772–780)
		81	Other personal services (770–771, 781–799)
38	Entertainment and recreation services	82	Entertainment and recreation services (800–811)
39	Hospitals	83	Hospitals (831)
40	Other health services	84	Health services, except hospitals (812–830, 832–840)
41	Educational services	86	Elementary and secondary schools (842–849)
		87	Colleges and universities (850)
		88	Other educational services (851–860)
42	Social services	89	Job training and vocational rehabilitation services (861)
		90	Child day care, including family homes (862–869)
		91	Other social services (870, 871)
		92	Religious and other membership organizations (873–889)
43	Other professional services	85	Legal services (841)
		93	Engineering, architectural, and surveying services (882–889)
		94	Research, development, and testing services (891)
		95	Management and public relations services (892)
		96	Other professional services (872, 890, 893–899)
44	Public administration	43	US Postal Service (412–419)
		97	Justice, public order, and safety (910–920)
		98	Other public administration (900–909, 921–939)

NOTES: Agriculture production (EEO #1, 1990 Census # 001–011), personal service in private households. (EEO # 78, 1990 Census #761), and the unemployed (EEO #99, 1990 Census # 000, 940–999) were eliminated.

[a]Weeden-Sørenson occupational classification number.

125-Category Occupation Recodes, United States

WS #[a]	Title	EEO #	EEO Title (1990 Census Code)
1	Financial managers	5	Financial managers (007)
2	Managers, marketing, advertising, and public relations	8	Managers, marketing, advertising, and public relations (013)
3	Administrators, education and related fields	9	Administrators, education and related fields (014)
4	Other specified managers	6	Personnel and labor relations managers (008)
		7	Purchasing managers (009–012)
		10	Managers, medicine and health (015)
		11	Postmasters and mail superintendents (016)
		12	Managers, food serving and lodging establishments (017)
		13	Managers, properties and real estate (018)
		14	Funeral directors (019–020)
		15	Managers, service organizations, not elsewhere classified (021)
5	Managers, executives, and administrators, not elsewhere classified	1	Legislators (001–003)
		2	Chief executives and general administrators, public administration (004)
		3	Administrators and officials, public administration (005)
		4	Administrators, protective services (006)
		16	Managers and administrators, not elsewhere classified salaried (022)
		17	Managers and administrators, not elsewhere classified self-employed (022)
6	Accountants and auditors	18	Accountants and auditors (023)
7	Personnel, training, and labor relations specialists	22	Personnel, training, and labor relations specialists (027)
8	Purchasing agents and buyers	23	Purchasing agents and buyers, farm products (028)
		24	Buyers, wholesale and retail trade, except farm products (029–032)
		25	Purchasing agents and buyers, not elsewhere classified (033)

(continued)

WS #[a]	Title	EEO #	EEO Title (1990 Census Code)
9	Inspectors and compliance officers	27	Construction inspectors (035)
		28	Inspectors and compliance officers, except construction (036)
10	Other management related occupations	19	Underwriters (024)
		20	Other financial officers (025)
		21	Management analysts (026)
		26	Business and promotion agents (034)
		29	Management related occupations, not elsewhere classified (037–042)
11	Engineers, architects	30	Engineers, architects (043)
12	Engineers, civil	37	Engineers, civil (053)
13	Engineers, electrical and electronic	39	Engineers, electrical and electronic (055)
14	Engineers, industrial	40	Engineers, industrial (056)
15	Engineers, mechanical	41	Engineers, mechanical (057)
16	Engineers, not elsewhere classified	31	Engineers, aerospace (044)
		32	Engineers, metallurgical and materials (045)
		33	Engineers, mining (046)
		34	Engineers, petroleum (047)
		35	Engineers, chemical (048)
		36	Engineers, nuclear (049–052)
		38	Engineers, agricultural (054)
		42	Engineers, marine and naval architects (058)
		43	Engineers, not elsewhere classified (059–062)
		44	Surveyors and mapping scientists (063)
17	Computer systems analysts and scientists	45	Computer systems analysts and scientists (064)
18	Operations and systems researchers and analysts	46	Operations and systems researchers and analysts (065)
19	Actuaries, statisticians, and mathematical scientists	47	Actuaries (066)
		48	Statisticians (067)
		49	Mathematical scientists, not elsewhere classified (068)
20	Chemists, except biochemists	51	Chemists, except biochemists (073)
21	Physicists, biologists, and other natural scientists	50	Physicists and astronomers (069–072)
		52	Atmospheric and space scientists (074)

(continued)

WS #[a]	Title	EEO #	EEO Title (1990 Census Code)
		53	Geologists and geodesists (075)
		54	Physical scientists, not elsewhere classified (076)
		55	Agricultural and food scientists (077)
		56	Biological and life scientists (078)
		57	Forestry and conservation scientists (079–082)
		58	Medical scientists (083)
22	Health-diagnosing occupations	59	Physicians (084)
		60	Dentists (085)
		61	Veterinarians (086)
		62	Optometrists (087)
		63	Podiatrists (088)
		64	Health diagnosing practitioners, not elsewhere classified (089–094)
23	Registered nurses	65	Registered nurses (095)
24	Other health assessment and treatment occupations	66	Pharmacists (096)
		67	Dietitians (097)
		68	Respiratory therapists (098)
		69	Occupational therapists (099–102)
		70	Physical therapists (103)
		71	Speech therapists (104)
		72	Therapists, not elsewhere classified (105)
		73	Physicians' assistants (106–112)
25	Teachers	74–103	Postsecondary teachers, all disciplines (113–154)
		104	Teachers, preschool and kindergarten (155)
		105	Teachers, elementary school (156)
		106	Teachers, secondary school (157)
		107	Teachers, special education (158)
		108	Teachers, not elsewhere classified (159–162)
26	Social scientists and urban planners	112	Economists (166)
		113	Psychologists (167)
		114	Sociologists (168)
		115	Social scientists, not elsewhere classified (169–172)

(continued)

WS #[a]	Title	EEO #	EEO Title (1990 Census Code)
		116	Urban planners (173)
27	Social and recreation workers	117	Social workers (174)
		118	Recreation workers (175)
28	Lawyers and judges	121	Lawyers (178)
		122	Judges (179–182)
29	Writers, artists, entertainers, and athletes	123	Authors (183)
		124	Technical writers (184)
		125	Designers (185)
		126	Musicians and composers (186)
		127	Actors and directors (187)
		128	Painters, sculptors, craft-artists, and artist printmakers (188)
		129	Photographers (189–192)
		130	Dancers (193)
		131	Artists, performers, and related workers, not elsewhere classified (194)
		132	Editors and reporters (195–196)
		133	Public relations specialists (197)
		134	Announcers (198)
		135	Athletes (199–202)
30	Other professional specialty occupations	109	Counselors, educational and vocational (163)
		110	Librarians (164)
		111	Archivists and curators (165)
		119	Clergy (176)
		120	Religious workers, not elsewhere classified (177)
31	Licensed practical nurses	140	Licensed practical nurses (207)
32	Health technologists and technicians	136	Clinical laboratory technologists and technicians (203)
		137	Dental hygienists (204)
		138	Health record technologists and technicians (205)
		139	Radiologic technicians (206)
		141	Health technologists and technicians, not elsewhere classified (208–212)
33	Electrical and electronic technicians	142	Electrical and electronic technicians (213)

WS #[a]	Title	EEO #	EEO Title (1990 Census Code)
34	Industrial and mechanical engineering technicians	143	Industrial engineering technicians (214)
		144	Mechanical engineering technicians (215)
35	Drafting and surveying technicians	146	Drafting occupations (217)
		147	Surveying and mapping technicians (218–222)
36	Other engineering and science technicians	145	Engineering technicians, not elsewhere classified (216)
		148	Biological technicians (223)
		149	Chemical technicians (224)
		150	Science technicians, not elsewhere classified (225)
		152	Air traffic controllers (227)
		153	Broadcast equipment operators (228)
37	Airplane pilots and navigators	151	Airplane pilots and navigators (226)
38	Computer programmers	154	Computer programmers (229–232)
39	Technicians, not elsewhere classified	155	Tool programmers, numerical control (233)
		156	Legal assistants (234)
		157	Technicians, not elsewhere classified (235–242)
40	Supervisors and proprietors	158	Supervisors and proprietors, sales occupations, salaried (243–252)
		159	Supervisors and proprietors, sales occupations, self-employed (243–252)
41	Finance and other business services sales occupations	160	Insurance sales occupations (253)
		161	Real estate sales occupations (254)
		162	Securities and financial services sales occupations (255)
		163	Advertising and related sales occupations (256)
		164	Sales occupations, other business services (257)
42	Sales representatives, commodities, except retail	165	Sales engineers (258)
		166	Sales representatives, mining, manufacturing, wholesale (259–262)
43	Cashiers and counter clerks	175	Sales counter clerks (275)
		176	Cashiers (276)

(*continued*)

WS #[a]	Title	EEO #	EEO Title (1990 Census Code)
44	Retail and personal service sales workers	167	Sales workers, motor vehicles and boats (263)
		168	Sales workers, apparel (264)
		169	Sales workers, shoes (265)
		170	Sales workers, furniture and home furnishings (266)
		171	Sales workers, radio, TV, hi-fi, appliances (267)
		172	Sales workers, hardware and building supplies (268)
		173	Sales workers, parts (269–273)
		174	Sales workers, other commodities (274)
		177	Street and door-to-door sales workers (277)
		178	News vendors (278–282)
45	Other sales-related occupations	179	Demonstrators, promoters, and models, sales (283)
		180	Auctioneers (284)
		181	Sales support occupations, not elsewhere classified (285–302)
46	Supervisors, administrative support occupations	182	Supervisors, general office (303)
		183	Supervisors, computer equipment operators (304)
		184	Supervisors, financial records processing (305)
		185	Chief communications operators (306)
		186	Supervisors, distribution, scheduling, and adjusting clerks (307)
47	Computer and peripheral equipment operators	187	Computer operators (308)
		188	Peripheral equipment operators (309–312)
48	Secretaries	189	Secretaries (313)
49	Stenographers and typists	190	Stenographers (314)
		191	Typists (315)
50	Receptionists	195	Receptionists (319–322)
		193	Hotel clerks (317)
		194	Transportation ticket and reservation agents (318)
		196	Information clerks, not elsewhere classified (323–324)
51	Other information clerks	192	Interviewers (316)

WS #[a]	Title	EEO #	EEO Title (1990 Census Code)
52	File clerks	202	File clerks (335)
53	Records processing occupations, except financial	197	Classified-ad clerks (325)
		198	Correspondence clerks (326)
		199	Order clerks (327)
		200	Personnel clerks, except payroll and time-keeping (328)
		201	Library clerks (329–334)
		203	Records clerks (336)
54	Bookkeepers, accounting, and auditing clerks	204	Bookkeepers, accounting, and auditing clerks (337)
55	Payroll and timekeeping clerks	205	Payroll and timekeeping clerks (338)
56	Other financial records processing occupations	206	Billing clerks (339–342)
		207	Cost and rate clerks (343)
		208	Billing, posting, and calculating machine operators (344)
57	Telephone operators	212	Telephone operators (348–352)
58	Mail and message distributing occupations	214	Postal clerks, except mail carriers (354)
		215	Mail carriers, postal service (355)
		216	Mail clerks, except postal service (356)
		217	Messengers (357–358)
59	Production coordinators, expediters, and dispatchers	218	Dispatchers (359–362)
		219	Production coordinators (363)
		224	Expediters (373)
60	Traffic, shipping, and receiving clerks	220	Traffic, shipping, and receiving clerks (364)
61	Stock and inventory clerks	221	Stock and inventory clerks (365)
62	Other material recording and distributing clerks	222	Meter readers (366–367)
		223	Weighers, measurers, checkers, and samplers (368–372)
		225	Material recording, scheduling, and distributing clerks not elsewhere classified (374)
63	Adjusters and investigators	226	Insurance adjusters, examiners, and investigators (375)
		227	Investigators and adjusters, except insurance (376)

(*continued*)

WS #[a]	Title	EEO #	EEO Title (1990 Census Code)
		228	Eligibility clerks, social welfare (377)
		229	Bill and account collectors (378)
64	Data-entry keyers	233	Data-entry keyers (385)
65	Other administrative support occupations	209	Duplicating machine operators (345)
		210	Mail preparing and paper handling machine operators (346)
		211	Office machine operators, not elsewhere classified (347)
		213	Communications equipment operators, not elsewhere classified (353)
		230	General office clerks (379–382)
		231	Bank tellers (383)
		232	Proofreaders (384)
		234	Statistical clerks (386)
		235	Teachers' aides (387–388)
		236	Administrative support occupations, not elsewhere classified (389–402)
66	Guards and protective service occupations, not elsewhere classified	250	Crossing guards (425)
		251	Guards and police, except public service (426)
		252	Protective service occupations, not elsewhere classified (427–432)
67	Police, sheriffs, firefighters, and related occupations	242	Supervisors, firefighting and fire prevention occupations (413)
		243	Supervisors, police and detectives (414)
		244	Supervisors, guards (415)
		245	Fire inspection and fire prevention occupations (416)
		246	Firefighting occupations (417)
		247	Police and detectives, public service (418–422)
		248	Sheriffs, bailiffs, and other law enforcement officers (423)
		249	Correctional institution officers (424)
68	Food preparation and service occupations	253	Supervisors, food preparation and service occupations (433)
		254	Bartenders (434)
		255	Waiters and waitresses (435)
		256	Cooks (436–437)

WS #[a]	Title	EEO #	EEO Title (1990 Census Code)
		257	Food-counter, fountain, and related occupations (438)
		258	Kitchen workers, food preparation (439–442)
		259	Waiters'/waitresses' assistants (443)
		260	Miscellaneous food preparation occupations (444)
69	Dental assistants, health aides, and nursing aides	261	Dental assistants (445)
		262	Health aides, except nursing (446)
		263	Nursing aides, orderlies, and attendants (447)
70	Cleaning and building service occupations	264	Supervisors, cleaning and building service workers (448)
		265	Maids and housemen (449–452)
		266	Janitors and cleaners (453)
		267	Elevator operators (454)
		268	Pest control occupations (455)
71	Recreation attendants, guides, ushers, and bellhops	272	Attendants, amusement and recreation facilities (459–460)
		273	Guides (461)
		274	Ushers (462)
		275	Public transportation attendants (463)
		276	Baggage porters and bellhops (464)
72	Other personal service occupations	269	Supervisors, personal service occupations (456)
		270	Barbers (457)
		271	Hairdressers and cosmetologists (458)
		277	Welfare service aides (465)
		278	Family child care providers (466)
		279	Early childhood teacher's assistants (467)
		280	Child care workers, not elsewhere classified (468)
		281	Personal service occupations, not elsewhere classified (469–472)
73	Agricultural service occupations, fishers, and hunters	288	Marine life cultivation workers (483)
		289	Nursery workers (484)
		290	Supervisors, related agricultural occupations (485)

(*continued*)

(continued)

WS #[a]	Title	EEO #	EEO Title (1990 Census Code)
		291	Groundskeepers and gardeners, except farm (486)
		292	Animal caretakers, except farm (487)
		293	Graders and sorters, agricultural products (488)
		294	Inspectors, agricultural products (489–493)
		295	Supervisors, forestry and logging workers (494)
		296	Forestry workers, except logging (495)
		297	Timber cutting and logging occupations (496)
		298	Captains and officers, fishing vessels (497)
		299	Fishers (498)
		300	Hunters and trappers (499–502)
74	Supervisors, mechanics and repairers	301	Supervisors, mechanics and repairers (503–504)
75	Automobile mechanics, except automobile body	302	Automobile mechanics, except apprentices (505)
		303	Automobile mechanic apprentices (506)
76	Industrial machinery repairs	311	Industrial machinery repairers (518)
77	Electronic and communication equipment repairs	313	Electronic repairs, communications, and industrial equipment (523–524)
78	Heating, air conditioning, and refrigeration mechanics	319	Heating, air conditioning, and refrigeration mechanics (534)
79	Other mechanics and repairers	304	Bus, truck, and stationary engine mechanics (507)
		305	Aircraft engine mechanics (508)
		306	Small engine repairers (509–513)
		307	Automobile body and related repairers (514)
		308	Aircraft mechanics, except engine (515)
		309	Heavy equipment mechanics (516)
		310	Farm equipment mechanics (517)
		312	Machinery maintenance occupations (519–522)
		314	Data processing equipment repairers (525)
		315	Household appliance and power tools repairers (526)

WS #[a]	Title	EEO #	EEO Title (1990 Census Code)
		316	Telephone line installers and repairers (527–528)
		317	Telephone installers and repairers (529–532)
		318	Miscellaneous electrical and electronic equipment repairers (533)
		320	Camera, watch, and musical instrument repairers (535)
		321	Locksmiths and safe repairers (536–537)
		322	Office machine repairers (538)
		323	Mechanical controls and valve repairers (539–542)
		324	Elevator installers and repairers (543)
		325	Millwrights (544–546)
		326	Specified mechanics and repairers, not elsewhere classified (547–548)
		327	Not specified mechanics and repairers (549–552)
80	Supervisors, construction occupations	328	Supervisors, brickmasons, stonemasons, and tile setters (553)
		329	Supervisors, carpenters and related workers (554)
		330	Supervisors, electricians and power transmission installers (555)
		331	Supervisors, painters, paperhangers, and plasterers (556)
		332	Supervisors, plumbers, pipefitters, and steamfitters (557)
		333	Supervisors, construction, not elsewhere classified (558–562)
81	Carpenters	338	Carpenters, except apprentices (567–568)
		339	Carpenter apprentices (569–572)
82	Electricians	341	Electricians, except apprentices (575)
		342	Electrician apprentices (576)
83	Painters, construction and maintenance	344	Painters, construction and maintenance (579–582)
84	Plumbers, pipefitters, and steamfitters	347	Plumbers, pipefitters, and steamfitters, except apprentices (585–586)

(*continued*)

WS #[a]	Title	EEO #	EEO Title (1990 Census Code)
		348	Plumber, pipefitter, and steamfitter apprentices (587)
85	Other construction trades	334	Brickmasons and stonemasons, except apprentices (563)
		335	Brickmason and stonemason apprentices (564)
		336	Tile setters, hard and soft (565)
		337	Carpet installers (566)
		340	Drywall installers (573–574)
		343	Electrical power installers and repairers (577–578)
		345	Paperhangers (583)
		346	Plasterers (584)
		349	Concrete and terrazzo finishers (588)
		350	Glaziers (589–592)
		351	Insulation workers (593)
		352	Paving, surfacing, and tamping equipment operators (594)
		353	Roofers (595)
		354	Sheetmetal duct installers (596)
		355	Structural metal workers (597)
		356	Drillers, earth (598)
		357	Construction trades, not elsewhere classified (599–612)
86	Extractive occupations	358	Supervisors, extractive occupations (613)
		359	Drillers, oil well (614)
		360	Explosives workers (615)
		362	Mining occupations, not elsewhere classified (617–627)
87	Supervisors, production occupations	363	Supervisors, production occupations (628–633)
88	Tool and die makers	364	Tool and die makers, except apprentices (634)
		365	Tool and die maker apprentices (635)
89	Machinists	367	Machinists, except apprentices (637–638)
		368	Machinist apprentices (639–642)
90	Sheet metal workers	375	Sheet metal workers, except apprentices (653)

WS #[a]	Title	EEO #	EEO Title (1990 Census Code)
		376	Sheet metal worker apprentices (654)
91	Other precision metal workers	366	Precision assemblers, metal (636)
		369	Boilermakers (643)
		370	Precision grinders, filers, and tool sharpeners (644)
		371	Patternmakers and model makers, metal (645)
		372	Lay-out workers (646)
		373	Precious stones and metals workers (jewelers) (647–648)
		374	Engravers, metal (649–652)
		377	Miscellaneous precision metal workers (655)
92	Precision textile, apparel, and furnishings occupations	382	Dressmakers (666)
		383	Tailors (667)
		384	Upholsterers (668)
		385	Shoe repairers (669–673)
		386	Miscellaneous precision apparel and fabric workers (674)
93	Precision food production occupations	394	Butchers and meat cutters (686)
		395	Bakers (687)
		396	Food batchmakers (688)
94	Precision inspectors, testers, and related workers	397	Inspectors, testers, and graders (689–692)
		398	Adjusters and calibrators (293)
95	Plant and systems operators	399	Water and sewage treatment plant operators (694)
		400	Power plant operators (695)
		401	Stationary engineers (696–698)
		402	Miscellaneous plant and system operators (699–702)
96	Other precision production occupations	378	Patternmakers and model makers, wood (656)
		379	Cabinetmakers and bench carpenters (657)
		380	Furniture and wood finishers (658)
		381	Miscellaneous precision woodworkers (659–665)
		387	Hand molders and shapers, except jewelers (675)

(*continued*)

(continued)

WS #[a]	Title	EEO #	EEO Title (1990 Census Code)
		388	Patternmakers, lay-out workers, and cutters (676)
		389	Optical goods workers (677)
		390	Dental laboratory and medical appliance technicians (678)
		391	Bookbinders (679–682)
		392	Electrical and electronic equipment assemblers (683)
		393	Miscellaneous precision workers, not elsewhere classified (684–685)
97	Metalworking and plastic working machine operators	403	Lathe and turning machine set-up operators (703)
		404	Lathe and turning machine operators (704)
		405	Milling and planing machine operators (705)
		406	Punching and stamping press machine operators (706)
		407	Rolling machine operators (707)
		408	Drilling and boring machine operators (708)
		409	Grinding, abrading, buffing, and polishing machine operators (709–712)
		410	Forging machine operators (713)
		411	Numerical control machine operators (714)
		412	Miscellaneous metal, plastic, stone, glass working machine operators (715–716)
98	Fabricating machine operators	413	Fabricating machine operators, not elsewhere classified (717–718)
99	Metal, plastic, and wood processing machine operators	414	Molding and casting machine operators (719–722)
		415	Metal plating machine operators (723)
		416	Heat treating equipment operators (724)
		417	Miscellaneous metal and plastic processing machine operators (725)
		418	Wood lathe, routing, and planing machine operators (726)
		419	Sawing machine operatives (727)
		420	Shaping and joining machine operators (728)

WS #[a]	Title	EEO #	EEO Title (1990 Census Code)
		421	Nailing and tacking machine operators (729–732)
		422	Miscellaneous woodworking machine operators (733)
100	Printing machine operators	423	Printing press operators (734)
		424	Photoengravers and lithographers (735)
		425	Typesetters and compositors (736)
		426	Miscellaneous printing machine operators (737)
101	Textile machine operators, except sewing	427	Winding and twisting machine operator (738)
		428	Knitting, looping, taping, and weaving machine operators (739–742)
		429	Textile cutting machine operators (743)
		434	Miscellaneous textile machine operators (749–752)
102	Textile sewing machine operators	430	Textile sewing machine operators (744)
103	Packaging and filling machine operators	436	Packaging and filling machine operators (754)
104	Furnace, kiln, and oven operators, except food	445	Furnace, kiln, and oven operators, except food (766–767)
105	Other specified machine operators	431	Shoe machine operators (745–746)
		432	Pressing machine operators (747)
		433	Laundering and dry cleaning machine operators (748)
		435	Cementing and gluing machine operators (753)
		437	Extruding and forming machine operators (755)
		438	Mixing and blending machine operators (756)
		439	Separating, filtering, and clarifying machine operators (757)
		440	Compressing and compacting machine operators (758)
		441	Painting and paint spraying machine operators (759–762)
		442	Roasting and baking machine operators, food (763)

(*continued*)

WS #[a]	Title	EEO #	EEO Title (1990 Census Code)
		443	Washing, cleaning, and pickling machine operators (764)
		444	Folding machine operators (765)
		446	Crushing and grinding machine operators (768)
		447	Slicing and cutting machine operators (769–772)
		448	Motion picture projectionists (773)
		449	Photographic process machine operator (774–776)
106	Miscellaneous and not specified machine operators	361	Mining machine operators (616)
		450	Miscellaneous machine operators, not elsewhere classified, nondurable goods (777–778)
		451	Miscellaneous machine operators, not elsewhere classified, durable goods (777–778)
		452	Miscellaneous machine operators, not elsewhere classified, nonmanufacturing (777–778)
		453	Machine operators, not specified, nondurable goods (779–782)
		454	Machine operators, not specified, durable goods (779–782)
		455	Machine operators, not specified, nonmanufacturing (779–782)
107	Welders, cutters, solderers, and brazers	456	Welders and cutters (783)
		457	Solderers and brazers (784)
108	Assemblers	458	Assemblers (785)
109	Hand-working occupations	459	Hand cutting and trimming occupations (786)
		460	Hand molding, casting, and forming occupations (787–788)
		461	Hand painting, coating, and decorating occupations (789–792)
		462	Hand engraving and printing occupations (793–794)
		463	Miscellaneous hand working occupations (795)
110	Graders and sorters, except agricultural	467	Graders and sorters, except agricultural (799–802)

WS #[a]	Title	EEO #	EEO Title (1990 Census Code)
111	Production inspectors, testers, and weighers	464	Production inspectors, checkers, and examiners (796)
		465	Production testers (797)
		466	Production samplers and weighers (798)
112	Truck drivers	469	Truck drivers (804–805)
113	Driver-sales workers	470	Driver-sales workers (806–807)
114	Other motor vehicle operators	468	Supervisors, motor vehicle operators (803)
		471	Bus drivers (808)
		472	Taxicab drivers and chauffeurs (809–812)
		473	Parking lot attendants (813)
		474	Motor transportation occupations, not elsewhere classified (814–822)
115	Rail and water transportation occupations	475	Railroad conductors and yardmasters (823)
		476	Locomotive operating occupations (824)
		477	Railroad brake, signal, and switch operators (825)
		478	Rail vehicle operators, not elsewhere classified (826–827)
		479	Ship captains and mates, except fishing boats (828)
		480	Sailors and deckhands (829–832)
		481	Marine engineers (833)
		482	Bridge, lock, and lighthouse tenders (834–842)
116	Supervisors, material moving equipment operators	483	Supervisors, material moving equipment operators (843)
117	Crane, hoist, and winch operators	486	Hoist and winch operators (848)
		487	Crane and tower operators (849–852)
118	Excavating, grading, and dozer machine operators	488	Excavating and loading machine operators (853–854)
		489	Grader, dozer, and scraper operators (855)
119	Other material moving equipment operators	484	Operating engineers (844)
		485	Longshore equipment operators (845–847)
		490	Industrial truck and tractor equipment operators (856–858)
		491	Miscellaneous material moving equipment operators (859–863)

(*continued*)

(continued)

WS #[a]	Title	EEO #	EEO Title (1990 Census Code)
120	Supervisors, handlers and laborers, not elsewhere classified	492	Supervisors, handlers, equipment cleaners, and laborers, not elsewhere classified (864)
121	Helpers, craft and production	493	Helpers, mechanics and repairers (865)
		494	Helpers, construction trades (866)
		495	Helpers, surveyor (867)
		496	Helpers, extractive occupations (868)
		498	Production helpers (874)
122	Laborers	497	Construction laborers (869–873)
		507	Laborers: manufacturing, nondurable goods (889–992)
		508	Laborers: manufacturing, durable goods (889–992)
		509	Laborers: transportation, communications, utilities (889–992)
		510	Laborers: wholesale and retail trade (889–992)
		511	Laborers: all other industries (889–992)
123	Freight, stock, and material handlers	499	Garbage collectors (875)
		500	Stevedores (876)
		501	Stock handlers and baggers (877)
		502	Machine feeders and offbearers (878–882)
		503	Freight, stock, and material handlers, not elsewhere classified (883–884)
124	Service station occupations and vehicle washers	504	Garage and service station related occupations (885–886)
		505	Vehicle washers and equipment cleaners (887)
125	Hand packers and packagers	506	Hand packers and packagers (888)

NOTE: Private household workers (EEO #237–241, 1990 Census #403–412), farmers and farm managers (EEO #282–287, 1990 Census #473–482), and the unemployed with no recent civilian labor force experience (EEO #512, 1990 Census #903–999) are eliminated from the data.

[a]Weeden-Sørensen occupational classification number.

CONCLUSION

CHAPTER NINE

The Past, Present, and Future of Occupational Ghettos

The rise of egalitarian values and reform is a defining feature of modernity and postmodernity. Although egalitarian reform has played out in many institutional domains, it has been especially prominent in the area of gender relations and stratification. Indeed, one might conclude that the forces for equalization are straightforwardly triumphing in this domain, given such well-known achievements as (a) the rapid diffusion of egalitarian views about gender roles, (b) the elimination (and even reversal) of the gender gap in educational investment, and (c) the continuing growth in rates of female labor force participation. This evidence of equalizing change has emboldened some commentators to conclude that "sex equality is our inevitable destiny" (Jackson 1998, p. 271).

Unfortunately, the story of gender stratification is replete with counterpoints to this equalizing trend, counterpoints that suggest that at least some forms of inequality are organic and possibly intractable features of the modern and postmodern condition. These inertial forces are revealed, for example, in the persistence of a hypersegregated occupational structure. That is, women and men continue to work in gender-typed "occupational ghettos," with women crowding into the nonmanual sector and, in particular, the less desirable occupations within that sector (sales, service, and clerical positions). To be sure, there is evidence of desegregation in many regions of the occupational structure, yet any careful observer will note its unevenness and the resulting pockets of persisting hypersegregation. The slow pace of desegregative change contrasts starkly with the more precipitous declines in other forms of gender inequality (see Figure 1.1).

This evidence suggests that sex segregation, far from being an ascriptive holdover, is actively advanced by dynamics that are integral to the functioning of contemporary labor markets. We have sought to identify the sources of such resistance to equalization. This task is usefully approached, we have argued, by identifying and resolving some of the core empirical puzzles in the field: Why does the typical pattern of sex segregation fail to accord with the common view that male power and privilege allows men to dominate the best occupations? Why is there so much disagreement and disarray in interpreting evidence on cross-national differences in segregation? Why is segregation most extreme in countries that are widely recognized for their family-friendly policies and gender-egalitarian reforms (such as Sweden and Norway)? And why has integration occurred relatively slowly and in such piecemeal fashion?

We argued in the preceding chapters that these puzzles can be resolved by recognizing that segregation regimes are two-dimensional and that distinct segregative logics underlie the two dimensions. The logic of "male primacy," which represents men as more status worthy than women, underlies the vertical segregation of women into subordinate occupations within the manual and nonmanual sectors. By contrast, horizontal segregation is generated and maintained through a logic of "gender essentialism," whereby women are presumed to excel in personal service, nurturance, and social interaction (nonmanual pursuits) and men are presumed to excel in technical tasks, outdoor work, and strenuous physical labor (manual pursuits). In the modern context, these two cultural tenets coexist, thus generating a fundamentally hybrid character to segregation regimes. The theme of this book is that the persistence of hypersegregation, the failure of egalitarian reform to eliminate some types of hypersegregation, and other puzzling features of contemporary segregation regimes become understandable when the hybrid character of modern segregation is appreciated.

Although this line of argument was formalized in Chapter 4, it was developed less formally in the other empirical chapters of our book. It may be useful, therefore, to explicitly review our results and their implications for our larger argument. The following sections discuss how our two-dimensional model provides new insights into the four core puzzles of contemporary segregation research.

PUZZLE #1: DO MEN DOMINATE
THE BEST OCCUPATIONS?

We began our analysis by asking whether conventional descriptions of the contours of sex segregation are adequate. There is surprisingly little relevant research; in fact, because index-based analysis has been so dominant, scholars have typically sought to characterize segregation regimes by the amount of inequality they display rather than the type or kind. When they *are* developed, descriptive profiles almost invariably incorporate the assumption that men crowd into the most desirable occupations, either because women have substantial domestic responsibilities that reduce their incentive to invest in demanding careers, or because employers exercise tastes for discrimination through hiring decisions and personnel practices that systematically advantage men. In its simplest form, the resulting "queuing model" implies that labor markets should have a strongly vertical character, with men tending to dominate the best-paying, most prestigious, and otherwise desirable occupations.

This conventional formulation, which is implicit in much segregation theorizing, fails to explain the structure of real data. We have shown that a three-parameter specification is required to represent the patterning of segregation at the major occupational level (see, especially, Chapter 4). This specification includes a "horizontal gap" parameter that absorbs the overrepresentation of women in the nonmanual sector, a "nonmanual slope" parameter that absorbs the tendency for men to dominate the most desirable nonmanual occupations, and a "manual slope" parameter that absorbs the corresponding tendency for men to dominate the most desirable manual occupations. The empirical deficiencies of queuing theory and other unidimensional formulations can therefore be attributed to the hybrid character of sex segregation. Although men indeed dominate the best occupations within each sector, queuing theory cannot explain the disproportionate allocation of women into the nonmanual sector itself ("horizontal segregation"), nor can it explain differences across sectors in the strength of the vertical principle. It is not possible, moreover, to salvage queuing theory by simply resorting to more detailed occupational data. As shown in Chapter 4, the vertical principle is even weaker when disaggregate data are analyzed, a result that contradicts the long-standing presumption that male privilege is revealed in stronger and purer forms as more detail is introduced.

We are unconvinced by the criticism that formal modeling of the sort advocated here is unduly complex (see Jacobs 2001). To the contrary, a mere three parameters suffices to capture the structure of aggregate segregation, thus rendering the modeling task only marginally more complicated than prevailing index-based approaches. This three-parameter model provides a tractable framework within which comparative analyses of different cities, countries, time periods, and subpopulations may be carried out. At the same time, there is room to elaborate and improve this model, perhaps most obviously by directly measuring nurturance, service orientation, physicality, and other presumed essentialist traits. In our view, the manual-nonmanual distinction is merely a proxy for some of these essentialist traits, and not necessarily an especially good proxy at that.[1] Likewise, our operationalization of the vertical effect could be readily improved, not only by developing a more defensible measure of overall desirability (see Jencks, Perlman, and Rainwater 1988) but also by decomposing desirability into its many components (pay, prestige, authority, and others).

PUZZLE #2: IS THERE A WORLDWIDE
SEGREGATION REGIME?

The field has similarly failed to reach consensus on the seemingly simple question of how much cross-national variability in segregation practices can be found. Among quantitative scholars, the long-standing view has been that labor markets differ mainly in the extent to which egalitarian practices have been institutionalized at the point of socialization, hiring, and promotion. These accounts, which assume that universalistic practices emerge in "modern" labor markets, imply that cross-national variability principally takes the form of across-the-board differences in the *extent* of segregation (Goode 1963; Ramirez 1987; Jackson 1998). By contrast, area studies scholars presume that sex segregation varies in more complicated and multidimensional ways by virtue of the distinctive cultures, political traditions, or institutional practices that emerge and live on in nation-states.

Can these opposing positions be reconciled? In Chapter 3, we suggested that the structure of cross-national variability is not as simple as quantitative survey analysts have suggested, but neither is it as idiosyncratic and complicated as area studies scholars have assumed. The quantitative tradition falls short because there are important cross-national differences in the underlying profile of segregation. By implication, all forms of index-based analysis, even that based on our own A, will conceal much cross-national variation that does not take the form of simple differences in the extent of segregation. We also found, however, that such complexity emerges most prominently at the level of detailed occupations, where local and particularistic forces determine the extent and direction of gender-typing. At the level of major occupational groups, we uncovered a deep structure to segregation regimes that holds in all countries, subject only to minor variations within prescribed ranges and limits. The area studies tradition has failed to appreciate such commonalities.

We explored the underlying structure of this shared segregation regime in Chapter 4. Although aggregate variability cannot be captured in a single parameter (as survey analysts have typically assumed), we found that it can be adequately summarized in our three-parameter model. It follows that aggregate segregation is generated in modern industrial countries by mixing vertical and horizontal principles in different proportions. Because segregation regimes are "loosely coupled," segregative practices in one sector of the labor market are often combined with more integrative practices in another, thereby undermining efforts to characterize segregation regimes unidimensionally. We might remind ourselves that such regimes have not been fashioned from on high to correspond with generalized commitments to equality or difference. Rather, they are a congeries of complicated institutional practices, each one affecting some subset of the parameters that govern segregation.

The preceding conclusions pertain to a limited set of advanced industrial countries. In future analyses, one might usefully examine the structure of segregation in other countries, especially non-European and less developed ones. If our model were applied more widely, only some of the parameters would likely remain within the constricted range characterizing our Eurocentric sample. The vertical parameters might, for example, reflect the wide variations in educational practices that obtain in a more diverse sample of countries. By contrast, the horizontal parameter may be less variable, given that essentialist definitions of male and female labor appear to be widely shared across many countries (see Williams and Best 1990).

PUZZLE #3: WHY ARE GENDER-EGALITARIAN
COUNTRIES EXTREMELY SEX SEGREGATED?

We have argued that competing views on the structure of cross-national variability are best reconciled by developing a core model that reveals the common theme to segregation as well as characteristic forms of variability around that theme. In applying this model, we have focused on the puzzling result that many so-called progressive countries (such as Sweden and Norway) have failed to make substantial headway in reducing sex segregation, whereas countries with more traditional gender politics and policies (Japan, Italy) have relatively integrated labor markets. This well-known result suggests that egalitarian principles, even when rigorously implemented, may fail to reduce sex segregation. Although present-day segregation is sometimes represented as a mere holdover from a less egalitarian past, it is difficult to reconcile this view with evidence that egalitarian policy tends not to deliver as promised.

How does our three-parameter model resolve this puzzle? We have found that Sweden and other Scandinavian countries register high index scores because horizontal segregation is especially well developed in those cases. In interpreting this result, one should bear in mind that liberal egalitarianism may delegitimate overt inequalities of opportunity, but it does not prevent individuals from understanding their own competencies and those of others in terms of standard essentialist visions of masculinity and femininity. As liberal egalitarianism spreads, women increasingly enter into higher education and the paid labor market, yet they do so in ways that reflect their own "female" preferences, the social and interpersonal sanctions associated with gender-inappropriate work, and the essentialist prejudices of employers. This coloring of employer tastes and worker choices allows for ongoing horizontal distinctions and the associated hypersegregation of manual and nonmanual work. It follows that sex segregation in modern egalitarian countries is shaped by a "different but equal" conception of gender and social justice.

The logic of egalitarian policy is quite consistent, then, with the persistence of horizontal forms of segregation. By contrast, we found that egalitarianism does undermine vertical forms of segregation, albeit mainly in the nonmanual sector. For employers of nonmanual labor, the social cost of continuing to segregate can be substantial, owing to the public visibility of elite professional and managerial positions and the consequent heightening of political pressures to conform to equal opportunity laws and norms of gender equality. Moreover, because qualifications for managerial and professional jobs must usually be formally demonstrated (via credentials), the processes governing allocation to such positions are likely to be more meritocratic. These arguments imply that the costs of exercising discriminatory tastes should become especially high in the nonmanual sector.

The structural side of modernization has, by contrast, principally segregative implications. The main structural process of interest, postindustrialism, undermines many of the integrative effects of egalitarianism because it tends to be well developed in countries that are also strongly egalitarian. As was shown in Chapter 4, the compositional effect of postindustrialism increases horizontal segregation, whereas the adaptive effect strengthens vertical segregation in the nonmanual sector. The compositional effect arises because nonmanual occupations are increasingly performed within those postindustrial service industries, such as commerce and communications, that tend to recruit or attract women. This structural shift strengthens horizontal segregation by increasing the proportion of nonmanual occupations that are service-based and hence female-dominated. The adaptive effect arises because service-sector expansion increases the demand for routine nonmanual labor beyond what can be met by simply drawing further on the pool of single women. This demand is therefore met by drawing wives and mothers into a routine nonmanual sector that has been made increasingly family-friendly by reducing the costs of intermittent labor force participation and otherwise fashioning a workplace that does not preclude a continuing commitment to domestic labor. As these workplace adaptations become more prominent, the routine nonmanual sector has been gradually defined and labeled as the default home for women (especially those with traditional domestic responsibilities), and men have become even less likely, by virtue of the label, to be drawn to this sector. The resulting stream of women into the routine nonmanual sector may well offset any weakening of vertical segregation brought about by egalitarianism.

The "Swedish puzzle" is solved, therefore, by recognizing that the integrative effects of cultural egalitarianism are muted because (a) the logic of egalitarian policy is not inconsistent with the persistence and even growth of horizontal forms of segregation, and (b) the egalitarianism of Sweden and other Scandinavian countries has emerged in the context of a strong postindustrial economy that unleashes processes that increase horizontal segregation as well as vertical inequalities within the nonmanual sector. The distinction between vertical and horizontal segregation is accordingly crucial in making sense of the initially puzzling patterns of cross-national variability.

PUZZLE #4: WHY HAS GENDER INTEGRATION
OCCURRED RELATIVELY SLOWLY AND IN SUCH
PIECEMEAL FASHION?

We have developed much the same story line in interpreting recent trends in sex segregation. In the existing literature on trends, what is perhaps most puzzling is the relatively modest rate at which overall levels of sex segregation have declined, a result that contrasts with more precipitous declines in the size of other prominent "gender gaps" (in labor force participation and educational attainment). The evidence also indicates that some occupations have desegregated more rapidly than others. We have found, for example, that horizontal forms of segregation have remained largely intact, whereas vertical forms of segregation have often weakened, especially in the nonmanual sector (see Chapters 5, 6, and 7).

These results imply that vertical and horizontal segregation have not changed together or at the same pace and that distinct forces may therefore underlie them. In understanding such uneven trends, we have again found it useful to conceptualize the modernizing process as a contest between egalitarianism and postindustrialism, where these are understood as the dominant cultural and structural forces influencing sex segregation today. When this formulation is adopted, the persistence of horizontal inequalities may again be attributed to (a) the compatibility of egalitarian cultural ideals with essentialist distinctions, and (b) the segregative effects of postindustrial economic restructuring. The cultural and structural forces commonly associated with modernity thus generate opposing integrative and segregative effects that resolve into quite limited net change in overall segregation indices. The historical dynamics of segregation cannot, then, be adequately understood without moving beyond standard index-based methods that assume across-the-board increases or decreases in segregation.

The foregoing pattern will inevitably play out in idiosyncratic ways as country-specific institutional features modify the generic effects of egalitarianism and postindustrialism. We chose to focus on Japan, the United States, and Switzerland in part because their labor markets are idiosyncratic in instructive ways, allowing us to put our generic formulation to especially revealing test. The Japanese segregation regime is of special interest because it is characterized by unusually weak horizontal segregation. This weakness may be attributed to a lifetime employment system that allows some males to use nonmanual jobs, especially routine ones, as staging posts for individual mobility. The question that then arises is whether the modernizing forces that protect and extend horizontal segregation (such as postindustrialism) can overcome particularistic Japanese institutional forces that undermine it. Although the evidence relevant to this question is too complicated to easily summarize here (see Chapter 6), it bears noting that at least some of it reveals the persistence and possible resurgence of Western-style horizontal segregation, an outcome that may be partly attributed to a weakening commitment in Japan to the lifetime employment system. This result suggests that our generic model may have some currency even in cases far from its home ground.

In the Swiss case, the large immigrant population poses yet another potential threat to our generic theory, because immigrants could replace women as the main labor source to which employers turn to meet the growing demand for service-sector employment. If male immigrants are functional equivalents of native women, employers will no longer need to implement workplace adaptations (provisions for maternal leave, flexible scheduling) that render the nonmanual sector a default home for women; and the effects of postindustrialism on horizontal segregation will accordingly be weakened.

The evidence on this argument, as presented in Chapter 7, is somewhat mixed. To be sure, Swiss employers do rely on immigrant men to fill many lower-level sales and service positions, but they are also relying increasingly on native women to fill mid-level clerical and associate professional positions. In the end, these countervailing forces appear to have generated a rough stability in horizontal sex segregation, suggesting that the "reserve army" of Swiss immigrants may have warded off what would have otherwise been a strengthening of sex segregation across the manual-nonmanual divide.

We appreciate that the puzzle of long-term trends is far from resolved by these analyses and our conjectures about their implications. As we see it, there is good reason to elaborate and extend our trend analyses, based as they are on a small sample of (potentially idiosyncratic) countries and on admittedly speculative interpretations of the model parameters. There is much to be said, in particular, for recasting the analyses of Chapters 5 through 7 in terms of a formal model of horizontal and vertical mobility (see Chapter 4). If such a model were estimated, we could more readily assess whether a three-parameter "leaning-N" profile prevails in all time periods, whether the parameters governing that profile are changing as hypothesized, and whether cross-national variability in trends accords with the stylized formulation advanced here. This model might therefore yield insights into long-term trend that cannot be gleaned from the less formal (albeit more readable) analyses presented in Chapters 5–7.[2]

THE FUTURE OF SEX SEGREGATION

We close by offering our thoughts on the future of gender segregation and inequality (also see Blau, Brinton, and Grusky, forthcoming).[3] Although we cannot offer a fully developed discussion here, our segregation model may lend some insights into the competing forces at work, if not necessarily into the ways in which they will ultimately resolve themselves. We proceed by laying out a range of plausible futures rather than emphasizing any particular one as inevitable or even likely. In carrying out this analysis, we again feature the distinction between vertical and horizontal inequality because we suspect that these dimensions will continue to define the basic structure of segregation, although they may well express themselves in new ways.

The future of vertical segregation may be quickly dispensed with given that straightforward extrapolation seems in this case to be in order. The diffusion of liberal egalitarianism, which undergirds the decline in vertical segregation, is one of the most dramatic developments of our time and does not appear to be losing momentum, the arguments of Faludi (1991) and others notwithstanding. This diffusion should continue to erode vertical segregation through the same supply-side and demand-side processes that have long operated (see Table 1.1). On the supply side, the spread of egalitarianism means that women will increasingly aspire to high-status work, evaluate themselves as capable of performing it, and invest in the requisite training and credentials.[4] At the same time, demand-side discrimination against women should recede, both because employers are less likely to have tastes for discrimination and because personnel policies will become increasingly woman-friendly. These developments should in turn precipitate "feedback effects" (Blau et al. 2002) whereby new cohorts of women come to appreciate that sanctions against gender-atypical employment have diminished and that investments in such employment may accordingly have real payoff.[5]

Are there, however, sectors of the labor market that may hold out indefinitely against the forces of liberal egalitarianism? The analyses that we have presented are certainly consistent with the interpretation that desegregative processes operate mainly in the nonmanual sector (see Chapters 5–7). There are two main reasons why the manual sector, by contrast, may continue to desegregate relatively slowly and thus remain resistant to egalitarian pressures. First, women seeking manual employment are, on average, less educated and less committed to the labor force than their counterparts seeking employment in the nonmanual sector. This means that they can bring less social and political capital to bear on employers and that they may have less interest in exercising the power they do have. Second, there is more opportunity for employers, customers, and coworkers to exercise discriminatory tastes in the manual sector, given that hiring decisions in this sector rely on informal networks (rather than formal credentials). These discriminatory tastes may take the form of employers preferring to hire male craft workers, customers preferring to interact with male craft workers, and coworkers drawing on male referral networks to help employers fill vacant craft slots.

Taken together, these considerations suggest that vertical segregation may erode relatively slowly in the manual sector, but not necessarily that this process will stall altogether. For a variety of reasons, liberal egalitarianism gained its initial foothold in the nonmanual middle class, yet the attitudes, aspirations, and personnel practices associated with it have already begun to trickle down. As they do, women in less advantaged market situations should become increasingly unwilling to accept positions as operatives or semiskilled laborers, preferring instead to compete with men for the relatively well-rewarded positions at the top of the manual hierarchy. The resulting forays into upper-manual occupations will meet with increasing public, institutional, and even legal support as segregation recedes elsewhere and renders male domination of the upper manual sector visibly at odds with prevailing practice.

The available evidence suggests that desegregative processes of this sort are already playing out. For example, all-female construction companies have found a niche in at least some cosmopolitan labor markets, with anecdotal evidence suggesting that "progressive" customers infused with liberal-egalitarian values are often willing to pay a premium for such labor, thereby revealing a taste for "reverse discrimination." We are not, then, entirely unsympathetic to the claim that "sex equality is our inevitable destiny" (Jackson 1998, p. 271), but we would immediately tack on the qualifiers that (a) such a destiny holds, at best, for vertical segregation alone, and (b) it will likely be achieved in the manual sector on a very slow and protracted schedule. This slow decline in vertical inequality may be understood as a "first revolution" in gender segregation that is largely consistent with conventional functionalist and neoinstitutionalist accounts of egalitarian change (see, e.g., Parsons 1970; Meyer 2001).

Will there be a "second revolution" that leads to an analogous decline in horizontal segregation? In answering this question, conventional functionalist and neoinstitutionalist accounts fall short because they fail to recognize that horizontal segregation proceeds from an essentialist ideology that can persist, even thrive, in the context of liberal egalitarian norms of equal opportunity. The second qualifier, therefore, to the optimistic pronouncements of Jackson (1998) and others (e.g., Parsons 1970) is that much modern segregation is backed by essentialism and is accordingly durable.

In the contemporary context, men and women are presumed to have rather different tastes and aptitudes, and liberal egalitarianism works merely to ensure that such differences, however they might be generated, can then be pursued or expressed in a fair (gender-neutral) contest. The presumption that men and women have fundamentally different tastes and capacities is reinforced in various social settings, not just in families (with their gender-specific socialization practices) and work organizations (with their discriminatory hiring practices) but in other institutional contexts as well. By way of (trivial) example, consider the practice among American fast-food restaurants of providing gender-specific toys to children, a practice of interest only because it is widely diffused and evidently unobjectionable to all but a small minority of "gender progressives." If these same restaurants distributed toys on the basis of racial or class standing, the practice would be deemed absurd at best. This example suggests that, at least in the United States, it is less legitimate to interpret racial or class-based inequalities in essentialist terms than to interpret gender segregation and inequality in these terms. In this regard, gender inequality is not just another form of ascription destined to wither away (see Parsons 1970), but a very special form distinguished by the durability of its essentialist legitimation.

The question at hand, of course, is whether such essentialism will continue to color labor market outcomes even as liberal egalitarian norms diffuse. These liberal norms, which stress the importance of providing equal opportunities to all workers, can be reconciled with massive horizontal segregation because male and female workers are presumed to come to the market with different social and cultural identities, different beliefs about their occupational capacities, and accordingly different occupational aspirations. At the same time, employers also behave under the influence of internalized essentialist beliefs and may presume, either rightly or wrongly, that gender provides a useful signal of individual capacities for particular lines of work. The resulting segregation, generated through supply-side variability in aptitudes or demand-side judgments about capacities, need not be interpreted as in any way inconsistent with equal-opportunity norms.[6] In addition, an essentialist logic can even coexist with a version of egalitarianism that stresses the importance of equal outcomes, at least insofar as "equality" in this context implies that men and women have *equally valued* outcomes (as measured, for example, by earnings, prestige, and intrinsic rewards) rather than *identical* ones. The "separate but equal" logic that underlies essentialist forms of segregation is accordingly quite consistent with those variants of egalitarianism that have widely diffused with advanced industrialism.[7]

It follows that essentialist segregation may coexist with egalitarianism of either the "equal outcomes" or "equal opportunity" form. In the long run, it is of course possible that a yet deeper form of egalitarianism will emerge and delegitimate (a) the tendency of males and females to develop different tastes, aspirations, and market capacities, and (b) the tendency of employers to make judgments about productivity through essentialist lenses. There are indeed many signs that just such a form of egalitarianism is developing. Most notably, conventional sociological understandings of the role of socialization, social exchange, and power differentials in generating preferences have diffused widely in contemporary industrial societies, suggesting that preferences and choices formerly regarded as sacrosanct are increasingly treated as outcomes of unequal and unfair social processes. This deeper form of egalitarianism is reflected in some parents' attempts to minimize gender bias in the socialization of their children, at least in the early years of childrearing before the unremitting influence of societywide essentialism typically undermines their efforts. It is surely plausible that this deeper egalitarianism will ultimately take hold (see Ramirez 1987, p. 270). For our part, we would merely stress that prevailing forms of egalitarianism do not fully delegitimate essentialist processes and that a true "second revolution," one that establishes this new and broader definition of equality, will therefore be needed to eliminate essentialist segregation.

This second revolution, were it to unfold, would require three major developments, none of which may be regarded as inevitable. First, ongoing public dialogue about the sources of gender-based difference in tastes and aptitudes would have to turn more definitively to social-constructivist accounts, with greater attention to the process by which essentialist scripts are generated and sustained in social institutions (including families, schools, and work organizations). Second, a consensus would have to emerge that these socially constructed differences (and perhaps biological ones as well) should be suppressed rather than celebrated, again hardly an inevitable development given that diverse constituencies (social conservatives, "gender-difference" feminists, and others) are arrayed against any such suppression. Third, even if this political consensus were to emerge, the project of realizing it by eliminating deeply essentialist assumptions in primary socialization and other micro-level interaction is surely a formidable one.

This three-stage revolution thus involves (a) recognizing that the content of essentialist beliefs can be manipulated, (b) agreeing that a particular form of manipulation (suppression) should be attempted, and (c) rooting out essentialist practices that are deeply embedded in our core social institutions. The latter stage, in particular, will likely unfold slowly, given that it is no easy task to convert abstract political commitments into new patterns of interaction that are truly gender-neutral (see Ridgeway, forthcoming). In part, this third stage might proceed in grassroots fashion as gender progressives closely monitor and scrutinize their own everyday interactions for hints of gender essentialism, much as some well-meaning individuals may attempt to root out residual racist sentiments through an ongoing self-censoring of thoughts and behaviors that are inconsistent with their egalitarian commitments. Although there is some precedent for change of this kind, there should be no illusions about how formidable the remaining barriers are. The "second revolution" is accordingly unlikely to unfold in the near term.

In the meantime, some form of essentialist segregation will persist, though not necessarily the same version that is found in present-day advanced industrial economies. Indeed, the content of essentialist beliefs is clearly malleable (within some evident limits), meaning that all manner of gender differences have been interpreted in various time periods and societies as natural and inevitable (cf. Williams and Best 1990). The question that then emerges is whether we should anticipate much change over the near term (say fifty years) in the underlying content of essentialist beliefs and the associated structure of essentialist segregation. We lay out the most likely changes in such beliefs in the next section.

The Rise of Female-Disadvantaging Essentialism

In asking whether the content of gender-essentialist beliefs might change, it bears emphasizing that modern horizontal segregation emerged during the early industrial period, a moment in history when manual labor was a central factor of production (see Kessler-Harris 1982; Milkman 1987). By contrast, manual labor is now becoming almost peripheral to production, particularly in advanced economies that are experiencing deindustrialization through the twin forces of labor-reducing technological change and globalization of production.

We have shown in Chapters 3 and 4 that the characteristic male-typing of manual work has remained in force despite these developments. Over the next half-century, the ongoing transition to a "postmanual" system may nonetheless begin to spur men to resist those pieces of the essentialist package, such as an emphasis on male physicality, that relegate them to increasingly peripheralized and devalued pursuits. Barring some dramatic intensification in the pace of deindustrialization, it seems unlikely that horizontal segregation will quickly wither away, but it may gradually weaken as men come to eschew dying manual occupations that are part of a largely superseded economic system.

This gradual decline in segregation across the manual-nonmanual divide, were it indeed to occur, need not trigger any associated decline in other forms of essentialist segregation. We suggest, then, that essentialism may be transformed and reshaped, but will not necessarily be weakened across the board. For instance, the long-standing belief that women excel in personal service and nurturance will likely remain unchallenged, thus providing continuing ideological support for the segregation of women into occupations that call upon such skills (nursing, childcare, teaching, among others).

Although "gender egalitarians" may applaud *any* breakdown in essentialist beliefs, a decreasing emphasis on male physicality would have ambiguous implications for women's status because it involves undermining one of those relatively rare manifestations of essentialism that benefits women rather than men. That is, contemporary horizontal segregation is all about women crowding into nonmanual occupations that, on average, confer more pay and prestige than manual occupations.[8] If horizontal segregation ultimately breaks down, this female-advantaging effect is lost; and the remaining forms of essentialist segregation disadvantage women (in terms of pay and prestige) at virtually every turn.

This raises the question of precisely how widespread other forms of essentialist segregation are. We cannot answer this question definitively without measuring essentialist segregation more exhaustively than we so far have. The available evidence nonetheless suggests that female-disadvantaging forms of essentialism are ubiquitous; after all, a great many occupations are regarded as nurturant or service-oriented, and such occupations tend to be less well rewarded than comparable "male" occupations (see, e.g., Kilbourne et al. 1994).

This form of essentialism shows up in almost every profession. For example, the presumption that women are especially nurturant supports the crowding of female medical students into pediatrics, a specialty that is low on extrinsics (pay, prestige) relative to comparable "male" medical specialties (internist, surgeon, cardiologist). The same female-typing of nurturant fields appears in law (family law), academia (psychology), business (personnel management), and many of the lower-status professions as well. In all of these areas, the female-typed specialty provides fewer extrinsic rewards than the comparable male-typed specialty, thus constituting a female-disadvantaging form of essentialism that will presumably live on even as those rare female-advantaging forms (based on the male physicality assumption) do not. The persistence of such "negative essentialism" will, by definition, perpetuate female disadvantage in the labor market. Although we have argued that overt vertical segregation is likely to (gradually) disappear, there is nothing in our model or larger framework that prevents female disadvantage from persisting when it is undergirded by essentialist processes.[9]

The foregoing account may be regarded, then, as a relatively minor elaboration of our larger argument that liberal egalitarianism works to undermine vertical segregation but not essentialist segregation. We are now suggesting that essentialist principles may live on even as the content of essentialist beliefs change in ways that exacerbate and legitimate male advantage. It is altogether possible that we are moving toward an end state of this sort. If so, it follows that desegregation efforts will effectively stall once vertical segregation is eliminated, because all remaining segregation will at that point have clear essentialist underpinnings.

This account implies, for example, that pediatricians will continue to be disproportionately female by virtue of the presumption that women are nurturant, naturally disposed to caring for children, and hence uniquely suited to such positions. Although committed egalitarians may complain that these (disproportionately female) pediatricians are paid less than other comparably trained physicians, their concerns will never gain traction because of the compelling essentialist story that legitimates such segregation. Namely, liberal egalitarians will understand essentialist segregation as arising, in part, from the (exogenous) tastes of women, thereby implying that the wage penalty they suffer is compensated by the extra utility they derive from realizing their tastes for nurturant work. These liberal egalitarian defenders will also continue to be attracted to the good sense of matching women to occupations that appear to exploit their particular talents. By liberal egalitarian logic, one should only defend the right of women to fairly compete for any occupation to which they aspire, thus leaving unchallenged the sociological forces that generate predictably sex-typed differences in aspirations.

The Decline of Female-Disadvantaging Essentialism?

The preceding account rests on the assumption that a liberal egalitarian logic will continue to underlie the institutions of contemporary labor markets and provide the main lens through which inequalities are judged. Although liberal egalitarianism is arguably the dominant labor market logic of our time, it exists in tension with competing logics that could eventually rise in prominence and make it possible to address the negative essentialism that liberal egalitarianism takes to be largely unproblematic.

Among these competing logics, the most prominent are those of "reward equalization" and "complete equalization," both of which appear to have revolutionary potential over the long run. The logic of "reward equalization" delegitimates residual gender inequalities in pay and other rewards (yet allows essentialist segregation to persist), while the more radical logic of "complete equalization" challenges the legitimacy of essentialist segregation itself. If either of these logics were to diffuse, it would produce a segregation regime quite different from that associated with liberal egalitarianism in its pure form. We review each of these logics below and then close by considering the likelihood that either will come to influence the development of labor market institutions.

In its contemporary form, the logic of "reward equalization" treats the gender gap in labor market rewards as fundamentally inconsistent with core egalitarian values, no matter how that gap is explained or justified. The liberal egalitarian justification, which interprets essentialist inequality as an expression of differential tastes, aptitudes, and investments, is regarded as problematic either because overt discrimination is presumed to account for much of the gender gap, or because tastes, aptitudes, and investments are regarded as outcomes of institutional forms and practices that are socially constructed (through gender-role socialization, the domestic division of labor, or power differences between the sexes). Although this gender differential in tastes, aptitudes, and investments could conceivably be eliminated, such equalization is unlikely given how intractable essentialist processes are. By virtue of such supply-side stickiness, advocates of "reward equalization" see no alternative, then, but to redress female disadvantage by equalizing the extrinsic rewards associated with comparable male-typed and female-typed pursuits. This approach should be understood as the fullest possible expression of "separate but equal" essentialism. That is, the separation of men and women into separate spheres is treated as an inevitable, if unfortunate, by-product of essentialism, but one that can at least be ameliorated by insisting on equal remuneration for comparable "male" and "female" occupations.

It is at least plausible that our labor market institutions will come to embody a logic of this sort. The comparable-worth initiatives of the 1980s, which may be understood as state-sponsored efforts to establish reward equalization, ultimately failed to garner much judicial support (see Nelson and Bridges 1999), but despite setbacks in the judicial arena many public and private organizations continue to attempt to rationalize job evaluation and remuneration policies in ways that putatively reduce gender bias (also see England 1992; Acker 1989). These efforts suggest an incipient interest in reward equalization that could well be transformed over time from a relatively minor grassroots movement into something more far-reaching. Indeed, this interpretation is consistent with the growing public interest in the raw gender gap (in wages), an interest that does not appear to stand or fall on any complicated analysis of whether that gap is generated by intervening processes that are consistent with a liberal egalitarian account. If public interest in the pay gap is truly animated by a commitment to equal outcomes, we might expect employees, unions, and watchdog organizations to increasingly scrutinize intrafirm pay policies, thereby increasing the social disapprobation experienced by recalcitrant firms that fail to practice extrinsic equalization (up to some accepted threshold). This development would of course imply that a new labor market logic is beginning to challenge or at least supplement that of liberal egalitarianism.

As noted above, an egalitarian attack on negative essentialism may be carried out in two main ways, either by reducing inequalities of reward ("reward equalization") or by addressing the occupational segregation that generates inequalities of reward ("complete equalization"). The latter possibility, which we have not yet discussed in any detail, would presumably unfold through a gradual weakening of (a) the supply-side tendency of males and females to develop different tastes, aptitudes, and aspirations, and (b) the demand-side tendency of employers to make judgments about productivity in terms of essentialist stereotypes.

As Ridgeway (forthcoming) and others (e.g., Reskin 2000) have stressed, essentialist precepts are difficult to root out because they are deeply embedded in the micro-level interactions that underlie primary and secondary socialization. There is, however, no denying that diffuse anti-essentialist sentiments continue to spread, thus raising the possibility that a viable alternative ideology might eventually emerge. To date, the impact of such anti-essentialist egalitarianism has been weakened because it takes the form of a thin, highly politicized veneer that is overlaid on a deeper essentialist base. That is, some girls now learn from their parents that they have every right, perhaps even an obligation, to pursue conventionally male-typed professions (such as scientist or mathematician), but this "surface veneer" of egalitarianism does not easily override deep essentialist sentiments formed by long interaction with popular culture, the media, and significant others.

How might segregation evolve in the context of this increasingly hybrid socialization process? Surely, the thin veneer of egalitarianism is not so thin as to be entirely meaningless, as some girls indeed develop preferences for, train for, and ultimately enter male-typed occupations. Although overt and egregious forms of negative essentialism may therefore come under attack, we ought not conclude that negative essentialism will entirely disappear. Instead, given that essentialist precepts are so entrenched in micro-level interaction, they will likely be reexpressed in less overt ways that are protected from politicized attack (see Abbott 2001; Reskin and Roos 1990; Williams 1989).

There is much anecdotal and qualitative evidence supporting such an account: (a) the recent (minor) influx of U.S. women into road-construction occupations is conjoined with personnel practices that shunt these new entrants into positions that are physically undemanding or people-oriented (such as "flagman"); (b) the influx of men into nursing is coupled with the presumption that they should take on technical specialties that are regarded as essentially male (such as nurse-anesthetist); and (c) the rising number of female military recruits has been accommodated by allocating them into noncombat billets and, in particular, female-typed nonmanual specialties in the noncombat labor force (clerical, medical, and dental specialties).

In each of these cases, the initial headway in reducing essentialist segregation is followed by occupational resegregation (again along essentialist lines), albeit now at a more detailed level. This new form of segregation may be so submerged as to be protected from exposure and delegitimation. Alternatively, the new form may eventually be "outed" and subjected to fresh egalitarian attack, which may in turn precipitate a new round of resegregation at an even more submerged level. In either case, essentialist segregation lives on, but in weakened and more specialized forms.[10]

The preceding discussion suggests that the future of gender inequality rests on a struggle between egalitarian and essentialist forces that is not quite as one-sided as modernization theorists have sometimes claimed (see, e.g., Parsons 1970; Jackson 1998). If gender segregation is especially durable, it is precisely because it has such a deep essentialist undergirding. We suspect that other forms of occupational segregation (including ethnic, racial, and class) are less extreme precisely because their essentialist bases are not as well developed.

The relevant thought experiment in this regard involves identifying stereotypical pairings of a particular occupation with a particular ethnic group (Japanese gardener), racial group (African-American jazz musician), or class background (upper-class investment banker). We submit that such a thought experiment yields relatively few consistent pairings of these kinds. To be sure, one finds localized ethnic typecasting during periods of extraordinary immigration, but it often attenuates as assimilative forces play out and ethnic enclaves dissipate. Likewise, racist occupational stereotypes were once legion in the United States (and other countries), but now are largely discredited and live on in weakened form. Finally, class-based stereotypes are exceedingly well developed in the caste systems of certain societies, but elsewhere are only found in residual or weakened form, typically for a small number of elite occupations that are presumed to demand long and intensive exposure to the requisite cultural capital (such as art critic). This is all to suggest that gender inequality is a uniquely cultural form that rests heavily on essentialist processes. As we have shown, essentialist stereotypes about gender proliferate and typecast entire regions of the occupational structure, thereby creating durable occupational ghettos that color the workplace experiences of a great many women and men.

We would not rule out the possibility that our egalitarian commitments will ultimately develop in ways that attack the essentialist foundations of gender inequality. In fact, we have laid out several pathways to this "second revolution," all of which involve radical extensions and reinterpretations of our egalitarian legacy. We have stressed that such extensions are indeed radical; that is, although pathways to full equality can be identified, we would not dare suggest that they constitute some "inevitable destiny" (Jackson 1998, p. 271) that will be straightforwardly realized provided that contemporary integrative dynamics continue to play out. To the contrary, the second revolution will have to overcome many formidable barriers, not the least of which is an entrenched tradition of classical liberalism that celebrates individual choice and thus supports and sustains those forms of inequality that can be represented as consistent with it.

Chapter One: The Four Puzzles of Sex Segregation

1. There is obviously much cross-national variability in the patterning and extent of these changes. The trend line in female labor force participation is especially variable, with countries such as Italy, Ireland, and Greece seeing muted change relative to the experiences of most advanced industrial countries (see Brewster and Rindfuss 2000, p. 276).

2. In the United States at the turn of the twenty-first century, women constituted 83.3 percent of all elementary school teachers, 98.9 percent of all secretaries, and 93.6 percent of all licensed practical nurses (see U.S. Census Bureau 2001, p. 381).

3. The contribution of establishment-level segregation is far less impressive. As reported by Petersen and Morgan (1995), only 24.3 percent of the wage gap can be explained by establishment segregation alone, whereas 89.1 percent of the wage gap can be explained when occupational and establishment segregation are simultaneously taken into account.

4. Although most of our own analysis focuses on occupation-level segregation, we appreciate that economic sectors, industries, and firms are sex segregated in ways that are worth studying as well. As exemplified in Chapter 8, our general modeling approach may be usefully extended to other forms of segregation, such as industrial segregation.

5. The association between gender and occupation remains largely unexplained by a model that constrains the gender composition of occupations to be a function of occupational status (e.g., Charles and Grusky 1995; see also Blackburn, Brooks, and Jarman 2000).

6. There is a long history of scholarship in which these dimensions have been invoked (e.g., Hakim 1992; Wright and Baxter 1995; Rubery, Smith, and Fagan 1999; Semyonov and Jones 1999; Blackburn, Jarman, and Brooks 2000). However, they have not typically been featured in comparative analyses of sex segregation (cf. Blackburn, Jarman, and Brooks 2000), nor has the horizontal distinction been equated explicitly with the manual-nonmanual divide.

7. Similarly, industries are desegregating very slowly, at least relative to the pace of change in female labor force participation and educational attainment (e.g., Müller, Willms, and Handl 1983; OECD 1985; Jacobs and Lim 1992).

8. The spread of bureaucracy is itself sometimes attributed to the efficiency of this organizational form (e.g., Weber 1956).

9. These principles may well have functionalist sources. In societies characterized by high fertility, low productivity, and short life expectancy, a sexual division of labor in which women specialize in bearing and rearing children may result in large economic efficiency gains for families and communities. Likewise, in societies that rely heavily on physical strength (such as hunting and gathering societies), men may leverage their advantage on this trait into power over women. Whatever their origins, these gender distinctions become deeply institutionalized over time, allowing them to persist even after the originating economic or social pressures disappear.

10. To some extent, conventional understandings of masculinity and femininity are variable and contingent, differing across social groups defined by race, ethnicity, sexual orientation, and other institutionalized categories (Flax 1990; Baca Zinn and Thornton Dill 1996). We focus here on the shared symbolic meanings associated with masculinity and femininity that appear consistently across most social groups.

11. The highly successful self-help book *Men Are from Mars, Women Are from Venus* (Gray 1992) may be regarded as an especially explicit rendering of gender essentialism.

12. Although the social effects of "high culture" are perforce limited, it bears noting that some strains of feminist theory also celebrate and thereby propagate essentialist world views (e.g., Daly 1978; Gilligan 1982; see J. Williams 2000 for an excellent review of this literature).

13. The familial division of labor may also be understood in essentialist terms. That is, women specialize in nurturance, personal service, and the care of young children, spouses, and parents, while men specialize in tasks that involve physical labor and interaction with things (rather than people).

14. Although the male-breadwinner model has always been unsustainable for poor and working-class families, this ideal undoubtedly influenced the ways in which many jobs and wages were structured.

15. The textile industry, which offered low pay and was female-dominated, is an obvious exception to this characteristic male-typing of blue-collar work. The forces of vertical inequality operated within the blue-collar sector by allocating women disproportionately to less desirable positions within that sector.

16. This conversion process is discussed in C. Tilly 1998 (also see Connell 1987; Chafetz 1988; Epstein 1988).

17. The latter mechanism generates additional feedback effects insofar as women opt against investing in human capital precisely because they believe that a

discriminatory "glass ceiling" prevents them from reaping the benefits of such an investment (see Table 1.1, line A4).

18. The available cross-national and historical data suggest that variability in gender attitudes is indeed associated with variability both in occupational aspirations and in the sexual division of labor (see, e.g., Shu and Marini 1998; Crompton and Harris 1999). There is also a well developed literature on the relationship between cultural values and cognition (see DiMaggio 1997 for an instructive review).

19. The continuing lure of gender essentialism is evident even in the feminist movement. There are, for example, well known disagreements within the movement about whether equality of the sexes is tantamount to "sameness," and whether the special needs and circumstances of women should be taken into account by policy makers (see, e.g., J. Scott 1988; Crompton 1999; and Epstein 1999 on the "equality-versus-difference" debate).

20. Throughout this book, we focus on horizontal segregation as one of the most important realizations of essentialist precepts, but we appreciate that such precepts generate other forms of segregation as well. For example, the presumption that women are especially nurturant generates a disproportionately large number of female pediatricians, a form of essentialist segregation that disadvantages women insofar as pediatricians secure less pay and prestige relative to comparable "male" specialties within the medical profession (e.g., internist, surgeon). Although essentialist segregation of the latter sort is not captured in our formal models (see Chapter 4), this should be regarded as a deficiency in our operationalization of essentialism rather than an unduly narrow conceptualization of its effects (see Chapter 9 for a relevant discussion).

21. This pattern also emerges in recent trends in attitudes toward homosexuality. Between 1973 and 1998, essentialist stereotypes about gays and lesbians proved to be extremely resilient, despite a marked decline of support for policies restricting the civil liberties of these groups (Loftus 2001).

22. In the elite professions, essentialist processes continue to express themselves in submerged form, affecting the types of detailed occupations that women and men fill. Among medical doctors, for example, women are overrepresented within the pediatrician category, presumably by virtue of its association with (female-typed) nurturing behavior (Crompton, Le Feuvre, and Birkelund 1999).

23. Although Oppenheimer (1970) refers to both industries and occupations as "female-demanding," it is the industrial distinction (i.e., the effect of industrial composition on occupational gender composition) that is of interest here.

24. We are not suggesting that service-sector expansion accounts for *all* observed increases in horizontal segregation. The suppressed demand in the manual sector is also relevant here; that is, given that the skilled manual sector continues to contract and that new manual hiring is accordingly limited, we would expect the nonmanual sector to serve as the principal destination for newly entering women (see, e.g., Rubery, Smith, and Fagan 1999).

25. The degree to which employers rely on women rather than other second-ary laborers (e.g., immigrants, racial minorities) to fill new service jobs varies across national and historical contexts (see Chapter 7 on the role of immigrant labor in the Swiss economy).

26. The labor force in these countries also includes women who are forced into the market by financial pressures (thus giving a bimodal cast to female labor supply).

27. This effect on vertical segregation appears principally in the nonmanual sector because female labor force entry is spurred largely by growing opportunities in lower nonmanual occupations.

28. We suspect that this conceptualization is also reinforced by the routine and automatic application of summary indices. Segregation is, in other words, often understood as "whatever D measures."

29. This "marginal sensitivity" is all the more problematic given that both the size of the female labor force and the structure of the economy are commonly cited as causal factors in the generation and maintenance of sex segregation. The com-plex causal relationships among these variables cannot be examined when margin-sensitive measures are employed.

30. The "size-standardized" dissimilarity index, D_s, has long served as the favored revision of D (Gross 1968; Cortese, Falk, and Cohen 1976; F. Blau and Hendricks 1979; Jacobs 1989a; Hakim 1992; Jacobs and Lim 1992). This revision is, however, flawed because it exchanges one form of marginal dependency for an-other; that is, D_s is indeed invariant to changes in the occupational structure, but it is dependent on rates of female labor force participation (Charles and Grusky 1995).

31. We have restricted our analysis to industrial countries because official la-bor market data in developing countries are even more fragmented and potentially misleading than those for the industrial world. Moreover, our hypotheses about the structure of sex segregation and variability therein have been developed for the in-dustrial context, where the distinction between domestic and market work is highly salient. Because sex segregation may be differently structured and generated in so-cieties where this distinction is more ambiguous, we will not attempt to generalize our results and conclusions beyond industrial market economies.

32. We provide data and sample programs for estimating our models on www.segregation.com.

33. On Japanese and Swiss gender-role traditionalism, see McLendon 1983; Simona 1985; Brinton 1988; Popenoe 1988; and Yu 2001.

Chapter Two: Toward Linking Theory and Method

1. For example, a modern analysis of gender discrimination entails regressing the relevant labor market outcome (e.g., earnings) on a vector of variables, one of which is of course gender. The extent of gender discrimination is then equated with

the size of the gender coefficient, not with some hypothetical estimate of how many women are affected by discrimination. In the following sections, we apply a similar modeling approach to the analysis of segregation, thus allowing us to fit and assess models that correspond to competing hypotheses about the structure of segregation.

2. In a perfectly segregated labor market, A is undefined because M_j equals 0 in all female-dominated occupations.

3. This is not to suggest that segregation regimes evolve in strict isolation from one another. To the contrary, the gender labels that are characteristically attached to occupations tend to diffuse across countries (and time periods), thus generating cross-national (and temporal) similarities in the discriminatory tastes of employers and the sex-typed aspirations of workers.

4. It is appropriate to use A_M (as well as A) when the segregation data are consistent with Models 1–5 of Table 2.2.

5. It is no easy task to choose among scalar indices when the multiplicative shift model fails to fit. In this context, one must either (a) distort the data at the point of estimating the model, or (b) apply a model that fits perfectly and then summarize the many parameters of that model in a single scalar index (thereby introducing "distortions" of a different sort). Although some information will necessarily be lost with either approach, we advocate the latter because the resulting index (i.e., A) is sensitive to all departures from perfect integration rather than merely those that emerge under a particular representation of the common segregation profile.

6. The marginal effects for this model can be identified by constraining the parameters for the first row or column to equal one (i.e., $\beta_{1k} = \gamma_{1k} = 1$).

Chapter Three: The Underlying Structure of Sex Segregation

1. The Statistical Office of the European Communities coordinates a "Labour Force Survey" (LFS) administered annually in twelve countries. We analyzed these data for an earlier version of this chapter, but ultimately decided that the LFS samples were too small to allow sufficient disaggregation.

2. The purpose of these efforts was not to devise a new classification distinct from ISCO-88, but rather to better "implement ISCO-88 for census and survey coding purposes" (Elias and Birch 1993, p. 1).

3. It is impossible to eliminate all cross-national inconsistencies in the criteria used to determine whether the wives of farmers are bona fide members of the formal labor force. We have nonetheless included agricultural workers in our analyses, since we prefer to represent all occupations in the national economy. It is reassuring in this context that our results remain much the same when the agricultural work force is excluded from our samples. (These supplementary results are available on request.)

4. The case of Luxembourg is more complex than we have allowed here. Al-

though Luxembourg has completed its mapping process and ISCO-88-COM classifications are therefore available, we decided not to include it in our archive because the available tabulations are based on small samples. Likewise, data for the former German Democratic Republic (GDR) are available, but the analyses reported here all pertain to the labor force of the original Federal Republic of Germany (West Germany) because we thought it important to restrict our analyses to market-based economies.

5. It is well known that the Swedish occupational structure includes very large clerical, service, and semiprofessional categories. The Japanese economy, by contrast, is characterized by sizable agricultural and manufacturing sectors.

6. We have normalized these coefficients by forcing them to sum to zero.

7. The values of A_M and A are typically quite similar, but there are a few discrepancies of interest. Most notably, we find that Japan, Belgium, and France show lower relative levels of segregation under A_M than under A.

8. This correlation increases somewhat ($r = 0.44$) when Japan is excluded from our ten-nation sample.

Chapter Four: Revisiting Parsimony

1. If the two vertical segregation lines are parallel, the distance between them is of course constant. However, insofar as the slopes of these lines are allowed to differ, the size of the horizontal parameter will depend on the implicit zero point of the vertical scale (see note 12).

2. Although egalitarianism has an attenuating effect on vertical segregation (in the nonmanual sector), it bears noting that postindustrialization has a countervailing effect on this parameter. We suspect that the former effect outweighs the latter.

3. This is not to suggest that horizontal segregation is the only form of segregation generated by gender essentialism. That is, horizontal segregation stems principally from the essentialist precept that women are poorly suited for physical tasks, whereas other forms of segregation (such as the female-typing of pediatricians) arise from the associated (but distinct) precepts that women are nurturant, service-oriented, and socially skilled. We discuss this broader conceptualization of essentialist segregation in Chapter 9.

4. This conventional operationalization amounts to equating horizontal segregation with the combined effects of (a) segregation across the manual-nonmanual divide, (b) omitted vertical segregation that is not captured by a socioeconomic index (SEI), and (c) omitted horizontal segregation that is not captured by our manual-nonmanual specification.

5. Among the ten countries considered here, this hypothetical baseline comes closest to being realized in Italy and Portugal (see Figure 3.3).

6. To some extent, such service-sector expansion is associated with more opportunities to outsource domestic work (such as house cleaning and child care),

thereby facilitating female employment in professional or managerial occupations and reducing vertical sex segregation. Although an "outsourcing effect" of this sort undoubtedly operates in most countries, it is likely swamped by the adaptive effect emphasized here.

7. In this regard, the heading of this section ("parsimony in causal dynamics") is something of a rhetorical flourish, since a great many macro-level variables are likely to affect segregation outcomes. However, given that our main objective is to explain why sex segregation is an organic feature of contemporary systems, a parsimonious specification suffices.

8. By design, the manual-nonmanual distinction figures prominently in the ILO's definition of major occupational groups, with only one group, "laborer," including both manual and nonmanual workers (according to ILO characterizations of the detailed occupations that comprise major occupational groups). However, given that the overwhelming majority of laborers perform tasks that require substantial physical effort (e.g., construction, manufacturing, domestic work), we have designated all occupations in this group as manual, thereby following convention. We have also experimented with models that measure horizontal inequality at the detailed occupational level by distinguishing manual and nonmanual occupations within this laborer category. These models do not fit much better than those that rely on the more conventional aggregate distinction.

9. For Switzerland, the 1990 score on this item was unavailable from the WVS, so we drew instead on the 1995 WVS. The egalitarianism scores for the other countries did not substantially change between 1990 and 1995.

10. For our postindustrialism variable, the value of Cronbach's alpha is .76.

11. Obviously, we lack evidence on the sources of this association between SEI and gender composition, but we suspect that it arises from male advantage in the competition for desirable occupations as well as degradation in the income and education of occupations that become female-labeled (see, e.g., England 1992; Catanzarite 2002).

12. Under this specification, the two vertical parameters no longer generate parallel lines, meaning that the estimated size of the horizontal parameter depends on the implied zero point of the socioeconomic scale. We have fixed the zero point of this scale at 37 (which is the midpoint between the score for the lowest nonmanual category [40] and the highest manual category [34]). The two vertical segregation lines are furthest from one another at this point (assuming that the nonmanual slope is weaker than the manual one).

13. We have also estimated a model that operationalizes the horizontal dimension at the disaggregate level by distinguishing manual and nonmanual occupations at that level (see note 8). This model modestly increases the percentage of disaggregate variability that is explained ($L^2 = 803,515$; d.f. $= 477$).

14. The socioeconomic scale has been renormalized for the interactive specification (see note 12 for details). The macro-level coefficients for this

specification (see Table 4.5, panel B) are sensitive to the zero point on the scale and must therefore be interpreted carefully.

15. These percentages are held down because some of the aggregate variability is not captured by our two-parameter or three-parameter specifications (see Table 4.3) and cannot be explained, therefore, by macro-level variables that are constrained to operate through these (imperfect) specifications.

16. All else being equal, this hypothetical increase in the egalitarianism score would weaken the socioeconomic effect by .0088 (.0003 × (87.93 − 58.46) = .0088), which amounts to a 14.2 percent decline in the estimated effect for Germany (.0088/.062 = .142).

17. To be sure, the new labor force entrants may also elect to enter low-status manual jobs, because these too can be combined with substantial domestic obligations. The routine nonmanual option should nonetheless be more frequently exercised because nonmanual positions (a) are more prestigious than most manual positions, (b) are more easily reconciled with part-time schedules and intermittent employment, and (c) do not require transgressing traditional gender norms.

18. This intercept is not identified because it is embedded in the sex-by-occupation interaction terms (δ_{ij}).

19. The agriculture coefficient is strongly negative in Table 4.6 and hence counter to the expected pattern (given that the SEI score for this category, 23, is relatively low). However, because this category is numerically small in most of the countries in our sample, it contributes rather little to the parameter estimates reported in Table 4.5. The macro-level hypotheses that we have advanced pertain principally to the dynamics underlying urban labor markets and cannot be expected to explain cross-national variability in agricultural segregation.

20. The latter effect arises because the negative coefficient for low-status operatives is stronger than the negative coefficient for high-status craft workers. The agriculture and laborer coefficients are less relevant in explaining the results of Table 4.5 because they are numerically small (see note 19).

21. The results reported in Table 4.6 are quite robust. When the data were weighted to generate identical sample sizes in each country, the only change of any consequence was a small decline in the effect of gender egalitarianism on managerial segregation. The parameter estimates also remained largely unchanged when univariate models were estimated and when a control for female educational attainment was applied.

22. The underlying structure of college-major segregation has been modeled by Charles and Bradley (2002).

Chapter Five: Profiles of Change

I acknowledge David B. Grusky and Maria Charles for their invaluable suggestions; Jesper B. Sørensen for sharing his GAUSS command files; and Karen Aschaffenburg, Mariko Lin Chang, Joon Han, Jacqueline Olvera, Jesper B. Sørensen,

Szonja Szelényi, and Nancy B. Tuma for their thoughtful comments. Models were estimated in GLIM 4.0 and GAUSS 3.0. Correspondence may be directed to Kim Weeden, Department of Sociology, Cornell University, 323 Uris Hall, Ithaca, N.Y., 14853 (kw74@cornell.edu).

1. This project was undertaken well before all of the Integrated Public Use Microdata Samples ("IPUMS;" Ruggles and Sobek 2003; see also www.ipums.org), which are an extraordinarily rich historical series of individual census records, became available. Even if one were to start afresh, though, it is not clear that IPUMS is ideal for studying long-term trends in sex segregation: first, the series does not yet include the 1930 census; and second, in reconciling occupation codes across more recent censuses, IPUMS researchers assumed a simple one-to-one match of codes rather than retaining the sex-specific, and often very complex, relationship between adjacent occupation schemes (see "Data" section). The latter feature may introduce nontrivial biases into segregation trends calculated from IPUMS data, while the former obviously makes it impossible to tease out Depression-era changes in the level or pattern of segregation.

2. Although bureaucratic organizations may institutionalize segregation, they are putatively grounded in universalistic principles (Weber 1978) and may ultimately be forces for integrative change (e.g., Yamagata et al. 1997; Jackson 1998).

3. This does not preclude changes in a particular organization's hiring or promotion practices (see, e.g., Tomaskovic-Devey and Skaggs 1999). However, unless there is some shock to the system that encourages a substantial number of organizations to change their practices simultaneously (and with the same consequences for segregation), the aggregate impact of organizational transformations is likely null or, at best, minute. A similar argument applies to the aggregate effects of attitudinal shifts among individuals.

4. The applicability of punctuated-equilibrium theory to social rather than biological systems is still debated (see Somit and Peterson 1992). In this chapter, "punctuated equilibrium" is used merely as an apt metaphor of change.

5. Although Current Population Surveys (CPSs) can provide detailed data for intercensal years, mixing data sources is problematic. CPS data from the 1970s, for example, show less integration than census data from the same period (Bianchi and Rytina 1986). For calculations of D and D_s based on 1997 CPS data, see Wells 1999 and Jacobs 2001.

6. D is 0.6 percentage points lower (67.1 vs. 67.7) and D_s is 0.7 percentage points higher (70.5 vs. 69.8) in the PUMS data than in the original 1910 tables.

7. The later definition included new workers who were seeking work, but effectively excluded seasonal workers, inmates of institutions, and retired or disabled individuals (A. Edwards 1943; Conk 1980; Moen 1988). There is little reason to believe that these changes would have a significant impact on sex segregation.

8. Some scholars exclude agricultural workers on the grounds that (a) the farm sector is outside of the modern industrial system, and (b) declining counts in

farming occupations will strongly affect segregation indices (Jacobs 1989a). The latter issue is moot when margin-free measures are used, and the former issue arguably misrepresents U.S. farming in the latter half of the century. As noted, though, the results are qualitatively similar when farmers are excluded.

9. In order to include 1970 data in the secondary array, it was necessary to use a 1970 table that was published as part of the 1980 Census and translated (by the Census Bureau) into the 1980 scheme (U.S. Census Bureau 1982), rather than the table, published as part of the 1970 Census, that contributed data to the primary array. The labor force gender composition differs across tables (compare the right-most columns of Tables 5.2 and 5.3), presumably because the Census Bureau modified its sampling weights and corrected (or introduced) errors in the later release.

After deflating the sample sizes to approximate the actual number of cases on which the published occupation tables are based, the secondary data array contains 87,223,960 cases.

10. For example, if occupations with fewer than ten incumbents of either sex are reclassified, the 1940 value of A is 83 percent of its 1910 value, whereas D_s is roughly 96 percent of its 1910 value. Note, too, that if the observed changes between 1930 and 1940 were simply due to sampling error, we would expect to see volatility in the trajectories, not continued integration in later decades.

11. Given the sample size, any change in the model is likely to generate significance according to the log-likelihood test statistic, and no (unsaturated) model is likely to fit. Moreover, all models generate large positive BIC values. For these reasons, the discussion of log-likelihood contrasts is supplemented with a discussion of the change in Δ, the percentage of cases misallocated under a given model.

12. The universal association model has an L^2 of 397,451 with 60 $d.f.$ and misclassifies 2.1 percent of cases. The multiplicative shift effect model has a L^2 of 332,005 with 57 $d.f.$ and misclassifies 1.9 percent of cases.

13. This multilevel model constrains the nine major-category effects and the detailed-category effects within them to sum to zero in each decade. As discussed in previous chapters, one advantage of this approach is that it purges the major-category data of compositional effects generated at the level of detailed occupations.

14. The major-category trends in Figure 5.3 appear less dramatic than the downward shift in A in Figure 5.1 for two reasons. First, the summary index captures both within- and between-category change, whereas the values in Figure 5.3 only capture change between major categories. In these data, integration and re-segregation occur at both the detailed- and major-category levels. Second, even if all of the variation took place at the major-category level, the trend lines in Figure 5.3 would replicate the trend in A only if the each major category's value were weighted by the number of detailed occupations constituting that category.

15. If marriage bars had been applied universally, we would expect the labor force participation rates of married women to drop precipitously between 1930

and 1940; the historical record, however, shows the opposite trend (see, e.g., Goldin 2000, figure 8).

16. $\text{Exp}[2.4] = 11.2$; $\exp[1.8] = 6.8$. This means that the female-to-male ratio declined relative to the ratios in other occupations, not necessarily that women's share of clerical and service work declined.

17. Black urban migration was greater during the wars than in the interwar period (G. Davis and Donaldson 1975; Johnson and Campbell 1981), but wartime migrants entered a wider range of jobs (Wilson 1980; Lieberson 1980).

18. Note that if the pre-1940 undercount of women farmers (Abel and Folbre 1990) were dominating the results, we would expect an artificial *increase* in female representation in farming in 1940, not the observed decrease. This lends further credence to the claim that changes in census practices are not driving these results.

19. These eight occupation groups are professional, managerial, clerical, sales, service, construction and repair, production and transportation, and farm. Because of the structure of the twenty-one-category scheme, it was not possible to estimate parameters for nine major occupation groups comparable to those estimated in the primary analysis.

Chapter Six: Gender and Age in the Japanese Labor Market

1. For example, a weakening of patriarchal norms in Japanese families, a growing service sector, and increases in female university attendance are likely to first effect change in the labor market behavior of rather narrowly defined age cohorts.

2. Indeed, some analysts have attributed the relative integration of clerical work in Japan to the creation of gender-specific job ladders from common clerical ports of entry—a dead-end track for "office ladies" (who are generally excluded from permanent employment), and an upward-bound managerial track for men (see, e.g., Ogasawara 1998).

3. These figures still differ considerably from those for the United States. In 1993, 10 percent of the U.S. labor force reported self- or family-employment, and 73 percent worked in the service sector (ILO 1995).

4. Even the most highly educated women are often discontinuously employed in Japan. In fact, recent research suggests a weak (sometimes negative) association between elite education and labor-market persistence following childbirth. This contrasts with patterns found in the United States, and may reflect normative pressures on educated women to withdraw from the labor force and attend to the socialization and education of their children (Brinton 1988; National Institute of Employment and Vocational Training 1988; Hirao 1996, 2001; Lee and Hirata 2001).

5. Sex segregation by institution type (junior college versus university, for example) and by field of study nonetheless remains substantial (Charles and Bradley 2002).

6. Although expectations for a more continuous labor force career may have generalized effects on women's occupational aspirations and employers' hiring decisions, this model implies that the strongest effects will be for individuals with the most intensive domestic obligations.

7. Before 1950, the "gainfully employed worker" approach was used to define the labor force, whereas subsequent years are based on the more inclusive "economically active" definition (see Japanese Bureau of Statistics 1974 for details).

8. Until 1985 the retirement age for women and men was 50 and 55, respectively. In 1985 it was raised to 55 for women and 60 for men.

9. Supplementary analyses were conducted for a "pooled" sample that was restricted to 20–49 year-olds. Results did not differ substantially from those reported here.

10. Remaining empty cells were handled by replacing zero with the estimated value from a model that constrained the sex ratio to be the same across adjacent time periods.

11. Despite the economic slowdown that commenced in the early 1990s, no decline in women's share of the labor force was evident between 1990 and 1995. Rather than laying off female workers, employers may be relying increasingly on temporary and part-time employees to reduce labor costs.

12. As can be seen in the last column of Table 6.2, women's share of the labor force increased sharply during the five-year period between 1990 and 1995, precisely when these two indices diverge.

13. The 1995 scale value for this major occupational category was 1.75 $[\exp(1.75) = 5.75]$.

14. Since 1965 there has been a steady trend toward gender integration of the major manufacturing category. By 1995 the scale value for this category was .00, indicating proportional representation of men and women in the average manufacturing occupation. Contributing to this integration were dramatic declines in female representation in silk, textile, and apparel production occupations.

15. Prevalence of family-run enterprises contributes to occupational integration because the counterpart to the female "family worker" is often a "self-employed" male shop owner.

16. Trends in two female-dominated semiprofessional occupations, "nurses and midwives" and "other teachers," contributed as well.

17. In fact, by 1995 the cohort aged 45–49 showed the highest overall level of sex segregation. As we will see further on, this can be attributed in part to the persistent overrepresentation of older women in service and manufacturing occupations in Japan.

18. $\exp(1.16) = 3.19$; $\exp(.09) = 1.09$; $3.19/1.09 = 2.93$. Ironically, women's overrepresentation in the professional category has contributed to the higher overall levels of sex segregation found for the youngest cohort during this period (Table 6.2).

19. Exp(.30) = 1.35; exp(.59) = 1.80; 1.80/1.35 = 1.34; exp(.13) = 1.14; exp(.35) = 1.42; 1.42/1.14 = 1.24.

20. Recall that in the context of our modeling framework female representation is assessed relative to that in other occupations.

21. The spike in female professional representation shown for the 25–29-year-old cohort between 1980 and 1990 may be partly attributable to volatility in the agriculture and transport/communication scale values during this period (see Figure 6.3, panels 5 and 6).

22. In the interest of historical consistency, we have here elected to conform as much as possible to the national classificatory scheme. However, for the cross-national comparative analyses presented in Chapter 3, occupations were reclassified so that "professions" and "semiprofessions" could be distinguished.

23. Among 25–29-year-old workers, women's representation increased by a factor of 2.27 exp(−1.92) = .15; exp(−1.08) = .34; .34/.15 = 2.27. For the 25–29-year-old cohort, the corresponding figure was 2.31.

24. This is likely to have had a particularly strong effect on women's opportunities in management. Women who are confined to part-time, temporary jobs are effectively shut out of managerial promotion lines.

25. By 1995 the scale value is in fact *lower* for this cohort than for any other.

26. The absolute number of older female clerical workers has also increased substantially since 1970 (see Appendix Figure A6.1).

27. As can be seen in Appendix Figure A6.1, older women are absorbing a growing share of service jobs. The downward trend lines shown for the 40–44- and 45–49-year-old cohorts in the last panel of Figure 6.3 can be attributed to older women's inroads into other occupations (especially clerical work) during this period.

28. Because breakdowns by age are not available before 1970, we cannot determine when these age-specific trends commenced. However, we suspect that they cannot be attributed entirely to the cost-saving efforts of Japanese employers, because overall increases in female clerical representation are evident before the recession of the 1970s (see Figure 6.2).

29. Recall again that the downward trend means that the average female-to-male ratio in service occupations declined *relative to that in other occupations*, not that women actually moved out of these occupations.

Chapter Seven: Gender, Nativity, and Occupational Segregation in Switzerland

1. In 2001 the Swiss per capita gross national product was the highest in the industrialized world (OECD 2001).

2. On cross-national variability in school-to-work linkages, see Haller et al. 1985; DiPrete and McManus 1996; Shavit and Müller 1998.

3. In 1990, 80 percent of school-leavers aged 15–17 years were enrolled in

traditional apprenticeship programs (Buchmann 1994; see Buchmann and Charles 1993 on historical trends).

4. Although more than half of resident foreign women are economically active, females represented only about one-third of the foreign labor force in Switzerland between 1970 and 1990 (and only slightly more than one-third in 2000).

5. Language-group membership also constitutes an important dimension of individual identity in multilingual Switzerland. However, such distinctions are considerably less salient in the process of labor market stratification than are those based on national citizenship.

6. The majority of workers coded to major category 6 are proprietors of family farms. These are generally operated by married couples and subsequently inherited by a son. There is evidence of historical shifts in the formal definition of women's activities in these enterprises, with wives increasingly reporting themselves as "occupationally active" farmers (Charles 1995). Although agricultural positions are thus allocated in distinctive ways, we have decided to retain this category in our analyses; preliminary analyses showed that its inclusion did not substantially affect other parameter estimates.

7. In 1970 and 1980, only those working six or more hours per week at paid employment were defined as occupationally active. In 1990, Switzerland adopted the standard of one hour per week, which is recommended by the International Labour Office.

8. Specifically, figures for A suggest that women were over- or underrepresented in the average occupation by a factor of 5.49 in 1980, compared to 4.37 in 1990. The values of D indicate that nearly half of Swiss women would have had to change occupational categories in all three census years in order to achieve a proportional distribution of the sexes across occupations.

9. By 1990 only about one-third of women with young children were occupationally active in Switzerland. Among Swiss nationals, this figure was 28 percent (Charles 1995), with most employed mothers working only a few hours a week. By contrast, approximate participation rates for mothers of young children were 80 percent in Sweden, 60 percent in the United States, 55 percent in France, and 37 percent in Germany (Tölke 1989; Joshi and Davis 1992; Sandqvist 1992; U.S. Census Bureau 1992). Age-specific figures for Japan (Chapter 5, Table 2) also suggest low rates of labor force participation among young mothers. However, Japanese women are more likely than their Swiss counterparts to resume paid employment when their children reach school age. Multivariate analysis of individual-level data indeed indicates that the labor force participation of Swiss women is more sensitive to family status than is that of either black or white American women (Charles et al. 2001).

10. During the 1990s, the economic security of Swiss families was generally reduced, in part due to the detrimental economic effects of growing single motherhood (Budowski, Tillmann, and Bergman 2002).

11. In absolute terms, the most pronounced expansion of female employment

occurred in the associate professional and clerical categories, which together added more than 200,000 women between 1970 and 1990. Although a substantial number of men moved into the associate professions during this period, most growth in the male labor force occurred at higher levels of the occupational structure (i.e., in management and professions).

12. Exp(2.00) = 7.39; exp(1.52) = 4.57.

13. "Corporate and general managers" is a particularly heterogeneous category that includes positions ranging from small business operator to elite corporate leader.

14. Women's growing presence in the "other associate professionals" can be attributed primarily to the gender integration of business services since 1970.

15. Since this detailed category included a very large number of women from the outset, historical shifts in its gender composition were necessarily less dramatic than those observed in some previously male-dominated occupations (which were able to double or quadruple their female-to-male ratios with the addition of just a few hundred women). But, in absolute terms, the feminization that has occurred is certainly noteworthy: women's share of "secretarial and office" jobs increased from 51 to 63 percent over this twenty-year period (see Appendix Table A7.1).

16. Men were nearly ninety-three times more likely than women to work in this category in 1970, but "only" twenty-seven times more likely in 1990 (exp(4.53) = 92.76; exp(3.30) = 27.11). See Appendix Table A7.1.

17. The declining female presence in some of these craft and manufacturing occupations may reflect structural adjustments *within* the twenty-five ISCO categories: trends across the (nonstandardized) Swiss national categories (not shown) suggest that economic rationalization has been accompanied by elimination of many of the less-skilled, previously female-dominated craft and manufacturing jobs. In the contracting agricultural category, female representation has changed very little between 1970 and 1990. This is not surprising, since substantial shifts in the gender composition of farm occupations would require fundamental changes in family inheritance practices.

18. Contributing to the reduction in native men's share of the labor force were longer educational careers among younger men and earlier retirements among older men (Bundesamt für Statistik 1993, p. 195).

19. Accordingly, the absolute numbers of Swiss-born men and women working in the professions increased sharply between 1970 and 1990. No such growth was evident among foreign men or foreign women (see Appendix Table A7.1).

20. For example, foreign men's share of restaurant waiting jobs increased from 14 percent to 25 percent between 1980 and 1990, while the number of native Swiss men working as waiters actually declined (Charles 1995). The same national breakdowns suggest that increasing native-male representation in the "personal and protective services" category is primarily due to the expansion of the protective service occupation.

21. Multivariate analyses (Charles 2000) suggest growing immigrant-male

presence in some, but not all, female-dominated occupations between 1980 and 1990.

22. The one exception in this regard is for the clerical category, which showed a more modest increase between 1980 and 1990 in the earlier table. This discrepancy most likely reflects integrative trends in the relatively small "cashiers and customer service" category (see Appendix Table A7.1).

23. Vocational students make binding occupational choices as early as age 14 in Switzerland. Adolescence is a developmental stage when approval of peers is of enormous concern, when reluctance to transgress norms about gender-appropriate activities is often at its peak, and when knowledge about the practical disadvantages of female-typed employment is limited (Entwisle and Greenberger 1972; Gaskell 1985; Eder 1995).

Chapter Eight: A Framework for Analyzing Industrial and Occupational Sex Segregation in the United States

We are grateful to David B. Grusky and Maria Charles for support and advice, and to Mariko Lin Chang, Paula England, Joon Han, Jacqueline Olvera, and Annemette Sørensen for extremely helpful suggestions, but we are responsible for all opinions expressed herein. Models were estimated in GAUSS 3.0. Please direct correspondence to Kim Weeden, Department of Sociology, Cornell University, 323 Uris Hall, Ithaca, N.Y. 14853 (kw74@cornell.edu).

1. Other permutations of the relationship between occupational and industrial segregation are of course possible, but we focus our illustrative analysis on those that will be of most substantive interest. We assume, for example, that readers have a good sense of the pattern of occupational segregation in the United States (see also Chapter 5).

2. One could, for example, fit models that impose one or more external scales on the industry-by-sex association, where the external scales correspond to theoretically salient features of industries (such as density of union membership). For a related approach, see Chapter 4.

3. There are several weaknesses in the segmented labor market argument. First, the organizational characteristics that purportedly drive patterns of sex segregation do not map cleanly onto industries or groups of industries (see, e.g., Baron and Bielby 1980; Bridges 1982; Kalleberg and Berg 1987). Second, the theory ignores situations in which the interests of the individual employer and those of the capitalist class or male gender conflict (Burris and Wharton 1982; Milkman 1987). Finally, it is not clear that crowding serves core employers' interests in dividing workers; after all, industry boundaries are not obviously linked to hierarchies of pay and authority, and are thus unlikely to be a particularly salient source of internal differentiation among workers. In spite of these shortcomings, segmented labor market theory and its cousins are still often brought to bear in contemporary discussions of segregation (e.g., Kaufman 2002).

4. Note that the imprinting argument does not carry any necessary implications for the strength of occupational sex segregation across industries, except that it would be historically dependent.

5. Some of the log-multiplicative models represented here could also be written as simpler log-linear models. We retain the log-multiplicative specification in order to give the reader a better sense of the relationship between the models.

6. To identify this model, we constrain the occupational scale values within each industry to sum to zero. An alternative specification of the saturated model would constrain the scale values to sum to zero only over the full set of industries, fit a global ϕ, and absorb industry variations in the strength of the occupation-by-gender association in the μ_{ik}. We prefer our parameterization because it retains the distinction between strength and pattern of occupational segregation.

7. At the time this chapter was written, the corresponding 2000 census data had not yet been released.

8. We experimented with other values for this constant. The results, which are available on request, were stable across conditions.

9. Viewed differently, occupational sex segregation reduces the unexplained association from the industrial segregation model (Model 3) by 87.7 percent.

10. The overrepresentation of men is computed with $1/e^{\psi\nu}$, so $1/e^{(3.757^* - 0.257)}$ = 2.63.

11. $1/e^{(3.757^* - 0.236)} = 2.43$.

12. $e^{(3.757^* - .047)}$ .84, $e^{(3.757^* .096)} = 1.43$. Note that because we are calculating the overrepresentation of women, there is no need to take the inverse of the exponentiated term.

13. $e^{(3.757^* .102)} = 1.47$, $e^{(3.757^* .354)} = 3.78$.

14. The dual labor market hypothesis could be tested more formally by conditioning the industry scale values on the level of capital intensity. Analogous tests could be devised to evaluate the other explanations. We leave these tasks to future work. For related models in the one-dimensional case, see Charles and Grusky 1995 and Chapter 4 of this volume.

15. The mean correlation across the 968 unique industry pairs is 0.82; the maximum correlation is 0.95, and the minimum correlation is 0.59. The full 44-by-44 correlation matrix is available upon request.

16. For the purposes of this table, an occupation in which women are overrepresented is defined as one in which $e^{(\phi k^* \mu ik)} < .90$, where ϕ_k is the industry-specific strength of association between occupation and sex and μ_{ik} is the occupation- and industry-specific scale value. Male overrepresentation is defined as $e^{(\phi k^* \mu ik)} > 1.10$. Both values are generated from the saturated model (6). Of course, Table 8.2 conceals what may be substantial interindustry differences in the degree of female over- or underrepresentation. For example, women are overrepresented in "cashier and counter clerk" occupations in all forty-four industries, but the value of the multiplier ranges from 2.50 in rubber and plastic goods manufacturing to

27.52 in transportation equipment manufacturing [$e^{(.043*21.287)} = 2.50$; $e^{(.161*20.590)} = 27.52$].

17. Mean = 2.0 industries; standard deviation = 3.5.

Chapter Nine: The Past, Present, and Future of Occupational Ghettos

1. The many weaknesses of our proxy are discussed in the final section of this chapter.

2. The data and programs used in our historical and comparative analyses are available at www.segregation.com.

3. This section draws heavily on discussions with Shelley Correll as well as her reactions to earlier drafts of our work. We are grateful for her insightful commentary.

4. This is not to suggest that vertical segregation will disappear altogether. Indeed, insofar as the domestic division of labor remains intact, women will be unable to commit as deeply as men to the formal labor force. This particular type of inertia makes it clear that even vertical segregation is affected by the durability of essentialist precepts. That is, the domestic division of labor is ultimately under-girded by essentialism (such as the presumption that women are naturally inclined toward nurturance and personal service), but it is an especially perverse form of essentialism because it reduces incentives for women to invest in human capital and thus serves to preserve *vertical* segregation.

5. We have ignored here the countervailing effects of postindustrialism and service-sector expansion. In many advanced industrial countries, this expansion has by now fully succeeded in redefining routine nonmanual labor as "women's work," and there is little room for further redefinition that would generate substantial increases in vertical segregation. We accordingly emphasize the effects of egalitarianism in this section.

6. We are merely referring here to the way in which segregation is understood by workers and employers. That is, our argument is that some forms of segregation may be readily interpreted as consistent with equal-opportunity norms, even though they may arise from overt discrimination or other processes that are inconsistent with such norms. The insidiousness of essentialism is that it clothes segregation in voluntarist terms.

7. This "separate but equal" logic has a long tradition in academic scholarship (see Chapter 1 for details), and not just within feminist circles. When Baron-Cohen (2003), for example, argued that the female brain is hardwired for empathy and the male brain for systematizing, he felt obliged to reassure that "*overall* one is not better or worse than the other" (p. 185; italics in original).

8. Obviously, women are especially likely to enter less desirable nonmanual occupations, which is precisely why our models include vertical segregation effects. We are interested here in the net effect of horizontal segregation after such vertical effects are purged.

9. It would be useful to develop formal models that parameterize not only horizontal segregation but other instances of essentialist segregation as well (see Chapter 4 for related comments). Indeed, if the future of essentialist-backed segregation rests principally with these residual female-disadvantaging forms, it is all the more important to build them explicitly into our segregation model.

10. In many cases, essentialist segregation at the suboccupational level appears to have predated the influx of women or men into the larger occupational category, implying that the influx merely made existing essentialist practice more visible. It is also possible, however, that some forms of micro-segregation are new responses to the influx. Although there are many important case studies of these processes (e.g., Williams 1989), a supplementary survey analysis of detailed segregation arrays (disaggregated by time) might assist in determining whether desegregation at the major occupational level tends to be followed by resegregation among the constituent detailed categories.

REFERENCES

Abbott, Andrew. 2001. *Chaos of Disciplines*. Chicago: University of Chicago Press.

Abel, Marjorie, and Nancy Folbre. 1990. "A Methodology for Revising Estimates: Female Market Participation in the U.S. before 1940." *Historical Methods* 23 (4): 167–76.

Abrahamson, Mark, and Lee Sigelman. 1987. "Occupational Sex Segregation in Metropolitan Areas." *American Sociological Review* 52: 588–97.

Acker, Joan R. 1980. "Women and Stratification: A Review of Recent Literature." *Contemporary Sociology* 9: 25–39.

———. 1989. *Doing Comparable Worth*. Philadelphia: Temple University Press.

Agresti, Alan. 1990. *Categorical Data Analysis*. New York: John Wiley.

Aiba, Keio, and Amy S. Wharton. 2001. "Job-Level Sex Composition and the Sex Pay Gap in a Large Japanese Firm." *Sociological Perspectives* 44: 67–87.

Albeda, Randy P. 1986. "Occupational Segregation by Race and Gender, 1958–1981." *Industrial and Labor Relations Review* 39: 404–11.

Allison, Paul. 1980. "Analyzing Collapsed Contingency Tables without Actually Collapsing." *American Sociological Review* 45: 123–30.

Altham, Patricia M. E. 1970. "The Measurement of Association of Rows and Columns for an r × s Contingency Table." *Journal of the Royal Statistical Society* 32: 63–73.

Anker, Richard. 1998. *Gender and Jobs: Sex Segregation of Occupations in the World*. Geneva: International Labour Office.

Arat, Yesim. 1989. *The Patriarchal Paradox: Women Politicians in Turkey*. London: Associated University Press.

Arrow, Kenneth. 1976. "Economic Dimensions of Occupational Segregation: Comment I." *Signs* 1: 233–37.

Baker, David P., and Deborah Perkins Jones. 1993. "Creating Gender Equality: Cross-national Gender Stratification and Mathematical Performance." *Sociology of Education* 66: 91–103.

Baron, James N. 1984. Organizational Perspectives on Stratification. *Annual Review of Sociology* 10: 37–69.

Baron, James N., and William T. Bielby. 1980. "Bringing the Firms Back In: Stratification, Segmentation, and the Organization of Work." *American Sociological Review*, 45: 737–65.

Baron, James N., Brian S. Mittman, and Andrew E. Newman. 1991. "Targets of Opportunity: Organizational and Environmental Determinants of Gender Integration within the California Civil Service, 1979–1985." *American Journal of Sociology* 96: 1362–1401.

Baron-Cohen, Simon. 2003. *The Essential Difference: The Truth about the Male and Female Brain*. New York: Basic Books.

Baunach, Dana Michelle. 2002. "Trends in Occupational Sex Segregation and Inequality, 1950–1990." *Social Science Research* 31: 77–98.

Bayard, Kimberly, Judith Hellerstein, David Neumark, and Kenneth Troske. 1999. "New Evidence on Sex Segregation and Sex Differences in Wages from Matched Employee-Employee Data." Working Paper 7003. Cambridge, Mass.: National Bureau of Economic Research.

Beck, E. M., Patrick Horan, and Charles M. Tolbert. 1978. Stratification in a Dual Economy: A Sectoral Model of Earnings Determination. *American Sociological Review* 43: 704–20.

———. 1980. Industrial Segmentation and Labor Market Discrimination. *Social Problems* 28: 113–30.

Becker, Gary S. 1971. *The Economics of Discrimination*. Chicago: University of Chicago Press.

———. 1975. *Human Capital*. New York: Columbia University Press.

———. 1985. "Human Capital, Effort, and the Sexual Division of Labor." *Journal of Labor Economics* 3 (1): S33–S58.

———. 1991. *A Treatise on the Family*. Cambridge, Mass.: Harvard University Press.

Becker, Mark P., and Clifford C. Clogg. 1989. "Analysis of Sets of Two-Way Contingency Tables Using Association Models." *Journal of the American Statistical Association* 84: 142–51.

Beck-Gernsheim, Elisabeth, and I. Ostner. 1978. "Frauen verändern—Berufe nicht?" *Soziale Welt* 29: 257–87.

Beggs, John J. 1995. "The Institutional Environment: Implications for Race and Gender Inequality in the U.S. Labor Market." *American Sociological Review* 60 (4): 612–33.

Bell, Daniel. 1973. *The Coming of Post-Industrial Society*. New York: Basic Books.

Bell, Wendell. 1954. "A Probability Model of the Measurement of Ecological Segregation." *Social Forces* 32: 357–64.

Beller, Andrea. 1982. "Occupational Segregation by Sex: Determinants and Changes." *Journal of Human Resources* 17: 371–92.

———. 1984. "Trends in Occupational Segregation by Sex and Race, 1960–1981." In Barbara Reskin, ed., *Sex Segregation in the Workplace: Trends, Explanations, Remedies*, pp. 11–26. Washington, D.C.: National Academy Press.

Berkovitch, Nitza. 1999. *From Motherhood to Citizenship: Women's Rights and International Organizations*. Baltimore, Md.: Johns Hopkins University Press.

Bianchi, Suzanne, and Nancy Rytina. 1986. "The Decline in Occupational Sex Segregation during the 1970s: Census and CPS Comparisons." *Demography* 23 (1): 79–86.

Bielby, William T. 1991. "The Structure and Process of Sex Segregation." In Richard R. Cornwall and Phanindra V. Wunnava, eds. *New Approaches to Economic and Social Analyses of Discrimination*, pp. 97–112. Westport, Conn.: Praeger.

Bielby, William T., and James N. Baron. 1984. "A Woman's Place Is with Other Women: Sex Segregation within Organizations." In Barbara Reskin, ed., *Sex Segregation in the Workplace: Trends, Explanations, and Remedies*, pp. 27–55. Washington, D.C.: National Academy Press.

———. 1986. "Men and Women at Work: Sex Segregation and Statistical Discrimination." *American Journal of Sociology* 95: 616–58.

Bielby, Denise D., and William T. Bielby. 1988. "She Works Hard for the Money: Household Responsibilities and the Allocation of Work Effort." *American Journal of Sociology* 93: 1031–59.

Bishop, Yvonne M., Stephen E. Fienberg, and Paul W. Holland. 1975. *Discrete Multivariate Analysis: Theory and Practice*. Cambridge, Mass.: MIT Press.

Blackburn, R. M., B. Brooks, and J. Jarman. 2001. "Occupational Stratification: The Vertical Dimension of Occupational Segregation." *Work, Employment and Society* 15: 511–38.

Blackburn, Robert M., Jennifer Jarman, and Bradley Brooks. 2000. "The Puzzle of Gender Segregation and Inequality: A Cross-National Analysis." *European Sociological Review* 16: 119–35.

Blackburn, Robert M., Jennifer Jarman, and Janet Siltanen. 1993. "The Analysis of Occupational Gender Segregation over Time and Place: Considerations of Measurement and Some New Evidence." *Work, Employment and Society* 7: 335–62.

Blair-Loy, Mary. 2001. "It's Not Just What You Know, It's Who You Know: Technical Knowledge, Rainmaking and Gender among Finance Executives." *Research in the Sociology of Work* 10: 51–83.

———. 2003. *Competing Devotions: Career and Family among Women Executives*. Cambridge, Mass.: Harvard University Press.

Blalock, Hubert M. 1967. *Toward a Theory of Minority-Group Relations*. New York: Wiley.

Blankenship, Kim. 1983. "Sectoral Influences on Occupational Sex Segregation." In Ida and Richard Simpson, eds., *Research in the Sociology of Work (II): Peripheral Workers*, pp. 69–99. JAI Press.

Blau, Francine, and W. Hendricks. 1979. "Occupational Segregation by Sex: Trends and Prospects." *Journal of Human Resources* 12: 197–210.

Blau, Francine D., and Lawrence M. Kahn. Forthcoming. "The Gender Pay Gap:

Going, Going, . . . but Not Gone." In Francine D. Blau, Mary C. Brinton, and David B. Grusky, eds., *The Declining Significance of Gender?* New York: Russell Sage Foundation.

Blau, Francine D., Mary C. Brinton, and David B. Grusky. Forthcoming. "The Future of Gender Inequality." In Francine D. Blau, Mary C. Brinton, and David B. Grusky, eds., *The Declining Significance of Gender?* New York: Russell Sage.

Blau, Francine D., Marianne A. Ferber, and Anne E. Winkler. 2002. *The Economics of Women, Men, and Work.* 4th ed. Upper Saddle River, N.J.: Prentice-Hall.

Blau, Francine, Patricia Simpson, and Deborah Anderson. 1998. "Continuing Progress? Trends in Occupational Segregation in the United States over the 1970s." *Feminist Economics* 4: 29–71.

Blau, Peter M., and Otis Dudley Duncan. 1967. *The American Occupational Structure.* New York: Wiley.

Blekher, Feiga. 1979. *The Soviet Woman in the Family and in Society.* New York: Wiley.

Blitz, Rudolph C. 1974. "Women in the Professions, 1870–1970." *Monthly Labor Review* 97: 34–39.

Blossfeld, Hans-Peter. 1984. "Bildungsexpansion und Tertiarisierungsprozess: Eine Analyse der Entwicklung geschlechtsspezifischer Arbeitsmarktchancen von Berufsanfängern unter Verwendung eines log-linearen Pfadmodells." *Zeitschrift für Soziologie* 13: 20–44.

Bluestone, Barry, Patricia Hanna, Sara Kuhn, and Laura Moore. 1981. *The Retail Revolution: Market Transformation, Investment and Labor in the Modern Department Store.* Boston: Auburn House.

Bonacich, Edna. 1972. A Theory of Ethnic Antagonism: The Split Labor Market. *American Sociological Review* 49: 308–22.

Bose, Christine E. 2001. *Women in 1900: Gateway to the Political Economy of the Twentieth Century.* Philadelphia: Temple University Press.

Boserup, Ester. 1970. *Woman's Role in Economic Development.* London: George Allen and Unwin.

Bourdieu, Pierre. 2001. *Masculine Domination.* Cambridge, England: Polity Press.

Bradley, Harriet. 1989. *Men's Work, Women's Work: A Sociological History of the Sexual Division of Labour in Employment.* Cambridge, England: Polity Press.

Bradley, Karen. 2000. "The Incorporation of Women into Higher Education: Paradoxical Outcomes?" *Sociology of Education* 3: 1–18.

Bradley, Karen, and Maria Charles. 2003. "Uneven Inroads: Understanding Women's Status in Higher Education." *Research in Sociology of Education* 14: 247–74.

Bradley, Karen, and Francisco O. Ramirez. 1996. "World Polity and Gender Parity: Women's Share of Higher Education, 1965–85." *Research in Sociology of Education and Socialization* 11: 63–91.

Braverman, Harry. 1974. *Labor and Monopoly Capital: The Degradation of Work in the Twentieth Century.* New York: Monthly Review Press.

Brenner, Johanna, and Maria Ramas. 1984. "Rethinking Women's Oppression." *New Left Review* 144: 33–71.

Brewster, K.L., and R.R. Rindfuss. 2000. "Fertility and Women's Employment in Industrialized Nations." *Annual Review of Sociology* 26: 271–96.

Bridges, William. 1980. "Industry Marginality and Female Employment: A New Appraisal." *American Journal of Sociology* 45: 58–75.

———. 1982. "The Sexual Stratification of Occupations: Theories of Labor Stratification in Industry." *American Journal of Sociology* 88: 270–95.

Brinton, Mary C. 1988. "The Social-Institutional Bases of Gender Stratification: Japan as an Illustrative Case." *American Journal of Sociology* 94: 300–34.

———. 1993. *Women and the Economic Miracle: Gender and Work in Postwar Japan.* Berkeley: University of California Press.

———. 2001. "Married Women's Labor in East Asian Economies." In Mary C. Brinton, ed., *Women's Working Lives in East Asia*, pp. 1–37. Stanford, Calif.: Stanford University Press.

Brinton, Mary C., and Takehiko Kariya. 1998. "Institutional Embeddedness in Japanese Labor Markets." In Mary C. Brinton and Victor Nee, eds. 1998. *The New Institutionalism in Sociology*, pp. 181–207. New York: Russell Sage.

Brinton, Mary C., and Victor Nee, eds. 1998. *The New Institutionalism in Sociology.* New York: Russell Sage.

Brinton, Mary C., and Hang-Yue Ngo. 1993. "Age and Sex in the Occupational Structure: A United States–Japan Comparison." *Sociological Forum* 8: 93–111.

Browning, Harley L., and Joachim Singelmann. 1978. "The Transformation of the U.S. Labor Force: The Interaction of Industry and Occupation." *Politics and Society* 8: 481–509.

Buchmann, Marlis. 1994. "Adolescence in Switzerland." In Klaus Hurrelmann, ed., *International Handbook of Adolescence*, pp. 386–99. Westport, Conn.: Greenwood Press.

Buchmann, Marlis, and Maria Charles, with Stefan Sacchi. 1993. "The Lifelong Shadow: Social Origins and Educational Opportunity in Switzerland." In Yossi Shavit and Hans-Peter Blossfeld, eds., *Persistent Inequality: Changing Educational Attainment in 13 Countries*, pp. 177–92. Boulder, Colo.: Westview Press.

Buchmann, Marlis, and Maria Charles. 1995. "Organizational and Institutional Factors in the Process of Gender Stratification: Comparing Social Arrangements in Six European Countries." *International Journal of Sociology* 25: 66–95.

Buchmann, Marlis, Irene Kriesi, Andrea Pfeifer, and Stefan Sacchi. 2002. *Halb Drinnen—Halb Draussen: Analysen zur Arbeitsmarktintegation von Frauen in der Schweiz.* Zurich: Rüegger.

Buchmann, Marlis and Stefan Sacchi. 1998. "The Transition from School to Work in Switzerland: Do Characteristics of the Educational System and Class Barriers Matter?" In Yossi Shavit and Walter Müller, eds. *From School to Work: A Comparative Study of Educational Qualifications and Occupational Destinations*, pp. 407–42. New York: Clarendon Press.

Budowski, Monika, Robin Tillmann, and Manfred Max Bergman. 2002. "Poverty, Stratification and Gender in Switzerland." *Swiss Journal of Sociology* 28: 297–317.

Bundesamt für Statistik. 1993. *Eidgenössische Volkszählung 1990: Erwerbsleben.* Bern: Bundesamt für Statistik.

———. 1994a. *Familien heute.* Bern: Bundesamt für Statistik.

———. 1994b. *Harmonisierter Personenrecord für die Volkszählungen von 1970, 1980 und 1990.* Bern: Bundesamt für Statistik.

———. 2003. "Beruflich Tätigkeit nach ISCO nach Zähljahr, Geschlecht und Nationalität." Unpublished data table. Neuchâtel: Bundesamt für Statistik.

Burris, Valerie, and Amy Wharton. 1982. "Sex Segregation in the U.S. Labor Force." *Review of Radical Political Economics* 14: 42–56.

Burt, Ronald. 1983. *Corporate Profits and Co-optation: Networks of Market Constraints and Directorate Ties in the American Economy.* New York: Academic Press.

Butler, Richard J. 1987. "New Indices of Segregation." *Economics Letters* 24: 359–62.

Cain, Pamela Stone. 1984. "Commentary." In Barbara F. Reskin, ed., *Sex Segregation in the Workplace*, pp. 87–90. Washington, D.C.: National Academy Press.

Calonder Gerster, Anita E. 1990. *Zur Situation der erwerbstätigen Frau.* Bern: Bundesamt für Industrie, Gewerbe und Arbeit.

Caplow, Theodore. 1954. *The Sociology of Work.* Minneapolis: University of Minnesota Press.

Carlson, Susan. 1992. "Trends in Race/Sex Occupational Inequality: Conceptual and Measurement Issues." *Social Problems* 39: 268–90.

Carrington, William J., and Kenneth R. Troske. 1998. "Sex Segregation in U.S. Manufacturing." *Industrial and Labor Relations Review* 51 (3): 445–64.

Carter, Michael J., and Susan Boslego Carter. 1981. "Women's Recent Progress in the Professions or, Women Get a Ticket to Ride after the Gravy Train Has Left the Station." *Feminist Studies* 7: 477–504.

Cartwright, Bliss, and Patrick Ronald Edwards. 2002. "Gender Segregation Measured by Job Groups and Industry." Working paper, U.S. Equal Employment Opportunity Commission.

Catanzarite, Lisa. 2002. "Race-Gender Composition and Occupational Pay Degradation." *Social Problems* 50: 14–37.

Chafe, William H. 1972. *The American Woman: Her Changing Social, Economic, and Political Role, 1920–1970.* London: Oxford University Press.

Chafetz, Janet Saltzman. 1984. *Sex and Advantage: A Comparative, Macro-Structural Theory of Sex Stratification*. Totowa, N.J.: Rowman and Allanheld.

———. 1988. "The Gender Division of Labor and the Reproduction of Female Disadvantage: Toward an Integrated Theory." *Journal of Family Issues* 9: 108–31.

———. 1999. "The Varieties of Gender Theory in Sociology." In *Handbook of the Sociology of Gender*, pp. 2–23. New York: Kluwer.

Chan, Tak Wing. 1999. "Revolving Doors Reexamined: Occupational Sex Segregation over the Life Course." *American Sociological Review* 64 (1): 86–96.

Chang, Mariko. 2000. "The Evolution of Sex Segregation Regimes" *American Journal of Sociology* 105: 1658–1701.

———. 2004. "Cross-National Variation in Sex Segretation in Sixteen Developing Countries." *American Sociological Review* 69: 114–37.

Charles, Maria. 1990. *Occupational Sex Segregation: A Log-Linear Analysis of Patterns in 25 Industrial Countries*. Ph.D. dissertation. Stanford University, Department of Sociology.

———. 1992. "Cross-national Variation in Occupational Sex Segregation." *American Sociological Review* 57: 483–502.

———. 1995. *Berufliche Gleichstellung—ein Mythos? Geschlechter-Segregation in der schweizerischen Berufswelt*. Bern: Bundesamt für Statistik.

———. 1998. "Structure, Culture, and Sex Segregation in Western Europe." *Research in Social Stratification and Mobility* 16: 89–116.

———. 2000. "Divisions of Labor: Social Groups and Occupational Allocation." *European Sociological Review* 16: 27–42.

———. 2002. "Schweizerische Besonderheiten im Vergleich mit anderen westlichen Ländern." In Marlis Buchmann, Irene Kriesi, Andrea Pfeifer, and Stefan Sacchi, *Halb Drinnen—Halb Draussen: Analysen zur Arbeitsmarktintegation von Frauen in der Schweiz* pp. 207–28. Zurich: Rüegger.

Charles, Maria, and Karen Bradley. 2002. "Equal but Separate? A Cross-National Study of Sex Segregation in Higher Education." *American Sociological Review* 67: 573–99.

Charles, Maria, and Marlis Buchmann. 1994. "Assessing Micro-Level Explanations of Occupational Sex Segregation: Human Capital Development and Labor Market Opportunities in Switzerland." *Swiss Journal of Sociology* 20: 595–620.

Charles, Maria, and David B. Grusky. 1995. "Models for Describing the Underlying Structure of Sex Segregation." *American Journal of Sociology* 100: 931–71.

Charles, Maria, Marlis Buchmann, Susan Halebsky, Jeanne Powers, and Marisa M. Smith. 2001. "The Context of Women's Market Careers: A Cross-National Study." *Work and Occupations* 8: 371–96.

Cheng, Mariah Mantsun. 1997. "Becoming Self-Employed: The Case of Japanese Men." *Sociological Perspectives* 40: 581–600.

Chodorow, Nancy J. 1978. *The Reproduction of Mothering: Psychoanalysis and the Sociology of Gender*. Berkeley: University of California Press.

Clark, Rodney. 1979. *The Japanese Company*. New Haven, Conn.: Yale University Press.

Clark, Roger. 1991. "Contrasting Perspectives on Women's Access to Prestigious Occupations: A Cross-National Investigation." *Social Science Quarterly* 72: 20–32.

Clement, Wallace, and John Myles. 1994. *Relations of Ruling: Class and Gender in Postindustrial Societies*. London: McGill-Queen's University Press.

Clogg, Clifford C. 1982. "Using Association Models in Sociological Research: Some Examples." *American Journal of Sociology* 88: 114–34.

Clogg, Clifford C., and Scott R. Eliason. 1987 "Some Common Problems in Log-Linear Analysis." *Sociological Methods and Research* 16: 8–44.

———. 1988. "A Flexible Procedure for Adjusting Rates and Proportions, Including Statistical Methods for Group Comparisons." *American Sociological Review* 53: 267–83.

Clogg, Clifford C., James W. Shockey, and Scott R. Eliason. 1990. "A General Statistical Framework for Adjustment of Rates." *Sociological Methods and Research* 19: 156–95.

Cockburn, Cynthia. 1991. *In the Way of Women: Men's Resistance to Sex Equality in Organizations*. Ithaca, N.Y.: Industrial and Labor Relations Press.

Cohen, Philip N., and Matt L. Huffman. 2003. "Occupational Segregation and the Devaluation of Women's Work across Labor Markets." *Social Forces* 81 (3): 881–908.

Cohn, Samuel. 1985. *The Process of Occupational Sex Typing: The Feminization of Clerical Labor in Great Britain*. Philadelphia: Temple University Press.

———. 2000. *Race and Gender Discrimination at Work*. Boulder, Colo.: Westview Press.

Coleman, Samuel. 1983. "The Tempo of Family Formation." In David Plath, ed., *Work and Lifecourse in Japan*, pp. 156–82. New York: State University of New York Press.

———. 1985. *The Process of Occupational Sex-Typing*. Philadelphia: Temple University Press.

Collins, Randall, Janet Saltzman Chafetz, Rae Lesser Blumberg, Scott Coltrane, and Jonathan H. Turner. 1993. "Toward an Integrated Theory of Gender Stratification." *Sociological Perspectives* 36: 185–216.

Conk, Margo Anderson. 1978. "Occupational Classification in the United States Census: 1870–1940." *Journal of Interdisciplinary History* 9:111–30.

———. 1980. *The United States Census and Labor Force Change: A History of Occupation Statistics, 1870–1940*. Studies in American History and Culture, no. 11. Robert Berkhofer, Series Editor. Ann Arbor, Mich.: University Microfilms International.

Connell, R. W. 1987. *Gender and Power: Society, the Person and Sexual Politics*. Stanford, Calif.: Stanford University Press.

Conway, Michael, M. Teresa Pizzamiglio, and Lauren Mount. 1996. "Status, Communality, and Agency: Implications for Stereotypes of Gender and Other Groups." *Journal of Personality and Social Psychology* 71: 25–38.

Correll, Shelley J. 2001. "Gender and the Career Choice Process: The Role of Biased Self-Assessments." *American Journal of Sociology* 106:1691–1730.

———. 2004. "Constraints into Preferences: Gender, Status, and Emerging Career Aspirations." *American Sociological Review* 69: 93–113.

Cortese, Charles F., R. Frank Falk, and Jack C. Cohen. 1976. "Further Considerations on the Methodological Analysis of Segregation Indices." *American Sociological Review* 41: 630–37.

Coser, Lewis A. 1975. "Presidential Address: Two Methods in Search of Substance." *American Sociological Review* 40: 691–700.

Cotter, David A., Joann M. DeFiore, Joan M. Hermsen, Brenda Marsteller Kowalewski, and Reeve Vanneman. 1995. "Occupational Gender Desegregation in the 1980s." *Work and Occupations* 22: 3–21.

Cotter, David A., Joan M. Hermsen, and Reeve Vanneman. 2001. "Women's Work and Working Women: The Demand for Female Labor." *Gender and Society* 15: 429–52.

Cotter, David A., Joann M. DeFiore, Joan M. Hermsen, Brenda Marsteller Kowalewski, and Reeve Vanneman. 1995. "Occupational Gender Desegregation in the 1980s." *Work and Occupations* 22: 3–21.

———. 1997. "All Women Benefit: The Macro-Level Effect of Occupational Integration on Gender Earnings Equality." *American Journal of Sociology* 62: 714–34.

———. 1998. "The Demand for Female Labor." *American Journal of Sociology* 103: 1673–1712.

Coulter, Philip B. 1989. *Measuring Inequality*. Boulder, Colo.: Westview Press.

Crompton, Rosemary. 1999. "The Decline of the Male Breadwinner: Explanations and Interpretations." In Rosemary Crompton, ed., *Restructuring Gender Relations and Employment: The Decline of the Male Breadwinner*, pp. 1–25. Oxford: Oxford University Press.

———. 2001. "The Gendered Restructuring of the Middle Classes." In Janeen Baxter and Mark Western, eds. *Reconfigurations of Class and Gender*, pp. 29–54. Stanford, Calif.: Stanford University Press.

———, with Nicky Le Feuvre. 1996. "Paid Employment and the Changing System of Gender Relations: A Cross-National Comparison." *Sociology* 30: 427–45.

Crompton, Rosemary, and Fiona Harris. 1999. "Attitudes, Women's Employment, and the Changing Domestic Division of Labour: A Cross-National Analysis." In Rosemary Crompton, ed., *Restructuring Gender Relations and Employment: The Decline of the Male Breadwinner*, pp. 105–27. Oxford: Oxford University Press.

Crompton, Rosemary, and Kay Sanderson. 1990. *Gendered Jobs and Social Change*. London: Unwin Hyman.

Crompton, Rosemary, Nicky Le Feuvre, and Gunn Elisabeth Birkelund. 1999. "The Restructuring of Gender Relations within the Medical Profession." In

Rosemary Crompton, ed., *Restructuring Gender Relations and Employment: The Decline of the Male Breadwinner*, pp. 179–200. Oxford: Oxford University Press.

Daly, Mary. 1978. *Gyn/Ecology: The Metaethics of Radical Feminism*. Boston: Beacon Press.

———. 2000. *The Gender Division of Welfare: The Impact of the British and German Welfare States*. New York: Cambridge University Press.

D'Andrade, Roy. 1995. *The Development of Cognitive Anthropology*. New York: Cambridge University Press.

Davies, Margery. 1975. "Woman's Place Is at the Typewriter: The Feminization of the Clerical Labor Force." In Richard Edwards, Michael Reich, and David Gordon, eds. *Labor Market Segmentation*, pp. 279–96. Lexington, Mass.: D. C. Heath.

Davis, George A., and O. Fred Donaldson. 1975. *Blacks in the United States: A Geographic Perspective*. Boston: Houghton Mifflin.

Davis, Kingsley. 1984. "Wives and Work: The Sex Role Revolution and Its Consequences." *Population and Development Review* 10: 397–417.

Davis, Kingsley, and Wilbur E. Moore. 1945. "Some Principles of Stratification." *American Sociological Review* 10: 242–49.

Deaux, Kay, and Mary Kite. 1987. "Thinking about Gender." In B. Hess and M. Ferree, eds., *Analyzing Gender: A Handbook of Social Science Research*, pp. 92–117. Newbury Park, Calif.: Sage.

DiMaggio, Paul. 1997. "Culture and Cognition." *Annual Review of Sociology* 23: 263–87.

DiMaggio, Paul, and Walter W. Powell. 1983. "The Iron Cage Revisited: Institutional Isomorphism and Collective Rationality in Organizational Fields." *American Sociological Review* 48: 147–60.

DiPrete, Thomas A., and Patricia A. McManus. 1996. "Education, Earnings Gain, and Earnings Loss in Loosely and Tightly Structured Labor Markets: A Comparison between the United States and Germany." In Alan C. Kerckhoff, ed., *Generating Social Stratification: Toward a New Research Agenda*, pp. 201–21. Boulder, Colo.: Westview Press.

Dobbin, Frank, John R. Sutton, John W. Meyer, and W. Richard Scott. 1993. "Equal Opportunity Law and the Construction of Internal Labor Markets." *American Journal of Sociology* 88: 396–427.

Dodge, Norton. 1971. "Women in the Soviet Economy." In Athena, Theodore, ed., *The Professional Woman*, pp. 207–23. Cambridge, Mass.: Schenkman.

Duncan, Otis D. 1968. "Social Stratification and Mobility: Problems in the Measurement of Trends." In Eleanor B. Sheldon and Wilbert E. Moore, eds., *Indicators of Social Change*, pp. 675–719. New York: Russell Sage.

———. 1975. *Introduction to Structural Equation Models*. New York: Academic Press.

———. 1979. "How Destination Depends on Origin in the Occupational Mobility Table." *American Journal of Sociology* 4: 793–803.

————. 1984. Foreword. In Leo A. Goodman, *The Analysis of Cross-Classified Data Having Ordered Categories*, pp. ix–xii. Cambridge, Mass.: Harvard University Press.

Duncan, Otis D., and Beverly Duncan. 1955. "A Methodological Analysis of Segregation Indexes." *American Sociological Review* 20: 210–17.

Eagly, Alice H., and Antonio Mladinic. 1994. "Are People Prejudiced against Women? Some Answers from Research on Attitudes, Gender Stereotypes, and Judgments of Competence." *European Review of Social Psychology*, 5: 1–35.

Edelman, Lauren B. 1992. "Legal Ambiguity and Symbolic Structure: Organizational Mechanism of Civil Rights Law." *American Journal of Sociology* 97: 1531–76.

Eder, Donna. 1995. *School Talk: Gender and Adolescent Culture*. New Brunswick, N.J.: Rutgers University Press.

Edwards, Alba. 1943. *Comparative Occupation Statistics for the United States, 1870 to 1940*. Sixteenth Census of the United States: 1940. Washington, D.C.: U.S. Government Printing Office.

Edwards, Richard C. 1979. *Contested Terrain: The Transformation of the Workplace in the Twentieth Century*. New York: Basic Books.

Elias, Peter, and Margaret Birch. 1993. "Establishment of Community-Wide Occupational Statistics." Working paper, Institute for Employment Research, University of Warwick.

————. 1994. "Harmonising Occupational Information across the European Union: Progress on the Labour Force Survey. Working paper, Institute for Employment Research, University of Warwick.

Ellis, Lee. 1993. *Social Stratification and Socioeconomic Inequality*. Vols. 1 and 2. Westport, Conn.: Praeger.

Elvin-Nowak, Ylva, and Heléne Thomsson. 2001. "Motherhood as Idea and Practice: A Discursive Understanding of Employed Mothers in Sweden." *Gender and Society* 15: 407–28.

England, Paula. 1979. "Women and Occupational Prestige: A Case of Vacuous Sex Equality." *Signs* 5: 252–65.

————. 1981. "Assessing Trends in Occupational Sex Segregation, 1900–1976." In Ivar Berg, ed., *Sociological Perspectives on Labor Markets*, pp. 273–95. New York: Academic Press.

————. 1982. "The Failure of Human Capital Theory to Explain Occupational Sex Segregation." *Journal of Human Resources* 17: 358–70.

————. 1984. "Wage Appreciation and Depreciation: A Test of Neoclassical Economic Explanations of Occupational Sex Segregation." *Social Forces* 62: 726–49.

————. 1992. *Comparable Worth: Theories and Evidence*. New York: Aldine de Gruyter.

England, Paula, Marilyn Chassie, and Linda McCormack. 1982. "Skill Demands and Earnings in Female and Male Occupations." *Sociology and Social Research* 66: 147–68.

England, Paula, George Farkas, Barbara S. Kilbourne, and Thomas Dou. 1988. "Explaining Occupational Sex Segregation and Wages: Findings from a Model with Fixed Effects." *American Sociological Review* 53: 544–58.

England, Paula, Lori L. Reid, and Barbara S. Kilbourne. 1996. "The Effect of the Sex Composition of Jobs on Starting Wages in an Organization: Findings from the NLSY." *Demography* 33: 511–21.

Entwisle, D. R., and E. Greenberger. 1972. "Adolescents' Views of Women's Work Role." *American Journal of Orthopsychiatry* 42: 648–56.

Epstein, Cynthia Fuchs. 1988. *Deceptive Distinctions: Sex, Gender, and the Social Order*. New Haven, Conn.: Yale University Press.

———. 1992. "Tinkerbells and Pinups: The Construction and Reconstruction of Gender Boundaries at Work." In Michèle Lamont and Marcel Fournier, eds., *Cultivating Differences: Symbolic Boundaries and the Making of Inequality*, pp. 232–56. Chicago: University of Chicago Press.

———. 1999. "Similarity and Difference: The Sociology of Gender Distinctions." In Janet Saltzman Chafetz, ed., *Handbook of the Sociology of Gender*, pp. 45–61. New York: Plenum.

Erikson, Robert, and John H. Goldthorpe. 1992. *The Constant Flux*. New York: Oxford University Press.

Estévez-Abe, Margarita, Torben Iversen, and David Soskice. 2003. "Social Protection and the Formation of Skills: A Reinterpretation of the Welfare State." In Peter A. Hall and David Soskice, eds. *Varieties of Capitalism: The Institutional Foundations of Comparative Advantage*, pp. 145–83. New York: Oxford University Press.

Etzioni, Amitai, ed. 1969. *The Semi-Professions and Their Organization: Teachers, Nurses, and Social Workers*. New York: Free Press.

EUROSTAT (Statistical Office of the European Communities). 1992. *Labour Force Survey: Methods and Definitions*. Luxembourg: Office for Official Publications of the European Communities.

Evans, M. D. R., and Karen Oppenheim Mason. 1996. "Currents and Anchors: Structure and Change in Australian Gender Role Attitudes." In James N. Baron, David B. Grusky, and Donald J. Treiman, eds. *Social Differentiation and Social Inequality*, pp. 275–302. Boulder, Colo.: Westview Press.

Faludi, Susan. 1991. *Backlash: The Undeclared War against American Women*. New York: Crown.

Featherman, David L., and Robert M. Hauser. 1978. *Opportunity and Change*. New York: Academic Press.

Featherman, David L., F. Lancaster Jones, and Robert M. Hauser. 1975. "Assumptions of Mobility Research in the United States: The Case of Occupational Status." *Social Science Research* 4: 329–60.

Fenstermaker, Sarah, and Candace West, eds. 2002. *Doing Gender, Doing Difference: Inequality, Power, and Institutional Change.* New York: Routledge.

Firestone, Shulamith. 1970. *The Dialectic of Sex.* New York: William Morrow.

Fiske, Susan T. 1998. "Stereotyping, Prejudice, and Discrimination." In T. Gilbert, S. T. Fiske, and G. Lindzey, eds., *Handbook of Social Psychology*, pp. 357–411. New York: McGraw-Hill.

Fitzsimons, Annette. 2002. *Gender as a Verb.* Burlington, Vt.: Ashgate.

Fossett, Mark A., and Scott J. South. 1983. "The Measurement of Intergroup Income Inequality: A Conceptual Review." *Social Forces* 61: 855–71.

Fossett, Mark A., Omer R. Galle, and William R. Kelly. 1986. "Racial Occupational Inequality, 1940–1980: National and Regional Trends." *American Sociological Review* 51: 421–29.

Fuchs, Victor R. 1975. "A Note on Sex Segregation in Professional Occupations." *Explorations in Economic Research* 2: 105–11.

———. 1988. *Women's Quest for Economic Equality.* Cambridge, Mass.: Harvard University Press.

Fukumoto, Ivan, and David B. Grusky. 1992. "Social Mobility and Class Structure in Early-Industrial France." In Andrew Miles and David Vincent, eds., *Building European Society: Occupational Change and Social Mobility in Europe, 1840–1940*, pp. 40–67. Manchester, England: Manchester University Press.

Galenson, Marjorie. 1973. *Women and Work: An International Comparison.* Ithaca, N.Y.: New York State School of Industrial and Labor Relations.

Ganzeboom, Harry B. G., and Donald J. Treiman. 1996. "Internationally Comparable Measures of Occupational Status for the 1988 International Standard Classification of Occupations." *Social Science Research* 25: 201–39.

Ganzeboom, Harry B. G., Ruud Luijkx, and Donald J. Treiman. 1989. "Intergenerational Class Mobility in Comparative Perspective." *Research in Social Stratification and Mobility* 8: 3–84.

Gaskell, J. 1985. "Course Enrollments in the High School: The Perspective of Working-Class Females." *Sociology and Education* 58: 48–59.

Gaskin, Katherine A. 1979. *Occupational Differentiation by Sex: An International Comparison.* Ph.D. dissertation. University of Michigan, Department of Sociology.

Gelb, Joyce. 1989. *Feminism and Politics: A Comparative Perspective.* Berkeley: University of California Press.

Gerson, Kathleen. 1993. *No Man's Land.* New York: Basic Books.

———. 2002. "Moral Dilemmas, Moral Strategies, and the Transformation of Gender: Lessons from Two Generations of Work and Family Change." *Gender and Society* 16: 8–28.

Gibbs, Jack P. 1965. "Occupational Differentiation of Negroes and Whites in the United States." *Social Forces* 44: 159–65.

Gilligan, Carol. 1982. *In a Different Voice: Psychological Theory and Women's Development*. Cambridge, Mass.: Harvard University Press.

Glass, Jennifer. 1990. "The Impact of Occupational Segregation on Working Conditions." *Social Forces* 68: 779–96.

Glenn, Norval D. 1977. *Cohort Analysis*. Newbury Park, Calif.: Sage.

Goffman, Erving. 1977. "The Arrangement between the Sexes." *Theory and Society* 4: 301–31.

Goldin, Claudia. 1983. "Historians' Consensus on the Economic Role of Women in American History: A Review Essay." *Historical Methods* 16 (2): 74–81.

———. 1990. *Understanding the Gender Gap*. Oxford: Oxford University Press.

———. 2000. "Labor Markets in the Twentieth Century." In S. Engerman and R. Gallman, eds., *The Cambridge Economic History of the United States*, Vol. 3, pp. 549–624. New York: Cambridge University Press.

Goldin, Claudia, and Cecilia Rouse. 2000. "Orchestrating Impartiality: The Impact of 'Blind' Auditions on Female Musicians." *American Economic Review* 90: 715–41.

Goldthorpe, John W., and Keith Hope. 1974. *The Social Grading of Occupations: A New Approach and Scale*. Oxford, England: Clarendon.

Goode, William J. 1963. *World Revolution and Family Patterns*. New York: Free Press.

Goodman, Leo A. 1979a. "Multiplicative Models for the Analysis of Occupational Mobility Tables and Other Kinds of Cross-Classification Tables." *American Journal of Sociology* 84: 804–19.

———. 1979b. "Simple Models for the Analysis of Association in Cross-Classifications Having Ordered Categories." *Journal of the American Statistical Association* 70: 755–68.

———. 1981a. "Association Models and Canonical Correlation in the Analysis of Cross-Classifications Having Ordered Categories." *Journal of the American Statistical Association* 76: 320–34.

———. 1981b. "Criteria for Determining Whether Certain Categories in a Cross-Classification Table Should Be Combined, with Special Reference to Occupational Categories in an Occupational Mobility Table." *American Journal of Sociology* 87: 612–50.

———. 1991. "Measures, Models, and Graphical Displays in the Analysis of Cross-Classified Data." *Journal of the American Statistical Association* 86: 1085–1111.

Gould, Roger V. 2002. "The Origins of Status Hierarchies: A Formal Theory and Empirical Test." *American Journal of Sociology* 107: 1143–78.

Granovetter, Mark. 1981. "Toward a Sociological Theory of Income Differences." In Ivar Berg, ed., *Sociological Perspectives on Labor Markets*, pp. 11–48. New York: Academic Press.

———. 1995. "Afterword." *Getting a Job: A Study of Contracts and Careers*. 2d ed. Chicago: University of Chicago Press.

Gray, John. 1992. *Men Are from Mars, Women Are from Venus.* New York: HarperCollins.

Gross, Edward. 1968. "Plus Ça Change . . . ? The Sexual Structure of Occupations over Time." *Social Problems* 16: 198–208.

Grusky, David B., and Maria Charles. 1998. "The Past, Present, and Future of Sex Segregation Methodology." *Demography* 35: 497–504.

———. 2001. "Is There a Worldwide Sex Segregation Regime?" In David B. Grusky, ed., *Social Stratification: Class, Race, and Gender in Sociological Perspective,* pp. 689–703. 2d ed. Boulder, Colo.: Westview Press.

Grusky, David B., and Robert M. Hauser. 1984. "Comparative Mobility Revisited: Models of Convergence and Divergence in 16 Countries." *American Sociological Review* 49: 19–38.

Grusky, David B. and Jesper B. Sørensen. 1998. "Can Class Analysis be Salvaged?" *American Journal of Sociology* 103: 1187–1234.

Guthrie, Doug, and Louise Marie Roth. 1999. "The State, Courts, and Maternity Policies in U.S. Organizations: Specifying Institutional Mechanisms." *American Sociological Review* 74: 41–63.

Gwartney-Gibbs, Patricia. 1988. "Sex Segregation in the Paid Workforce: The New Zealand Case." *Australia and New Zealand Journal of Sociology* 24: 264–78.

Haavio-Mannila, Elina. 1989. "Gender Segregation in Paid and Unpaid Work." In K. Boh et al., eds., *Changing Patterns of European Family Life: A Comparative Analysis of 14 European Countries,* pp. 124–40. London: Routledge.

Haberman, Shelby J. 1974. "Log-Linear Models for Frequency Tables with Ordered Classifications." *Biometrics* 30: 589–600.

Hakim, Catherine. 1992. "Explaining Trends in Occupational Segregation: The Measurement, Causes, and Consequences of the Sexual Division of Labour." *European Sociological Review* 8: 127–52.

———. 1994. "A Century of Change in Occupational Segregation 1891–1991." *Journal of Historical Sociology* 7: 435–54.

———. 1996. *Key Issues in Women's Work: Female Heterogeneity and the Polarisation of Women's Employment.* London: Athlone.

———. 2000. *Work-Lifestyle Choices in the 21st Century: Preference Theory.* New York: Oxford University Press.

Haller, Max, Wolfgang König, Peter Krause, and Karin Kurz. 1985. "Patterns of Career Mobility and Structural Positions in Advanced Capitalist Societies: A Comparison of Men in Austria, France, and the United States." *American Sociological Review* 50: 579–603.

Handl, Johann. 1984. "Chancengleichheit und Segregation: Ein Vorschlag zur Messung ungleicher Chancenstrukturen und ihrer zeitlichen Entwicklung." *Zeitschrift der Soziologie* 13: 328–45.

Hannan, Michael T., and John Freeman. 1989. *Organizational Ecology.* Cambridge, Mass.: Harvard University Press.

Hanson, Sandra L., Maryellen Schaub, and David Baker. 1996. "Gender Strati-fication in the Science Pipeline: A Comparative Analysis of Seven Countries." *Gender and Society* 10: 271–90.

Hart, Nicky. 1991. "Procreation: The Substance of Female Oppression in Modern Society." *Contention* 1 (1): 90–108; (2): 66–88.

Hartmann, Heidi I. 1976. "Capitalism, Patriarchy, and Job Segregation by Sex." *Signs* 1: 137–69.

———. 1981. "The Unhappy Marriage of Marxism and Feminism: Towards a More Progressive Union." In Lydia Sargent, ed., *Women and Revolution: A Discussion of the Unhappy Marriage of Marxism and Feminism*, pp. 1–41. Boston: South End Press.

———. 1987. "Changes in Women's Economic and Family Roles in Post–World War II United States." In Lourdes Beneria and Catharine R. Stimpson, eds., *Women, Households and the Economy*, pp. 33–64. New Brunswick, N.J.: Rutgers University Press.

Hauser, Robert M. 1978. "A Structural Model of the Mobility Table." *Social Forces* 56: 919–53.

———. 1984. "Vertical Mobility in Great Britain, France, and Sweden." *Acta Sociologica* 27: 87–110.

Hauser, Robert M., and David L. Featherman. 1977. *The Process of Stratification.* New York: Academic Press.

Hauser, Robert M., and David B. Grusky. 1988. "Cross-National Variation in Occupational Distributions, Relative Mobility Chances, and Intergenera-tional Shifts in Occupational Distributions." *American Sociological Review* 53: 723–48.

Hauser, Robert M., and John Robert Warren. 2001. "Socioeconomic Indexes for Occupations: A Review, Update, and Critique." In David B. Grusky, ed., *Social Stratification: Class, Race and Gender in Sociological Perspective*, 2d ed., pp. 281–86. Boulder, Colo.: Westview Press.

Hirao, Keiko. 1996. "The Effect of Higher Education on the Rate of Labor Force Exit for Married Japanese Women." Paper presented at the Annual Meeting of the American Sociological Association, New York.

———. 2001. "Mothers as the Best Teachers: Japanese Motherhood and Early Childhood Education." In Mary C. Brinton, ed., *Women's Working Lives in East Asia*, pp. 180–203. Stanford, Calif.: Stanford University Press.

Hodson, Randall. 1983. *Worker's Earnings and Corporate Economic Structure.* New York: Academic Press.

Hoffmann-Nowotny, Hans-Joachim. 1986. "Switzerland." In Tomas Hammar, ed., *European Immigration Policy: A Comparative Study*, pp. 206–36. Cambridge: Cambridge University Press.

Hout, Michael. 1984. "Status, Autonomy, and Training in Occupational Mobility." *American Journal of Sociology* 89: 1379–1409.

———. 1988. "More Universalism, Less Structural Mobility: The American Occupational Structure in the 1980s." *American Journal of Sociology* 93: 1358–1400.

———. 1996. "The Politics of Mobility." In Alan C. Kerckhoff, ed., *Generating Social Stratification: Toward a New Research Agenda*, pp. 293–316. Boulder, Colo.: Westview Press.

Hout, Michael, and John A. Jackson. 1986. "Dimensions of Occupational Mobility in the Republic of Ireland." *European Sociological Review* 2:114–37.

Huber, Joan. 1988. "A Theory of Family, Economy, and Gender." *Journal of Family Issues* 9: 9–26.

———. 1999. "Comparative Gender Stratification." In Janet Saltzman Chafetz, ed., *Handbook of the Sociology of Gender*, pp. 65–80. New York: Kluwer.

Huffman, Matt L., and Steven C. Velasco. 1997. "When More Is Less: Sex Composition, Organizations, and Earnings in U.S. Firms." *Work and Occupations* 24: 214–44.

ILO (International Labour Office). Various Years. *Yearbook of Labour Statistics.* Geneva: ILO.

———. 1989. *Women in the World of Work: Statistical Analyses and Projections to the Year 2000.* Geneva: ILO.

———. 1990a. *International Standard Classification of Occupations ISCO-88.* Geneva: ILO.

———. 1990b. *Yearbook of Labour Statistics: Retrospective Edition on Population Censuses 1945–89.* Geneva: ILO.

———. 1991. *Yearbook of Labour Statistics 1991.* Geneva: ILO.

Inglehart, Ronald. 1997. *Modernization and Postmodernization: Cultural, Economic, and Political Change in 43 Societies.* Princeton, N.J.: Princeton University Press.

Inglehart, Ronald, and Wayne E. Baker. 2000. "Modernization, Cultural Change, and the Persistence of Traditional Values." *American Sociological Review* 65: 19–51.

Inglehart, Ronald, and Pippa Norris. 2003. *Rising Tide: Gender Equality and Cultural Change Around the World.* New York: Cambridge.

Inkeles, Alex, and David Smith. 1974. *Becoming Modern.* Cambridge, Mass.: Harvard University Press.

Ishida, Hiroshi. 1998. "Educational Credentials and Labour-Market Entry Outcomes in Japan." In Yossi Shavit and Walter Müller, eds., *From School to Work: A Comparative Study of Educational Qualifications and Occupational Destinations*, pp. 287–309. Oxford: Oxford University Press.

Izraeli, Dafna N. 1979. "Sex Structure of Occupations: The Israeli Experience." *Work and Occupations* 6: 404–29.

Jackson, Robert Max. 1998. *Destined for Equality: The Inevitable Rise of Women's Status.* Cambridge, Mass.: Harvard University Press.

Jacobs, Jerry. 1986. "Trends in Workplace Contact between Men and Women, 1971–1981." *Sociology and Social Research* 70: 202–5.

———. 1989a. "Long-Term Trends in Occupational Segregation by Sex." *American Journal of Sociology* 95: 160–73.

———. 1989b. *Revolving Doors: Sex Segregation and Women's Careers.* Stanford, Calif.: Stanford University Press.

———. 1992. "Women's Entry into Management: Trends in Earnings, Authority and Values among Salaried Managers." *Administrative Science Quarterly* 37: 282–301.

———. 1996. "Gender Inequality and Higher Education." *Annual Review of Sociology* 22: 153–85.

———. 1999. "The Sex Segregation of Occupations: Prospects for the 21st Century." In Gary N. Powell, ed., *Handbook of Gender and Work*, pp. 125–41. Newbury Park, Calif.: Sage.

———. 2001. "Evolving Patterns of Sex Segregation." In I. Berg and A. L. Kalleberg, eds., *Sourcebook of Labor Markets: Evolving Structures and Processes*, pp. 535–50. New York: Kluwer Academic /Plenum.

———. 2003. "Detours on the Road to Equality: Women, Work and Higher Education." *Contexts* 2: 32–41.

———, ed. 1995. *Gender Inequality at Work.* Thousand Oaks, Calif.: Sage.

Jacobs, Jerry A., and Suet T. Lim. 1992. "Trends in Occupational and Industrial Sex Segregation in 56 Countries, 1960–1980." *Work and Occupations* 19: 450–86.

Jacobsen, Joyce P. 1994. "Trends in Work Force Sex Segregation, 1960–1990." *Social Science Quarterly* 75 (1): 204–11.

———. 1997. "Trends in Workforce Segregation: 1980 and 1990 Census Figures." *Social Science Quarterly* 78 (1): 234–35.

Japanese Bureau of Statistics. 1974. *Comparison of Employed Persons by Occupations in the Population Census: 1930 through 1970.* Tokyo: Statistic Bureau, Prime Minister's Office.

———. 1976. *Population Census of Japan, 1975.* Tokyo: Statistic Bureau, Prime Minister's Office.

———. 1982. *Population Census of Japan, 1980.* Tokyo: Statistic Bureau, Prime Minister's Office.

———. 1986. *Population Census of Japan, 1985.* Tokyo: Statistic Bureau, Prime Minister's Office.

———. 1994. *Population Census of Japan, 1990.* Tokyo: Statistic Bureau, Prime Minister's Office.

———. 1998. *Population Census of Japan, 1995.* Tokyo: Statistic Bureau, Prime Minister's Office.

James, David R., and Karl E. Taeuber. 1985. "Measures of Segregation." In Nancy Tuma, ed., *Sociological Methodology 1985*, pp. 1–32. New York: Jossey-Bass.

Jencks, Christopher, Lauri Perlman, and Lee Rainwater. 1988. "What Is a Good Job? A New Measure of Labor-Market Success." *American Journal of Sociology* 93: 132–57.

Johnson, Daniel M., and Rex R. Campbell. 1981. *Black Migration in America: A Social Demographic History.* Durham, N.C.: Duke University Press.

Jones, JoAnn, and Rachel A. Rosenfeld. 1989. "Women's Occupations and Local Labor Markets: 1950–80." *Social Forces* 67: 666–92.

Jonung, Christina. 1984. "Patterns of Occupational Segregation by Sex in the Labor Market." In Günther Schmid and Renate Weitzel, eds., *Sex Discrimination and Equal Opportunity*, pp. 44–63. Hampshire, England: Gower.

———. 1998. "Occupational Segregation by Sex and Change Over Time." In Inga Persson and Christina Jonung, eds., *Women's Work and Wages*, pp. 36–71. New York: Routledge.

Joshi, Heather, and Hugh Davis. 1992. "Day Care in Europe and Mothers' Forgone Earnings." *International Labour Review* 132: 561–79.

Kalleberg, Arne L., and Ivar Berg. 1987. *Work and Industry: Structures, Markets, and Processes.* New York: Plenum Press.

Kalleberg, Arne L., and James R. Lincoln. 1988. "The Structure of Earnings Inequality in the United States and Japan." *American Journal of Sociology* 94 Supplement: Sl21–Sl53.

Kanter, Rosabeth Moss. 1977. *Men and Women of the Corporation.* New York: Basic Books.

Karmel, T., and M. MacLachlan. 1988. "Occupational Sex Segregation—Increasing or Decreasing?" *Economic Record* 64: 187–95.

Kaufman, Robert L. 2002. "Assessing Alternative Perspectives on Race and Sex Employment Segregation." *American Sociological Review* 67: 547–72.

Kennelly, Ivy. 2002. "'I Would Never Be a Secretary': Reinforcing Gender in Segregated and Integrated Occupations." *Gender and Society* 16: 603–24.

Kerckhoff, Alan C., ed., 1996. *Generating Social Stratification: Toward a New Research Agenda.* Boulder, Colo.: Westview Press.

Kerr, Clark, John T. Dunlop, Frederick H. Harbison, and Charles A. Myers. 1960. *Industrialism and Industrial Man.* Cambridge, Mass.: Harvard University Press.

Kessler-Harris, Alice. 1982. *Out to Work: A History of Wage-Earning Women in the United States.* New York: Oxford University Press.

———. 1990. *A Woman's Wage: Historical Meanings and Social Consequences.* Lexington: University of Kentucky Press.

Kilbourne, Barbara Stanek, Paula England, George Farkas, Kurt Beron, and Dorothea Weir. 1994. "Returns to Skill, Compensating Differentials, and Gender Bias: Effects of Occupational Characteristics on the Wages of White Women and Men." *American Journal of Sociology* 100: 689–719.

King, Mary. 1992. "Occupational Segregation by Race and Gender, 1940–1980." *Monthly Labor Review* 115: 30–37.

Kiyoko, Kamio Knapp. 1995. "Still Office Flowers: Japanese Women Betrayed by the Equal Employment Opportunity Law." *Harvard Women's Law Journal* 83: 409–23.

Kuhn, Sarah, and Barry Bluestone. 1987. "Economic Restructuring and the Female Labor Market: The Impact of Industrial Change on Women." In Lourdes Beneria and Catharine R. Stimpson, eds., *Women, Households, and the Economy*, pp. 3–32. New Brunswick, N.J.: Rutgers University Press.

Kumazawa, Makoto. 1996. *Portraits of the Japanese Workplace: Labor Movements, Workers, and Managers*. Boulder, Colo.: Westview Press.

Lam, Alice C. L. 1992. *Women and Japanese Management: Discrimination and Reform*. London: Routledge.

Lamont, Michèle. 2000. *The Dignity of Working Men: Morality and the Boundaries of Race, Class, and Immigration*. New York: Russell Sage.

Lapidus, Gail W. 1985. "The Soviet Union." In Jennie Farley, ed., *Women Workers in Fifteen Countries*, pp. 13–32. New York: ILR Press.

Lee, Yean-Ju, and Shuichi Hirata. 2001. "Women, Work, and Marriage in Three East Asian Labor Markets: The Case of Taiwan, Japan, and South Korea." In Mary C. Brinton, ed., *Women's Working Lives in East Asia*, pp. 96–124. Stanford, Calif.: Stanford University Press.

Leidner, Robin. 1993. *Fast Food, Fast Talk: Service Work and the Routinization of Everyday Life*. Berkeley: University of California Press.

Leira, Arnlaug. 1992. *Welfare States and Working Mothers: The Scandinavian Experience*. New York: Cambridge University Press.

Levy, René, Dominique Joye, Olivier Guye, and Vincent Kaufmann. 1997. *Tous égaux? De la stratification aux representations*. Zürich: Seismo Verlag.

Lieberson, Stanley. 1969. "Measuring Population Diversity." *American Sociological Review* 34: 850–62.

———. 1980. *A Piece of the Pie: Blacks and White Immigrants since 1880*. Berkeley: University of California Press.

———. 1981. "An Asymmetrical Approach to Segregation." In Ceri Peach, Vaughan Robinson, and Susan Smith, eds., *Ethnic Segregation in Cities*, pp. 61–82. Athens: University of Georgia Press.

Lipset, Seymour Martin, Reinhard Bendix, and Hans L. Zetterberg. 1959. "Social Mobility in Industrial Society." In Seymour Martin Lipset, Reinhard Bendix, and Hans L. Zetterberg, eds., *Social Mobility in Industrial Society*, pp. 11–81. Berkeley: University of California Press.

Loftus, Jeni. 2001. "America's Liberalization in Attitudes toward Homosexuality, 1973 to 1998." *American Sociological Review* 66: 762–82.

Lorber, Judith. 1993. *Paradoxes of Gender*. New Haven, Conn.: Yale University Press.

Lorence, Jon. 1992. "Service Sector Growth and Metropolitan Occupational Sex Segregation." *Work and Occupations* 19: 128–56.

Loury, Glenn. 2002. *The Anatomy of Racial Inequality*. Cambridge, Mass.: Harvard University Press.

Lovenduski, Joni. 1986. *Women and European Politics: Contemporary Feminism and Public Policy*. Amherst: University of Massachusetts Press.

Lyson, Thomas A. 1986. "Industrial Transformation and Occupational Sex Differentiation: Evidence from New Zealand and the United States." *International Journal of Comparative Sociology* 27 (1–2): 53–68.

Maki, Omori. 1993. "Gender and the Labor Market." *Journal of Japanese Studies* 19: 79–102.

Mann, Michael. "A Crisis in Stratification Theory? Persons, Households/Families/Lineages, Genders, Classes and Nations." In Rosemary Crompton and Michael Mann, eds. *Gender and Stratification*, pp. 40–56. Cambridge, England: Polity Press.

Marini, Margaret Mooney. 1989. "Sex Differences in Earnings in the United States." *Annual Review of Sociology* 15: 343–80.

Marini, Margaret Mooney, and Mary C. Brinton. 1984. "Sex Typing and Occupational Socialization." In Barbara Reskin, ed., *Sex Segregation in the Workplace: Trends, Explanations, and Remedies*, pp. 192–232. Washington, D.C.: National Academy Press.

Mason, William M., and Stephen E. Fienberg, eds. 1985. *Cohort Analysis in Social Research: Beyond the Identification Problem*. New York: Springer-Verlag.

Massey, Douglas S., and Nancy A. Denton. 1988. "The Dimensions of Residential Segregation." *Social Forces* 67: 281–315.

———. 1993. *American Apartheid: Segregation and the Making of the Underclass*. Cambridge, Mass.: Harvard University Press.

McAdam, Doug, and Dieter Rucht. 1993. "The Cross-National Diffusion of Movement Ideas." *Annals of the American Academy of Political and Social Science* 528: 56–74.

McCall, Leslie. 2001. *Complex Inequality: Gender, Class and Race in the New Economy*. New York: Routledge.

McLendon, James. 1983. "The Office: Way Station or Blind Alley?" In David Plath, ed., *Work and Lifecourse in Japan*, pp. 156–82. New York: State University of New York Press.

Melkas, Helina, and Richard Anker. 2001. "Occupational Segregation by Sex in Nordic Countries: An Empirical Investigation." In Martha Fetherholf Loutfi, ed., *Women, Gender and Work: What Is Equality and How Do We Get There?*, pp. 189–213. Geneva: ILO.

Meyer, John W. 2001. "The Evolution of Modern Stratification Systems." In David B. Grusky, ed., *Social Stratification: Class, Race and Gender in Sociological Perspective*, 2d ed., pp. 881–90. Boulder, Colo.: Westview Press.

Meyer, John W., and Brian Rowan. 1977. "Institutionalized Organization: Formal Structure as Myth and Ceremony." *American Sociological Review* 83: 340–63.

Meyer, John W., John Boli, and George M. Thomas. 1987. "Ontology and Rationalization in the Western Cultural Account." In George M. Thomas, John W. Meyer, Francisco O. Ramirez, and John Boli, eds., *Institutional Structure: Constituting State, Society and the Individual*, pp. 12–37. Newbury Park, Calif.: Sage.

Meyer, John W., John Boli, George M. Thomas, and Francisco O. Ramirez. 1997. "World Society and the Nation State." *American Journal of Sociology* 103: 144–81.

Milkman, Ruth. 1987. *Gender at Work: The Dynamics of Job Segregation by Sex during World War II.* Urbana: University of Illinois Press.

Milkman, Ruth, and Eleanor Townsley. 1994. "Gender and the Economy." In Neil J. Smelser and Richard Swedberg, eds., *The Handbook of Economic Sociology*, pp. 600–619. Princeton, N.J.: Princeton University Press.

Mincer, Jacob. 1985. "Intercountry Comparisons of Labor Force Trends and of Related Developments: An Overview." *Journal of Labor Economics* 3: S1–S32.

Mincer, Jacob, and Solomon Polachek. 1974. "Family Investments in Human Capital: Earnings of Women." *Journal of Political Economy* 82: S76–S108.

Moen, Jon. 1988. "From Gainful Employment to Labor Force: Definitions and a New Estimate of Work Rates of American Males, 1860 to 1980." *Historical Methods* 21: 149–58.

Müller, Walter, Angelika Willms, and Johann Handl. 1983. *Strukturwandel der Frauenarbeit 1880–1980.* Frankfurt: Campus.

National Institute of Employment and Vocational Training. 1988. *Jyosei no shoku-gyo keireki* (Work History of Women). Vol. 77. Tokyo: National Institute of Employment and Vocational Training.

Nelson, Robert L., and William P. Bridges. 1999. *Legalizing Gender Inequality: Courts, Markets, and Unequal Pay for Women in the United States.* New York: Cambridge University Press.

Nermo, Magnus. 1996. "Occupational Sex Segregation in Sweden, 1968–91." *Work and Occupations* 23: 319–32.

———. 2000. "Models of Cross-National Variation in Occupational Sex Segregation." *European Societies* 2: 295–333.

Nuss, Shirley, and Lorraine Majka. 1983. "The Economic Integration of Women: A Cross-National Investigation." *Work and Occupations* 10: 29–48.

Oakley, Ann. 1974. *Woman's Work: The Housewife, Past and Present.* New York: Pantheon Books.

OECD (Organization for Economic Cooperation and Development). 1980. *Women and Employment.* Paris: OECD.

———. 1985. *The Integration of Women into the Economy.* Paris: OECD.

———. 1998. *The Future of Female-Dominated Occupations.* Paris: OECD.

———. 2001. *OECD in Figures: Statistics on the Member Countries.* Paris: OECD.

Ogasawara, Yuko. 1998. *Office Ladies and Salaried Men: Power, Gender, and Work in Japanese Companies.* Berkeley: University of California Press.

Okamoto, Dina, and Paula England. 1999. "Is There a Supply Side to Occupational Sex Segregation?" *Sociological Perspectives* 42: 557–82.

Oppenheimer, Valerie K. 1970. *The Female Labor Force in the United States:*

Demographic and Economic Factors Governing Its Growth and Changing Composition. Berkeley, Calif.: Institute for International Studies.

———. 1973. "Demographic Influence on Female Employment and the Status of Women." *American Journal of Sociology* 78: 946–61.

Orloff, Ann Shola. 1993. "Gender and the Social Rights of Citizenship: The Comparative Analysis of Gender Relations and Welfare States." *American Sociological Review* 58: 303–28.

Parkin, Frank. 1971. *Class Inequality and Political Order: Social Stratification in Capitalist and Communist Societies.* New York: Praeger.

Parsons, Talcott. 1954. *Essays in Sociological Theory.* Glencoe, Ill.: Free Press.

———. 1970. "Equality and Inequality in Modern Society, or Social Stratification Revisited." In Edward O. Laumann, ed., *Social Stratification: Research and Theory for the 1970s*, pp. 14–72. Indianapolis: Bobbs-Merrill.

Parsons, Talcott, and Robert F. Bales. 1955. *Family, Socialization, and Interaction Process.* Glencoe, Ill.: Free Press.

Peach, Ceri. 1975. *Urban Residential Segregation.* London: Longman.

Petersen, Trond, and Laurie A. Morgan. 1995. "Separate and Unequal: Occupation-Establishment Sex Segregation and the Gender Wage Gap." *American Journal of Sociology* 101: 329–65.

Petersen, Trond, Ishak Saporta, and Marc-David Seidel. 2000. "Offering a Job: Meritocracy and Social Networks." *American Journal of Sociology* 106: 763–816.

Phelps, Edmund S. 1980. "The Statistical Theory of Racism and Sexism." In Alice H. Amsden, ed., *The Economics of Women and Work*, pp. 206–10. New York: St. Martin's Press.

Pietilä, H., and J. Vickers. 1990. *Making Women Matter: The Role of the United Nations.* Atlantic Highlands, N.J.: Zed Books.

Polachek, Solomon. 1979. "Occupational Segregation among Women: Theory, Evidence, and a Prognosis." In Cynthia Lloyd, Emily Andrews, and Curtis Gilroy, eds., *Women in the Labor Market*, pp. 137–57. New York: Columbia University Press.

———. 1981. "Occupational Self-Selection: A Human Capital Approach to Sex Differences in Occupational Structure." *Review of Economics and Statistics* 63: 60–69.

Polachek, Solomon, and W. Stanley Siebert. 1993. *The Economics of Earnings.* Cambridge, England: Cambridge University Press.

Popenoe, David. 1988. *Disturbing the Nest: Family Change and Decline in Modern Societies.* New York: Aldine de Gruyter.

Poster, Winifred R. 1998. "Globalization, Gender and the Workplace: Women and Men in an American Multinational Corporation in India," *Journal of Developing Societies* 14: 40–65.

Presser, Harriet B., and Sunita Kishor. 1991. "Economic Development and Occupational Sex Segregation in Puerto Rico: 1950–80." *Population and Development Review* 17: 53–85.

Preston, Samuel H. 1989. *Census of the Population, 1910 [United States]: Public Use Sample*. Philadelphia: University of Pennsylvania. Population Studies Center [producer]. Ann Arbor, Mich.: Inter-university Consortium for Political and Social Research [distributor].

Pyle, Jean Larson. 1990. *The State and Women in the Economy: Lessons from Sex Discrimination in the Republic of Ireland*. Albany: State University of New York Press.

Raftery, Adrian E. 1986. "Choosing Models for Cross-Classifications. *American Sociological Review* 51: 145–46.

———. 1995. "Bayesian Model Selection in Social Research (with discussion)." In Peter V. Marsden, ed., *Sociological Methodology 1995*, pp. 111–96. Cambridge, Mass.: Blackwells.

Ramirez, Francisco O. 1987. "Global Changes, World Myths, and the Demise of Cultural Gender: Implications for the United States." In Terry Boswell and Albert Bergesen, eds., *America's Changing Role in the World System*, pp. 257–73. New York: Praeger.

———. Forthcoming. "Progress, Justice, and Gender Equity: World Models and Cross-National Trends." In Walter W. Powell and Daniel L. Jones, eds., *Bending the Bars of the Iron Cage: Institutional Dynamics and Processes*. Chicago: University of Chicago Press.

Ramirez, Francisco O., and Jane Weiss. 1979. "The Political Incorporation of Women." In John W. Meyer and Michael Hannan, eds. *National Development and the World System: Educational, Economic and Political Change 1950–1970*, pp. 238–49. Chicago: University of Chicago Press.

Ramirez, Francisco O., and Christine Min Wotipka. 2001. "Slowly but Surely? The Global Expansion of Women's Participation in Science and Engineering Fields of Study, 1972–92." *Sociology of Education* 74: 231–51.

Ramirez, Francisco O., Yasemin Soysal, and Suzanne Shanahan. 1997. "The Changing Logic of Political Citizenship: Cross-National Acquisition of Women's Suffrage Rights, 1890 to 1990." *American Sociological Review* 62: 735–45.

Reskin, Barbara F. 1988. "Bringing the Men Back In: Sex Differentiation and the Devaluation of Women's Work." *Gender and Society* 2: 58–81.

———. 1993. "Sex Segregation in the Workplace." *Annual Review of Sociology* 19: 241–70.

———. 2000. "The Proximate Causes of Employment Discrimination." *Contemporary Sociology* 29: 319–28.

Reskin, Barbara F., and Debra Branch McBrier. 2000. "Why Not Ascription? Organizations' Employment of Male and Female Managers." *American Sociological Review* 65: 210–33.

Reskin, Barbara F., and Irene Padavic. 1994. *Women and Men at Work*. Thousand Oaks, Calif.: Pine Forge Press.

Reskin, Barbara F., and Patricia A. Roos. 1987. "Status Hierarchies and Sex Segregation." In Christine Bose and Glenna Spitze, eds., *Ingredients for Women's Employment Policy*, pp. 3–21. Albany: State University of New York Press.

———. 1990. *Job Queues, Gender Queues: Explaining Women's Inroads into Male Occupations*. Philadelphia: Temple University Press.

Reskin, Barbara F., Debra B. McBrier, and Julie A. Kmec. 1999. "The Determinants and Consequences of Workplace Sex and Race Composition." *Annual Review of Sociology* 25: 335–61.

Ridgeway, Cecilia L. 1997. "Interaction and the Conservation of Gender Inequality: Considering Employment." *American Sociological Review* 62: 218–35.

———. Forthcoming. "Gender as an Organizing Force in Social Relations: Implications for the Future of Inequality." In Francine D. Blau, Mary C. Brinton, and David B. Grusky, eds., *The Declining Significance of Gender?* New York: Russell Sage Foundation.

Rogoff, Natalie. 1953. *Recent Trends in Occupational Mobility*. Glencoe, Ill.: Free Press.

Roos, Patricia A. 1985. *Gender and Work: A Comparative Analysis of Industrial Societies*. New York: State University of New York Press.

Roos, Patricia, and Barbara Reskin. 1984. "Institutional Factors Contributing to Sex Segregation in the Workplace." In Barbara Reskin, ed., *Sex Segregation in the Workplace: Trends, Explanations, and Remedies*, pp. 235–60. Washington, D.C.: National Academy Press.

Rosaldo, Michelle Z. 1974. "Women, Culture, and Society: A Theoretical Overview." In Michelle Z. Rosaldo and Louise Lamphere, eds., *Women, Culture, and Society*, pp. 17–42. Stanford, Calif.: Stanford University Press.

Rosaldo, Michelle Z., and Louise Lamphere, eds. 1974. *Women, Culture, and Society*. Stanford, Calif.: Stanford University Press.

Rose, Sonya O. 1992. *Limited Livelihoods: Gender and Class in Nineteenth-Century England*. Berkeley: University of California Press.

Rosenfeld, Rachel. 1983. "Sex Segregation and Sectors: An Analysis of Gender Differences in Returns from Employer Changes." *American Sociological Review* 48: 637–55.

Rosenfeld, Rachel, and Heike Trappe. 2000. "Occupational Sex Segregation in State Socialist and Market Economies: Levels, Patterns, Change in East and West Germany, 1980s and 1998." Paper presented at the Annual Meetings of the American Sociological Association, Washington, D.C.

Rosenfeld, Rachel, and Arne L. Kalleberg. 1991. "Gender Inequality in the Labor Market: A Cross-National Perspective." *Acta Sociologica* 34: 207–25.

Rubery, Jill. 1988. "Women and Recession: A Comparative Perspective." In Jill Rubery, ed., *Women and Recession*, pp. 253–87. London: Routledge.

———. 1998. "Women in the Labour Market: A Gender Equality Perspective." OECD Working Paper no. 75, Vol. 6. Paris: OECD.

Rubery, Jill, and Colette Fagan. 1995. "Gender Segregation in Societal Context." *Work, Employment and Society* 9: 213–40.

Rubery, Jill, Mark Smith, and Colette Fagan. 1999. *Women's Employment in Europe: Trends and Prospects*. New York: Routledge.

Ruggie, Mary. 1984. *The State and Working Women: A Comparative Study of Britain and Sweden*. Princeton, N.J.: Princeton University Press.

Ruggles, Steven, and Matthew Sobek. 2003. *Integrated Public Use Microdata Series: Version 3.0*. Minneapolis: Historical Census Projects, University of Minnesota.

Safilios-Rothschild, Constantina. 1975. "A Cross-Cultural Examination of Women's Marital, Educational and Occupational Options." In Martha T. S. Mednick, Sandra S. Tangri, and Lois W. Hoffman, eds., *Women and Achievement: Social and Motivational Analyses*, pp. 48–70. New York: Wiley.

Sainsbury, Diane. 1996. *Gender, Equality, and Welfare States*. New York: Cambridge University Press.

Sakuma, Ken. 1988. "Change in Japanese-Style Labor-Management Relations." *Japanese Economic Studies* 16: 3–48.

Sanday, Peggy Reeves. 1981. *Female Power and Male Dominance: On the Origins of Sexual Inequality*. London: Cambridge University Press.

Sandqvist, K. 1992. "Sweden's Sex-Role Scheme and Commitment to Gender Equality." In S. Lewis, D. N. Izraeli, and H. Hootsmans, eds., *Dual Earner Families: International Perspectives*, pp. 80–98. Newbury Park, Calif.: Sage.

Schmitter Heisler, Barbara. 1988. "From Conflict to Accommodation. The 'Foreigners Question' in Switzerland." *European Journal of Political Research* 16: 683–700.

Scott, Alison MacEwen. 1986. "Industrialization, Gender Segregation and Stratification Theory." In Rosemary Crompton and Michael Mann, eds., *Gender and Stratification*, pp. 154–89. Cambridge, England: Polity Press.

———. 1994. "Gender Segregation in the Retail Industry." In Alison MacEwan Scott, ed., *Gender Segregation and Social Change: Men and Women in Changing Labour Markets*, pp. 235–70. Oxford: Oxford University Press.

———, ed. 1994. *Gender Segregation and Social Change: Men and Women in Changing Labour Markets*. Oxford: Oxford University Press.

Scott, Joan W. 1988. "Deconstructing Equality-Versus-Difference: Or, the Uses of Poststructuralist Theory for Feminism." *Feminist Studies* 14: 33–50.

Scott, W. Richard, and John W. Meyer. 1987. "Environmental Linkages and Organizational Complexity: Public and Private Schools." In Henry M. Levin and Tom James, eds., *Comparative Public and Private Schools*, pp. 128–60. New York: Falmer.

Scriven, Jeannie. 1984. "Women at Work in Sweden." In Marilyn J. Davidson and Cary L. Cooper, eds., *Working Women: An International Survey*, pp. 153–81. New York: Wiley.

Semyonov, Moshe. 1980. "The Social Context of Women's Labor Force Participation: A Comparative Analysis." *American Journal of Sociology* 86: 534–50.

Semyonov, Moshe, and Frank L. Jones. 1999. "Dimensions of Gender Occupational Differentiation in Segregation and Inequality: A Cross-National Analysis." *Social Indicators Research* 46: 225–47.

Semyonov, Moshe, and Richard Ira Scott. 1983. "Industrial Shifts, Female Employment, and Occupational Differentiation: A Dynamic Model for American Cities 1960–1970." *Demography* 20: 163–76.

Semyonov, Moshe, and Yehouda Shenhav. 1988. "Investment Dependence, Economic Development, and Female Employment Opportunities in Less Developed Countries." *Social Science Quarterly* 69: 961–78.

Sewell, William H., Robert M. Hauser, and Wendy C. Wolf. 1980. "Sex, Schooling, and Occupational Status." *American Journal of Sociology* 86: 551–83.

Shavit, Yossi, and Walter Müller. 1998. *From School to Work: A Comparative Study of Educational Qualifications and Occupational Destinations.* New York: Oxford University Press.

Shimada, Haruo, and Yoshio Higuchi. 1985. "An Analysis of Trends in Female Labor Force Participation in Japan." *Journal of Labor Economics* 3: S355–74.

Shirahase, Sawako, and Hiroshi Ishida. 1994. "Gender Inequality in the Japanese Occupational Structure: A Cross-National Comparison with Great Britain and the United States." *International Journal of Comparative Sociology* 35: 188–206.

Shu, Xiaoling, and Margaret Mooney Marini. 1998. "Gender-Related Change in Occupational Aspirations." *Sociology of Education* 71: 44–68.

Silber, Jacques G. 1989. "On the Measurement of Employment Segregation." *Economics Letters* 30: 237–43.

Silén, Birgitta. 1988. "Women and Power." *Scandinavian Review* 76: 91–101.

Siltanen, Janet, Jennifer Jarman, and Robert M. Blackburn. 1995. *Gender Inequality in the Labour Market: Occupational Concentration and Segregation.* Geneva: International Labour Office.

Simona, Ilda. 1985. "Switzerland." In Jennie Farley, ed., *Women Workers in 15 Countries: Essays in Honor of Alice Hanson Cook*, pp. 147–53. Ithaca, N.Y.: ILR Press.

Singelmann, Joachim, and Harley L. Browning. 1980. "Industrial Transformation and Occupational Change in the U.S., 1960–1970." *Social Forces* 59: 246–64.

Singelmann, Joachim, and Marta Tienda. 1985. "The Process of Occupational Change in a Service Society: The Case of the United States, 1960–80." In Bryan Roberts, Ruth Finnegan, and Duncan Gallie, eds., *New Approaches to Economic Life*, pp. 48–67. Manchester, England: Manchester University Press.

Smelser, Neil J. 1968. *Essays in Sociological Explanation.* Englewood Cliffs, N.J.: Prentice Hall.

Smith, James P., and Finis Welch. 1984. "Affirmative Action and Labor Markets." *Journal of Labor Economics* 2: 269–301.

Smith, Tom W. 1999. "The Emerging 21st Century American Family." GSS Social Change Report No. 42, National Opinion Research Center, Chicago, Ill.

Sobel, Michael E., Michael Hout, and Otis D. Duncan. 1986. "Saving the Bath Water: An Invited Comment on Krauze and Slomczynski's 'Matrix Representation of Structural and Circulation Mobility.'" *Sociological Methods and Research* 14: 271–84.

Sokoloff, Natalie J. 1987. "The Increase of Black and White Women in the Professions: A Contradictory Process." In Christine Bose and Glenna Spitze, eds., *Ingredients for Women's Employment Policy*, pp. 53–72. Albany: State University of New York Press.

Somit, Albert and Stephen A. Peterson, eds. 1992. *The Dynamics of Evolution: The Punctuated Equilibrium Debate in the Natural and Social Sciences.* Ithaca, N.Y.: Cornell University Press.

Sørensen, Jesper B. 1992. "Locating Class Cleavages in Inter-Generational Mobility: Cross-National Commonalities and Variations in Mobility Patterns." *European Sociological Review* 8 (3): 267–81.

Soysal, Yasemin. 1994. *Limits of Citizenship: Migrants and Postnational Membership in Europe.* Chicago: University of Chicago Press.

Stafford, M. Therese, and Mark A. Fossett. 1989. "Occupational Sex Inequality in the Nonmetropolitan South, 1960–1980." *Rural Sociology* 54: 169–94.

Statistics Bureau of Japan. 1984. *1980 Population Census of Japan.* Vol. 4, pt. 1. Tokyo: Statistics Bureau.

Stearns, Linda Brewster, and Charlotte Coleman. 1988. "Occupational Segregation by Sex in High- and Low-Technology Manufacturing Industries." *Research in the Sociology of Work* 4: 289–310.

Stier, Haya, and David B. Grusky. 1990. "An Overlapping Persistence Model of Career Mobility." *American Sociological Review* 55: 736–56.

Stinchcombe, Arthur L. 1965. "Social Structure and Organizations." In James G. March, ed., *Handbook of Organizations*, pp. 142–93. Chicago: Rand-McNally.

Stockard, Jean, and Miriam M. Johnson. 1980. *Sex Roles: Sex Inequality and Sex Role Development.* Englewood Cliffs, N.J.: Prentice Hall.

Stockard, Jean, and Jeanne McGee. 1990. "Children's Occupational Preferences: The Influence of Sex and Perceptions of Occupational Characteristics." *Journal of Vocational Behavior* 36: 287–303.

Stolzenberg, Ross M., and Ronald J. D'Amico. 1977. "City Differences and Non-differences in the Effect of Race and Sex on Occupational Distribution." *American Sociological Review* 42: 937–50.

Straits, Bruce C. 1998. "Occupational Sex Segregation: The Role of Personal Ties." *Journal of Vocational Behavior* 52: 191–207.

Strober, Myra H. 1984. "Toward a General Theory of Occupational Sex Segregation: The Case of Public School Teaching." In Barbara F. Reskin, ed., *Sex Segregation in the Workplace*, pp. 144–56. Washington, D.C.: National Academy Press.

Strober, Myra H., and Agnes Miling Kaneko Chan. 1999. *The Road Winds Uphill All the Way: Gender, Work, and Family in the United States and Japan.* Cambridge, Mass.: MIT Press.

Swidler, Ann. 1986. "Culture in Action: Symbols and Strategies." *American Sociological Review* 51: 273–86.

Szelényi, Szonja. 1988. *Social Mobility and Class Structure in Hungary and the United States.* Ph.D. dissertation. University of Wisconsin-Madison, Department of Sociology.

Szelényi, Szonja and Winifred R. Poster. 1991. "The Transformation of the Hungarian Class Structure, 1943–1980." Unpublished manuscript. Stanford University, Department of Sociology.

Taeuber, Karl E., and Alma F. Taeuber. 1965. *Negroes in Cities: Residential Segregation and Neighborhood Change.* Chicago: Aldine.

Thomas, George M., John W. Meyer, Francisco O. Ramirez, and John Boli, eds. 1987. *Institutional Structure: Constituting State, Society and the Individual.* Newbury Park, Calif.: Sage.

Thurow, Lester C. 1975. *Generating Inequality: Mechanisms of Distribution in the U.S. Economy.* New York: Basic Books.

Tienda, Marta, and Vilma Ortiz. 1987. "Intraindustry Occupational Recomposition and Gender Inequality in Earnings." In Christine Bose and Glenna Spitze, ed., *Ingredients for Women's Employment Policy*, pp. 23–51. Albany: State University of New York Press.

Tienda, Marta, Shelley A. Smith, and Vilma Ortiz. 1987. "Industrial Restructuring, Gender Segregation, and Sex Differences in Earnings." *American Sociological Review* 52: 195–210.

Tijdens, Kea G. 2001. "Are Secondary Part-Time Jobs Marginalized? Job Characteristics of Women Employed Less Than Twenty Hours a Week in the European Union." In Tanja Van der Lippe and Liset Van Dijk, eds., *Women's Employment in A Comparative Perspective*, pp. 203–19. New York: Aldine De Gruyter.

Tilly, Charles. 1998. *Durable Inequality.* Berkeley: University of California Press.

Tilly, Louise A., and Joan W. Scott. 1978. *Women, Work, and Family.* New York: Holt, Rinehart and Winston.

Tolbert, Charles M., Patrick Horan, and E. M. Beck. 1980. "The Structure of Economic Segmentation: A Dual Economy Approach." *American Journal of Sociology* 85: 1095–1116.

Tölke, Angelika. 1989. *Lebensverläufe von Frauen: Familiäre Ereignisse, Ausbildungs- und Erwerbsverhalten.* Munich: Juventa.

Tomaskovic-Devey, Donald. 1993. *Gender and Racial Inequality at Work: The Sources and Consequences of Job Segregation.* Ithaca, N.Y.: IRL Press.

Tomaskovic-Devey, Donald, and Sheryl Skaggs. 1999. "Degendered Jobs? Organizational Processes and Gender Segregated Employment." *Research in Social Stratification and Mobility* 17: 139–72.

Tomaskovic-Devey, Donald, Arne L. Kalleberg, and Peter V. Marsden. 1996. "Organizational Patterns of Sex Segregation." In Arne L. Kalleberg, David Knoke, Peter V. Marsden, and Joe L. Spaeth, eds., *Organizations in America: Analyzing Their Structures and Human Resources Practices,* pp. 276–301. Thousand Oaks, Calif.: Sage.

Tomaskovic-Devey, Donald, Catherine Zimmer, Corre Robinson, Tiffany Taylor, and Jamie W. Wolf. 2003. "Documenting Desegregation: EEO-1 Estimates of U.S. Gender and Ethnic Segregation, 1966–2000." Unpublished manuscript. Department of Sociology and Anthropology, North Carolina State University.

Trappe, Heike, and Rachel A. Rosenfeld. 2001. "A Comparison of Gender Earnings Inequality for Young Adults in the Former East Germany and the Former West Germany." In Tanja Van der Lippe and Liset Van Dijk, eds., *Women's Employment in A Comparative Perspective,* pp. 109–50. New York: Aldine De Gruyter.

Treiman, Donald J. 1970. "Industrialization and Social Stratification." In Edward O. Laumann, ed., *Social Stratification: Research and Theory for the 1970s,* pp. 207–34. Indianapolis: Bobbs-Merrill.

———. 1977. *Occupational Prestige in Comparative Perspective.* New York: Academic Press.

Treiman, Donald J., and Heidi I. Hartmann. 1981. *Women, Work, and Wages: Equal Pay for Jobs of Equal Value.* Washington, D.C.: National Academy Press.

Treiman, Donald J., and Kermit Terrell. 1975. "Women, Work and Wages: Trends in the Female Occupational Structure." In K. Land and S. Spilerman, eds., *Social Indicator Models,* pp. 157–99. New York: Russell Sage Foundation.

United Nations. 1991. *The World's Women: Trends and Statistics, 1970–1990.* New York: United Nations Publications.

———. 2000. *The World's Women 2000: Trends and Statistics.* New York: United Nations Publications.

U.S. Census Bureau. 1958. "Occupational Trends in the United States: 1900 to 1950," by David L. Kaplan and M. Claire Casey. Working Paper no. 5. Washington, D.C.: U.S. Government Printing Office.

———. 1961. "Table 201: Detailed Occupation of the Experienced Civilian Labor Force, by Sex, for the United States: 1960 and 1950." In *1960 Census of the Population.* Vol. 1: *Characteristics of the Population,* part 1. Washington, D.C.: U.S. Government Printing Office.

———. 1968. "Changes between the 1950 and 1960 Occupation and Industry Classifications—With Detailed Adjustments of 1950 Data to the 1960 Classifications," by John Priebe. Technical Paper no. 18. Washington, D.C.: U.S. Government Printing Office.

———. 1972. "1970 Occupation and Industry Classification Systems in Terms of Their 1960 Occupation and Industry Elements," by John A. Priebe, Joan Heinkel, and Stanley Greene. Technical Paper no. 26. Washington, D.C.: U.S. Government Printing Office.

———. 1973. "Table 221: Detailed Occupation of the Experienced Civilian Labor Force and Employed Persons by Sex: 1970 and 1960." In *1970 Census of the Population*. Vol. 1: *Characteristics of the Population*, part 1. Washington, D.C.: U.S. Government Printing Office.

———. 1982. "Table 276: Detailed Occupation of the Experienced Civilian Labor Force and Employed Persons by Sex: 1980 and 1970." In *1980 Census of the Population*. Vol. 1: *Characteristics of the Population*, part 1. Washington, D.C.: U.S. Government Printing Office.

———. 1984. "Detailed Population Characteristics." *1980 Census of Population*. Vol. 1. Washington, D.C.: U.S. Government Printing Office.

———. 1989. "The Relationship between the 1970 and 1980 Industry and Occupation Classification Systems." Technical Paper no. 59. Washington, D.C.: U.S. Government Printing Office.

———. 1992. *Statistical Abstract of the United States*. Washington, D.C.: Government Printing Office.

———. 1993a. *Census of Population and Housing, 1990; Summary Population and Housing Characteristics*. Washington, D.C.: Census Bureau.

———. 1993b. *Census of Population and Housing, 1990; Equal Employment Opportunity (EEO) Supplemental Tabulations File*. Machine-readable data files. Washington, D.C.: Census Bureau.

———. 1993c. *Census of Population and Housing, 1990; Equal Employment Opportunity (EEO) Supplemental Tabulations File Technical Documentation*. Washington, D.C.: Census Bureau.

———. 2001. *Statistical Abstract of the United States*. Washington, D.C.: U.S. Government Printing Office.

———. 2002a. "Table P067: Sex by Occupation for the Employed Civilian Population 16 Years and Over." Census 2000 Supplemental Survey Summary Tables. Available at http://factfinder.census.gov/servlet/DTTable?ds_name=D&geo_id=D&mt_name=ACS_C2SS_EST_G2000_P067&_lang=en, last accessed July 26, 2002.

———. 2002b. "About the Census 2000 Supplemental Survey." Available at http://www.census.gov/c2ss/www/About/index.htm, last accessed July 26, 2002.

———. 2002c. "Accuracy of the Data (2000)." Available at http://www.census.gov/c2ss/www/Downloads/Accuracy00.pdf, last accessed July 26, 2002.

Upham, Frank K. 1987. *Law and Social Change in Postwar Japan*. Cambridge, Mass.: Harvard University Press.

Walby, Sylvia. 1986. *Patriarchy at Work*. Cambridge, England: Polity Press.

———. 1990. *Theorizing Patriarchy*. Oxford, England: Blackwell.

Wallace, Michael, and Chin-fen Chang. 1990. "Barriers to Women's Employment: Economic Segmentation in American Manufacturing, 1950–1980." *Research in Social Stratification and Mobility* 9: 337–61.

Wandersee, Winifred. 1981. "The Economics of Middle-Income Family Life: Working Women during the Great Depression." *Journal of American History* 65: 60–74.

Watts, Martin. 1992. "How Should Occupational Sex Segregation be Measured?" *Work, Employment, and Society* 6: 475–87.

———. 1994. "A Critique of Marginal Matching." *Work, Employment, and Society* 8: 421–31.

———. 1998. "Occupational Gender Segregation: Index Measurement and Econometric Modelling." *Demography* 35: 489–96.

Weber, Max. [1956] 1978. "Bureaucracy." In *Economy and Society*, Vol. 2. Ed. Guenther Roth and Claus Wittich. Berkeley: University of California Press.

Weeden, Kim A. 1998. "Revisiting Occupational Sex Segregation in the United States, 1910–1990: Results from a Log-Linear Approach." *Demography* 35: 475–87.

Weiss, Jane A., Francisco O. Ramirez, and Terry Tracy. 1976. "Female Participation in the Occupational System: A Comparative Institutional Analysis." *Social Problems* 23: 593–608.

Wells, Thomas. 1999. "Changes in Occupational Sex Segregation during the 1980s and 1990s." *Social Science Quarterly* 80: 370–80.

West, Candace, and Don H. Zimmerman. 1987. "Doing Gender." *Gender and Society* 1: 125–51.

Wharton, Amy. 1986. "Industry Structure and Gender Segregation in Blue-Collar Occupations." *Social Forces* 64: 1025–31.

———. 1989. "Gender Segregation in Private-Sector, Public-Sector, and Self-Employed Occupations, 1950–1981." *Social Science Quarterly* 70: 923–40.

White, Michael J. 1983. "The Measurement of Spatial Segregation." *American Journal of Sociology* 88: 1008–18.

Williams, Christine. 1989. *Gender Differences at Work: Women and Men in Nontraditional Occupations*. Berkeley: University of California Press.

Williams, Gregory. 1979. "The Changing U.S. Labor Force and Occupational Differentiation by Sex." *Demography* 16: 73–87.

Williams, Joan. 2000. *Unbending Gender: Why Family and Work Conflict and What to Do About It*. New York: Oxford University Press.

Williams, John E., and Deborah L. Best. 1990. *Measuring Sex Stereotypes: A Multination Study*. Newbury Park, Calif.: Sage.

Willms, Angelika. 1982. "Modernisierung durch Frauenarbeit? Zum Zusammenhang von wirtschaftlichem Strukturwandel und weiblicher Arbeitsmarktlage in Deutschland, 1882–1939." In Toni Pierenkemper and Richard Tilly, eds., *Historische Arbeitsmarktforschung: Entstehung, Entwicklung und Probleme der Vermarktung von Arbeitskraft*, pp. 37–71. Göttingen: Vandenhoeck and Ruprecht.

Willms-Herget, Angelika. 1985. *Frauenarbeit: Zur Integration der Frauen in den Arbeitsmarkt*. Frankfurt: Campus.

Wilson, William Julius. 1980. *The Declining Significance of Race: Blacks and Changing American Institutions*. 2d ed. Chicago: University of Chicago Press.

Winship, Christopher. 1977. "A Reevaluation of Indexes of Residential Segregation." *Social Forces* 55: 1058–66.

World Bank. 1993. *World Development Report 1993*. New York: Oxford University Press.

Wright, Erik Olin. 1997. *Class Counts: Comparative Studies in Class Analysis*. New York: Cambridge University Press.

Wright, Erik Olin, and Janeen Baxter, with Gunn Elisabeth Birkelund. 1995. "The Gender Gap in Workplace Authority: A Cross-National Study." *American Sociological Review* 60: 407–35.

Wright, Rosemary, and Jerry Jacobs. 1994. "Male Flight from Computer Work: A New Look at Occupational Resegregation and Ghettoization." *American Sociological Review* 59: 511–36.

Wuthnow, Robert. 1989. *Communities of Discourse: Ideology and Social Structure in the Reformation, the Enlightenment, and European Socialism*. Cambridge, Mass.: Harvard University Press.

Xie, Yu. 1992. "The Log-Multiplicative Layer Effect Model for Comparing Mobility Tables." *American Sociological Review* 57: 380–95.

Xie, Yu, and Kimberlee A. Shauman. 1997. "Modeling the Sex-Typing of Occupational Choice: Influences of Occupational Structure." *Sociological Methods and Research* 26: 233–61.

———. 2003. *Women in Science: Career Processes and Outcomes*. Cambridge, Mass.: Harvard University Press.

Yamagata, Hisashi, Kuang S. Yeh, Shelby Stewman, and Hiroko Dodge. 1997. "Sex Segregation and Glass Ceilings: A Comparative Statics Model of Women's Career Opportunities in the Federal Government over a Quarter Century." *American Journal of Sociology* 103: 566–632.

Yamaguchi, Kazuo. 1983. "The Structure of Intergenerational Occupational Mobility: Generality and Specificity in Resources, Channels, and Barriers." *American Journal of Sociology* 88: 718–45.

———. 1987. "Models for Comparing Mobility Tables: Toward Parsimony and Substance." *American Sociological Review* 52: 482–94.

Yu, Wei-hsin. 2001. "Family Demands, Gender Attitudes and Married Women's Labor Force Participation: Comparing Japan and Taiwan." In Mary C. Brinton, ed., *Women's Working Lives in East Asia*, pp. 70–95. Stanford, Calif.: Stanford University Press.

Zaretsky, Eli. 1986. *Capitalism, The Family, and Personal Life*. New York: Harper and Row.

Zoloth, Barbara S. 1976. "Alternative Measures of School Segregation." *Land Economics* 52: 278–98.

DATE DUE

GAYLORD			PRINTED IN U.S.A.

SHANAHAN LIBRARY
MARYMOUNT MANHATTAN COLLEGE
221 EAST 71 STREET
NEW YORK, NY 10021